There is no "I" in TEAM,
but there are two "I's" in IDIOT.

Coach Sam Rutigliano

If You Wore the Uniform You're a Brown

Volume 1

by Barry Taylor
& Shannon Duffy

If You Wore the Uniform, You're a Brown *Volume 1*
by Barry Taylor & Shannon Duffy

ISBN 0975509578 / ISBN-13 9780975509579 (Paperback)
©2012 All Rights Reserved

Library of Congress Control Number 2012942241

Published by Blue Leaf Publications
"A New Leaf in the Publishing Industry…"
Website: http://www.BlueLeafPub.com

All images used with permission

Cover images source Cleveland Browns
Cover art by Dehanna Bailee

CONTENTS

Features:

SOURCE: J. LAWLER

Introduction

When I was approached by Barry and Shannon to write the introduction to this book, I jumped at the opportunity. I'm the biggest Cleveland fan in the world. I love the Cavaliers and attend any Indians or Browns games possible on my busy schedule. If I can't be there, I am tuned into Satellite or XM Radio.

Although I was born in Memphis, my father worked for the Ford Motor Plant when I was a mere Prince. The plant closed and my family relocated to Amherst, Ohio, so my father could continue working for his company. Because of our proximity to Cleveland Stadium, my dad would take my brothers and myself to games.

It was at this time that I started soaking up the rich heritage and storied history of the Cleveland teams. Coach Paul Brown was a genius, and watching the epic duels between Jim Brown (no relation) and Sam Huff was as thrilling as it could get for a child my age.

They say that your first love in Pro sports is your only love. I know this is true for me. Even though my family moved back to our home in Memphis, my heart and home in Pro sports remain in Cleveland. No other teams matter. I live and die for my Cleveland teams.

Fortunately, the WWE has our great wrestling shows in Cleveland several times a year and I get to attend games on a regular basis. I have become friends with many Cleveland players, coaches, and administration, some of which are in this book. In fact, it's become a mutual admiration society in a way. I can look into the audiences at our WWE shows in Cleveland and see a plethora of Browns, Indians, and Cavaliers cheering me on, just like I cheer them.

Tony Bennett once sang about leaving his heart in San Francisco; my heart resides in Cleveland, Ohio and always will.

I'm sure you'll enjoy this book as much as I will as a true "River Rat."

Yours truly,

Jerry "The King" Lawler
WWE Hall of Fame

Foreword

One important phase that was virtually overlooked in the excitement created by the return of the Cleveland Browns in 1999 was the new organization's emphasis on its Alumni program. Ownership immediately took the posture that the franchise was not to be known as an expansion team, but as **The Cleveland Browns.**

Former players, whether they played in one or one-hundred fifty games and regardless of their geographical location, were invited to home games and to be a part of the Browns' family.

Their community involvement has played an integral part in the success of hundreds of charitable causes.

It was a pleasure to root for them as a fan. It was a greater pleasure to have the opportunity to work with them in the Public Relations Department. And now, it's not only a pleasure, but a privilege to be associated with such a distinguished group that once wore the colors of Brown and Orange.

Dino Lucarelli

Former Alumni Director

CHRIS, MY FAVORITE (COMPETITOR) GO BREWOS!!! Barry Taylor

SOURCE: B. TAYLOR

Acknowledgements

A person spends his entire life thinking the world will be this way forever. Then you wake up to life itself. The world isn't a perfect place, no matter what anyone tells you. I always thought my father would only be as far away as the end of a telephone call. Yet, less than two months after his fifty-second birthday, he drew his last breath due to cancer. After having passed away twenty-three years ago, thoughts of him still cloud my mind, things like wanting to discuss a recent construction problem or questions of how to deal with the many personal issues of my existence. Fifty-two also just happens to be my current age, and I am starting to look at some of the ghosts that haunted him. I thought I was invincible; work all day long and play all night long. Always having my family's welfare in mind first, but constantly running to keep up with my next appointment, the next scheduled time I had to be somewhere.... Six years ago, a surgery left me unable to fulfill my duties as a pipefitter and my twenty-five-year career came to an abrupt end. However, through the encouragement of my wife, co-writer, friends, and family, I came up with the idea of writing about something that interests me: The Cleveland Browns. It helped that the River Rats Browns Backers had given me the responsibility to run their annual Celebrity Golf Outing where, at the first tournament, we had the pleasure of having several celebrities sitting at a meet-and-greet, and we listened to the stories that Lance Mehl of the New York Jets and George Lilja from the Cleveland Browns were trading across the table. As I sat there, I thought about how many other people in the world would also be fascinated with these two competitors' ramblings, and, thus, the idea for this book was born. Working on this project has been a great labor of love; kind of like the whip cream, nuts, and cherry to finish up the perfect Banana Split.

I dedicate this book to my dad. I still miss him. *Go Browns!!!*

Sincerely,

Barry Taylor

Don Shula

When one talks about Don Shula, they have to talk about achievements. Walt Michaels considered Don a good football player, but even knew then he was going to be a coach. Walt told me that Don studied football from every aspect of the game. He not only knew what his responsibilities were, but the duties of all the players around him as well. Don was traded to the Baltimore Colts in what was, at that time, the largest NFL player trade ever made, involving fifteen players. The Colts traded tackle Mike McCormack, defensive tackle Don Colo, linebacker Tom Catlin, defensive back John Petitbon, and guard Herschel Forester to the Browns for Shula, defensive back Bert Rechichar, defensive back Carl Taseff, linebacker Ed Sharkey, end Gern Nagler, quarterback Harry Agganis, tackle Dick Batten, tackle Stu Sheets, guard Art Spinney, and guard Elmer Willhoite. The only larger trade was the October 13, 1989, trade starting with Hershel Walker being traded from the Dallas Cowboys to the Minnesota Vikings. Shula and Carl Taseff were teammates at John Carroll University, with the Browns, and with the Colts. He only played there one-and-a-half years, but his tutelage with Paul Brown has been carried on to the field ever since. Blanton Collier helped finish out his football education at the University of Kentucky in 1959. As a defensive coordinator at Detroit from 1960-62, Don moved into his first head coaching job with the Baltimore Colts. Blanton Collier moved into the head coaching position with Cleveland that same year and they met in the Championship Game in 1964. The Browns won 27-0, but that didn't discourage Don Shula. From there, all he did was win and his list of accomplishments includes:

- two-time Super Bowl champion (VII, VIII)
- five-time AFC Championship winner (71, 72, 73, 82, 84)
- NFL Championship winner (1968 before the Super Bowl)
- eleven-time Division title winner
- most regular-season wins (328)
- most Super Bowl appearances as head coach (6)
- 328-156-6 (Regular season)

- 19-17 (Post season)
- 347-173-6 (Overall)
- four-time NFL Coach of the Year
- NFL 1970s All-Decade Team
- 1972 Perfect Season

- **What was it like to walk on the field the first time as a Cleveland Brown?**

I grew up about thirty miles from Cleveland. The Browns started in 1946 and that was my team. I became a fan. I played in a small college just outside of Cleveland called John Carroll University. Our coach was a fan of Paul Brown and we used the Browns playbook and copied everything the Browns did. Then to be drafted by the Browns, and to make the Browns team, was like a dream come true.

- **When did you decide you wanted to be a professional football player?**

I evolved into it. I was a small college player and I had no idea whether or not I would be good enough to play professional football. My senior year, we scheduled Syracuse University and played and beat them in Cleveland Stadium. Paul Brown and his whole staff were there watching the game. I had a big night and my teammate, Carl Taseff, did too. We both got drafted by the Browns out of that one ball game.

- **When did you decide you were going to be a coach?**

I played as a player for seven years and football was a game that I loved. I could have tried to come back and played an eighth year, but I knew my career was coming to an end as a player. When I had the opportunity to go into coaching, I didn't hesitate.

- **Was there any one person who inspired you to play professional football?**

The guy that had the biggest influence on my career was Coach Blanton Collier. Blanton was the assistant coach to Paul Brown when I broke into the Browns in 1951. I played under him and then coached under him. It was all Paul Brown football. I was a guy that paid attention to every detail and worked hard, both physically and mentally, to be in the best shape that I could be in. I wanted to know what my responsibility was, but also the responsibility of everybody around me, and why we were being asked to do what we are being asked to do. I continued to ask the coaches the "why" questions. When I became a coach, I wanted my players to ask me the "why" questions, because that meant they wanted to know more and more about their responsibilities. It was my nature not only to know what my responsibility was, but the philosophy behind the whole thing.

- **What kind of parental influence did you have growing up?**

My dad came over from the old country and, when he was about eighteen, met and married my mom over here. He didn't know anything about American football or sports. When I started to play high school football and then college football, he became a fan and started to become interested and go to games whenever he could.

- **Where were you born?**

Thirty miles from Cleveland in Grand River, Ohio, which is a small fishing village where the Grand River lets out into Lake Erie.

- **Who was your favorite player when you were getting involved with the Browns?**

Without a doubt, it was Otto Graham. He was unbelievable. All he ever did was win championships. They had so many other great players such as Marion Motley, Lou Rymkus, Abe Gibron, Dante Lavelli, Frank Gatski; a lot of Hall of Famers.

- **Where did you go to high school and what kind of an influence did your high school coach have on your career?**

I went to Painesville Harvey High. Painesville was the biggest town right outside of Grand River that had a high school. My high school coach was Clarence Mackey. He had a big influence on my career. But the coach that had the biggest influence was a high school track coach, Don Martin, who was an assistant football coach. He saw me in my physical education class when I was a sophomore, and I wasn't out for football. He asked me why, and I told him that I had been sick when football practice started and went out and couldn't handle it, so I quit the team. He told me to get back out there, because "you have some talent and should be on the team." I also ran track for him. He was—and is—a great influence on my career. The first coach I coached under was Joe Jenkins. He was with the fifth and sixth grade at St. Mary's Grade School. That was the first organized football I played. We used to play games before the high school game on Friday nights. We would play early, and the high school game would start around 8:00.

- **What position did you play in grade school and high school?**

I was always a running back and I also played defensive back. I played both ways always in high school and college until I got into Pro ball.

- **Who was your coach at John Carroll?**

Herb Eisele. He had a two-man coaching staff, two assistant coaches: Bill Balanchek and Dan Mormile.

- **How did your teams do at that time?**

My senior year we ended up 9-2, which was the year we beat Syracuse. We played in a bowl game, The Great Lakes Bowl, in Cleveland Stadium. We beat Niagara in that game.

- **Is that still a trophy that they pass back and forth?**

No, after we left John Carroll, they sort of watered it down. They play in a lower division now. After we beat Syracuse, the teams did not want to schedule us because they had nothing to gain and everything to lose.

- **What was your experience like being drafted by the Browns?**

I was drafted in round nine by the Browns in 1951 and I was the only rookie to make the team. Carl Taseff, my teammate, ended up being drafted and was put on the taxi squad and then activated so he, too, made it his first year. So, we had two guys from John Carroll that made the Browns in 1951 with a thirty-three man roster.

- **What was it like playing for Paul Brown?**

It was unbelievable for me because I was in awe of him in high school and then in college. We would go to the Cleveland Browns games whenever we could and, in college, if you wore your letter sweater, you could sit in the end zone for fifty cents, which later became the "Dawg Pound." So, we all wore our letter sweaters. They did that because we were college students or players who were close by. All Paul Brown did was win beginning in 1946 with the Browns. When the leagues merged in 1950, they opened the season with that great win against the Philadelphia Eagles. They went on to win the Championship, too. Everybody thought they couldn't compete when the two leagues merged, but they continued to win championships.

- **What did you think of Weeb Eubank?**

Weeb was Paul's assistant and, when I got traded to Baltimore in 1953, the owner down there asked us who we would recommend from the Browns staff to be a head coach. He was looking for a head coach from the Cleveland staff of assistants. We all recommended Blanton Collier. He talked to Blanton, but he was reluctant to leave or to talk to him about the head coaching position. So, they talked to Weeb, and he was interested. They ended up hiring him to be the head coach, which turned out to be a great decision.

- **Who was your coach the one year you were with Washington in 1957?**

Joe Kurhajec.

- **What players did you enjoy playing with?**

Otto Graham; two great wide receivers, Max Speedie and Dante Lavelli; on defense they had Lenny Ford; on offense they had Lou Rymkus, Abe Gibron, Frank Gatski, Rex Bumgardner, Marion Motley, Horace Gilliam. They were all great guys and great players. My claim to fame is not in the record books. It was when we were playing the Bears in the game where Dub Jones scored six touchdowns. I scored a touchdown in that game. I intercepted a pass and ran it back ninety-six yards for a touchdown. It was called back with a penalty. Lenny Ford had hit Johnny Lujack as he was throwing the ball. They called him for roughing the passer and nullified my touchdown. That catch would have been a record for yardage on an interception return at that time.

- **Who were the team leaders when you were playing?**

Otto Graham was a team leader. Bill Willis was another great, great player. Abe Gibron, Marion Motley. Paul would send in all the plays. He sent them in by messenger guard. Chuck Noll was one of the "messenger guards" when he played. Before that, it was Abe Gibron. He would send in a play with a guard, and the guard would give it to Otto in the huddle. Then Otto would call the play, and another guard would come in, substitute for the guard that was in there, and give the next play. That was before they had transmitters in the helmet where the coach could talk to the quarterback from the sideline. It was called the "Messenger Guard System." As far as I know, Paul Brown was one of the first people to do that. He was also one of the first that put the radio in the helmet. I think the league outlawed it. Why should you have to go through a messenger system or hand system? If you are going to call the plays, make it as easy as possible to call them. Technology has changed over the years.

- **Jim Brown came into the league after you had left. Did he have an influence on the Browns that is still around today?**

Certainly, he does. He has to be maybe the best player that has ever played the game, or certainly one of the top best that has played the game.

- **Is your influence still felt in Miami?**

I would hope so, because I spent twenty-six years there. We had some pretty good records; it is hard to beat 17-0. The next year we went 15--2 and won back-to-back Super Bowls.

- **You, being a Baltimore coach and player and being at Cleveland, what is your opinion on the Browns leaving Cleveland and going to Baltimore?**

The fans hated to see that happen, but the owner, Art Modell, was put into a situation where the city wouldn't help them at all with the stadium. It needed help. He had an opportunity to go somewhere where they were anxious to have them and help them as much as they could. So, he made the decision to leave after he gave Cleveland every chance to keep him.

- **Being a business decision, should the fans understand more about the business side of football?**

I think the fans are so emotionally involved with the team that something like that would hurt them. I know Art and like him. I know that he didn't want to do that, but it was something he felt was the right thing to do for himself and for the franchise.

- **Now that you are a sports announcer as well as an analyst, you spend a lot of time watching television and looking at games. Ohio State/Michigan has been said to be the best college rivalry; Cleveland/Pittsburgh has been said to be the best Pro rivalry. What is your opinion on this?**

Cleveland/Pittsburgh is a great Pro rivalry, and certainly Ohio State/Michigan. You've got some other great college rivalries like Alabama/Auburn; Southern Cal/Notre Dame, too. The years I coached, I had great rivalries with Vince Lombardi and with George Allen and other guys that were great coaches.

- **On the field when you were coaching, who was your nemesis?**

I would have to say Jim Kelly. When I was coaching the Dolphins, we were in five Super Bowls. I was in one Super Bowl coaching the Colts so, actually, I was a coach in six Super Bowls. I could have coached in a lot more Super Bowls if it hadn't been for Buffalo, Marv Levy, Jim Kelly, Bruce Smith, Thurman Thomas, and the great teams they had. They knocked us out of four Super Bowls that they went to and lost. All four Super Bowls. They were 0-4 in Super Bowls, but the fact that they were in those four was what knocked us out of two or three of them. Jim Kelly was a great player and Marv Levy was a great coach.

- **Do you still feel like you are part of the Cleveland Browns organization?**

I was just there for 1951. When the season was over, I was in the Ohio National Guard and our unit got activated. I missed the training camp in 1952, but when the Korean War was over and we got discharged at the end of 1952, I called Paul and told him that we were discharged. He told me to get there as soon as I could because Tommy James, a defensive end, got hurt in practice and he was not going to be able to play. He said, "I can use you for Sunday." I got there on a Friday and played against the Eagles that Sunday. I was there that year and a half and got traded to Baltimore. I played four years with Baltimore and then one year with the Redskins. I feel more like I am a Baltimore Colt. I played with them for four years, came back, and coached them for seven. Eleven years of my early adult life, I spent with a horseshoe on my helmet with the Colts.

- **Who are the best fans in the NFL?**

I think the Browns have great fans. I think the Bears have great fans. I think that the Colts have great fans. It is hard to pick out just one. Certainly, Green Bay has to be proud of their Packers. Detroit always had great fans. Oakland has great fans. When you play the Raiders, you don't know what to expect. I think it is great what the Browns are doing by keeping the Browns Backers Clubs alive and being part of the organization.

- **You were accepted into the Hall of Fame in 1997 as a coach. What did that mean to you?**

It meant everything. That was really the highlight of my life, being recognized by your peers. The ultimate recognition you can get in football is being inducted into the Hall of Fame and be part of the history in Canton, Ohio. That is something that you will always be proud of.

- **Do you have a funny story that you laugh about still today from anytime in your NFL career?**

In Baltimore, one of my roommates was Arty Donovan and he was a great storyteller. We had a lot of laughs and a lot of great times together. Gino Marchetti was also in that group; he was one of the best defensive ends to ever play the game.

- **What was the saddest thing that ever happened in your NFL career?**

Losing Super Bowl VII to the Jets when we were a seventeen-point favorite. Namath came out and predicted that the Jets were going to win and they won. My relationship with the owner of the Colts, Carol Rosenbloom, was never quite the same after that. I lasted another year with the Colts and then moved on to Miami.

- **What was the most memorable game in your career?**

The perfect season of 17-0. We were playing the Redskins in the Super Bowl, and were ahead 14-0 in the game. I went for a field goal with only two minutes to go. If we had kicked that field goal, the score would have been 17-0 in a 17-0 perfect season. Garo Yepremian screwed it up. It was a bad snap and he picked it up and tried to throw a pass, which was intercepted. They ran in for a touchdown and now the score is 14-7 with about two minutes to go in a game we completely dominated. When I look back, that had to be the greatest moment, when that game was over and it was the end of a perfect season, which was something that nobody had done before that and nobody has done it since. When it is all over, the reason they keep score is to see who won the game. The team that has the most points wins, and the team that has the most wins is the best team. Otherwise, why do you keep score?

- **What can you tell us about the 1964 championship game when you coached against the Browns?**

Blanton Collier was the coach, and after I had coached under him in Kentucky, I got the job with Baltimore as a head coach. He got the job with the Browns as a head coach. We played them in the championship game and they beat us. The next year, we got even and beat them in the big game.

- **What was it like to go head-to-head with Paul Brown?**

To me it was unbelievable because I grew up idolizing him, from when I was a fan and a player at John Carroll and then as a player under Paul. To have the opportunity to come back as a young coach and coach against him was certainly one of the thrills and highlights of my coaching career. Later on, I became a member of the NFL Competition Committee and Paul was also a member. We got to know each other and spend time together with that type of a relationship. I went full circle with my relationship with Paul. I got to know him on several different levels.

- **Should players today be more fan conscious?**

There are a lot of players today that are very fan conscious. I don't know how much different it is than when I played or when I first started coaching. You respect fans and realize how important they are. We had great fans in Cleveland and in Baltimore, and when I came back as a coach with the Dolphins, too. The fan support was always something we cherished.

- **What is your job today?**

I am retired, and I do a lot of motivational speaking. I'm also involved in the restaurant business. I follow and support the Dolphins as best I can. My son, Mike, was the head coach of Alabama, so I followed them for a while. Now he is at Jacksonville with the Jaguars, so I will be following them.

- **Do you take an active part in your restaurant?**

My son, Dave, is the one that goes around to all the restaurants and works on a daily basis. My wife, Mary Anne, and I go to all of the openings and promotional activities. Anytime we are in the vicinity, we will go out to eat in one of the restaurants.

- **Are you really an Angus expert?**

We have people that are. We take a lot of pride in the advertisement "The Best Beef Money Can Buy." We advertise that and we try to make it the best dining experience you can have when you come to our restaurant.

- **What are your hobbies?**

Golf is the hobby I enjoy the most.

- **Do you enjoy being the analyst with the crews?**

I don't want to do anything that requires me to be somewhere every week of my life. I did that for thirty-three years as a coach and when I got out of coaching, I said, "I want to get to know my kids and my grandkids and travel with my wife. I want to do the things we weren't able to do because of the demands and restrictions in the coaching profession."

- **Any plans for more television work?**

I am going to do some things on Monday Night Football, half-time radio, and some occasional television work.

- **Don, what did you get out of your NFL career?**

So many great memories, and I was able to meet so many people on different levels; players, coaches, owners, fans. That was forty-three years I will always cherish. The Hall of Fame was the crowning memory of my career in the NFL.

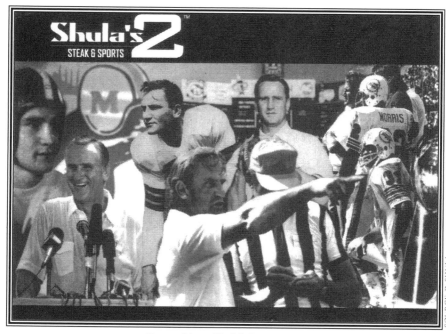

Postcard from Shula's 2 restaurant

Season	Team	Games	Defense				Fum	Total	
			INT	Yds	Avg	TD		Points	
1951	CLE	12	4	23	5.8	0	0	0	
1952	CLE	5	0	0	0	0	0	0	
1953	BAL	12	3	46	15.3	0	0	0	
1954	BAL	12	5	84	16.8	0	0	0	
1955	BAL	9	5	64	12.8	0	0	0	
1956	BAL	12	1	2	2	0	0	0	
1957	WAS	11	3	48	16	0	0	0	
Career		73	21	267	12.7	0	0	0	

Don Shula

DB/HC 1951-1995

John Carroll (OH)

Season	Team	Punt Ret.				Kick Ret.			
		PR	Yds	Avg	TD	KR	Yds	Avg	TD
1951	CLE					1	6	6	0
1956	BAL					1	0	0	0
Career		0	0	0	0	2	6	3	0

Season	Team(s)	Other Stats							
1953	BAL	Rec: 1/6yds							
1954	BAL	Rush: 2/3yds							

"The Cleveland Browns have one of the most storied and fascinating histories and backgrounds of any team in the NFL. We have heroes. We have villains. The community is so wedded to the concept of the Browns, it's right up there with family and religion..."

— *Carmen Policy, President/CEO (1999-2003)*

"An Ode to the Browns Fan"

By Brad Hiener
A River Rats Browns Backer

There's this sport called football that I love to watch
I'm not sure why, cause it pisses me off
I root for a team called the Cleveland Browns
Sundays are filled with boos and frowns
Every once in a while we can clap and cheer
But mostly it's just cursing and spilling of beer
It seems sometimes like they suck on purpose
Like it is fun for them to purposely irk us
Soon enough though we'll have our day
When the Browns show up and ready to play
Not just for one game or some unknown reason
Yet for us, the fans they'll have a winning season
Furthermore, they won't stop there
They'll continue on through the bitter cold air
When every game is in the dead of winter
We'll go very deep like a really bad splinter
Into the playoffs that is, like the rest of the teams
Whom do really well and fulfill their fans dreams
They will surprise us all, but most of all us
The die harders who cry and cuss
The ones that stand by them, week in and week out
Year after year, we come with no doubt
That this is the year we've been waiting for
Yet, we get to the Red Zone and still can't score
Field goals don't…match up all that well
To the touchdowns against us…oh, what the hell
There's always next year has become the team motto
But that will soon change; come on, man, it's got to

One of these years, when we least expect it
Our team will be great and make the others respect it
We will play in THAT game, the biggest of all
Finally, our season won't be over at the end of fall
We will take the title of our respected division
And we will play and perform like we've always envisioned
So hold your heads high, my fellow Browns fans
Losing, restructure, new players…all part of the plan
We'll fire and hire new coaches at will
'Til we find the right ones that can fulfill
The very thing we've all waited for
To take the right path, or the right door
That will lead us to victory and glory abound
Have faith and have hope, that we'll get that first down
And the next one…and the one after that
Before you know it, we'll be right there where we want to be at
In the big game, against the best of the best
We'll take the Lombardi and put the losing to rest
But, for now…we'll do what we've always done
We'll run when we should pass and pass when we should run
We will accept six wins as a pretty good season
Hoping to lose for draft picks, even though it feels like treason
Third down and sixteen, we'll throw it for eight
In the fourth quarter, we'll make a comeback, but it will be too late
We'll rack up penalties like they're a good thing to have
Our very best players will pull muscles in their calves
We will challenge a play that is clearly in favor
Of the other team and they'll surely savor
The sweet taste of victory, we will relinquish to them
We will hold our red flag and give them first and ten
Even though they fumble and we pick it up
Our defense could have scored, but that's just our luck
So, one of these days, probably when the Earth itself ends
The Browns will be Champions and I'll be wearing Depends

2

Gene Hickerson

One of the classiest and most humbled of men to play the game of football, Gene Hickerson, was respected by many during his time on the field, just as much as he is to this day. Gene passed away on October 20, 2008, due to complications associated with his battle with diabetes, Alzheimer's, and vascular dementia. One year earlier, in 2007, the wheelchair-bound hulk of an offensive tackle took to the stage as he was inducted into the Pro Football Hall of Fame. Jim Brown (inducted in 1971), Leroy Kelly (inducted in 1994), and Bobby Mitchell (inducted in 1983) were all carried on the back of Gene as he helped them to the Hall of Fame years earlier. Now they accompanied him to his date with infamy as they pushed his wheelchair to his place of honor on that stage. Rarely will one ever see a picture of any of the three of these running backs coming out of the backfield without Hickerson leading the way. Many would argue that the prestigious honor was thirty-four years overdue, but not Gene. Not once did he lobby sportswriters for his induction into the Hall of Fame. His sharp wit and humor will be gravely missed by family and friends.

- **When did you decide that you wanted to be a professional football player?**

I was at Ole Miss and at that time. We had eleven professional ballplayers. Johnny Vought, an Admiral in the Navy, was the head coach. When I was a freshman, Paul Brown called me about playing for him. Bruiser Kinard, one of the best football players ever in history and a super guy, was the one who told me that Paul Brown had called for me. I told him there was no way Paul Brown called for me. I soon became the rave of the campus for two or three weeks. I told Paul Brown I didn't know what to do and he told me that Bruiser had told him what I needed to do. He didn't want to break up any traditions Old Miss (University of Mississippi) had, but two years later, they drafted me. In fact, they drafted me one year early. They take care of their kids at Old Miss. I know we didn't lose more than two games for about seven or eight years. The coaches at Old Miss played there and they came back. They never said a swear word.

- **What did you do when you were drafted by Cleveland?**

They brought me to Cleveland and I bought myself a new Cadillac. Down south, in the hot weather, you cannot run fast enough to get cool. They moved the All-Star game to Chicago and I said it was cooler than what we were used to. We were there for three weeks, but we practiced for two weeks and then we got in a car coming to Cleveland. We couldn't believe how cool, nice, and pretty it was. I had a very good time. Lou Groza was too old to tell stories. He was a super, super human being. He never knocked on anyone. He was still kicking in his last three or four years. So, if he missed one, nobody said anything. On occasion, everyone is going to miss one. When they built the new stadium, the Browns gave us tickets to the games. I told Lou that I was going to walk down there and pick up about eight or ten tickets for my seats. He had no idea that I was going to be behind him. His kids still use his tickets.

- **What was it like to play for Paul Brown?**

Mr. P.B.—Paul Brown was a gentleman and a super human being like all the coaches at Old Miss (University of Mississippi). I knew about half of the players in the league when I began to play. Paul Brown said we would have fun, but at certain times, we would sit down and rest, laugh a little bit. And we did. Paul Brown thought the world of the people from Ole Miss, because they were straight-laced. At that time, I had not played a ball game for him. I was quick old beans. The ballplayers thought the world of him. He could chew your butt and three minutes later, he would be fine with you.

- **What was it like to play for Blanton Collier?**

The same situation, he said to just do our best. When Paul Brown and Blanton Collier were in Cleveland, we won a lot of ball games.

- **What was it like to play for Nick Skorich?**

Uncle Nick. He was in the same mode as Paul Brown. Of course, when Paul left, I think Nick coached three or four seasons. I enjoyed playing on Sunday, but the practice through the week hit me terribly hard.

- **A lot of people write and talk about how your quickness and speed was what helped Jim Brown gain so many yards; is that correct?**

I could run within three yards of him for the 100-yard sprint. I was quick, and I could move. I think he played nine years and he took off to the West coast and was in three or four movies. Then we didn't have any Jim Brown.

- **What players did you enjoy playing with?**

Monte Clark, Dick Schafrath, John Wooten, Doug Dieken, Lou Groza. Dieken had three brothers. His mom and dad used to come to the ballgames because they could get on the turnpike and come straight to

Cleveland from Streator, Illinois. Dieken came from a family of farmers. I think they used to hook Dieken to a plow so he could pull it. Anytime you have a ball club that is winning, it is very, very nice. Anytime you are happy, you are having fun. It finally came down to me, I was there fifteen years, and I was tired, so I was done. Groza retired about two years before me and he told me I had a sharp life and not to walk off and leave it now. I retired three times and they kept bringing me back, but this time I was done.

- **What kind of leadership role did you take when you were playing?**

I never yelled and screamed at anyone because I could make mistakes, too. I would try to jig them up a little bit, though. It got thin the last part of my years. I kept telling them that I was not coming back anymore. Well, they had me coming back three years. Then they wanted a fourth year. I told them I was not coming back because I was tired. I played football, but I worked a full time job. I sold metal for Anchor Tool and Dye in Cleveland, Ohio, on Brookpark Road. Metal was the best thing to sell in Cleveland because the city would use most of it. George Dowling was the Director of Purchasing there and in Cleveland. In Youngstown, Ohio, they had a big stadium, and I was the first one to ever call on that stadium. Sometimes I enjoyed selling more than playing football.

Hall of Famer Gene Hickerson leading a block for Hall of Famer Leroy Kelly
vs.the Cincinatti Bengals Dec 5, 1971

- **What were your feelings when the Cleveland Browns left Cleveland and went to Baltimore?**

I didn't like it. I knew they would eventually get another team. Art Modell was one of the greatest owners for the ballplayers.

- **What can you tell me about your Pittsburgh Steelers rivalry?**

When you heard Joe Greene's name, you would hear mine. He did not beat me too many times. He was big, but I was quicker.

- **Who was your nemesis on the field?**

They were all about the same. If you have a caliber of football players, they are all about the same.

- **Did you encounter any negatives while you were playing?**

No, they did not allow that, which was the best thing that ever happened. Paul Brown was the best coach in the world. If you try to do your job, he would never criticize you.

- **Do you still feel like you are part of the Cleveland Browns organization?**

If I'm down there, I do.

- **What did it mean to be one of the first players to be elected to the Cleveland Browns Hall of Fame?**

It was, and is, very nice, which is one reason why I stayed in Cleveland.

- **Are the Cleveland Brown fans the best in the NFL?**

Usually, the team that gets the most wins for two or three years in a row has the best and the most fans. It is up and down. Cleveland is one of the best places in the world and we live on the west side of Cleveland. I was the first ones to ever move across the river. Actually, I built a home before I retired. I have relatives in West Tennessee, Memphis, etc. We came from a family of ten. I had brothers who didn't want to go play Pro football, so they went through college and started their own careers.

- **Did Nick Skorich play on the field with you?**

He was one of our coaches for seven or eight years. He did know football. Nick was just a little short guy, but he used to blast people.

- **What are your hobbies now?**

I have a monster yard that I cut with a tractor. When I do that, I scatter the grass and then the birds come to eat off of it.

- **What stadium was the hardest place to play in?**

It was not so much the stadium as it was the dirt. It was hard! It was very hard on your knees. Detroit was where I first realized how hard the dirt was. I never had a fight out there, but I saw some rookies slugging it out.

- **As a player, what was the saddest thing that ever happened?**

I hated to see them pick up a ballplayer on a stretcher. That would be ugly.

- **I understand that Paul Brown didn't like to do any type of hazing, but did you still make the rookies stand up and sing their fight songs, etc?**

Yes. I think they enjoyed it, because it made them feel part of the team.

- **What did you get out of your NFL experience?**

It is up and down. When you win, you win, and you are very, very happy. When you lose a game, though, it is just terrible through the night and the next morning.

- **How did it happen that you were a friend of Elvis Presley?**

Eli, Eli...I called him Eli because I could never remember his name. We were in school together in North Memphis, I think in the second and third grade. My family got out of the slums, but Elvis's didn't. He and I would play tag football together as kids. We played every Sunday, rain or shine. I eventually moved to White Haven, Tennessee, and they moved to White Haven, too. His house was probably two blocks over from me and he came over one day and my mother and dad were the only ones living there at that time. They had no idea who Elvis Presley was. They knew the name, but they didn't realize he lived so close. My mother was so excited and kept saying Elvis was at her house. We remained friends for a long time. He would walk up to a car dealership and there would be people looking for a car and most of the people didn't know who Elvis was at the time. While doing this, he would buy two or three cars every month for somebody. He especially loved to buy cars for elderly people. He took care of his mother and father, too. Once the City of Memphis asked Jim Brown to come down and give a speech at some auditorium. Elvis came to it, but when it was over, he jumped up and ran before he got swamped. Elvis Presley just loved people.

Gene Hickerson				
Guard 1958-1973				
Mississippi				
Pro Football Hall of Fame 2007				
Season	Team	Games	Other Stats	Total Points
1958	CLE	12		0
1959	CLE	12		0
1960	CLE	12		0
1962	CLE	12		0
1963	CLE	14		0
1964	CLE	14		0
1965	CLE	14		0
1966	CLE	14		0
1967	CLE	14		0
1968	CLE	14		0
1969	CLE	14		0
1970	CLE	14		0
1971	CLE	14		0
1972	CLE	14		0
1973	CLE	14		0
Career		202		0

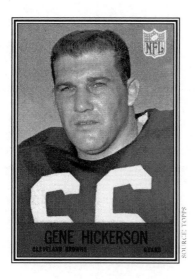
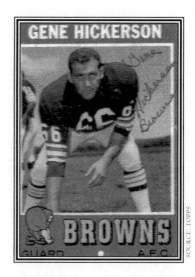

3

Ross Fichtner

In 1954, *Sports Illustrated* started production of its magazine. Since then, there have been over twenty-four-hundred covers. Athletes of all walks of life have graced the *Sports Illustrated* cover, however, is this privilege a crowning achievement or a curse? Almost forty percent of those individuals' covers have ended in a negative manner. Injuries, poor production, unexpected loss, or just bad luck have been the result shortly after issuance. Eddie Matthews was on one of the first *SI* covers, when the Milwaukee Brewers were in first place and Eddie had been doing well. Soon after, he broke his hand, missed seven games, and the Brewers missed out on their first pennant. Michael Jordan was on fifty-one covers and never saw the jinx on the court, but his last cover resulted in his wife filing for a divorce. September 2005 saw Donavan McNabb and Terrell Owens together on the cover. During that season, Owens ended up being removed from the team without pay, and McNabb suffered from a sports hernia. They bickered back and forth all season even though the headline read, "Philadelphia: Brotherly Love." Expecting Anna Kournikova to do well in the French Open, then seeing her defeated the day after her June 5, 2000, cover, *SI*, recognizing their own possibilities, put a black cat on their cover in 2002. And even Ross Fichtner felt the sting of the *SI* jinx (he explains below). Described by fellow players as a teacher, Ross helped many players in their assignments. Later, his intellect carried over to several coaching positions. He was also a member of a respected group of college quarterbacks that Paul Brown transformed into a solid defensive backfield. Ross was considered to be the Browns "disaster quarterback" in case the starting and backup quarterbacks were unable to play, however, that disaster never struck.

- **What was it like to walk on the field the first time as a Brown?**

I played in the College All-Star game in August of 1960. We played on Friday night. There were six of us on the All-Star team who were Cleveland Brown rookies. After the game, we flew to Detroit where the Browns were playing their first pre-season game. We joined up with the team at the hotel. The players were always taped at the hotel before the game. So, I saw my first veteran Browns when I went in to get taped. They were some of the older veterans and to me, being only twenty-one, they looked so mature. We played that game at the old Briggs baseball stadium in Detroit, so we entered the field through the dugout. As I recall, at that time, the only football stadiums were Lambeau Field, the Los Angeles Coliseum, Chicago's Soldier Field, the Cotton Bowl in Dallas, and Franklin Field in Philadelphia. In all the other cities, we played in the baseball stadiums. That first time, when I emerged from the dugout in my No. 20 Browns uniform, I felt like I was in a fantasy world. In a dream. It was surreal. It was in every way a once-in-a-lifetime experience and is indelibly etched in my mind. During my nine years and 185 games as an NFL player, I have only one other memory of running out onto the playing field. It was the last game of my rookie year, the Sunday afternoon I came on to the field in Yankee Stadium. I felt the aura of the great names and games of that place. The year prior, when I was a college senior, my dad and I had attended the championship game there between the New York Giants and the Baltimore Colts. And, now, I was running on to that famous field and my father was watching me. Compared to those two, even coming on to the field for the 1964 World Championship Game has barely left a memory. Going back to that first game in Detroit as a Cleveland Brown, we rookies were as green as could be. We were wearing Browns uniforms, but we'd not yet been to a practice or even a team meeting. We didn't know the defense or the terminology. We didn't know anything. So, they just sent us in to cover some kickoffs. But I was happy. I was a Cleveland Brown. They had been my favorite team, even though I'd grown up in Pittsburgh. Television was new when I was in seventh grade and a friend had one. The first thing I ever saw on television was the Browns/Los Angeles Rams Championship game. That's how I became a Browns fan. So, that added to the thrill of wearing a Browns uniform that first game.

- **How were you drafted into the Browns?**

I was the third round draft choice in 1960. Defensive end Jim Houston was first. Then Prentice Scott, a running back from Oklahoma was second. And I was third. There were twelve teams in the National Football League. It was also the first year and the first draft of the American Football League. The AFL team in Buffalo drafted me as a quarterback. The success of this new league was unsure so, naturally, I chose the Browns and the opportunity to play under Paul Brown and to be a teammate of legends such as Jim Brown and Lou Groza.

- **When did you decide that you wanted to be a professional player?**

I started playing midget league football in fifth grade. I knew I wanted to be a professional player when I saw that televised game when I was in seventh grade. But, first, I had dreams of being on the high school team. I would lie in my bed with a football, which I would throw up toward the ceiling and I would catch it. Every day, when my mom made my bed, she'd flip that football up and down and then place it by my pillow. She was having dreams for me, too. I dreamed that I was going to be the captain or the most valuable player and I was going to play in the high school all-star game; that

I would go to a university and be the captain and most valuable player and play in the college all-star game. Then I would go to an NFL team, and I was going to be captain and most valuable player. My mind used to run rampant. I had a good work ethic. I worked out every day during the off-season. I was small and a lot of guys would laugh because I was working out all the time. All of a sudden when I became a junior, things started changing. Then when I was a senior, I was one of the fastest guys in the state. My high school coach knew what motivated me, so he used to play mental games with me by saying I couldn't do this or I couldn't do that. And I'd counter him saying that I could. And I did. We were both happy. I didn't date, drink, or smoke. I didn't even know how to dance. I was always into football and track. I worked out during the summer. I know I would have never accomplished anything if I had not done that. I can't say I was a fantastic athlete, but I was a decent athlete with a good work ethic, and it paid off.

- **Was there any one person that inspired you to play football?**

My high school coach was one of the most instrumental people in my life. I believe most athletes would say that their high school coach was influential. I think because you are developing the things you learn at that time are very important. I was fortunate that I had a chance to play under a great high school coach. So he, Duke Wiegel, was the most influential. I was also with an excellent coach at Purdue, Jack Mollenkopf. Playing for Paul Brown and Blanton Collier—well, they were the gold standard of coaching.

- **What kind of a parental influence did you have?**

My dad and mom were divorced when I was nine months old. There was no male in the family and my mom worked three jobs. I was raised by a grandmother and my mom encouraged me to go into sports. My mom was very, very supportive. She would come to all of my midget league and high school games. When I played for Purdue, she came out to at least two of the home games and one of the away games that we played at Ohio State or Michigan State. When I became professional, she came to a lot of the games in Cleveland. She was very encouraging and supported what I chose to do.

- **What was it like playing for Paul Brown?**

I really enjoyed playing for Paul Brown. I always felt it was an honor to play for him. I respected him very much. I played for him three years, at the end of his career in Cleveland. I know that when he got fired, some of the guys on the team made derogatory statements about him as he was leaving, but I did not. One thing about Paul Brown, which made it very easy to play for him, was that he basically required just one thing: To totally concentrate on what you were supposed to do.

- **What was it like to play for Blanton?**

It was the same as playing for Paul Brown. There was nothing different. They had worked together for so long. If you didn't know better, you would

21

think that it was Paul up there talking with a different voice. Blanton was one of those guys who wanted you to carry out the details of your assignment. That was the main thing about our teams back in those days. We were very detail oriented.

- **Who were the team leaders?**

When I first got there, the team leaders were Ray Renfro on offense and Walt Michaels on defense. After they retired, Galen Fiss and Paul Wiggin were leaders. By leadership, I mean that they exhibited a good work ethic, game preparation, on the field performance, and respect for the coaching staff and team policy. Jim Brown led by production. He didn't say much, but when players saw him fighting for that extra yard and consistently giving extra effort, it inspired us to do our best. Actually, there was leadership demonstrated throughout our team.

- **What kind of leadership role did you take?**

I was known for being a competitor. I was very feisty. I was a butt-slapping type of encourager to my teammates. I played hard, and I felt like I was a physical player. There are a lot of guys who play professional football that are fairly decent players, but they are not physical. They might not stick their nose in the propeller. I put my head in a couple of propellers that I probably shouldn't have, resulting in concussions and then in epilepsy about twenty years after I retired. To me, the most important thing in evaluation was the respect of my teammates and how they felt about the job I was doing. That was my barometer. When my teammates said I was a hard hitter, to me that was the greatest compliment I could get. Not that the press said it, not that anybody else said it. It was what my teammates said. I always felt that if I ever got to the point where my teammates started thinking that I was not doing my job, that would be the time for me to retire. Most of the time, your teammates know more about your performance than even the coaches do. Coaches watch and they analyze film, but no one is as close to your performance as your teammates and the opposing teams.

- **What players did you enjoy playing with?**

I enjoyed playing with all my teammates. When you are with a team, you get closer to some guys than you do to others. I was close to Lou Groza and John Morrow. Every day in practice for eight years, I took snaps from center John Morrow and held the ball for Lou, "The Toe." I must have held the ball for him ten thousand times. After practice during training camp, the three of us stayed behind as he kicked his thirty or forty balls. We were the last guys off the field, and the last ones to join a group of veterans at a local bar to have our traditional couple of beers before dinner. During the off-season, Jim Kaniki and I spent a lot of time together and I was close to my training camp roommate, Gary Collins. Jim Kaniki and I used to go out on Friday nights to see area high school games. The night before a game, Frank Ryan and I always went out for a beer. We would talk about the opposing teams, offensive and defensive points of, we talked about any of our weaknesses and tendencies that the other team might have picked up, and what we could do to counteract it. We finished these discussions each time by having a toast to Christmas in Cleveland, which meant we'd be in the playoffs.

- **Tell us about your *Sports Illustrated* cover.**

When that happened, I guess I got what was called the "*Sports Illustrated* jinx." It was in 1966, when I had eight interceptions in the first six games of the season. We were playing in Atlanta and, on the way to the hotel, I was told that *Sports Illustrated* would interview me at the hotel that evening. They were doing an article on the best deep defenders in the NFL. The next day, during pre-game warm-up at the stadium, it seemed that every time I turned around an *SI* photographer was taking pictures. Finally, I said, "How many pictures do you need?" He said he needed quite a few. When I asked him why, he said it was for the magazine cover. "The *cover* of *Sports Illustrated*?" I asked. "Yes, *the cover*." Over the next three days, during the game, at my home, and at practice, the camera was always clicking. Here's where the jinx came in. For the last eight games of that season, not only did I have any more interceptions, but there was never a ball even thrown to my area of coverage. I was either under the jinx, or the other teams were giving me a lot of respect by avoiding me. Nonetheless, I finished that season being second in the league for interceptions for the second time in my career. Oh, and here's an interesting twist to the *SI* cover story: It all depended on a boxing match. The heavyweight championship between Cassius Clay and "Big Cat" Williams was about that time. If "Big Cat" had upset Cassius Clay, he would have made the cover—and maybe I would have ended up leading the league in interceptions!

- **Was it the three interceptions during the Cowboys game that helped get you on or was it just the eight interceptions?**

I think it was probably the three interceptions against Dallas. The thing that was really amazing is that, for the week before the game, I woke up four or five times during the night after picturing myself intercepting all these passes. I even told my roommate I was having these strange dreams. I wish I could have intentionally manufactured those dreams and had them come true during some other years in my career.

- **Tell us about your all-Pro season in '66?**

The one thing that I was probably most disappointed in is the fact that the two or three years I was voted to the Pro Bowl, and I never went. Each team had a limit on how many guys go, and we had a few guys whose contracts stipulated that they go whether they had a good year or not. After the game, the opposing coaches would vote for two offensive and defensive players that they felt most deserved it. We played the third from the last game in 1966 in L.A., which was where they used to have the Pro Bowl. There was a big article in their local sports section about the Pro Bowl and they named the players who were in town for the L.A. vs. Browns game who were going to be on the Pro Bowl team. I was one of the guys that they named. In fact, I think that year I had the most votes for a defensive back. But, when they announced the team, they didn't name me. That was really very disappointing. Two of the years that I was voted in for sure were '65 and '66, yet, I didn't go, even though I was voted onto the team. When I renegotiated my contract the next year, I mentioned it to them and they gave me an extra raise because of it. I would have rather gone to the Pro Bowl than have the extra money. I was very let down.

- **What were your feelings when the Browns went to Baltimore?**

I was disappointed, but the one thing I am the most appreciative is that the city of Cleveland filed suit to the NFL to keep our records in Cleveland. Otherwise, if someone wanted to look up when I played, they would have to find me in the Baltimore Ravens Yearbook with an asterisk noting I'd played with the Browns. So, I am still a Cleveland Brown. They even sued to keep the colors from leaving Cleveland. If they hadn't, they would have gone down with the brown, orange, and white to Baltimore, just like the Colts took their uniforms and colors to Indianapolis. To me, the Baltimore Colts are not the Indianapolis Colts, although the uniforms are exactly the same. I really appreciate that the people in Cleveland stood up for that. Art Modell took the players, but he took nothing else; everything else stayed there, the records, the colors.

- **ESPN said that the Ohio State/Michigan is the best college rivalry and the Browns/Steelers is the best Pro rivalry. What is your opinion?**

Cleveland and Pittsburgh has always been one of the best rivalries. I believe the reason is because they are both in the same conference, as well as the proximity of the two cities—being only two and a half hours distant. Browns fans go to the games in Pittsburgh, and vice versa. There are Cleveland fans living in Pittsburgh and Pittsburgh fans living in Cleveland. This makes for a lot of fan rivalry between neighbors and family, which is fun for them. The rivalry is long-standing, going back to the 50's. I'm enjoying a unique position now because my son, Randy, is in his second year as the Steelers wide receivers coach so, overnight, I became a proud Steelers fan. Blood is thicker than my old team loyalty. Also, in the Pros you can't leave out the Packers and Bears. It's a rivalry made in heaven, with the states adjoining, being in the same division, and their long history. I coached for both the Packers and the Bears. I have to mention what die-hard fans the Packers have, proud to come out in all weather. And during the four years I coached with them, there was never a game we played away from home where there weren't loyal fans waiting to greet us. Ohio State and Michigan play the last game of the college season and it's almost always for the Big Ten title. This makes for a great college rivalry. Proximity is also a contributing factor for the fans because they only have about a two-hour drive. My middle son, Rusty, played for Michigan under Bo Schembechler, so our family was able to take part in that traditional rivalry for a few years.

- **Who was your nemesis on the field; who gave you the most trouble?**

Of all the guys I played against, and I played against a lot of the good ones, I think the tight end from the Philadelphia Eagles was probably one that I had to worry about the most. There were a lot of good ones, though. Jacquie Smith from St. Louis; John Mackey from Baltimore; Mike Ditka from the Bears; and Aaron Thomas from the New York Giants. They were all really good. Basically, the toughest one that I worried about the most, the guy that ran the best patterns, and was the toughest, was Pete. He would be very closely followed by Jacquie Smith.

- **Do you still feel like you are a part of the Brown Organization?**

Yes, I do, because the Browns have been very respectful of the guys that have played there before. I am active in playing a lot of the charity golf tournaments. The ownership has treated the old team very well. This is one reason why I think the new owners have done so. For the time Cleveland was without a team, the veterans took part in a lot of things to keep the Browns name in front of the public. We went places and did things just as if the Browns were still there. I think they are very appreciative of that and they have done a great job in making the alumni feel like we are still a part of that legacy. I feel I could go over there at any time and go to their facility and be very welcome. We, the alumni, are very appreciative that they have done some things for us. When we had our forty-year reunion for our Championship team, they flew guys in with their families and picked up the hotel tabs. We played in an era when we didn't get very many perks and the salaries were low. So, bringing us in to celebrate that anniversary, to see all your old teammates, and to see all the changes in the Browns facility—it was wonderful. I appreciate their generosity that is for sure.

- **Are Cleveland Brown fans the best in the NFL?**

The Browns were always great when I was there. Of course, every year that we were there, except when we broke even, we had a winning record. When I was coaching in the NFL, we would go to different cities to play and fans would say the Browns and the Green Bay Packers have the most organized clubs, like yours. I coached the Packers for four years, and we would go to different cities and there would be Packer fans everywhere tailgating. I was talking to one fan and he said we are the second largest; Cleveland is the biggest. The Browns and the Packers are supposed to have the biggest fans around the country than all of the teams. I can't verify it. I just heard people saying it. I've seen what the Green Bay Packers have, but they even say they are second behind the Browns.

- **What is one of the funniest stories of your NFL experience?**

At Thanksgiving, the rookies were told there was a grocery store on the other side of town giving away free turkeys to the players. So, the rookies would sign up for a turkey and go to pick it up and our film guy would go ahead of time and would be out of sight filming as the men came up to the meat counter to claim their birds. The guy behind the counter, who was in on the prank, kept asking them what they were talking about, that he had no free turkeys. The players kept repeating that they were a Brown coming to get their promised Thanksgiving bird. After they filmed this, they showed it at the team meeting, and of course, all the guys would be dying laughing. A funny thing that happened to me was when I was coaching in Chicago. My wife's sister lived there at the time and we went to their apartment for a party. It was full of people and my brother-in-law came up to me and told me that a former Cleveland Brown was there. So, I walked over to him and said, "I understand you played with the Browns." He said, "Yeah." When I asked when he played, he told me the early '60's. Then I said, "I'm Ross Fichtner and I played in the early 60's, but I don't remember you." That guy left that party so fast....

In 1965, I got an invitation to speak at a banquet in a suburb of Cleveland. They were paying me $150, which was pretty good pay back then. I was to meet these guys at this tavern first. It was a year after our championship and I walked into this tavern and I gave the name of the man I was supposed to meet. They directed me to the back room where these guys were sitting around the table. They asked who I wanted; I told them, "I'm looking for so and so." He asked what I wanted. I said, "I'm Ross Fichtner. I'm supposed to be speaking at your banquet tonight." These guys started looking at each other with the biggest surprise on their faces. They said, "You aren't Ross Fichtner." I said that I was Ross and I was to come here and meet them. One guy slammed the table, "I'll be a son of a $#@%!" Then I found out what happened. After we'd won the championship, I left Cleveland for the season, but some guy went into the bar and said he was me and hung around there for about a week. He stayed at this guy's apartment, borrowed a car, borrowed $200 from a guy, then took off. So, they had set me up to pay me back by doing me some unnamed harm. They were embarrassed, and after we'd visited for a while, they paid me my $150 "speaking fee" and I left.... Another time, at the Browns practice facility, our equipment manager said the police wanted to talk to me. So, I went outside and there was a man with the police. The guy said, "This isn't him." I said, "What are you talking about?" They said they were looking for Ross Fichtner. I said I was Ross Fichtner. The guy looked surprised and apologized for his mistake. Someone had come into their bar and ran up a tab and left them hanging. So, he called the police and came to our practice facility to get his money. I must have been a favorite guy, or maybe one of those faces that nobody remembers, and so people thought it was easy to impersonate me. I think one of the best ones was when I was sitting in a restaurant with friends and a bottle of wine is brought over to our table. The waiter said, "I understand you are with the Cleveland Browns." He said that another patron had heard there was a Brown at our table and had sent over the wine. I walked over to his table, I asked who I needed to thank for the bottle of wine. The guy introduced himself and he said he wanted me to know that he was probably the best Browns fan in the city of Cleveland. He said that since the inception of 1946, he'd never missed a home game and went to at least two away games a year.

Then he asked my name. When I told him who I was he said, "Are you new with the team this year?" I told him it was my sixth year. So, the best fan in Cleveland didn't even know who I was.

- **What is the saddest thing that happened during your career?**

I think the saddest thing that happened was when Don Fleming was killed in an accident during the off-season one year. He and I were the starting safeties. The Browns flew us to Florida for the funeral and it was very tough.

- **Are players worth their salary? Should they be more fan conscious?**

I don't know how they are as far as being fan conscious anymore. I've been away from it. I would probably know a little bit more if I were coaching and observing things. I would assume they are not. I personally don't believe they are worth their salary. When I was playing, we played for a whole year for $10,000. Elvis Presley would make tens of thousands of dollars in one night. Now, *that* was out of whack. One way I used to look at it was to compare it with the huge amounts entertainers are paid. Football players are a type of entertainers. But they have short careers and they put themselves at risk for injury. Of course, in those days we didn't have huge salaries. But, I knew I was making at least three times what anybody else made when they graduated from college. So, we felt like we were paid well. We used to have to have off-season jobs, because we didn't make enough to retire on. However, I am still thankful that I played when I did, because the league was good then. The biggest problem in the NFL today is that most guys in the league can't play. They can't play against the best. There is such a big difference with thirty-two teams and sixty guys on a team. We had twelve teams with thirty-six guys on a team. The difference between the best athlete and the least athlete on the team was a lot closer than it is today.

- **What are your hobbies today?**

I have loved playing golf for quite a few years now. I especially enjoy playing in the many celebrity and charity golf tournaments, which have football-related sponsorships. I have always loved to hunt and ice fish, though I rarely get to do so anymore.

- **Tell us about the classes that you teach.**

I have done coaching conferences with Athletes in Action, a Christian ministry for athletes and coaches at all levels. The first conference is *How to Build Character Qualities in your Athlete*. The other part addresses how the coaching staff should relate to each other in front of the team in order for a team to be successful. I've done them both here and in Europe. I don't get paid for doing it. It is one of the things I give away. It is my gift to the Lord for being very generous to me in my lifetime. It is not a business.

- **What did you get out of your NFL experience?**

I got many really good friends and connections, which have lasted for decades. And there are a lot of things that you learn about yourself. You have to dig pretty deep to do some things. I gained confidence. Mostly it was just the experience of playing, and I can't say that it was financial. None of the guys that I played with would ever say it was financial. Although it wasn't bad; it wasn't like we were playing for nothing either.

Ross Fichtner									
Defensive Back 1960-1968									
Notre Dame									
Season	Team	Games	Defense				Fumbles	Total	
			Int	Yds	Avg	TD		Points	
1960	CLE	12	0	0	0	0	0	0	
1961	CLE	13	0	0	0	0	0	0	
1962	CLE	14	7	76	10.9	0	0	0	
1963	CLE	13	2	75	37.5	1	0	6	
1964	CLE	8	2	67	33.5	0	0	0	
1965	CLE	14	4	98	24.5	1	0	6	
1966	CLE	14	8	152	19	1	0	6	
1967	CLE	14	4	113	28.3	0	1	0	
1968	NO	4	0	0	0	0	0	0	
Career		106	27	581	21.5	3	1	18	

Season	Team(s)	Punt Ret.				Kick Ret.			
		PR	Yds	Avg	TD	KR	Yds	Avg	TD
1960	CLE					1	0	0	0
1961	CLE					1	11	11	0
Career		0	0	0	0	2	11	5.5	0

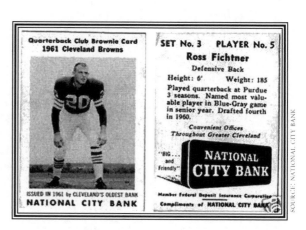

Jim Houston

Many players are not ones to pull their own chains. Most also don't talk about their accomplishments on or off the field. Jim Houston is one of those accomplished players. His first achievement at Ohio State was winning a National College Football Championship in 1957. Not bad for a first major feat in college football. The next year, he was the Number One receiver at Ohio State, a non-throwing team. By the end of the 1959 season, he had received the honor of All-American for both years and Team Captain for the latter. Jim was drafted in the first round by both the American Football Conference Buffalo Bills and the National Football Conference Cleveland Browns. He chose to sign with the Browns. Several years under Paul Brown were productive, but when Blanton Collier took over, he changed Jim from a defensive end to a linebacker. After that change, the honor of Pro Bowler followed him for four years. Jim Houston was elected to the Ohio State Varsity Hall of Fame in 1979, Ohio State Football All-Century Team in 2000, and the College Football Hall of Fame in 2006. Jim is an all-Ohio boy, playing with the Massillon Tigers, Ohio State University, and the Cleveland Browns.

- **What was it like the first time you walked on the field as a Cleveland Browns player?**

Oh, (laughs), it was interesting. The first exhibition game I played in against San Francisco, out in Oregon, I told the coach, "Bob St. Clair held me," and Paul Brown, being Paul Brown, said, "You don't let him hold you; that's just not done." So, that was the end of that. I'll back up a little bit—they had a special formation they ran that would be a sweep to our side, so they sent a substitute in and he said, "Hey listen, make sure you widen out a little bit." And, I did of course. St. Clair was 6'9" and weighed 270 pounds. I'm 6'3" and weighed 240 pounds. So, he reached out and grabbed my foot. Well, the middle linebacker and the corner man closed the play down, and as I was running off, Paul Brown put his head down and he just shook his head, like I was going to get cut. There was no question I was going to be cut. Well, I told him later that following Tuesday, "He held me," and Paul Brown said, "'Don't let them hold you." That's it, period. That was the biggest lesson.

- **You played linebacker and defensive end for Ohio State and Cleveland Browns from 1960 to 1972.**

I played at Ohio State as a defensive end and offensive end. I played both ways for the Buckeyes.

- **Did you play both ways for the Browns, too?**

No. I just played defense and special teams.

- **When did you decide you wanted to be a professional football player?**

Well, I played for a long time at Ohio State and my brother (Lin Houston) played for the Browns from 1946 to 1953. I had another brother that played for the Washington Redskins (Walt Houston) in 1955. I was drafted...actually, I went to the last game—Cleveland against San Francisco—as a guest of the San Francisco 49ers. They said, "Jim we are going to take you first." I said, "Great," so I thought I was going to San Francisco. That day, the 49ers beat them 21-20 and the Browns picked me first. So, I was lucky the whole way and, of course, playing for the Cleveland Browns is where I wanted to play, because I was born in Massillon, Ohio. I am the only Houston born in Massillon.

- **What round did the Browns draft you?**

I was drafted in the first round. I was the fifth guy overall taken.

- **When you got to Cleveland, were the crowds about the same as what you were seeing at Ohio State?**

Well, pretty much. There was a great orientation for anybody that was from Ohio State. There was no question about that.

- **Who inspired you to play professional football?**

Well, it was almost a process of elimination. Here I am going to go teach school, be a coach, and make $10,000 a year, or I am going to play football, goof off half of the year, and make $10,000. Well, I had a couple of choices, so I decided to play football. Of course, being with the Browns, they were my childhood idol. I don't know if you remember the stories, but in 1946, I used to go to the games, buy the tickets for a quarter, and sit in the end zone watching the games. My brother was playing as an offensive guard for Paul Brown. By the way, Lin (Lindell Houston) played for Paul Brown in high school, college at Ohio State, and then the Browns. That's how I followed that story.

- **What high school did you play football?**

Massillon High School in Massillon, Ohio.

- **Who did you play for at that time?**

It was Chuck Mather and Tom Harp. Chuck Mather my sophomore year—I didn't get to play much then—but as a junior and senior I played full time under Tom Harp, who later went to the United States Military Academy at West Point.

- **Was Massillon a powerhouse at that time?**

Oh, yes. We won the Ohio State Championship my junior year and we lost it my last year as a senior.

- **Do you still follow Massillon sports?**

Oh, yes. I only keep in touch by what is printed—I don't do anything else. Normally, I don't go to the games because Saturday is Ohio State University and Sunday is Cleveland Browns. Going on Fridays would make for a very busy weekend.

- **What kind of parental influence did you have growing up?**

My dad worked at the mill all his life. He walked to work and we never had a car here in Ohio. We came from Southern Illinois and my mom ruled the roost. Whatever she said, we had to do. She was about 5'9", weighed 200 pounds. If you didn't do what she said, you were in deep trouble—I don't care how big you were.

- **Are your parents still around?**

No, they died a long time ago. My dad died at age 68 in 1962, and my mom died at 81 in 1982.

- **How many siblings did you have?**

Five brothers and one sister. My sister is deceased, my oldest brother is deceased, the next brother is deceased, and the third one down is deceased. There are three of us left: Howard, Walt, and me.

- **Are they athletes as well as you are?**

Well, my oldest living brother is a double amputee, but was probably the best athlete in the family. He retired from the jewelry business. He had a store in Massillon all these years. My brother Walt is a retired businessman. He has a place in Naples and a place in Chagrin Falls, Ohio. He is probably the most successful of the bunch. Football though, I can't tell you how important it was to us. It made us do what we were supposed to do. Don't talk about what you want, get out there and do it; go and get it.

- **Was that the discipline you learned from sports?**

Well, the discipline from our parents and football—instant success or failure is a definite indication of whether you are going to have success or you're not. If you block that guy and knock him on his back, that is success. If he stuffs you, then it is not success!

- **What about Woody Hayes? How did he influence you?**

Woody, of course, was the guy who planned for everything. He was probably the individual that prepared his players for absolutely everything. The reason I say that is that Coach Hayes would plan for a lull in practice. Then on the practice field, (he would) go into a tirade to charge us, excite us a little bit, motivate us to get us going. If we were kind of lackluster—that was just the way Woody worked and he would take his hat off, and rip it apart—literally rip it apart. You and I can't rip that hat apart. He was caught by the manager snipping the strings in the hat in preparation for a lull in the practice, so he could emphasize something. It worked. He was a big enough guy, though, and he could stuff you if he wanted to.

- **It's been said that he [Woody Hayes] was a military genius and that he carried those military values on to the football field. Did you see that when you were coming through?**

He was a bright guy; a really bright guy. Everything he did was influenced by his military background. There was no question about it. After college, I was military-oriented. I went to advanced ROTC and I was in the service for two years and retired as a captain.

- **What was Paul Brown like?**

Oh, an astute technician. Great reputation. A lot of history. He drafted me first. I really feel he drafted me first because of his experience with my oldest brother. I was two-time All-American and all that stuff, but Lin was born in 1919 and I was born in 1937. I was the youngest of the group, and bigger than Lynn was, so he said, "Hey, I want him because I know of the experience with Lynn," so he drafted me first.

- **Was that work habit instilled by your parents?**

Oh, it was just understood. You had nothing, you deserve nothing, but you better bust your butt and get something. That is just the way it was.

- **What was it like to play for Blanton Collier?**

Oh, great. Blanton was probably Paul's henchman, or assistant coach, that provided all the nuances, changes, additions, corrections, etc. to the football plays. Blanton was an expert, there's no question about that, and he assisted Paul, who was an expert, also.

- **Did he follow Paul to Cincinnati?**

No. He was at Cleveland, he took over for Paul in Cleveland and stayed with Cleveland until 1967, I think. They probably communicated all the time.

- **Nick Skorich was a player's coach. What do you think about that?**

Yes, he was. He certainly was. He would say this is the way you do it, and if you don't do it this way, you are going to get run over. He's a friend of mine. As a matter of fact, a business partner, and Nick was forthright, direct in that. We owned some land together.

- **Several players say you were one of the leaders. How did you lead?**

I just did what I was supposed to do. For example, carry out my assignments on defense, carry out my assignments on the punting team, the kickoff team, all of those. It is kind of an understood thing in the game and all the players know that you have to carry out your responsibility. It is just being responsible is what it amounts to. I had played and prepared all my life for it—from Massillon, to Ohio State, to Cleveland. I was excited about it. It was a wonderful pleasure for me to be able to participate at the level in which I participated and have the success I had. A leader does what he is supposed to do! Be consistent!

- **What players did you enjoy playing with?**

What comes to mind are the 1964 guys. I can name the entire team for you. From when I served as captain at Ohio State. All the players I have played with. Young guys as they came in and all the experiences we had, kind of checking them and seeing how well they did. That was a pleasure for me. To start off, at age nine, watching my brother play for the Browns and then have it materialize to having finished my thirteenth year with the Browns…well, it was just a wonderful experience. I owe everything to the Browns.

- **What kind of influence did Jim Brown have on the team?**

It was kind of an understood influence. He was the greatest runner in history. The best run he ever made is on a highlight film, about a six or seven-yard run through about four or five guys into the end zone. I don't know which team we were playing or anything like that, but it is on his highlights. You will see it if you do happen to see the rehashing of his career. He was a beautiful, physical player. He weighed 236, 238, 240, 235 pounds—whatever his weight was. He was sharp. He was a smart player that knew what he was doing and had a great running ability. They say, "He didn't block that well," well, who cares whether he could block or not. He could block if he wanted to, but we wanted him to run.

- **Sportscasters have made the statement Ohio State vs. Michigan is the best rivalry in sports today. What is your experience?**

No question. Absolutely the best. I have friends from Michigan who played on the team and it was just an exciting time. In my three years, they whipped our butts once. We beat them in my sophomore and junior years. We lost there when I was a senior when I was a captain, so it was really hard to take.

- **Did you attend any Bowl Games?**

We went to the Rose Bowl my sophomore year and that was a key game in my college career. I caught a couple of passes and played the entire game— sixty minutes in 85-degree weather. I lost a little over twenty pounds and I didn't have anything to lose. *(This was the 1958 Rose Bowl and the Ohio State Buckeyes won the National Championship.)*

- **What about the Cleveland and Pittsburgh rivalry?**

Well, that is a storied competition, no question. In my era, and in my brother's era, Pittsburgh was second rate; however, from the 80's on, they have been first rate. I have friends there, too, but Pittsburgh is one hell of an organization and Mr. Rooney and all those people over there—God bless them, I hope they do well, but just so they don't beat the Browns.

- **Who is your nemesis?**

Not really anyone. I weighed about 245 as an outside linebacker and if the guy was going to knock me down, he had to really do the job, and I don't remember getting knocked down [laughs].

- **A few players always have one person in their mind that they always had trouble with, did you have anyone?**

Yes. Bill Brown played for the Minnesota Vikings. Bill was a short guy, six foot, weighed 230 pounds, and I couldn't get my hands around him. For some reason I could not get a hold of him. From a leverage standpoint, I could hold my own against anybody like that, but it just didn't work out. We lost to Minnesota, but we beat them many times, too. When I ran into Joe Capp, or Joe Capp ran into me, and the quarterback was involved some way, Capp got outside of our end and started to run up the field. I was deep in the secondary trying to help our cornerback, so I recovered and came back. I thought to myself, "This is a chance to put him out." Well, I hit him and I went out because the way I was hit, it knocked me out. I walked off the field I guess, I don't remember. Later, though I go to Washington, D.C., when I retired from football, and I was scouting for the Browns. A young kid came up to me and he said, "Hey, aren't you Jim Houston?" I thought holy-moly, they remember me after all these years...and he said, "You're the guy Joe Capp knocked out!" I almost swore at him, but I didn't [laughs]. The only time I have ever been knocked out was the previous day. I hurt my head and the next day I had a collision. It usually took two blows!

- **What were your feelings when the Browns left Cleveland?**

I was very disappointed, but understood with all of those circumstances. I think it was a mayoral problem in Cleveland. They didn't cross all their T's and dot all their I's. It was a general screwup by the administration, and an organization the size of the Cleveland Browns needs to have some input from the city. The city didn't provide that so that is why they moved.

- **Do you still feel like you are part of the Browns organization?**

Totally. I am the president of an LLC, which is called the 1964 Championship Team. What has happened is that we had an appearance at the Hyatt Center, the starting defense and starting offense only. We each received a pretty good stipend for doing that. What we are looking forward to now is a cruise that Bernie Parrish is working on; he is the treasurer of our group. I am the president, he is the treasurer, Monte Clark is the secretary, and John Wooten is the vice president. We are working on everything from a trip to Alaska, to a trip across Canada, a Caribbean trip, and a European trip with the Browns Backers. We should get about 1,000 fans to go on these trips because they will get an exclusive with all the players. That is a real possibility.

- **Were any of your six divisional championships more meaningful?**

No. A championship is a championship. Of course, the 1964 is the most important one, but still a championship.

- **Tell us about your 1964 shut out.**

Have you ever had anybody reach around your neck and hug you? Well, that is what we all did. We did that to everybody. All players had that kind of attitude. What that meant is that we wanted to portray, "I'll cover you—you cover me," and we are going to be there forever. The 1964 team should be the catalyst for an evaluation for any corporation. If you get that kind of attitude from your employees [like the 1964 Championship team], what do you think you are going to have? Nothing but a positive gain. We feel it; we won't run in front of a car for somebody, but anything they need…we take care of each other. We are very tight. It comes from a definite feeling for each other because we went through this special time.

- **Your interception and yardage rate is phenomenal. How did you do it?**

[Laughs] I'm fast—that's all—I'm fast.

- **How many touchdowns did you have in your career?**

Oh, three or four. Not that many. I don't even remember them. What is important is that we won the game. I do remember my 79-yard interception against New York. I ran out of gas at about the five-yard line, but thankfully, the lineman chasing me ran out of gas also.

- **You played in four Pro Bowls. Was that an honor for you?**

Oh, yes, it was an honor. Of course, the biggest one was in 1964, the year we won the Championship, and all that kind of thing, so I thought I deserved a chance to do that. What happened the other years—well, the team wasn't the champion, so the hell with Houston, that kind of thing. I felt I should have been there ten years, minimum, but I don't argue about that.

- **Are the Cleveland Browns fans the best in the NFL?**

Yes. No question about it. We have probably the greatest fan organization, called the Browns Backers, of any professional football team in the country or in the world. I say that because they were all for us and the Cleveland organization. Not for the visitors. You had your naysayers, or you had your Pittsburgh fans or Chicago fans, but they were a minimum number of people.

- **Where was the hardest place to play because of the opposing fans?**

The only negative experience I had was in Pittsburgh when we got hit with snowballs, not dog biscuits, but snowballs. A lot of my friends were opposition players.

- **What is the funniest experience you ever had in college?**

Well, one of the funniest experiences is a story I use in my speeches. Dick Schafrath and I were pretty tough players in college. We had a signal called, "run it, rack it, or got it." What that signal meant was if it was a "rack it" call, that was a double team with Dick and me on the guy right over Dick. If it was a "got it" call, that meant that Dick and the guard would take the guy over the guard. Or if it was a "run it" call, that meant single guys—one over me, one over the tackle, one over the guard. So, we were playing Iowa, and Iowa/Ohio State was always a tough game. We came to the line of scrimmage, and as Woody would always want to play three yards and a cloud of dust, so they ran a twenty-eight rack it call because the guy was over Dick, and Dick was the guy that made the calls at the line of scrimmage, and so Dick said "rack it." The guy he was playing against was a guy by the name of John Cline who was 6'5," 255 pounds, and the other tackle was Alex Karris. So, anyway, Schaft called "rack it" and Cline, as a big guy, would normally rush and was a high target and Schaft whacked him right in the chest with his helmet, and then of course his arms are up in the air trying to fight Dick off, and then I just blew him away. I came in just underneath his arm and knocked him down. I picked up the middle linebacker and we got an eighteen-yard run. That is the way things go, right? That is what Woody wants, but Woody has a tendency to repeat himself. So, about five plays later he says twenty-eight and whatever the blocking is and we go to the line of scrimmage and the guy is right over Dick again. Dick says "rack it" and John Cline's eyes got as big as saucers and he says "son-of-a-bitch." The team couldn't understand why Dick and I were laughing our asses off for about four plays. No kidding—that is the funniest experience that ever happened to me in football.

- **What is the saddest thing that ever happened during your experience?**

Some of the guys getting hurt really bad. That applies to any team, not just the Browns. You don't want that to happen. I was really happy I could run all day, participate, and contribute. That was my objective.

- **What is the difference between players then and now?**

I don't know; they are making fifty times more than we made. I was the first draft choice, fifth guy taken in the draft, and signed the contract for a $1,000 signing bonus and a $10,000 contract, and that was about three times the amount a teacher made, so I thought I was in hog heaven. The same draft choice today is $25 million. Hello? What does that mean? We are talking now about getting our pension increased. Our pension is $200 per year times the years of service pre-1982. If they increase that to $500, $600, or $700 times the years of service, we just increased our retirement incomes to over $100,000. That is crazy, but it is a strong possibility. So, the alumni are working on things like that. I am part of the players and alumni association. We have all kinds of problems with the administration for the NFLPA. The president, Gene Upshaw, is getting an awful lot of money ($7+ million including players incentive) and maybe he deserves it; but when there are so many players only receiving a few hundred dollars per month that is not good, that is not good at all and they deserve a heck of a lot more. We are actively working to get the amount increased so that a ten-year veteran can have $100,000 pension per year! (*Gene Upshaw died during the 2008 season*)

- **Are players worth their salary? Should they be more fan conscious?**

Oh, you can't judge that. Whatever the market allows is pretty much what you deal with. What was Jim Brown worth when he played for us? He made $90,000/year maximum of the nine years he played. I played thirteen years and my max was $55,000. I played, six or seven years after he retired. His was nine and mine was thirteen, but he was the real hero, a star.

- **Are agents good for the NFL today?**

No, I don't think so; but you can understand the business position to use them because these guys are actually oriented. I happen to sign my life insurance license when I was a senior in college so I was business-oriented all the time, so my best year I made a $55,000 salary from the Browns, but I made $200,000 from the insurance business. I was an independent guy, and $55,000 was great. Paul Brown said, "Nobody owes you a living nobody owes you anything."

- **What are your hobbies today?**

I love golf, I really love golf, and Ernie Kellermann knows that, and that is why he mentioned it in his interview.

- **Are you still working?**

Yes, I still write for several insurance companies, have a broker/dealership. I have been writing securities since 1965 and life insurance since 1959, my senior year in college. It is the greatest business.

- **What did you get out of your NFL experience?**

[Laughs] I was introduced to a lot of high-caliber, top-flight people. That is what football has given me. But, you have to remember, I started watching it when I was nine-years-old and had the connection because of my brothers, although I didn't get too much involved with the Redskins because my brother Walt was in Washington, D.C. The experience with the Browns, having played for Massillon and Ohio State and Cleveland—spending my entire time here—I am disappointed that Paul did not make it with the Browns or Art Modell, or whatever the circumstances were, because he was such a great coach. If Paul had stayed on the scene with Blanton Collier and the other assistants, he probably would still be here. I have been the luckiest guy in the world because my football experience has led me to a lot of different people that have become lifetime friends and I just want to continue that. Meeting people like you and others is an intricate part of all that process. I just remember the 1964 year and here we were eighteen-point underdogs against Baltimore and won 27-0. We took on people, all of us; we supported each other. That is rare. It is pretty much an individual accomplishment now with these guys making their millions of dollars; it is their individual accomplishment. They deserve this. Well, we didn't deserve anything and we knew that. I also knew that we had to earn whatever we got, and that is the 1964 team.

			Defense					Total	
Season	Team	Games	Int	Yds	Avg	TD	Fumbles	Points	
1960	CLE	12	0	0	0	0	0	0	
1961	CLE	14	0	0	0	0	0	0	
1962	CLE	14	0	0	0	0	0	0	
1963	CLE	14	1	0	0	0	0	0	
1964	CLE	14	2	86	43	1	0	6	
1965	CLE	12	2	32	16	0	0	0	
1966	CLE	14	2	27	13.5	0	0	7	
1967	CLE	13	3	97	32.3	2	0	12	
1968	CLE	14	3	11	3.7	0	0	0	
1969	CLE	14	0	0	0	0	0	0	
1970	CLE	14	1	25	25	0	0	0	
1971	CLE	14	0	0	0	0	0	0	
1972	CLE	14	0	0	0	0	0	0	
Career		177	14	278	19.9	3	0	25	

Jim Houston

Linebacker/Defensive End 1960-1972

Ohio State University

		Punt Ret.				Kick Ret.			
Season	Team	PR	Yds	Avg	TD	KR	Yds	Avg	TD
1968	CLE					1	0	0	0
1971	CLE					1	21	21	0
Career		0	0	0	0	2	21	10.5	0

Season	Team	Other Stats							
1966	CLE	Rec: 1/10yds,TD							

SOURCE: GAMMETT

5

Paul Warfield

When Paul Warfield called to set up a time to do the interview for this book, there were quite a few questions in my mind about how to conduct it. In truth, his call forced me to play my hand. Typically dumbfounded whenever I talked to Pro players at malls and card shows, I never really had the opportunity to have a more formal conversation with any players, except the few that had attended the River Rats Browns Backers Celebrity Golf Tournament. Of course, that was easy. Those talks were of a lighthearted nature, around a table, after a few drinks. Now, here was this eight-time Pro Bowler, five-time All-League, 1983 Pro Football Hall of Famer asking me how the interview would be done. After relating my intentions, we started talking and, luckily, the interview went off without a hitch. Sure, the sequencing was way off, but the intent of the chapter went better than ever expected. And Paul's eloquent manner and speech made the whole interview process that much more of a pleasure. *Sporting News* Top 100, '79 Ohio State Hall of Fame, 1970's NFL All-Decade Team, a reception average of 20.1, number of touchdowns in his career...all of this was downplayed by Paul. Instead, he talked about his team successes. The '64 Cleveland Browns Championship game, the Browns run on Championship games, the Super Bowl wins in VII and VIII—those were the topics of discussion. And of how this Warren G. Harding High School player excelled in football and set an Ohio State High School Record in the long jump. His Hall of Fame stats describe him as fast, super smooth, excellent blocker, sure-handed, as well as a premier wide receiver—and in this first, pressure-filled interview, he proved all that and more just through his kind demeanor and calm attitude. Thanks Paul.

- **What was it like when you walked on the field the first time to play?**

I had the full range of emotions, much like any young prospective entering the NFL. Certainly, a lot of things were going on in my mind. The opportunity to fulfill a dream was exciting. I grew up in northeast Ohio and became interested in athletics and professional sports. I followed the Cleveland Indians and Browns. The Indians were the most popular sports team in Cleveland during the mid-fifties. They had outstanding players. I recall going to a ball game at the original stadium, which was called Municipal Stadium. Later, it would be renamed as Cleveland Stadium. I remember very vividly sitting in those stands and thinking, "Boy, would I love being on that field playing baseball!" It was just a whimsical thought in my mind. Ironically, fifteen years later I found myself on that field in a uniform, not as an Indians, but rather with the Cleveland Browns. The dream came true, but with a slight twist. Nevertheless, being on that stage on a late summer's night in August 1964, was as Yogi Berra once said, "Like déjà vu all over again."

- **You were drafted both by the Browns and the Bills in 1964. Why did you decide to go to the Browns?**

There were two distinct professional football leagues in the early sixties. There was the National Football League, the reigning league of stature. It had been in existence for over fifty years at that time. The rival American Football League (AFL) was a newcomer, having just started in 1960. So, they were the upstart league, seeking to find a place in Pro football history, competing against the established NFL. Consequently, there were two leagues and two separate drafts. I was drafted by the Buffalo Bills of the AFL. A few years later, the AFL and NFL would merge and become a part of the one league that we all recognize today as the National Football League. While the Buffalo Bills of the then American Football League was busy seeking my services, the NFL was notably standing by. Luckily, I was also drafted by the Cleveland Browns of the National Football League. I indicated previously I was a fan growing up in nearby Warren, Ohio. I knew the Browns winning tradition and identified more with the established NFL. I wanted to be with the best football team in the best league, so the Browns and NFL were my choice.

- **When did you think you would become a Brown, before the draft?**

I had no idea that I would be going to the Browns until the day of the draft. I received a telephone call from club owner, Art Modell, just before they were getting ready to make their selection and he informed me that they were going to call my name for their first pick. I was bewildered, ecstatic, and happy. I had received inquiries from other NFL clubs, but not the Browns. I had visited their training camp a couple of years earlier. I had even met the legendary head coach, Paul Brown. Aside from that, there was no other communication between that organization and me. The common draft goes then, as it does today, most draft eligible college seniors don't know until the day of the draft which club will select them. The draft is set in sequential order, with the worst teams selecting first and better teams record-wise selecting towards the bottom. League policy forbids conversations until a club is on the clock during their time to select a player in any given round from one to round seven. So, the draft does not assure a club of getting the exact player a team covets, but hopefully a very good one who fits their needs. The only exception to that policy is the team that has the worst record. That team has a right to talk to any player before the draft.

- **What inspired you to be a professional football player?**

I was fortunate to grow up in a small community that provided opportunities for youngsters to play Little League baseball and other sports programs. I progressed from recreational to interscholastic programs, intercollegiate programs, and, ultimately, professional football. I loved competing. However, I never thought, at least initially, that I would be good enough to play professionally. I may have dreamed about it, but never thought I was talented enough to play any sport as a professional. My thoughts began to change when I played Junior American Legion Baseball. It was during my years of fifteen to seventeen that scouts from several major league clubs began to make inquiries about me. Baseball, initially, was the sport that opened my eyes to possibilities at the professional level. Actually, I thought about playing baseball right up to signing with the NFL. I made a decision to forgo baseball and play professional football. It was a decision I made in my senior year. A very difficult one, because baseball was very important to me. I honestly had not given much thought to playing football beyond Ohio State until my senior year.

- **Are you glad you made the choice to be a football player instead of the baseball player?**

I am not disappointed, but baseball was a real love. I have often wondered what would have been had I chosen my first love.

- **Did Woody Hayes make an impression on you?**

No, but Woody was very concerned that I was going to sign a baseball contract during a summer vacation. There was little reason to worry. I was committed to staying at Ohio State. However, the Pittsburgh Pirates made an offer that summer that was hard to refuse. But, I did, after consulting with my dad. He suggested, or perhaps convinced me, that I would be better served by finishing school first and assuming the challenges of baseball later.

- **What players did you really enjoy playing with?**

I had the privilege to play with great players and for two great organizations. I started in 1964, playing with an offensive unit. The incomparable Jim Brown was in that ball club, along with Ernie Green and, later, Hall of Fame runningback Leroy Kelly. We had a center offensive line in Gene Hickerson, John Wooten, Dick Schafrath, and Monty Clark. Frank Ryan was quarterback. Gary Collins was the receiver who played opposite of me. He probably was the best wide receiver I teamed with during my career. He was outstanding, a prototype for receivers today. He stood 6' 4", 225 pounds; not only a big man, but very nimble performer. He was a great threat. As a result, his presence on the field took a lot of pressure as a rookie. On defense, we had excellent leadership and fine players. Galen Fiss was our team captain, top linebacker Bernie Parrish was the leader of our secondary and like a coach on the field. Bob Gain played many years in the Browns organization, epitomized the Browns winning tradition. Dick Modzelewski joined our ball club in 1964, coming from the New York Giants where he had been part of their great defense, and Walter Beach who was an outstanding cornerback. We had great leadership and great players who were part of that Paul Brown system. Paul Brown was no longer the head coach, but in 1964 his top assistant, Blanton Collier had taken over. Blanton was a great coach in his own right. He led us to a title. So, we had an outstanding offensive football club and an excellent defensive unit as well. It was a great experience to be a part of a championship team my first year in the NFL.

- **What was it like to play with Jim Brown? What kind of impression did he have on the team?**

He was already a legend, playing in his eighth year in the league. I used the term "incomparable" and you really cannot compare him even by today's standards. Football is a team sport, and usually one individual does not have the ability to control the flow of the game offensively or defensively, but his running and his ability was unique. He was so awesome as a runner, he could literally control the flow of the game by himself. He was a dominate player in every sense of the word. While we had great talent at the receiving positions and otherwise, the entire focus of the defensive team opposing us was to stop him, and he couldn't be stopped.

- **Did that open up the rest of the field for good players like you?**

Yes, without question. My life was made a lot easier. I was a first round draft choice and felt no pressure. Opposing teams did not attempt to stop me; they set their defenses to stop the great Jim Brown. Consequently, through experience, I gained confidence and stature as a young player.

- **What did you learn from Coach Blanton Collier?**

He was a great coach. He was vastly underrated in Pro football. His winning percentage was right up there with some of the great coaches of his era. He won over seventy percent of his games, and an NFL title. He was an unassuming, mild-mannered, Southern gentleman who didn't seek to bring a lot of attention to himself. He was committed to football and had an extremely analytical mind, a tremendous teacher who could teach any position on offense or defense. He had a unique way of relating to his players and getting them to accept his philosophy about self-improvement to become a better football player.

- **Sam Rutigliano, what did you learn from him?**

I did not play for Sam, but I did work with him in the Browns organization. Sam, like Blanton, was a communicator and teacher. I thought his teaching credentials and his ability separated him from other coaches in his era. There were more coaches who were teachers and that's the key to developing talent through instruction. When the young men come from the colleges and universities, they are well schooled. Still, it is a learning aspect, and the difference between good and great in the National Football League is not whether you run a 4.3 or 4.2 forty, although it has importance. It is (more) from the shoulders up, because everyone has talent who plays at this level. You asked me about Jim Brown and, as great as he was with his physical gifts that he had, Jim Brown was an intellectual player. I mean he looked at every aspect of his game. He was intuitive, knew what people were trying to defend against him, how to stop him, and knew how to take advantage of me. He was, as I said, very intuitive and instinctive and then you combine that great intellect, the insight, the feel, the instincts of his play, which was from learned behavior but not only learned behavior, but study of his opponents. He knew precisely how the New York Giants would try to stop him. He knew precisely what Sam Huff would be doing on any given play. To be able to anticipate things and know things before going into a ball game only help those players who have outstanding talent to take the game to another level.

- **Did Jim Brown take his leadership skills into the locker room and off the field as well as on the field?**

Unquestionably, he was a leader on the field. He had this great obsession with winning and winning at the highest level. He was a very important part of our success and winning. He was truly a team player. That is a lesson younger players can learn today. Winning as a team was for individual sacrifice. Jim wanted to win at the highest level. He wanted team wins and championships. Consequently, he was willing, if necessary, to sacrifice his contribution if we had to win. By that, I mean, if we were in a tough ball game and we needed to throw the football to win, he was not upset with the fact that it might reduce his carries because winning, not his individual interest, was most important. Today, you find in too many instances where players are more concerned about themselves, whether it is running or catching the football on offense or making sacks on defense. However, they are not thinking about the team concept, which is the way to win at the highest level. The greatest teams in the history of professional sports, whether you're talking about the Boston Celtics of the sixties, Yankees, or even the Green Bay Packers. Those teams embodied the concept of team. Maybe I'm getting a little off the subject, but our teams today, amateur and even professional, are ridden with too many "me-type" players instead of "we" guys. Yes, we had talented athletes, but they were not meshed together as a team. In recent years, our country has lost its supremacy in Olympic Basketball competition and in the most recent world baseball competition. The reason being that our foreign competitors play the sports games better as a team. We now place too much emphasis on the individual.

- **Why aren't the teams, the Browns of today like they were pre 1999?**

The Browns are rebuilding. A structure or foundation must go into place. We have attempted to bring in the people administratively and in coaching who have a track record for winning to take us to the top level, with the leadership going on down to the field people with the hiring of their most recent coaches who have come in here with Mr. Crennel. He has hired his staff and now the personnel department is intact. Now the building blocks have been put in place. There is still more work to be done before this organization gets to where it needs to go, but I think they are falling in place and we are moving in the right direction.

- **What were your feelings when the Browns left for Baltimore?**

Well, I think it was unfortunate. This great area, with its great fan base, lost its football team. There were a number of factors that were involved and I don't know if I have all the answers to the situation, but it would be simplistic to point your finger in one direction. I don't think that would be fair or accurate. The most important thing is that Clevelanders have their football team and the Browns back. It is unproductive to hold grudges or look back. We only go forward to bigger and better things.

- **It's been said, and you have been involved with both of them, that the two biggest rivalries in sports history to this date are Ohio State/Michigan and Cleveland/Pittsburgh.**

Both are geographical rivalries. The State of Michigan borders Ohio, as does Pennsylvania. The University of Michigan over the years has had great teams and players. So has the Pittsburgh Steelers. Along with the great teams and players, it is the geography that makes the rivalries—the bragging rights, if you will, for the fan base of both states on a yearly basis.

- **Who was your nemesis on the field? Who did you have the most trouble with?**

In the early years, ironically, there was a cornerback by the name of Brady Keys who played for Pittsburgh who seemed to have a greater level of success against me. He was a feisty little guy, and perhaps ahead of his time in that he was a talker of so-called smack. He thought he could get into an opponent's head by talking constantly. However, in reality, I respected him because he was good in man-for-man coverage. He was consistent and centered. I had success against him later in my career, but he did present problems for me as a rookie.

- **The Cleveland Browns fans have the distinction of being labeled with certain plays: Red Right 88, The Drive, The Fumble, the Bottle Throwing Incident, the Rudd Penalty. Were you part of any of those?**

No. But I was with the Browns organization, and watched that ball game and the play. Red Right 88 now lives in infamy. That one play perhaps kept the Browns from advancing to the Super Bowl. However, one could never fault a player such as Brian Sipe, the quarterback who threw the interception. Brian was a competitive player who was trying to win. Consequently, you never penalize or criticize a player who gives a one-hundred percent effort towards winning. In that instance, you just pay homage to the

Oakland Raiders defender who made a great play against the Browns with intercepting the ball. Those things happen. Brian Sipe was trying to win the ball game. He was doing what he did best, playing with tenacity, playing with aggressiveness, courage, and playing to win. It just didn't work out. I don't think it was necessarily a bad call on the part of the coach and he was trying to win. It didn't work out, but being so close to a Super Bowl and yet end up being so far away from it, and the ball club was probably as close at that point as at any time. Hopefully, in the future an opportunity will be presented to rectify the call Red Right 88.

- **Are Cleveland Browns Fans really the best in the NFL?**

Unequivocally, they are great fans. I simply loved playing in the old stadium, and am sure I would have loved playing in the new Browns stadium because the fans are so loyal to the Cleveland Browns. Speaking of Mr. Modell, and while I think he did his best to get Cleveland the very best, there was some lean years occasionally. Yet, you would find sell-out crowds throughout each NFL season. That is an indicator of their loyalty. Today, the Browns still play to full houses.

- **You were an eight-time Pro bowler. What experiences did you have?**

The adulation of being selected as a player that is considered to be one of the top players of the game and playing against some of the great players of that era was a great feeling. It also was a good feeling to know your work is appreciated and that you're considered to be one of the top players of the period.

- **How has being in the Hall of Fame affected your life?**

In my opinion, the Hall of Fame belonged to players like Otto Graham or Marion Motley. I never dreamed that my play on the football field would be likened to that of legendary players. I wanted to be as good as I possibly could be, game in and game out. That was my objective to prepare myself physically, mentally, and to utilize all of my resources, to every given Sunday afternoon be the best I could be. If we lost, or if I didn't have a good game, then I was not very happy and was doggedly determined the following week to work even harder to improve as a player. It was not my objective to be in the Hall of Fame, but I was overwhelmed to be selected for induction. Moreover, this great honor was bestowed on me in all likelihood because my objective was to play the best football that I could game in and game out. A friend of mine, Brooks Robinson, baseball's great third baseman and Baseball Hall of Famer said, "My objective was to be the best baseball player that I could be every time I was on the field." As a result, the Hall of Fame goes to those who consistently set and achieve the highest standards of play. Then their play over a career is evaluated and the pundits determine who is worthy of this greatest of all honors.

- **You were with the Dolphins during the Undefeated Season.**

Yes. It was one of the great experiences I had. I joined a team that was at the bottom of the barrel, but turned it around overnight and became one of the great teams in NFL history. We were committed to the objective of winning, and establish a mark that has stood the test time for thirty years. That undefeated season was, and is, a monumental accomplishment for a group of men who change their image from losers to winners.

- **Who was most influential to you as a coach?**

My high school coach. Had it not been for him, I never would have played football, period. I met him when I was a junior high student. I had my first experience in junior high with tackle football and in my hometown of Warren, Ohio. There was a separate junior high school system of grades seven through nine. High school was only a three-year high school at that time, not four years. So, as a ninth grader, I played football. I was not anything special as a football player, but made it through that year. I played a lot, but as I was going into getting ready to go to high school the following year, I started thinking about which sports I was going to play in high school. I knew all of the older boys who played in high school. They were bigger and they were better athletes and football players than me. I was really good at track and field and was very good at baseball. I said, "Perhaps if there are any sports I am going to play in high school, I would probably be better suited and serve my interest better if it was either baseball or track and field." If I chose track and field in the spring, I could play baseball during the summers. I was much better in those two sports than football. Towards the end of the school term in the spring, the high school had just hired a new young head coach who came up from the southern part of the state of Ohio and he came over to our junior high school to encourage the ninth graders to come out for the football program. He was going to be doing some special things with football and was going to really put Warren High school football on the map, which he ultimately did. I had never heard, I was only thirteen or fourteen years old at the time, a more impressive speech, and I felt like I was compelled to go out for football later that summer, just to inquire what it was all about. I was so impressed with what he had to say and I felt that he was distinctly talking to me even though there were five or six other kids there. I identified very closely with him and lived on the edge of every word he said. A lot of things happened to me that felt right—things started to change overnight for me and became a very important part of the football program and evolved into quite a good high school player.

- **Did you have a lot of parental support when you were playing?**

Very much so. I had a very strong family base and my father played high school football himself, so I got the necessary encouragement. My mother was a little bit leery about my playing because she was afraid I would get hurt. I was doing what I wanted to do and my dad gave me his full encouragement. I had the necessary support system.

- **Did you have more influence as a leader before 1970 or after 1975?**

I think my role in professional football had not been one of an upfront leader in a vocal sense. I think that because of what I accomplished on the field and my work habits and work ethics, people may have seen me as a leader in that respect—more so than articulating leadership or taking leadership and respecting me for how hard I worked in practice—and saw that I had success and I was an individual who saw himself as a member of the team and did not try to separate myself from the team in one respect to another. I think the players respected that and valued what my contributions were.

- **Did that actually make you more of a role model than a leader?**

That is certainly a question we ask today in terms of young men who come into Pro football. We want to know whether their leadership has evolved; whether it is vocal or whether it is example or a combination of the two. I learned that Jim Brown was a real leader, in the sense he would be vocal, but I learned a lot just by watching him and watched the way he did things. I picked up on those things and incorporated a lot of things. He didn't necessarily have to tell me that. I knew what he was doing. I knew how much work and effort that he put into every play. I knew he was very meticulous about understanding how defenses tried to stop him. I learned to incorporate how defensive coverage affected me. Opposing teams would set coverages to try to stop me, double teams and so forth. Then I began to think a little bit beyond that. First, identifying that I've got to be aware of it. I am going to become a person they are going to try to direct defensive strategies toward. I have to be able to anticipate what they are going to do to me. I never want to go into any ball game that I'm surprised by what the opposition does strategy-wise. I've got to be able to anticipate every conceivable thing they may do. I have to have a counter move in order to be successful. I can't expect them to play a game in which they are going to cover me with just one man. I learned that from Jim Brown, and as I learned from Jim I am certain other players, because of my reputation and stature, learned by watching me or by asking me questions. That is a form of leadership. If you are willing to share that information. When you do the right things. When the coaches don't have to stress you're not working hard enough. When they see a Jim Brown come out on the field, and his commitment during that practice session, and they see the great results he's received over the year, they emulate that because they say that's the right way to do this job.

- **You seem to speak highly of Romeo Crennel.**

His resume certainly speaks to the success he has had as a defensive coordinator. He's been in winning situations. He is a part of the New England Patriots success. He has been with Bill Belichick, who is considered to be the top coach during this era of Pro football. He spent time with Bill Parcell, another top coach in modern day football. He's watched, he's observed, he's been a top coordinator, a tough strategist. He was Bellichick's top strategist in terms of organizing and putting together the defensives. He understands how to do that. Obviously, he has been involved with football for many,

many years. He has been among two great coaches in terms of observing and seeing—how they are organized, how they put things together, how they relate, how they communicate—but he is his own individual and he has his own individual style in terms of getting his concepts and ideas across and building toward what he intends to do is to bring a championship team to Cleveland. I feel confident he the right man for this job, and if all the rest of us who are associated with this organization do our parts, we are going to move in the right direction—hopefully in the direction that young Miami Dolphins team moved to getting to the top. To bring the Cleveland Browns back to where they should be as a flagship of the fleet team in the NFL.

- **Does Jim Brown still have an influence on players today?**

I certainly don't think it hurts and if I were a young player, and let me tell you, when I was a young player years ago, if I had a Jim Brown who was one of the greatest players who ever played this game and knowing what he accomplished, I would lean on every word that he had to say. I would want to know those secrets of being the best player I could be. When I was a young player joining the Cleveland Browns, when Jim Brown had something to say to me during the course of the ball game, I certainly leaned on every word he said. I knew he could provide me with some insight, because I was young and inexperienced. I wanted to find those answers, to have some success. I would hope the young players of today would be receptive because here is an individual who has climbed the highest mountains and certainly has advice to offer. I would want to be the recipient of that kind of advice.

- **Do you think Jim Brown is the greatest player who ever played?**

In my mind, I don't want to begrudge any of the other great, great players because there have been great players at other positions, so that is why I said one of the greatest. I can be fair and be accurate without someone in Chicago saying, "Are you kidding, Walter Payton is the greatest running back," or someone in Buffalo saying, "O. J. Simpson is the greatest running back." In my mind, I don't think there is a greater running back that has ever played this game. Today, someone in Detroit might say Barry Sanders is. Chicago might say Gale Sayers is. I appreciated his great talents. I played with him for two years. I watched him even before I played with him as a collegian and as a high school kid. I've seen the other great backs, but Jim Brown is one of the greatest football players this league has ever seen and perhaps the greatest running back.

- **What did you get out of your football experience with the Browns?**

I started out this conversation by indicating that I chose the Browns over the Bills, and the Bills were probably prepared to offer me the Taj Mahal and a place in Heaven to have gone to them over the Cleveland Browns. I grew up as a Northeastern Ohioan. I was a youngster who got highly interested in sports and had the opportunity to play for the team of your dreams, in a manner of speaking, and the team in your geographical area that you grew up in. That just doesn't happen. For things to really work out in terms of my playing for this organization, but having success for this organization, it was truly a dream come true. Certainly, my friends, my family, all the people in my home town were able to follow me from the time that I was playing high school football, were able to come up here and see me play, was the best experience I think a young man could have. To play for that team and to have some success for his hometown team.

- **Putting it all out there and letting the real fans look and see what the real players are all about, right?**

I can appreciate that from the standpoint that we're talking about Cleveland Browns fans and boosters and supporters who have been a great support for this organization over the years. I'm still vitally interested in it and want the very best for it. I can understand them wanting to have this close insight into those players who have played through different eras. What they're feeling when playing. I think most players who have played have had great experiences playing for the Browns organization in terms of what it represents in being a part of it. It's part of their life and their history, what they are most proud of.

- **The differences in the players in the different eras. The earlier players played because they loved the game. Other players played because they loved the game but then started making money. The latest players are bankers. Do you agree with any of that philosophy?**

Obviously, there have been some changes in attitude. I certainly don't begrudge any players for the amounts of money they make today. I can only say they had good fortune and God bless them. They are in a position where they have the opportunity to make money and, in some instances, their heirs' lives will be taken care of. I think that the attitudes have changed in players and, to a certain extent, you go through different kinds of generations. I am from the generation in which young people were told you have to earn your place, or you have to prove yourself, before you're in the position to make demands. I think we are in a generation that, rightly or wrongly, you're talking about families to some extent. I have always said that my dad wanted me to have a better life than him and that's quite natural for a man to want his offspring to have a better life than they had. My dad did honest work, was a steel worker, and it was a great life for us. We were not poor and we were not rich, but we always had clothing, food, a home, and we had the love of our parents. Now, I was able to do things that my dad was unable to do in terms of higher education, although my dad was a high school graduate. I was able to go on to college and receive a degree and play football professionally and so I did have a better life economically and so forth. Now, I am looking at my children and am I taking the position that I want my son to have a better life than I had. Well, the life he had wasn't too bad, because of his dad. Still, I wanted him to be competitive in society and for him to have an education and those things. Each generation, where does it go? Does it keep going up and up? Well, we now have young people who feel a sense of entitlement to a certain extent. I'm not saying that is necessarily my kids, because we tried certainly to guard against that, but we do follow some patterns, which means you want so much for your kids. We have a lot of young men who are playing this game who feel they are entitled to certain things, that they are entitled to millions of dollars. Those notions are placed in their minds by what they see on television, what they hear about these excessively inflated contracts to some degree, and also by agents. Each man has the right to do what he wants. Earlier, we talked about team concept, we talked about Boston Celtics, we talked about Yankees, and we talked about the great Browns teams, players of that era put team before everything else. If you talk about the Miami Dolphins team now, those teams in the 1970's, that's why those teams were so great. I would like to see players today, for the most part, if they could embody those concepts, and again, I am not saying I don't want to be too broad with the brush, painting the same individualism and self, but there's probably a little bit too much of it.

Paul Warfield in a publicity picture catching a pass

			Rushing				Recieving					Tot
	Paul Warfield											
	Wide Receiver 1964-1977											
	The Ohio State											
	Pro Football Hall of Fame 1983											

			Rushing				Recieving					Tot
Year	Team	Gm	Rn	Yds	Avg	Td	Rc	Yds	Avg	Td	Fum	Pts
'64	CLE	14	52	920	17.7	9	0	0	0	0	0	54
'65	CLE	1	3	30	10	0	0	0	0	0	0	0
'66	CLE	14	36	741	20.6	5	0	0	0	0	0	36
'67	CLE	14	32	702	21.9	8	2	10	5	0	0	48
'68	CLE	14	50	1,067	21.3	12	0	0	0	0	0	72
'69	CLE	14	42	886	21.1	10	2	23	11.5	0	0	60
'70	MIA	11	28	703	25.1	6	2	13	6.5	0	0	36
'71	MIA	14	43	996	23.2	11	9	115	12.8	0	3	66
'72	MIA	12	29	606	20.9	3	4	23	5.8	0	1	18
'73	MIA	14	29	514	17.7	11	1	15	15	0	1	66
'74	MIA	9	27	536	19.9	2	0	0	0	0	0	12
'76	CLE	14	38	613	16.1	6	1	3	3	0	3	36
'77	CLE	12	18	251	13.9	2	1	2	2	0	0	12
Career		157	427	8,565	20.1	85	22	204	9.3	0	8	516

Year	Team	Punt Ret.				Kick Ret.						
		PR	Yds	Avg	TD	KR	Yds	Avg	TD			
'64	CLE					1	4	4	0			
Career		0	0	0	0	1	4	4	0			
Year	Team	Other Stats										
'66	CLE	1 TD/Fum Rec										

Paul Warfield
Wide Receiver, 1964-1969, 1976-1977

Fluid receiver posted Cleveland's
first 1,000 yard receiving season
(1,067 yds in 1968)

SOURCE: HEROES DECK

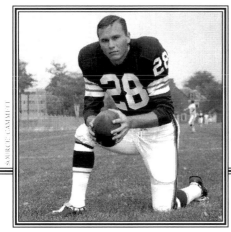

Ernie Kellermann

Blanton Collier, following in the offbeat coaching mannerisms of Paul Brown, obtained the contract for quarterback Ernie Kellermann and converted him into a defensive corner. Just the same way he did with Ross Fichtner and several other college quarterbacks. In his own rights, Ernie Kellermann was an outstanding quarterback at Miami of Ohio. He was a three-time, All Mid-American Conference player from 1962-64; still owns Miami's all-time total offensive leader with 3,978 yards; and set four passing records by completing 88 of 149 passes for 1,260 yards and a completion percentage of .591. Ernie's biggest game passing-wise came against the University of Houston in the Tangerine Bowl in 1962, completing 17 of 40 passes for 265 yards. He also engineered the upset defeat of Purdue in 1962. He played with Cleveland, Dallas, Cincinnati, and the Buffalo Bills. This 1965 draft choice is a quiet, humble man, and I almost had to drag the story about his interception for a touchdown on December 12, 1969, out of him. It was against the Green Bay Packers and the future Hall of Famer Bart Starr. Ernie intercepted the ball in the third quarter and ran it back forty yards to clinch the 13-7 game by making it 20-7.

- **What was it like to walk on the field the first time as a Browns player?**

It was the thrill of a lifetime, because I grew up in Cleveland. I had my opportunity to come back here because of Bo Schembechler. The Dallas Cowboys drafted me and I went to the last cut with them. Having said that, I called Bo, who I had played for at Miami. Long story short, he had coached with Blanton Collier and, through a bit of networking, put a call in on my behalf and talked me up to Collier. That gave me the chance to go to Cleveland. I was on their Taxi Squad in 1965, which was Jim Brown's last year. I didn't dress for any of the home games because I wasn't on the active roster but I practiced every day. I sat with the coaches when they graded the films, helping them chart the pass coverages. I heard them critiquing the players, especially the linebackers and defensive backs, and felt that went a long way to my making the team the next year. I had a better grasp on the coverages and what they were intended to do. As a safety, it behooved you to know where the linebackers were on pass coverages. It would allow you to play the weakness of coverage if you knew where your linebacker help was coming from. In 1966, I made the team in the third game. I was rushed in because Walter Beach got hurt. I stayed in as a regular for the next six years. From that point forward, we had a pretty cohesive unit with me as safety, Mike Howell at the corner position, Erich Barnes, and Ross Fichtner as free safety. I don't recall exactly how we finished up, but I know we had a winning record in 1966. It was the '67-'68 or '68 and '69 season we beat up Dallas for the Eastern Division Championship. When you can play professional football, realizing a boyhood dream, in your hometown, I think it makes it extra special. That is how it affected me. You didn't put a whole lot of thought into it at that point of your career because you are so busy learning your assignments and focusing on who you were playing the following week. Watching films and doing everything they expected of you to get you ready for the game. You practiced during the week and watched films, then come Sunday, you had it all in your brain, and you just went out there and played with a lot of reckless abandon. At the same time, you played with some intelligence. You would stay focused on the down and distance and what the opponent's tendencies had been. Every game, the coach prepared a playbook full of the previous games on the team you were playing. The harder you studied the opposition's tendencies, and got it engrained into your head, the better you played. My basic assignment on the pass was to cover the tight end. Jackie Smith was a premier tight end from St. Louis, Jerry Smith was another good one from Washington. We played Baltimore a couple of times back in the era when John Mackey was doing his thing. I tried to thoroughly study these guys, because some of the teams really featured the tight ends in their pass offense as much as they did the wide outs. I always had really good games against these so-called "better than average tight ends." Mackey made the Hall of Fame, as did Jackie Smith. Having said that, the guys I played with and against were classy and took a lot of pride in what they were doing. Back in the era I played, if you had two or three new guys from one year to the next on your team, that was a major overhaul. There was more continuity and guys played most of their career with one team. The guys that I played with on defense were there for most of the five or six years I played. When I tried out with Dallas, Tom Landry was the coach and they had guys like Mel Renfro and Cornell Greene, Warren Livingston, and Mike Gaechter. I thought I could play with those guys, and I went down to the very last cut thinking that I had made the team. Five days before the start of that season, they cut Brig Owens and that made me the sixth defensive back, which most teams carried then. I really got my hopes up after that. However, a couple days later, Landry called me in and said, "We are only going to go with five defensive backs this year." That is when I gave my old coach, Bo Schembechler, a call. He told me to get my graduate degree so I could coach with him. I told him no, that I thought I could play, and a couple weeks later, I was with the Browns working out with them on the cab squad. That was the beginning of it. It was a learning curve that particular year. The following year, I am on the active roster with the starting defensive unit. Things can change in a heartbeat, and they changed in my favor at that time.

- **Did anyone inspire you to play football?**

I grew up in an athletic family. My mother and father were good athletes. I vividly recall at age seven my mother being my first coach in baseball. Baseball was my first love. She was pretty instrumental in teaching me fundamentals and giving me the mindset to try to excel and be the best I could be and try to take it to the next level. Obviously, I had some innate ability and played all the different sports growing up in high school: football, basketball, baseball, and golf. I don't know if one single thing or person inspired me. I was always blessed with great coaches. My high school coach really talked me up when I was a senior. He promoted me enough to get a scholarship. I owe him quite a bit for talking me up. I went to Miami and only played quarterback. When I was drafted by the Cowboys, I was drafted as a defensive back. Back in that era, they were drafting quarterbacks with quickness, trying to switch them into defensive backs for whatever the reason. I knew the writing was on the wall with Dallas. I would have to make it as a defensive back. I was in the best shape of my life and thought I did well enough to make the team. What seemed to be a disaster at the time turned out to be a blessing in disguise by having the opportunity to come back to Cleveland.

- **What were your parental influences to play football?**

My parents encouraged myself, my two brothers, and my two sisters to play sports. My oldest brother was a pretty good high school wrestler. He didn't go to college because he went into the service. My two sisters were tomboys, and the younger brother came along when we were all teenagers. He ended up being the golfer of the family and went to Duke on a golf scholarship. My parents were always encouraging us to participate and be involved. They came to every football game I played in high school. I don't think they missed a game in college either. Miami played in a bowl game in Orlando in the Tangerine Bowl. My parents drove down there for that game. Houston beat us 49-21. They made trips to Purdue and Marshall. They jumped in the car every weekend and showed up at my games. The biggest influence in my life was sacrifices they made to get to the games and support me. My Mom and Dad were my biggest inspirations.

- **Where did you play high school football?**

St. Peters Channel in Bedford, Ohio. It was a brand new boys' parochial school. They had started this school and, in 1957, we were the first freshman class. There was only one class in 1957. They added one class every year, and we eventually became the first graduating class in 1961. We played a decent schedule. My junior and senior years, we played St. Edwards, which is a state power now. I remember beating them the last two years. The high school experience was memorable because it was a brand new school. We had a couple kids that went to Big 10 schools on scholarships and I got a scholarship to Miami, Ohio.

- **Who was your high school coach?**

Sam Revolo. I saw him not long ago in Las Vegas while I was there for a company trip. We were able to spend four or five hours together, talking about things. Sam was the coach who promoted me to the people at Miami. Sam told me he had sent some film on my behalf to Miami and the film came back. He said they never opened the film. He had it sealed in such a way that when it came back, he knew it had not been opened. A couple weeks later, John Pont, the head coach of Miami, called Sam and asked him if he knew of any quarterbacks that could help him out. He said, "Yes, I sent you the film on Kellermann." Pont said he was never made aware of the film. Again, Sam was telling Pont that his quarterback, Kellermann, should be his man. Long story short, he sent the film back and, shortly after, I received a visit from John Pont at home and he offered me a scholarship.

- **Who were the coaches at Miami?**

The first two years was John Pont and then he left to take a job with Yale University in my junior year. That was when Bo Schembechler came down from Ohio State University. I was in summer school, and he asked me, or kind of told me, that I was going to live with him during the summer. He said that since I was at summer school, he wanted to get into my heart and soul since I was the incumbent quarterback. That began a pretty neat relationship that we maintained even after I graduated from Miami. Of course, he helped me out big time to get the opportunity to come back with the Browns. After that, we kept in touch. I would see him from time to time when he would make recruiting trips from Michigan. It was very emotional for me when he died recently because he had a major impact on my entire career.

- **Anything else you would like to say about Bo Schembechler?**

We were both inducted into the Miami Hall of Fame in 1972. I have a neat picture inscribed by Bo on a Hall of Fame tribute that listed the participants who were inducted that year. At that time, he was head coach at Michigan, and on the picture he wrote, "To Ernie, the player who had the greatest influence by enhancing my coaching career." One year I was Honorable Mention All-American as a quarterback and he was always talking me up. He said that he wouldn't trade me for any quarterback in the country. He achieved much in his lifetime and was very revered at Michigan and Miami.

- **In 1962, who caught the 88-yard touchdown pass to beat Purdue 10-7?**

I was a sophomore and a fellow named Bob Jenks, the big split end (wide receiver as they are known as nowadays), was in our passing scheme. He was 6'5" and weighed 230, which back then was a pretty big player. He ran an out-and-up pass route and they were not expecting it. I remember going straight back and when he made the out move and took off, I launched it. The ball went fifty-five yards in the air, hit him in full stride, and he galloped into the end zone. We were a big underdog that game. Purdue had just beaten Notre Dame the week before and was ranked in the Top 10 at that time. That was one of Miami's biggest upsets and quite a thrill. It was so exciting the whole town of Oxford, Ohio, ripped the goal posts down in Oxford Stadium and dragged them uptown. The town was going crazy. They had to reroute traffic and they had a great big rally for us when we came back. That was the biggest, most thrilling moment in my Miami career. We beat the Big Ten two of the three years I was there. As great as those victories were with the Big Ten teams, we got knocked off by Ohio University (Athens, Ohio) the next week, which was the low point of my collegiate career.

- **Who did you get inducted into the Miami Hall of Fame with?**

In the Miami of Ohio University Hall of Fame, I was inducted with Bo Schembechler ''51; Bob Brown '49, basketball; Marvin Pierce '16, football; and Charles Shugert '32, football and shot put. I graduated in 1965.

- **What was it like to play for Blanton Collier?**

He was the one coach that was not a "holler guy." If you messed up, he would take you aside after the game or after a practice and walk you through your technique and try to get you to picture what you did wrong. That helped me greatly, because you were always looking for words of encouragement to improve. A lot of times, he would come up after you had made corrections in your techniques and would complement you. That helped impact me as a Pro because he was probably the only coach who came up and gave me a pat on the back, or the only coach who really walked me through the techniques. Blanton tried to get me to focus on how the coaches would see it.

- **What was it like to play with Nick Skorich?**

He was an assistant under Blanton. When he took over, that could have led to my demise. When he came, he brought in a lot of new coaches. I was never left with burner speed. I got by with savvy and technical knowhow. So, when this new guy named Ritchie McCabe came in as a defensive backfield coach, he thought that he would try to implement the bump-and-run coverage, even with the tight end. That was in 1971, and I was still with the team that year. In 1972, I went to camp with the Browns. I was cut and Walt Sumner took over at strong safety. It's not that I never got along with Ritchie McCabe, but he had a different philosophical outlook on what a defensive back was supposed to do. Whatever the reason, I was cut and picked up by the Bengals. They needed a defensive back in a backup roll. I went there and Paul Brown was still coaching. Having said that, I grew up as a kid watching these teams in the 50's, all those great teams with Otto Graham and Marion Motley. Jim Brown came along in 1957, which would have been my freshman year in high school. I played with some of these guys I grew up idolizing.

- **What was that like to be picked up by the Bengals?**

It was cool. I was striving to get ten years and thought maybe my career was going to be over. It also gave me an opportunity to play against my former teammates.

- **What was it like to play for Paul Brown?**

I met him when I went to Cincinnati. He was a living legend. Vince Costello was a player with the Browns, and a pretty good friend and all-Pro linebacker. Later, he wound up coaching under Paul Brown. He was responsible for putting a word in on my behalf. I went to Cincinnati and played for only one year. Paul had either mellowed or some of the stories I heard about him were pretty erroneous. Paul delegated a lot of authority to the assistant coaches. When he was at Cleveland, he had to have the last say in every decision made. It was a neat year, because I met new people. I met Ken Anderson that year, who was a rookie quarterback. They had guys like Bill Bergey, who was a big middle linebacker, and Bob Trumpy was still playing tight end. Bob Johnson was the center. Tommy Casanova was the #1 draft choice out of LSU. That was quite an interesting year, because Paul Brown was "The Main Man." You know, I had a not so funny experience with him. I was invited to come back to their training camp at the start of the '73 season at Wilmington College. Paul calls me into his inner sanctum. It was him and me, and he had this five-page letter from a gal who shall remain nameless. My wife-to-be, Mary Ann, was getting threats from this girl who said, "If you marry Ernie, I am going to kill you." She actually even called the church where we were going to be married, and the priest at the church somehow got her name. He called me and said, "Do you know some girl named 'So and so,'" because she just called and said if he performed the ceremony she was going to kill him, too. This was very bizarre and when he mentioned the name, I said I remembered signing an autograph for her and putting a couple lines together. She was having trouble with her parents, could never get along with them, and sounded troubled, so I was trying to play mini-psychologist. I sent a little note and a picture telling her to get along and encouraged her by saying that her parents meant well and she should abide by what they were telling her. When she mentioned her name, everybody put two-and-two together and the FBI tracked her down. They found out she was a girl who had had a lot of mental instability and had been in and out of institutions. It was not a fun time in our life. We were married in 1970 and two years later, she sends Paul Brown this five-page letter saying what a bum I was and we had this mad passionate love affair. The whole story was fabricated. I had to give a dissertation to Paul Brown because he was a man of high principles. I remember hearing stories about if you crossed him, you were gone the next day. That was the last year I was with the Bengals. I was the last guy cut and I thought that was it. Low and behold, I came back and was working at my off-season job and got a call three weeks into that season. Lou Saban, the Bill's Head Coach, said he had some injured defensive backs and could I come up and help them out for three or four games. I said yes, arrived there on a Thursday, and started the following Sunday. I stayed in as a regular the entire year. At 31, I was the oldest guy in a Bills uniform. They had a pretty good team that year. That is the year O.J. Simpson broke Jim Brown's rushing record. In 1973, he rushed for 2003 yards. Joe Ferguson was a rookie quarterback, Joe DeLamielleure was a rookie, and they had the makings of a great team. I was getting some pressure from my boss to hang it up and get on with my life. Before the '74 season, I asked Lou Saban if he would at least guarantee me some money if they thought so much of me through the pre-season of 1974. Lou didn't want to do it. So, I made a determination to retire before the 1974 season ever started. I had gotten knocked out a few times and was starting to get nicked up a little bit. I don't think I ever regretted that decision to hang my cleats up.

- **Who did you enjoy playing with?**

I enjoyed playing with Jim Houston, Walter Johnson, Paul Warfield, Gary Collins, Ernie Greene, Bo Scott, Leroy Kelley, and Bill Nelson. Bill Nelson and I used to hang out together a little bit on the off days. He just loved to have a good time. He was a character and had some great years with the Browns. We had two Eastern Conference Championship games when we beat the Cowboys back to back. Two years they were picked to win.

- **What were your feelings when the Browns left Cleveland?**

That was a gut-wrenching experience and unfortunately so was the negative legacy that Art Model would leave with Cleveland. Whether he was right or wrong in doing what he did, he was dead wrong in ninety-nine percent of the peoples' eyes I have talked with. When he was the owner of the Browns, when I played, he was always considered a fair, honest owner. The first time I met him was when the Browns assigned me to a contract. That was kind of a cute story when they tried to sign me to the cab squad, which was a much lesser payment than being on a regular team, but they also wanted to sign me to a contract for the following year. They offered me twenty grand to sign. I said, "I have to think about it." They said, "We would like to sign you now." I said, "Let me go talk to my agent." I really didn't have an agent. Bo Schembechler was my first agent. They said I could go call and I went into their private office. I called Oxford and Bo wasn't in. He was out recruiting. I stayed in there at least ten minutes then went back and said I did talk with Bo. That he thought the offer was really pretty low and I shouldn't sign for anything less than ten grand more. I said this with somewhat of a straight face, and they went along with it. Bo wanted part of my upgrade when I told him the story years later.

- **You said earlier baseball was your passion; did you ever get a chance to do anything in that field?**

I played a lot of sandlot ball in Cleveland during my high school years in some pretty good leagues. Baseball wasn't nearly as big as it is now, unless you were a pitcher that threw one-hundred miles per hour. They didn't have nearly the scouting either. I did pretty well pitching, but messed my arm up throwing curve balls at an early age. I could throw a football and it never did bother my arm. Throwing a baseball always affected it. At some point, I felt I had to make it in football because I had ability. I was able to get the scholarship for football and after that it became all football and the passion changed from what it might have been baseball to nothing but football.

- **Who was your nemesis on the field?**

I thought they were all pretty good tight ends, but Jackie Smith comes to mind initially. He was one of the premier tight ends in that era and played for St. Louis Cardinals. Later, he was traded to the Cowboys and is in the Hall of Fame. He was a great one; weighed 240 and ran like a deer. I would hook up against him twice every year. Jerry Smith was another premier tight end with the Washington Redskins in Sonny Jerguson's era. John Mackey, who we played every now and then, was another premier tight end. We played against some great tight ends and great backs: Jim Taylor, Paul Horning, and Gale Sayers from the Bears. One of the highlights of my whole career was when I brought Sayers down when it was him and me and the goal line. I made what I thought was a great open field tackle on him. We were watching films the next week and the coaches were critical of me because I didn't come up and be aggressive towards him. I kept in my back pedal and let him run out of all those moves and eventually made the tackle and prevented a touchdown. He was one of the greatest running backs of his time.

- **Do you still feel like you are a part of the Browns Organization?**

They have a fairly active alumni group and, unlike any other team in the NFL, if you played with the Browns and you want to attend games, they always have a couple tickets for you and your wife or whoever you take. I think they try to promote the tradition of the Browns. Cleveland was always rich in tradition and, yes, I do feel like I'm still a part of this organization.

- **Let's talk about your interception for a touchdown.**

There was the one against Green Bay, which was a pretty close game at the time. Boyd Dowler was running a slant pattern and was in sight of Bart Starr's arm. We had a different coverage called and were playing inside out and read the pass pattern correctly, stepped in front, made the pick. I ran forty yards untouched on a sloppy, cold, dreary day at the stadium. I had to side-step one guy. The Cleveland Plain Dealer had a picture of me eluding Forrest Gregg, and somehow it looked like he was going to wrap me up, but I got around him. That was a big thrill and the one and only time it happened. I had nineteen interceptions for the eight years I played. That was definitely a highlight and critical in helping us maintain a lead in that particular game.

- **Were any of your three divisional titles more important than others?**

Defeating the Cowboys was particularly gratifying because I was a small part of beating up on them two years in a row. We beat them here the first time in 1968 and we went to Dallas the next year. They were heavily favored down there and we beat them even worse. I think it was 40-17. Those two divisional games really stick out in my mind because they were against Dallas. Of course, that was the team that cut me.

- **You alluded to being a quarterback and drafted as a defensive back.**

There were three defensive backs that were ex-quarterbacks: you, Ross Fichtner, and Mike Howell. What can you tell me about that?

Back then, they were doing a lot of that. College offenses had a lot of roll-out option quarterbacks. The quarterbacks had quickness and speed. That is what Pro coaches were looking at. I don't know if they thought quarterbacks might have more savvy in switching us to the defense. I never did hear the official word on why that was happening so much. But you knew you had to make it as a defensive back. And that is why Dallas drafted me.

- **Are Cleveland Browns fans the best in the NFL?**

I think so. I have great memories of going into many different cities. Wherever we would go, the team would have this great reception. Whenever you got off a bus, or off a plane, there were people there waving signs and placards to give you a little bit more inspiration. The hometown fans from the era I played in were really terrific, loud, and very supportive. I think people are still very supportive. I played in different cities, such as Cincinnati, and fans are fans and they are going to cheer and cheer their guts out if you win.

- **What can you tell me about the Pittsburgh/Cleveland rivalry?**

It was always pretty intense when I was there. We played them several times as a Saturday night game. For some reason it was a big rivalry back then because we were so close to Pittsburgh. We were beating up on them when I played until Bradshaw came along. They got some great draft choices and had the "Steel Curtain." I would say our rivalry was very intense. Blanton Collier's theme was be consistent. Don't have a great game one week and be down the next week. He thought you should be consistent with all games. So, they always tried to mentally prepare you one week at a time, and the same for every team you played. However, I think the intensity level went up a few decibels whenever we played against the Steelers.

- **Where was the hardest place to play because of the opposing fans?**

I remember Baltimore being the loudest. They had old stands which were right near the field. That place was just deafening. During games, I was always responsible for calling out the forces to the cornerback and remember having some communication problems that game. We had to get some hand signals together and, somehow, would get the signals to Houston or the linebacker in front of me. He was a lot closer to me than the corner back was. It was called The Baltimore Memorial Stadium. I also thought Shea Stadium was pretty loud. I played a few games against Joe Namath when he was just coming up. He was one of the good ones. He had such a quick release and had a lot of class. He was a great quarterback in that era.

- **What was one of the funniest stories of your NFL career?**

I think it'd have to be of Ben Davis. He was a fiery little defensive back and returned a punt one time in a Pittsburgh game. He turned up field and was going to get hit. Instead of running out of bounds, he just turned back into this guy who eventually made the tackle. The guy was a little bit ticked off that Ben would try to run over him, because he outweighed him by thirty or forty pounds. I don't remember who it was, but he jumped up and said, "Davis, if you do this one more time, I am going to bite your head off." Davis shouted back, "If you do that, you big dummy, you will have more brains in your stomach than you do in your head." On another incident, Erich Barnes was our corner for a couple of years. He was brash and cocky and in the twilight of his career, always talking on the field. I remember one time he went down and was dinged in the head. I was the first guy to get to him. I was asking him how he was doing and he said, "Ernie, I'm fine, but how are the fans taking it?" He was certainly a character who was always talking to the receivers. The first couple of plays at the start of games, he would always make it a point to knock these guys in the head. He was a big defensive back who weighed about 215 and who would try to intimidate the guys.

- **What is the saddest story of your NFL experience?**

I remember somebody absorbing a wicked hit and their leg going in the total opposite direction at the knee. It was an awful hit, and the leg was sticking up in the air going one way and it was the wrong way. It was supposed to be pointed. I saw that and got pretty sick. It was always pretty traumatic when we lost a couple of games that would have eventually gotten us into the Super Bowl those two years. We beat up on Dallas in great victories then we lost to Minnesota badly one year and against the Colts in the other game.

- **What is your job today?**

I am an independent sales representative working for JIT Packaging. I got started in 1969 with a fellow who had a lot of interest in the Browns. Milt Lax became my business mentor at this time. In 1969, Milt asked if I would come interview with him. At that time, he was the president of Milrob Corporation, they sold industrial equipment and components. I joined Milt and Milrob in 1969 and continued to work with him for twenty-plus years. Milt is now a consultant to JIT Packaging. Milt was president of Milrob and sold it to a fellow who owned the packaging company in 1992. We joined forces with Dave Jones, who was a wide out with the Browns ('69-'71). I'd brought Dave into our business when it was called Milrob. Dave stayed on with that company for seven years. He did very well at his sales position with Milrob but wanted to get into management and that was not open to him then. So, he left the company in good graces and got into packaging. He eventually started JIT Packaging, selling corrugated containers to industry. In 1992, Dave and Milt got together and Milt sold the company to Dave, which reunited Dave and me. We'd been pretty good friends from when Dave was previously with the team.

- **What are your hobbies today?**

I like to play golf and play a pretty good game of ping-pong. I play golf in the summer and in the winter. I play platform tennis, which is an outdoor game played on a raised up platform. It is played in an enclosed chicken wire type of setting. It also has tennis-court-type lines, and it looks like a sawed-off version of a tennis court, and it is enclosed in this meshed in area. It is both a fun and very competitive sport.

- **Tell me about your Pro Bowl Experience?**

The year I was selected to be the starting safety in the 1970 Pro Bowl, the Dallas Cowboy coaching staff was coaching the Eastern Division All Stars. The team I was cut by in 1965. Emotionally, that really got my ticker going when I was re-introduced to Tom Landry and his staff. What I remember most, over and above our losing the game to the Western All Stars, was rubbing noses with all those great players of that era. Don Meredith, Fran Tarkenton, Mel Renfo, Bob Lilly, and Paul Warfield to name a few. Larry Wilson (elected to the Pro Football Hall of Fame in 1979), the great free safety for the St. Louis Cardinals, was especially interesting to meet and play with. I admired his style of play. He always had a nose for the ball and was a real playmaker. If was not making a key tackle, then [he was] breaking up or intercepting passes. He reminds me of the Steelers free safety [Troy Palamalu] with his reckless, aggressive style of play. But, at least I had the last laugh on the Cowboy coaching staff.

- **What did you get out of your NFL career?**

I got a lot of phenomenal memories. Growing up, I always had these boyhood dreams about playing a professional sport. I take great pride in the fact I have realized that dream. I have been blessed because I played with and against some of the greatest names in professional sports. I have been blessed also to have played under some of the greatest coaches: Blanton Collier, Paul Brown, Bo Schembechler, John Pont, and Tom Landry. I have learned a great deal under these men. Playing for the Browns allowed me to grow in stature and then parlay that into a successful business career in industrial sales. Being a member of the Browns enabled me, and our company, to successfully promote and sell our line of products. The Browns were instrumental in getting us an audience with decisionmakers of companies we were trying to sell. The Browns were a hot commodity and got our company a chance to bid and negotiate large contracts with credit-worthy customers. My wife, Mary Ann, and I still attend most home games as guests of the Browns. It is still a thrill to have been a small part of the organization; seeing old teammates and talking to avid fans who remember the teams and personnel from the 60's and 70's era. Football, to me, is the greatest team sport in existence today. Growing up in Cleveland, idolizing, and then playing with some of the all time great names in Browns' history was more than a boyhood dream come true. It was the Ultimate!

Ernie Kellermann								
Defensive Back 1966-1973								
Miami (OH)								
Season	Team	Games	Defense				Fum	Total
			Int	Yds	Avg	TD		Points
1966	CLE	14	3	23	7.7	0	0	0
1967	CLE	14	1	9	9	0	0	0
1968	CLE	14	6	29	4.8	0	1	0
1969	CLE	11	3	40	13.3	1	0	6
1970	CLE	14	1	18	18	0	0	0
1971	CLE	14	3	0	0	0	0	0
1972	CIN	14	0	0	0	0	0	0
1973	BUF	10	2	23	11.5	0	0	0
Career		105	19	142	7.5	1	1	6

Ernie Kellermann in a game against
the Houston Oilers on Nov. 22, 1970

7

Ben Davis

Ben's parents were well educated and both held jobs as teachers. Ben's father also started a service station business as it made more money for the family. It is not to reason why Ben graduated from high school at the age of fifteen. He attended another prep school until he was of age to attend Defiance College in Defiance, Ohio. When he went to college, he put down his band instruments and picked up a football. His abilities got him drafted by the Cleveland Browns in the seventeenth—and very last—round of the draft. As a running back at Defiance, he came to Cleveland to play alongside Hall of Famer Leroy Kelly, Bo Scott, and Ernie Green. Since the position was set, Ben started playing corner and returning punts. That year he ended up leading the league in punt returns with a 12.7 average. In 1974, Ben was traded to Detroit for Jim Cole of Ohio State University. Jim never really panned out for the Browns, but Ben went on with Detroit for two more years, where he had even more productive years. Ben's sister, Angela Davis, had a life in itself with enough drama to be written into a book.

- **What was it like to walk on the field the first time as a Cleveland Browns player?**

Well, the first time I walked into Municipal Stadium as a player was a very unique experience. I guess the Browns were trying to determine if I could make the team, not only as a punt/kickoff return player, but as a defensive back as well. We were playing an exhibition game against the Packers and they had just won the Super Bowl. Bart Starr was the quarterback, Max McGee, Boyd Dowler receivers, and I hadn't played defensive back at all. I was a running back in college. So I'm lined up against Boyd and they are marching in to score. He runs a post pattern inside and I bit real quick. He just took another couple of steps in and went back out towards the flag. We called it "post flag pattern," and I was way out of position and he was wide open. Bart Starr just lobbed the ball to him and I was able to recover well enough. I was maybe five or six yards away, but way underneath. It was a flat pass; I was able to knock it down. I had good success and I think the Browns felt that I could play after that particular play.

- **Were you one of the first in the trend of defensive backs to become punt returners?**

Well, the reason I was switched to defensive back is because Ernie Kellermann was a quarterback in college and he switched to defensive back. Mike Howell was a quarterback at Grambling and he switched to a defensive back. The trend was to take good athletes and make them defensive backs. In fact, we used to think the best athletes were on the defense anyway, but the reason I was switched is because I was told I would never make the team as a wide receiver. That was why the Browns initially drafted me. We had Paul Warfield and Gary Collins. A guy named Clifton "Sticks" McNeil went on to San Francisco and led the league in receptions. It would have been very difficult for me to make the team as a wide receiver. Now, Leroy Kelly was a punt return guy. His role was a bit diminished, because he was replacing Jim Brown at the running back position. He had done both duties as running back and punt return. I guess in 1966 and they were looking for someone who could return punts and play as a special-teams player. They give you two years as a special-teams player. If you don't make the team doing something else, then you pretty much move on. Blanton Collier had the foresight to switch me before camp started.

- **When did you decide you wanted to be a professional football player?**

Oh, I never decided that. It was decided for me. I went to a small school, Defiance College in Northwestern Ohio. To the best of my knowledge, no one ever played in the NFL from Defiance. It was something I thought I would try. I didn't even think about it until my senior year in college, when I had some success as an individual and on the team. The team did well. I thought it was possibile, but I still had the ability to teach if that didn't happen. I went to camp with the attitude that I wasn't losing anything. I just wanted to go and give it a try because I didn't want to say years later, "Hey, I should have tried it." I went there and things just started to happen. Ross Fichtner told me later, when he was coaching the Chicago Bears, that I wasn't supposed to make the cut. He was an eight or nine-year veteran when I arrived, and he was pretty tight with the coaches. He told me that they told him that I was going to be cut after the West Coast trip. I got into the 49er game, the last game of the West Coast trip, and I did pretty well. That bought me some time. It just happened that I became a professional football player.

- **Who inspired you to play football?**

I didn't play in high school. I played in the band and went to a prep school in Maine, which had about ninety-eight boys. I went out for every sport there because it was so isolated and that was a way of getting off campus. My coach there, Bob Walker, explained that if I went to Defiance College and went out for football, by my senior year I could be a starter there. He inspired me to continue and go out for college ball. Defiance was a smaller college and, at that time, an NAIA School.

- **Would you have played any other college sports if you had not have played football?**

No. I would not have. I wasn't an athlete until I went to prep school and football was my main love. I did track, wrestling, and all those things to help my football skills. So, I probably would not have done it if I had not of been playing football.

- **Where were you born?**

Birmingham, AL.

- **And you went to high school there for a while?**

Yes, I went to high school there for two years, to the same school that guys like Buck Buchanan, Lee May—the a baseball player—went to Birmingham. I was way ahead in terms of my age in grade, I graduated from high school when I was fifteen, so I hadn't even started to develop yet athletically, so that is why I bought some time at this prep school and began to enjoy sports.

- **What kind of parental influence did you have?**

My parents were educators—my mother was a teacher, my father was a teacher, and then he turned into a businessman. He had a service station in Birmingham. I had both sides in terms of the academia as well as the entrepreneurial. They were pretty firm, pretty strict discipline-type parents. Sports were more of a plaything back then anyway, so I never considered myself a Pro type of player.

- **What changed for you then from being a non-athlete to an athlete?**

Well, I always had a love for play and sports. The neighborhood always had pick-up games football, basketball, so I loved sports. I guess what changed it in terms of my getting involved was the situations that I found myself in. Nate Walleck was one of the Browns reporters back when I was playing. He use to go on his tours when we were going to visiting teams to play and he would say, "Here's a guy that went out for sports because there was no band at the next school he went to." So, that is halfway true—I did go out for sports, but I finally caught up with my class age and was able to compete. I guess I was waiting for a small-school environment for me to be able to go out and feel as if I could contribute.

- **What instrument did you play in the band?**

Trumpet, Baritone, mostly brass-type instruments where treble cleft was the music to read.

- **Do you still play?**

No. I don't have to, but I mess around at the piano every now and then. But to play brass instruments, you need your lips to be fine-tuned.

- **Who was your college coach?**

Kirk Mee, Kirk—that is an interesting story in and of itself. He went to Wilmington College and did his graduate work over at Ohio University. He was a young coach, but when he took over the program at Defiance College, he built the program so that by my sophomore to my senior year, he took us to an undefeated season my senior year. He moved on to some bigger schools and ended up in the front office of the Washington Redskins for over twenty-five years, as well as doing some coaching and some personnel work.

- **Is he still around?**

Yes, he is retired now and we get together at least once a year.

- **So, he had a pretty good influence on your career?**

Yes, he was probably why I had the success I did. His training, his ability to develop young athletes, it was just raw. We were out of school—what's equivalent to a Division III school now—back then was the NAIA. We didn't have scholarship money, didn't have a lot of the weight programs, training facilities, but he was creative enough to make it all work. He started with a bunch of guys that became successful in football.

- **Did you pay for your college?**

We used national defense loans and we had to pay them back. There was no free ride. They had jobs around the campus, monitoring the gym, opening and closing the gym, but we had to pay for college.

- **When you were at Defiance, did you play Marietta?**

Well, I am trying to remember…. No, Marietta was a little big for us.

- **What was it like playing for Blanton Collier?**

Well, I told someone recently that I was fortunate to come into professional sports under a person like that. The philosophy he had…he was a very intellectual type person that responded to your intellectual abilities. He didn't yell or holler, he explained it to you. He was a teacher. He would tell you what you needed to do and what was expected of you and either you complied or you didn't. If you didn't, you just weren't around very long. He prepared us extremely well and did not tolerate any mental mistakes. In fact, if you made too many mental mistakes, you were out of there. He would always say that, too. That he would not tolerate mental mistakes because, if you were in position, close to where you should be, you got an "atta boy" for that, but if you were totally out of position, then you were on your way out of there. I liked his approach—for example, I got beat one time, it didn't happen very often, but I got beat, and my parents were there. He came up to me before practice and said, "Ben I am going to use you as an example to talk to the team and I wanted to let you know that, but I want you to tell me why you got beat—what was your thinking on why you got beat." So, I appreciated that, that he was alerting me to the fact he was going to bring me up in front of the team, not to embarrass me, but he wanted to know what my thinking was regarding why I reacted like I did. I think I was much better off by being able to come in under Blanton than some of the other coaches of that day.

- **Was there a big difference under Blanton and Nick Skorich?**

Yes, yes, there was. I think when Nick took over, he wanted to develop a more physical team. Now we were successful, but I think Nick wanted to be able to hit a little harder, be a bit more intimidating by hitting harder. I don't think he was the teacher that Blanton was, either, so that was a big difference. Blanton had philosophies that carry on today. You might end up saying things or doing things that you can go back and say, "Because Blanton did it."

- **Who were the team leaders while you were playing?**

Well, the captains for the most part were Leroy Kelly and Jim Houston, but we also had Paul Warfield. We were a team early in my career. It was just guys that would go out and perform. You would think, "Well, this is the way it should be done." There wasn't a lot of talking going on in terms of what you should do. It was just those things that you learn by example.

- **What kind of leadership role did you take?**

Well, I was initially a cornerback. Erich Barnes was the man back then. We called him the "old man." He was a senior guy, until the early 70's, and then, at that point, I became the senior guy, so we stepped up and I guess my tactic, too, was just to try and perform and let people know that I am showing up every day. If I am a little hurt I still try and play and do the best I can.

- **Who gave you the most trouble?**

After my knee operations—I had a couple of knee operations on one knee— and moving into the American Football Conference, Isaac Curtis, probably, because we went up against Cincinnati twice, sometimes even three times. We played an exhibition game at Ohio State. Isaac had this loping-type speed and was very deceptive, but I could cover it. I could be close to it, could be on it, and all of a sudden he would just reach out and, some way or another, find a way to catch the ball. I think he is the one who stands out as one of the tougher receivers to cover. Now, I had receivers such as Monty Hayes—the world's fastest human—he was somebody I had to go up against. I had to go up against Warfield when he got traded to Miami, and guys like Harold Jackson, he is one of the fastest guys out there. It was pretty much there was a situation every week there was someone that could flat out get it.

- **Paul Warfield said in his interview he had a lot of trouble with you. He also made the statement, and maybe you can reinforce this a little, that the Browns came the closest to beating the Dolphins in the 1972 game than any other team the whole season. What was your experience?**

Yeah—we had them going into the fourth quarter. Well, it was the first playoff game. It was Miami against us. We were the wild card that year and just barely made it into the playoffs. We went down to the Orange Bowl and Mike Phipps was our quarterback, and they had Earl Morrell as their quarterback in that game, and we fought them tough. We fought them hard. In fact, we allowed them to begin a drive defensively on us and they drove the ball about seventy yards to score the go-ahead touchdown. If we could have held them there, we might have demoralized them. I can remember one particular play where Paul caught a pass, and I can remember him leaping over twenty-some feet to catch a ball, that Morrell just tried to throw away and come down with it for a first down. It kept the drive going.

- **Browns fans have the distinction of being labeled with several negative results: Red Right 88, the Drive, the Fumble, the Bottle Throwing Incident, the Rudd Penalty. Times when one thing happened to name an entire game. Did you experience this?**

Yep. I tell you. It began in '68. We had a team capable of going to and winning the Super Bowl. We had a really good team. And it came down to us and the Baltimore Colts. They came in and we were just totally flat that day. We had beaten them during the year but we just couldn't get anything going, so they beat us and they went on to lose to the Jets and that famous Joe Namath "I guarantee a Super Bowl." That was one year we should have won it, and the next year, 1969, although I was out for that year with a knee injury, we had an opportunity of playing the Vikings for the championship, the NFC Championship, and we lost to them. We went up there and they just blew us out. It was a pretty cold day and they just had our number that day. Those two years, we were one game away from participating in the Super Bowl. Then you just mentioned the 1972 season, where we could have beaten the Dolphins, we might have moved on. I always focus on the '68 and '69 seasons as those years we were capable of playing the Super Bowl.

- **ESPN said the Ohio State/Michigan and Browns/Steelers rivalries are the two best in sports today. What are your experiences?**

Well, certainly Ohio State/Michigan. I have friends that played at both institutions and it is always a source of ribbing during the season among professional teammates, so hands down that is probably one of the all-time rivalries. Pittsburgh/Cleveland—during the late 60's early 70's was a rivalry I participated in and I think the intensity was turned up in the early 70's. Late 60's, we pretty much owned the Steelers. We would play them here and over at Pitt Stadium and had successes most of the time. Now, the fans probably created more of a competition than the Steelers did back in those days. Once they moved into Three Rivers Stadium in 1970, the tide turned and they began to have our number. But, yes, there always a dogfight and it didn't matter who or what kind of teams were there, we could always beat them and, in the 70's, we could always beat them here, but never at Three Rivers. I guess the cities are so similar in nature, working-class people, people that love their football, that the traditions of the football teams go way back so, yes, it was a natural rivalry. I don't know how many remember, but we used to play the Steelers on a Saturday night. That was a great, great rivalry.

- **What were your feelings when the Browns left Cleveland?**

Well, I denied it. Even when I heard it was happening. It was my birthday, October 30th, and that weekend we had a party and a news reporter knocked at the door. He had his cameras and everything because he knew we had some Browns players there. He was the first one that I heard say, "Have you heard the rumor that the Browns are moving?" Like I said, we denied it. We told him he got his information wrong, that's not going to happen. The Browns will always be the Browns. I think we played Houston that Sunday. We went to the stadium and that is when it was verified. I don't know how it really broke, but I think someone from Baltimore came forward and confirmed it somehow. I didn't believe it was happening.

- **Were there any negatives that happened while you were playing?**

Probably the biggest thing I began to dislike about professional football was the insistent nature of what happens when you get hurt. As long as everything is going fine and you are producing then it is a wonderful game. When adversity comes along—for example, injuries—you are looked at in a manner that seems like you shouldn't be getting hurt, even though your injury is not of your own doing. That was probably one of the biggest things I realized immediately was that there is no place for people who are hurt or injured, and you are not doing any good until you are able to produce. If you are careful, you will take that philosophy over to your daily life.

- **When did that change and why did it change?**

For me, my experience happened with the ligament I had, and we needed some help in my position while I was out, so I tried to come back too soon. I kept pushing and tried to get back and tore the ligament in two, which kept me out for a full month. My knee, I still can't get it passed ninety-degrees in terms of being able to punt my leg up. Even afterwards, with the type of trauma I had to that knee, when I did recover I would reinjure it. It would be full of fluid and, of course, you were expected to play. I did my best, I tried to do my best and, in fact, I had one coach I told "I can't play, my knee is just too swollen." He said, "Well just go out there and let me determine whether or not you can play." I think it goes to the fact coaches have a lot of faith in players. They want to see them out there no matter what. And if you talk to Bill Nelson, he played hurt pretty much every game. So, the negative is the reality of professional sports is you are being paid to play and so you just got to suck it up and go.

- **Let's talk about your two touchdowns.**

Let's see—my rookie year—this is the Pittsburgh rivalry thing, too. I just took a punt on about fifty or sixty yards and ran it in for a touchdown against the Steelers, which pretty much put the game out of reach for the Steelers. I was amazed at all the reporters that came around the locker room after that. That was a good play. I had picked up blocking and I went out there and broke to the side, got behind a wedge, and just went on in. That was a punt return touchdown. The other one was with the Lions. I think Will Kurt was the quarterback. He was trying to hit Pruitt on a flare pass and Paul Naumoff, who was a linebacker for the Lions, just nicked the ball and it landed right in my lap. I ran about seventy yards back for the touchdown for the Lions. I think I only scored two touchdowns in my career. One for the Browns and one for the Lions against the Browns. I didn't want to leave the Browns, but I got traded. They were going in a different direction in terms of starting another defensive back going into the season, so I asked to be traded as much as I wasn't being considered as part of the Browns defense. They complied and traded me to Detroit. I think that with my play, that is what you try to prove, I guess you gave up on me a little too soon. You should have stayed with me, when you do something like that. The way it turned out, I had coaches tell me they would have done it a little differently, they wouldn't have traded me right away, they would have waited to see if the other guy worked out, those kind of things. It was satisfying, I felt pretty good. I was eight years into my career and it felt good that Greg Pruitt wasn't able to catch me. He was one of the faster guys in the NFL and that was rewarding.

- **Do you still feel like you are part of the Browns organization?**

Yeah—yeah, I mean, they do make the alumni feel a part of it. We were, the alumni, the only Browns that the team had here for three years, but they relied a lot on the alumni who lived in and around the city to keep the game going and keep the Browns alive in the community. We certainly felt a part of the organization back then and, with the new owner and team coming in, I think they appreciate the fact we did what we did. So yes, we are still involved in the community and the Browns—I have been in other cities and I have seen that the Browns community really encompasses the whole city and we're just a part of the city. Once a Brown, you are always a Brown.

- **Is that where you have maintained a home since day one?**

Well, that has a lot to do with it. The city certainly makes you feel welcome. I have maintained a home here because I have been a very successful business-wise. I don't know if it would have been as good in any other city.

- **Do you have any influence on the game today?**

Well, I like to think that I kind of showed the way for smaller guys to be successful playing. Philosophies going back and forth about guys under six feet not being big enough or strong enough to be good cornerbacks. I guess my influence is that guys that are small in stature are not to be discounted to play professional football. I came into the league at 5'10", 175 lbs. People will look at me and marvel at the fact I was playing professional football. I even tell kids today, "If it is something you want to do, play football. If you are small, that's ok. If you want to do it, just do it. You never know what is going to happen." That's kind of what my legacy might have been.

- **Are the Browns fans the best in the NFL?**

Well, from my experience, they are passionate about their football and passionate about their players so, yes, for a team that has not been to a Super Bowl yet, they are still hanging in there. I have seen them go through good times and bad times and the fans are still there. Now, I would like to say the Browns fans are probably the best. The fair-weather fans are probably Steelers—those people over there in Pittsburgh. Everybody can jump on the bandwagon and they have good fans now, because they are winning, and that is not always a true indication of how good your fans are.

- **Would Cleveland have gotten back a team if not for the fans?**

Well, first of all, there is a team and the tradition of professional football is really strong right here in Northeastern Ohio. You can go to Canton and see the Football Hall of Fame, so there is no way in the world that a city like Cleveland could not be represented with a football team in the NFL. So, one way or another, the Browns would have gotten a team back here. It was good the way it turned out; that we kept our name and our colors. The first best thing was not to lose our team. The second best thing is that we ended up doing it with keeping the team name.

- **Where was the hardest place to play because of the opposing fans?**

There were a couple of places. The Raiders, that was pretty tough. The Minnesota Vikings, that was tough—not so much of the fans, but for the fact you were standing almost next to the opposing bench. For fans though, Pittsburgh was tough. I would say probably Oakland and Pittsburgh.

- **Were you one of the players that taped the stadium demolition?**

No, I didn't get that on tape, but it was good to see. I had seven years—two good years, and then the rest—so I guess I did get a chance to have some successes over there in Pittsburgh. There are probably guys that played their entire career with the Browns and never did see a win in Pittsburgh.

- **Do you have any funny stories from your NFL experience?**

A lot of the funny stuff you just really can't talk about (laughs). I can't think of anything right now.

- **What is the saddest story while you were on the field?**

What comes to mind was seeing Blanton Collier go. I really hated to see him retire, although he went upstairs, but I hated to see him move on as a coach. I really thought he could continue.

- **What did Cleveland get out of your trade?**

I think it was a third or fourth rounder, I use to know that, but I can't remember who it was. They did well—I was a seventeenth rounder coming in and they got a third or fourth rounder coming out of it.

- **What is the difference between the players today and the players when you were playing?**

Well, from my perspective, my son is quite different than what I am; but the way the game has changed now, certainly. It is a good profession, but money is the driving force behind it. I think the business aspect of the players is so different now.

- **Are players worth their salary today?**

Well, I guess the players are worth it because the fans are buying the tickets. So, if you ask me if…the analogy I am looking for is Prince…I went to see a concert of Prince and it was over $100 to go in and see this guy sing. So, if no one was there, I am sure the prices would go down. Players today are making the type of money because the fans are driving the market. Are they worth it? Are corporate CEOs worth salaries of $800 million a year? I think just the way things are nowadays is, if you are an oddity or unique you can demand a lot of money. Worth and value are two different things.

- **Should players be more "fan conscious?"**

To try and cultivate that relationship is more difficult today than what it was back then. For instance, back in our day—and I am not trying to stick up for the athlete, I am just trying to look at it objectively—an autograph back in our day was worth the value of a kid receiving it. Nowadays there is a dollar value associated on both sides. If a player signs it and a fan has it, he is looking at it as this is twenty or twenty-five dollars right now. The raw sport, just the fact I like you because you are a fan, I like you because you are a player, that relationship is gone and I don't think it will ever be back.

- **Are agents good for the NFL today?**

You've got management and you've got labor. Now, if you worked in a situation where you could have worked fifteen hours in unfair conditions, well, in terms of agents, I think agents kind of protect the ballplayer to some extent. I was a seventeenth-round draft choice. I didn't have an agent. I didn't need an agent. I was able to get my signing bonus doubled from $500 to $1000 dollars. Bob Matheson was a first round draft choice. He had an agent, but he had an agent that, as I understand it, took advantage of him.

Now, I think that today a player needs someone to represent him because of the money we just talked about, but I think the agent has to have the interest of the player foremost in his mind.

- **What do you do today?**

I have an office equipment supply business but am kind of semi-retired doing that on a casual basis. I do a lot of investing, real estate and stocks.

- **Do you travel all over the country?**

Yes, I travel to different parts of the country. I don't do it as much anymore. I had a radio station in Tulsa, OK, and I would commute every week as a young man, but I don't enjoy doing that any more.

- **What are your hobbies?**

A little golf and I really like to do a combination of yoga and pilates. I do that because it helps some of these injuries I have had along the way. I still like sports. I like the Browns, the Cavaliers.

- **What did you get out of your NFL experience?**

The most obvious is I got a "base" to get on with my life's work, including sales, entrepreneurial experience, and I like to think my background in sports helped me as an employee and also as an employer. It helped me with my values as well. Fair competition, trying to win, and all that kind of good stuff.

Ben Davis in the Heisman Trophy pose

			Defense					Total
			Int	Yds	Avg	TD	Fumbles	
Season	Team	Game	Int	Yds	Avg	TD	Fumbles	PoIntS
1967	CLE	14	1	9	9	0	2	6
1968	CLE	14	8	162	20.3	0	4	0
1969	CLE	1	0	0	0	0	0	0
1970	CLE	7	1	0	0	0	0	0
1971	CLE	12	2	18	9	0	0	0
1972	CLE	14	3	10	3.3	0	0	0
1973	CLE	13	2	33	16.5	0	0	0
1974	CLE	9	1	14	14	0	0	0
1975	CLE	11	1	67	67	1	0	6
1976	CLE	14	0	0	0	0	0	0
Career		109	19	313	16.5	1	6	12

Ben Davis

Defensive Back 1967-1976

Defiance College

		Punt Return				Kick Return				
Season	Team	PR	Yds	Avg	TD	KR	Yds	Avg	TD	
1967	CLE	18	229	12.7	1	27	708	26.2	0	
1967	CLE	9	11	1.2	0	8	152	19	0	
Career		27	240	8.9	1	35	860	24.6	0	

"It seems like they breed little Browns babies there.
I went back a couple of years ago, it was an eye opener.
I didn't understand the magnitude when I was playing.
But there are some diehard fans, and that's their environment.
They believe in their Brownies..."

— *Joe "Turkey" Jones*

8

Jerry Rhome

"I love Cleveland Browns, I love the fans, my teammates—they were good people and the coaches were cool. I have stories, but not all I would care to repeat…" were the words spoken by Jerry Rhome, well before the interview ever started.

Jerry Rhome is a football wizard. Football has been an everyday part of his life for more than fifty years—from his days of playing the game to today where he evaluates and encourages players to achieve the skill level to which they can excel. Jerry became serious about his career at Dallas Sunset High school. His accomplishments were Texas All-State; All American; High School Hall of Fame, Waco, TX; M.V.P. in North-South All American Game; and a member of Texas High School Hall of Fame. At the University of Tulsa, his accomplishments were All American in 1964; Walter Camp Trophy Winner in 1964; broke 18 NCAA Records in 1964; Heisman Trophy runner-up in 1964; Oklahoma Sportsman of the Year in 1964; member of Oklahoma Sports Hall of Fame; member of College Football Hall of Fame; and a member of Tulsa University Hall of Fame. Jerry's services were used by the Dallas Cowboys, Cleveland Browns, Houston Oilers, and the Los Angeles Rams. In the NFL, his accomplishments included playing in three NFL Championship Games and in the famous Ice Bowl game, Dec. 31, 1967, in Green Bay. As a Brown, Jerry told me his favorite accomplishment was to have helped "coach" the Browns players and staff as they played against his former team, the Dallas Cowboys. The motive was not revenge, but just another in a long series of accomplishments for this players' coach. The list of Coach Rhome's coaching positions is long enough to be a book in itself. Now, he is an evaluator of talent. The list of players he has worked with includes Jim Zorn, Dave Krieg, Joe Theisman, Jay Schroeder, Doug Williams, Mark Rypien, Troy Aikman, Chris Chandler, Timm Rosenbach, Steve Beurlein, Warren Moon, Steve McNair, Kurt Warner, Brad Johnson, Daunte Culpepper, Steve Largent, Chris Carter, and Issac Bruce. Jerry Rhome is what football should be: No negatives. No skeletons. Just football.

- **What was it like to walk on to the field for the first time as a Cleveland Browns player?**

I loved it! And the thing I thought that would benefit me with Cleveland was the fact that their number one nemesis was the Cowboys. That was going to be an advantage to the Browns, since I knew so much about Dallas.

- **Was there any one person that inspired you to play football?**

Well, I grew up in a "football family." My father was a high school head coach and is in the Texas Coaches Hall of Fame. It wasn't hard to follow that, plus my second cousin was Ray Renfro, the all-Pro wide receiver for Cleveland. I had chances while growing up to visit with him every once in a while. Plus, with him being a member of the family, it was easy to talk with him about football. Ironically, in Dallas, they showed the Browns a lot. They showed the Lions and the Browns games, so I was able to watch them on television a lot of the time.

- **Did you play for your father during high school and, if so, which one ?**

Oh, yes, I played for him at Sunset High School in Dallas, Texas.

- **So your father had a lot of influence....**

Yes, from the very beginning—I rode a bus all over the state of Texas with him as the water boy. From the age of five, I was on that bus. The players even took care of me—but I took care of them, too. Snuck them water when coach wasn't looking.

- **Who was your coach at the college level?**

Well, I went to SMU for two years and, when I came out of high school, I had played in two All-American games and named the #1 football player in the state of Texas. Don Meredith, who ended up playing for Dallas, was playing for SMU and they were running the same offense that we ran at my high school. We kind of patterned ourselves after them. We were running the spread shotgun offensive when I was in high school, which was rare. I could have gone anywhere in country, but I kind of wanted to follow in those same footsteps. After two years, I started as a sophomore we went 5-5 and had a really good chance to have a great team the next year, but they fired the coach and brought in someone who just wanted to line up and run the ball. So, at the end of that year, I had a couple of coaches from Tulsa, Ken Ship and Sammy Baugh, come see me about transferring to Tulsa. I had this opportunity, but I wanted to go to Nebraska or Mississippi. Coach Johnny Vaught [the coach from Mississippi] informed me I would have to pay my first year there, which I couldn't afford. I ended up at Tulsa and that is where I played out my college career. The funny thing about this is that three years later, we played Mississippi in a bowl game and Coach Vaught was a real gentleman saying, "We would have rather had him on our team playing with us, instead of playing against him."

- **How were you acquired by the Browns?**

In a trade with the Cowboys. I think they gave them a third round pick.

- **What was it like to play from Blanton Collier?**

I loved him. Of all the head coaches, other than my father, I thought he was the one that had the most heart. He just had a way of putting his arms around the team, walking into a room, and talking to us. It just made you want to play.

- **Was Nick Scorich the quarterback coach at that time?**

Yes, he ran the offense. He was a very detail-oriented coach. Very efficient. The offense was not a complicated offense, but he liked changing a few things every week to cross the defense up when they tried to read where our backs were lined up. It wasn't near as complicated as Dallas' but it was very efficient. I guess that came from Paul Brown and Jim Brown. The thing I really liked about him was he took suggestions. Most of the good coaches do.

- **I talked to some guys who said you were a good team leader, not just because of being the quarterback, but an overall team leader. How?**

Oh, I don't know [laughs], maybe because I had so much coaching in my background. First, maybe because I played a position. Second, because I had so much experience as someone standing in front of a team and talking. I grew up listening to my father and I had my mind made up to coach since I was eight. Of course to play, but I couldn't think of anything else I wanted to do other than coach after my playing career. I think if you are going to coach, you better be a pretty good leader. Also, I was always a player's coach because I was a player and always liked that environment. I wanted to know what they felt. So, maybe because I was always talking to different guys about what we could do to be better, that might be where all of that came from.

- **What were your feelings when the Browns moved to Baltimore?**

I was pretty saddened by that. The fact the Browns had such great fans, and that was something that always impressed me about my time in Cleveland. Whenever you walked into that stadium there were 82,000 people and it was a bitter cold day and there they were. It was like that was all they could think about. Of course, that end zone down there [the Dawg Pound] was just super from the very beginning. At that time, they may not have even had it named. I don't know. When you got down to that end zone though, they were for you no matter what. There is just something about Cleveland. I even liked the city. It was kind of a throw back.

- **Do you still feel like you are a part of the Cleveland Browns?**

Oh, yes. That is my favorite team. I have people ask me, "Who do you root for on Sunday?" and I tell them the Cleveland Browns.

- **Are the Cleveland Browns fans the best in the NFL?**

I think so.

- **Have you been back lately?**

Oh, yes. My wife and I just went up there for two or three days. We were guests of Troy Aikman to his Hall of Fame induction, so we went on up to Cleveland before heading to Canton. We went to the stadium and Dino Lucarelli was so nice. He took us on the tour of stadium, went out on the field, took pictures. We were in the locker room with pictures of previous players, coaches. Then Dino took us up to where they had all the old clippings and he was kind enough to go back to 1969 and go through all the clippings page by page. There was a picture of me and my dog from the *Cleveland Plain Dealer*. I can't believe it. We were there four hours and he was so nice. We continue to talk every once in a while. I have to tell you that was my favorite team.

- **Who is second?**

Ok, now you have to set this by saying, "What kind of fans are you looking for?" I don't remember the Browns ever being, I am sure they were at some point, but I don't ever remember the Browns because we had a really good team, being against us, whereas everywhere I have ever been as a coach and playing they could turn on you. I coached at Cleveland against them a bunch of times.... Now, I don't know if you know what they use to put the visiting coaches? On top of the stadium was a little white house about the size of a small press box—like a one room, oh, I don't know, it was just very small. Just big enough to get about six guys in. You literally had to go out on top of the stadium, climb a little row of steps to get into it. You were looking almost straight down. It had a makeshift heater but you know how cold it is in Cleveland, so when we were there when it was cold, we still had to wear everything we could. We are up there trying to work and call plays with the phones and all of that and you were wearing stocking hats, multiple coats.... The wind would blow. The whole thing would shake. That is where the visiting coaches went. You had to leave the locker room fifteen minutes early to get there because you had to go through the stands, which was not good because they [the fans] would be yelling and booing. Then you had to go up an elevator, had to climb stairs, had to go outside, and climb stairs again. I tell you what, though, it was a great view. When we [my wife and I] were there, Dino took us to the [new] opposing coaches area and I asked him, "Do you remember where they used to put the opposing coaches?" He said, "Yeah, I sure do!"

- **Who was your nemesis on the field when you played?**

I would have to say Larry Wilson. He was the greatest safety. He was about 6' 1" 190 lbs. but he could knock your head off. Larry Wilson of the St. Louis Cardinals. He became the General Manager of the Cardinals when they moved to Arizona. He played during the late 60's, early 70's. Every

80

quarterback, when they played St. Louis, kept their eye on Wilson. He is the one who made the safety blitz what it is today. Obviously, Butkus always gave everybody problems, but as a quarterback it was Larry Wilson.

- **Who was the Center for the Browns when you played?**

Fred Hoaglin. We were good friends then, but later we became really good friends and associated more when we became coaches in the NFL.

- **What is your opinion about the Browns / Steelers rivalry?**

There wasn't a whole lot of rivalry with the Steelers when I played. The Browns were far more superior. At that time, it was the Cowboys.

- **Tell us about one of your funniest experiences in the NFL.**

Well, when I was with the Cowboys I almost choked to death on the sidelines. It was my rookie year and we were playing in New York. It was about ten degrees and we had these big coats to keep warm. They buttoned up with these old-time buttons. I was the holder for extra points and field goals so I ran out on to the field and held the ball then came back to the sidelines. I put all of this stuff back on and didn't realize the Giants had fumbled the kickoff and Dallas picked the ball up and ran it back in for a touchdown. So, I had to go right back on to the field for the extra point. Well, I just got all my stuff on, turned around, and somebody said, "You are supposed to be out there." Now, I start stripping all this stuff off and I can't get the top hook undone so I am trying to pull it over the top of my head. I am literally rolling around on the ground trying to get this stuff off and finally I get it pulled up and Coach Landry is standing over the top of me saying, "Do you think you are going to make it?" I say, "I guess not" and they ended up calling a timeout, which cost me a $200 fine...but he was just as calm.

- **Tell us about Tom Landry.**

Oh, I loved him. He was so laid back, but yet intense. When you were behind closed doors, one-on-one, he was down to earth, smiled, talked, but then you put him in front of people, he became serious, reserved, particularly by the book. He took his wife on every trip. He had a heart of gold…. I was actually in the room when he got fired. I had just gone from San Diego to Dallas to be the offensive coordinator. I was probably there two and a half weeks and, of course, rumors were going around about the owner of the Cowboys going to sell the team and there was the possibility Jerry Jones was going to buy it and Jimmy Johnson was going to become the coach. But, life goes on. You don't know if something like that is going to happen because of the rumors. It was Friday afternoon and Tom and I are sitting in the film room, looking at a bunch of Redskins footage on how to use the tight end. I had coached for the Redskins for five years. We are looking at the tape for about thirty minutes, talking, and about that time Tex Schram stuck his head in the door and asked to speak with Tom. He leaves the room, is gone about two minutes, comes back in, sits down, and he just sits there—in the total dark. Then after about thirty seconds, he turns the projector back on. He doesn't say a word—just lets it run. I am sitting there thinking, "What is going on?" I look over and from the light of the projector, I see big tears running down his face. He shuts the projector off. Now we are in the dark again. He goes, "Jerry, I am sorry I got you into this, they just fired me." He got up and walked out. Just disappeared for a while. He went home, got his wife, and they took off on an airplane. No one was even able to find him for quite a while. But, you know what—Jimmy Johnson was a very good coach.

- **Did he keep you on?**

Yes. Well, let me tell you another story. I have the record—it probably isn't on the books anywhere—but I have the record for most head coaches to work for in the shortest amount of time. This is the truth. I was at San Diego and it was in December. I was working for Al Saunders. At the very end of December, they fired him. So, that starts at about December 31st. January 8th they hired Dan Henning to be the head coach. I am still there, under contract. About January 10th, I get a phone call from the Cowboys asking me if I would like to come down and interview for the coordinator job. Well Dan Henning was going to run the offense so I went to Dan and talked to him about it and he said to go ahead. So I went to Dallas. Landry hired me. We are up to three coaches now—Saunders, Henney, Landry. I am there two or three weeks and Tom gets fired, and in comes Jimmy, so that makes four. Jimmy informs me he has his staff filled, but Don Shula is going to need a coach, so another coach and I who were in the same situation flew to Miami. So, I was visiting with Don Shula and he was telling me how much he wanted me to be a part of his staff, so he was going to make me a passing coordinator. I thought, "Great." Right then the phone rings and Coach Shula says, "Gosh, Gary. That is a surprise, okay," and he hangs up the phone. He says to me, "Jerry, I am sorry, but I am going to need to change my mind. That was Gary Stevens and he has decided to stay here." I thought for a second—and said, "Didn't Gary Stevens go to Dallas?" He said yes, but that he had changed his mind. I asked right then if I may use the phone and I called Jimmy. He was mad, but he said for me to get on a plane and head back to Dallas. So, that made five coaches in a very short period of time.

- **What was the saddest experience in the NFL?**

I guess when I hear about players dying or are crippled. Things like that. Not really any one experience. As far as coaches go, when Tommy Prothro died—he was a Rams coach—that was pretty sad.

- **Are players worth their salaries? Should they be more fan conscious?**

Well, the market brings what it brings. That same question could have been asked of the 1950 players talking about the 1970 players, and the 70's players talking about the 90's. That is just the way it is. Things keep getting bigger. Television has obviously made it huge and coaches are the same way. Coaches are making that kind of money now. I came into the league

82

as a coach for Seattle making $24,000 in 1976, which I thought was really good. As far as being more "fan" conscious, that is always the case. Fans are the blood and players should be aware, and I think there are a whole lot who are. There were always those who held out, wanted more, complained about their contract, no matter what era. I think now though, because the spotlight is brighter, it gets noticed more as there are more people playing, more people watching, more involvement from the media that everything is now magnified. A player today can't take his shoes off in public without somebody knowing about it. Example: If I was to do something that was against the law, criminal or something—not anything serious, something minor—and I was to be taken in, my sister within five hours would probably hear about it, and she lives in Anchorage, Alaska. The point I am trying to make is the microscope is so strong. All the things players do, being impolite to fans, unappreciative...well, there were guys like that in 1970 even 1960. It just wasn't under a microscope. How about our government? How many times can you look back and see something done wrong in our government and it got brushed aside? Today, the whole world knows about it.

- **What do you do today?**

I am retired, but still work with players. I didn't really start what I do now, it just sort of came to me. After I retired, I knew a few agents around the country and they started calling, asking me to work with their quarterback. Get him ready for the draft, senior bowl, etc.—that kind of thing. My wife talked me into setting up a web site so then I started receiving e-mails from kids anywhere from ten to twenty-five that wanted special training. If I could work it out, great as some people want things for nothing and others actually want it done. It didn't take long to figure out who was fishing for information and who was serious. I got kids lined up for now through the end of summer. I must admit, every kid I worked with has been a gentleman. I haven't found anyone who has a "big head" and thinks they are already good.

- **What are your hobbies?**

I play a little golf, my wife and I go to a lot of movies, but I actually play a lot of pool. I have a pool table in my house and have the room fixed up kind of cool—a lot of old pictures, memories. Pictures of the Cleveland Browns. I was at an NFL alumni golf outing in Buffalo about three years ago and the banquet was going on. There were these three guys up front at the main table and they were the guys from the three different teams that helped organize the event. I was in the audience with my wife, but the defensive back for the Browns, Charlie Leigh, came up to me at that banquet and said, "Jerry, I just want to tell you how much I appreciated what you did for me." I said, "What did I do for you?" He said, "You made me. You helped me make that football team. Every time I got into the game, you threw balls to me because we were calling our own plays and you let me play. You gave me a chance to show what I could do and I made the team because of that. You did the same thing at practice and you were always supporting me." Unfortunately, he died of cancer about a year ago.

- **Let's hear a funny NFL story.**

Erich Barnes was an All-Pro defensive back and his nickname was the "Old Man." He was the veteran of the team. He was a strong leader and everyone looked up to him as "big daddy." So, we are sitting in the audience at this banquet and I am about four tables from the front sitting behind this really big guy—so I just yell out, "Hey, Old Man," and then I hid. Erich starts looking around the room, then he stops looking. So I yelled out again, "Old Man." I did it to him about five times—it was driving him crazy. See, this wasn't a Cleveland Browns alumni gathering, this was an NFL gathering, so he doesn't know who it is, where it is coming from, but he knows they are calling him. Finally, I stuck my head out and waved and he started laughing. "Old Man," what a great man. Do you know the turkey stories? Well, we had this rookie named Al Jenkins from Tulsa, which was my college. So, they told the rookies to go get their turkey and they send Al Jenkins clear on the other side of Cleveland to pick up all our turkeys. The phone rings. Erich Barnes answers and its Al Jenkins is on the other end of the phone. He says, "Old Man, they ain't got no turkeys down here," and Eric said, "Oh, yes, they do—YOU!" [Laughs]

- **Would you consider a head-coaching job if offered?**

Yes, but that isn't going to happen. I retired in 2001 and in 2005 Mike Tice called and asked if I would come and help coach, so I went the first of October and coached for about three months. That was a good time.

- **What did you get out of your NFL experience?**

Well, I got a lot of good friends, plus an avenue to be what I wanted to be, which was a coach. I am sure, because of my Pro career as a player, it propelled me into a situation where they were looking to see if I might turn out to be an NFL coach. I coached three years in college and we did pretty well. We had one of the top offenses, so the Director of Personnel with the Seahawks had just come on board, a guy by the name of Dick Mansburger, and he had been with the Cowboys as one of the top scouts. I suppose, as being a player from there, they respected me to some degree, knowing the offense and stuff. Plus, I had a little coaching blood in me. I sometimes did a little coaching on the side and that opened the door for me and coached in the NFL for twenty-five years. I am now sixty-five years old....

Jerry Rhome										
Quarterback 1965-1971										
Tulsa										
Seas	Team	Gam	Passing							
			Comp	Att	Comp %	Yds	Yd/Att	TD	Int	Pass Rating
1965	DAL	11	9	21	42.9	157	7.48	1	1	65
1966	DAL	7	21	36	58.3	253	7.03	0	1	68.4
1967	DAL	14	9	18	50	86	4.78	0	1	40.5
1968	DAL	1	0	0	0	0	0	0	0	
1969	CLE	11	7	19	36.8	35	1.84	0	2	5.7
1970	HOU	13	88	168	52.4	1,031	6.14	5	8	61.4
1971	LAM	14	5	18	27.8	66	3.67	1	1	37.7
Career		71	139	280	49.6	1,628	5.81	7	14	55.2

Rushing				Fumbles	Total Points
Rush	Yds	Avg	TD		
4	11	2.8	0	1	0
7	37	5.3	0	1	0
2	-11	-5.5	0	1	0
0	0	0	0	0	0
1	0	0	0	1	0
9	54	6	1	5	6
3	0	0	0	0	0
26	91	3.5	1	9	6

Rhome under center, Browns training camp

9

William Andrews

Art Modell set the stage. He had helped broker the television deals to get Monday Night Football to the NFL and fans across the country. Owners were worried about if this experiment would carry the interest of the audience. Would just two teams be able to hold the attention of all the individual team's fans? Many owners and stations were speculative about the fate of this preview game. It was Art who volunteered the Cleveland Browns to be the guinea pig, and the New York Jets hoped it would be a special event, too. As the Browns Bill Nelson and the Jets Joe Namath took the field with their respective teams, neither knew their fate. ABC had paid for the rights to broadcast this unique moment of time. The crowd of 85,703 watched and waited for that defining moment that could make or break the game. And there are times when one incident can create that defining moment in a career or a lifetime. That moment came for William "Billy" Andrews that Monday night on September 21, 1970, when he picked off a ball intended for Emerson Boozer. After his hands were "sticking" to the ball, and turning the wrong way, he finally righted himself for a twenty-five-yard touchdown. An interception for a touchdown that would be a first for Monday Night Football. As Bill himself said, "I went from being a nominal player to being a starter the rest of my career from just that one play...."

- **What was it like the first time you walked on the field as a Brown?**

It was incredible. It was an annual double-header. I don't know if they still do it now, but we played a double-header every year. It was against the Green Bay Packers. I was a rookie from Southeastern Louisiana University. As a late round draft choice, I wasn't expected to make the team so didn't tell them that I could snap punts. When it got down toward the last cut, they needed somebody that could snap punts. I said I could. They said, "No, you can't." I went out and showed them I knew how to snap the football. In the game, we were backed up on the five-yard line in the Dawg Pound end before it was called the Dawg Pound. I snapped it to an All-Pro, Gary Collins, with Ray Nitschke jumping over my head, saying there is a rookie in here. To tell you the truth, I was having a heart attack. I felt like the ball was too big to go through my legs and Gary Collins was standing back, about half way in the middle of the bleachers. After all that yelling and threats, Nitschke didn't even hit me. In those days, you could hit the center while the ball was snapped. Gary punted it to either Herb Adderley or Willie Wood. They were household names to me. I ran down the field and was the first man to the punt returner and nailed him like you dream about, thinking the ball went one way and the returner went the other. I was getting up to take my accolades when I turned around and all I saw was him spiking the ball in the end zone. I hadn't even fazed him. That was my introduction to my first real action in Cleveland Stadium. It was incredible.

- **When did you decide that you were going to be a professional player?**

I was nine years old, believe it or not. I was a wormy little boy that nobody thought was even able to chew gum and walk. Truthfully, I couldn't very well. The first time I ever played Pee-Wee football, that was my dream. The small town I grew up in had probably five-hundred people in it. It had little ones all the way up to age twelve or thirteen playing in the Pee-Wee league. The first time we ever played, I fell in love and that was it for me.

- **Who was your favorite player growing up?**

My favorite players were anybody with the Green Bay Packers. I didn't know who the Browns were until after I had been there about halfway through the season. The heritage, fame, and history they had. I didn't see a television until I was eight or nine. I'm just a country boy. I didn't know much about professional football, except that was what I wanted to do when I grew up. When the Browns drafted me, I was shocked. I heard from practically every team in the league, except the Browns. When they drafted me, it was out of the blue. When I went to Cleveland for the first mini-camp, I was in shock and awe of the all the players I saw. Everybody knew Jim Brown; he was a household name. He had retired in '66 and was gone the year before I was drafted. I went there in 1967. Leroy Kelley was coming into his own. I started hearing these names. Names I knew were famous like: Gary Collins, Frank Ryan, Leroy Kelley, Jim Brown, Gene Hickerson, Lou Groza, Paul Warfield, and Dick Modzelewski. People that were famous in my eyes. Then, the more I was there, the more heritage I saw in Cleveland Browns football. I saw the tradition; it was incredible. In later years, we won many games just because we were the Browns. It was because we were more talented than most teams we played. We had the tradition of winning and that is what we did.

- **You were the 333rd person taken in the draft. Did being a 13th rounder, 17th player taken for the Browns affect you?**

No. One thing I did not lack was confidence. I believed I could play just as well as anybody. Whether it is ignorance, naivety, or just not knowing any better, that's the way I was. The linebackers were Jim Houston, Johnny Brewer, Vince Costello, and Dale Lindsey. Bob Matheson was the number one draft choice when I was there. Cecil Dowdy, an all-American from Alabama, was drafted with us. Sydney Williams and several others. There were a lot of big name people. I still thought I could play; nobody else did though.

- **Who inspired you to play?**

My high school coach, Hubert Poke, was a tremendous inspiration. He was a tremendous teacher in the techniques of the game. He excelled in getting people in the positions they were best suited for. He was one inspiring man. He taught me the techniques of the game. I was a student, as well as a player. When I came to the Browns, Blanton Collier was the coach. He was a teacher of intricate details in every facet of the game. He would look at the player and say, "You have your foot three inches too far back. That is why this is happening to you. Your hands are right here and they need to be over there." He taught those intricate details of positioning on the field. I was already used to that. I was coached that way in high school and college. Being a detail person, this made me realize if I was supposed to take a block on my right shoulder, I was supposed to step with my proper foot. I did it. If you were supposed to fill this hole, I did it, etc. That was the way I was coached from the onset. That inspired me. I had a great love of the game from the mental vantage point as well as playing on the field. I have to say Coach Hubert Poke was probably the person that inspired me the most. The little town I grew up in, played football in, and live in (Clinton, Louisiana), it was called Football Town. We played in the playoffs. We won state championships year after year. It was a continuous tradition. It was like what I fell into with the Browns. It was a tradition to win, which is what we did.

- **How close are you to where you grew up?**

Actually, my mother still lives in the original homeplace. I am about seven miles from where I grew up. Home is home, it really is.

- **Who was your college coach and how did he influence you?**

Stanley Galloway. He influenced me on mental toughness. He was a man that demanded everything of his players. He was an old-school type. If he needed to kick you in the rear end, he would do it. He didn't cater to any prima-donna players. My high school coach told me that I would start as a freshman. Coach Galloway said, "No freshman ever starts for me and Billy may never ever start for me." I started after four games into my freshman year. We played both ways in those days. I started off playing defense. I took over about mid-season playing both offense and defense. He didn't pander to anybody. On this little college team, we had five guys that signed NFL contracts. That was unheard of in those days. Today, small colleges sign a lot of players, but in those days they didn't.

- **What five players came from there?**

Maxi Williams played eight years for the Dolphins and Oilers; he was selected in an extension draft. Ellis Johnson, the number two draft choice for the old Boston Patriots and Minnesota Vikings. Jerry Joe Donnaway and I can't remember the others.

- **Do you have any idea why so many players came from your high school team into the NFL draft?**

Clinton High school, which was B-class, was as small as it could get. We had Jimmy Davis who played for the Steelers and the Giants. He came out of this little town. Ken Phares was the number two draft choice for the Steelers. Corey Bradford played for the Green Bay Packers and Houston Texans. There have been ten players from this little town of five or six hundred people. People follow through and believe it can be done because somebody has done it before. They go right on with the tradition.

- **Tell us about Blanton Collier?**

Blanton Collier was the gentleman of all gentlemen. He was my type of coach; a coach that I needed. He had patience. He saw in me something that probably I don't believe any other coach had seen. He saw that heart plays a role in football. That you could overcome some physical abilities with the heart and knowledge of the game. He was such a gentleman. I never ran a mandatory sprint, nobody did for that matter. We never ran mandatory sprints while he was the head coach. With Blanton, mental mistakes were absolutely not tolerated, but being beaten physically could be overcome. He was astute on everything concerning the game. He was one of the first that believed special teams were twenty-five percent of your game. You played your best people. When I got there, that wasn't the procedure. If you were a starter, you didn't play on special teams. He said, "We can't give up twenty-five of our game and win." The first team started playing special teams. I covered and snapped punts my entire career. He used his best players. There was no phase of the game he didn't know, inside and out. He never played football, which to me was incredible. He sat and took notes. That is how Paul Brown noticed him and brought him on his staff. He was there and had all these detailed notes on all the characteristics of the game. I was told that was why Paul Brown hired him.

- **What was it like to play for Nick Skorich?**

I enjoyed playing for Nick Skorich. He came from a different school of thought on training. There was no more coming to camp and playing yourself into shape. The game had evolved far beyond this with the Kansas City Chiefs having won the Super Bowl largely due to the extreme conditioning and strength training of Alvin Roy. He was the first strength coach in the NFL. I was one of the few people that had trained with weights my entire life. I started weight training at eight or nine years old. Alvin Roy was from Baton Rouge, thirty miles from my hometown. This made it possible for my dad to get me to him. Dad could see my desire to play football. That was just the great providence of God that I had the opportunity to train with this man. He ended up being the Chargers strength coach then the Kansas City strength coach, when they won the Super Bowl in 1969. That was when everybody went to weight training. Nick Skorich took over in '71. My first year, I was blown away by the guys that didn't come to camp in shape. They came to camp and played themselves into shape. That was not the way I was brought up. I came in 100% condition and that is the way this training evolved. Now they train year around, there is no time that they are off. I personally liked Coach Skorich. He believed in me. When I came into camp in '73, I was named defensive captain and moved to middle linebacker. I started the first three or four games before Bob Babbich came in. I left with a ruptured disc. I tried to keep going until the fifth or sixth game. About November, I ended up having my back operated on. The next year, I felt like they should have moved me back to my starting position on the outside. That was not what they did. Mr. Modell told me if I would come back in 1974, after the surgery, and I can't make you happy, I will okay a trade. I made a prideful mistake and asked to be traded. When he traded me to Denver, I was all right with it. When I got to the Broncos, they wanted me to play middle linebacker. That was not what I started as. I started at outside linebacker for the last four years. I asked to be released from Denver. I came home and San Diego contracted me to join their team. I played a year there and retired. Paul Wiggin, head coach of the Chiefs, called me to come to Kansas City to play for him and Vince Costello. I loved the teams I played for and the experiences with each one.

- **What was it like to play for your friend Paul Wiggin?**

It was wonderful! When I got to Cleveland, he was the team captain and played defensive end. I didn't know he knew I existed. He loved to joke around. He told me he had followed me all the way through my career. I was the type of player he wanted and they needed me. I had retired from San Diego. He told me they needed an outside linebacker. He told me the position was mine if I could take it. I said, "I am coming." I believe if they had given him another year, he would have produced a team. When he got to Kansas City, all of the veterans had been there too long. I had the privilege of playing with Willie Lanier, Jim Lynch, and Emmett Thomas. We did pretty good, but we never did get over the hump. He didn't have time to develop a team because he didn't have any draft choices. The players had gotten older and that was why he needed somebody like me who could still play. I loved playing for him and Vince Costello.

- **Is it true you tried to choke Doug Dieken?**

I would have to jump up to choke him because of how tall he was. But, it wasn't Doug, it was Ernie Kellermann. There are so many of those tales, I can't remember all of them. I don't know what happened to me. I lost it in my sleep. I had my arms around him and my hand on his throat. They said I was just wild-eyed and had this look in my eyes like I was trying to kill him. All I know is what they told me. I didn't know what had gone on because I was still asleep. I wasn't really a sleepwalker. I must have been in bad shape.

- **Who were the team leaders when you were playing?**

I was the defensive captain in 1973. Offensively, there was Doug Dieken, who was a young player. There was Gene Hickerson; he was the silent leader. He never said anything. He was a major player those fifteen years in the league. Gene would do the job, so you just sat back and marveled at him. Bill Nelson was a fiery leader. There were young players like Thom Darden, Jerry Sherk. Jim Houston was the captain. Dale Lindsay was the type of player that played with heart. We had guys like Ron Snidow, Bob Briggs, and Nick Roman. People like that who came in there and contributed. They inspired us to play. We had Clarence Scott, the defensive back, and Ernie Kellermann. Ben Davis coming back off of that traumatic knee surgery. Erich Barnes was an inspiration, too. He would knock your behind off in the game. A lot of people don't remember when Miami went 17-0. We beat them on the field, but didn't beat them on the scoreboard. We had the blocked punt and interference on me, with Paul Warfield down on the eight-yard line. That is one that I didn't mention. How could I forget him? He was an inspiration just to watch him run his route. You had Gary Collins, with his hands and toughness, to catch the ball in a crowd. I told somebody not too long ago that when I left the game, I was still in awe. I was like a kid looking up to them, more than like a fellow player. I never really got over being in awe of them my whole career, even after I was the MVP in 1971, the Cleveland Touchdown Player of the Year.

- **Al Jenkins, who played for the Dolphins in the 1972 season, said that they had won the game against the Browns only by luck, that it was the only game where they were pressed to try to do something, and that, even though he was a Dolphin, he was very proud of the Browns.**

It was something incredible. Offensively, we had 400 yards total, they had 110 yards. We had a blocked punt that they managed to score off of. I interfered with Warfield down on the eight-yard line and the quarterback threw four or five interceptions that day. We could have won the game, even in the last seconds, as we were ahead 14-13. They went ahead of us 20-14 when I interfered with Warfield. When we got the ball back, we drove down the field and threw an interception in the end zone. That was one of those cases where we were the Cleveland Browns. We shut them down and we moved the ball.

- **You said that you were often challenged by your not being big enough or strong enough, yet you have proven that wrong. What do you attribute that to?**

I attribute it to believing in myself. If you want to know the truth, I think it was by the grace of God. I was a young man where football was my God. I lived for myself and to gratify that God, which was football and gratification of me. I believe it was the grace and an awesome God to get me to the point of humility to see that I was nothing. He saved my soul and then turned it all around to allow me to play the game that I loved. To me, it was a person who was able to realize something after being able to put it into proper perspective. There were a lot of other guys I haven't mentioned like John Garlington who died in 2000. He was my dearest friend. He was the second draft choice of the Browns. He played for ten years. There was a group of us, Don Cockroft, Bill Glass, Tom Beutler, John, and me. I came there as a hell-raising person, arrogantly prideful, trying to fulfill anything to satisfy my ego. I left the NFL a grateful, thankful, humble man having been able to play in such a great game with such a great team with such great players and great fans. I had come away experiencing the Browns and having come away as a man with a changed life and a new direction. I couldn't ask for any more in life than that. The Browns experience was a wonderful thing. When we came back to Cleveland for the Countdown to '99, Jim Brown was there. Jim Brown, Leroy Kelly, Ben Davis, and I were shooting the bull and he said, "Fellows, I want to tell you all something. This experience is something that nobody else can have. There is no other place; there is nobody that can take this away. This is something unique." When he said that, I thought to myself, "Is this what I have been feeling my entire career?" I was long out of a career then, but this is what it has been to me. An experience nobody, no matter what, can take away. I may not have been the biggest, strongest, fastest, but I played in championship games. I played against Johnny Unitas and Joe Namath. I was on the field with Jerry Sherk, Doug Dieken, Gene Hickerson, Jim Houston, and Don Cockroft. Nobody can take that away from me. This is what the Browns experience was all about. It was everything. In the NFL period, you narrow it down to the Cleveland Browns. It doesn't get any better than that.

- **Sports enthusiasts have classified the two greatest rivalries in sports as Ohio State/Michigan and Cleveland/Pittsburgh. Tell us about your experiences with the Pittsburgh Steelers.**

They used to play on Saturday night in Cleveland. It was all of the border-town people. They came in and already had their bets and wagers. They were having a good time. The fans were at each others' throats, and the Browns and the Steelers were at each others' throats. They may have won a game in there somewhere. They definitely won when Bradshaw got there. They began to get their team together. They split with us in 1971; 1972 was split again. It didn't matter who won the game, when you came out of there it was a dogfight from the word go. It was old time, old-fashioned NFL knock them, do anything to win. There was no good blood between the two teams. I had some good friends that played with the Steelers and I respect them. Even to this day, even with them being the AFC, even with them being a division, I can hardly pull for them at all. That is how deep it goes. I acknowledge the teams and players they put together and how they play the game. But there is no love lost to this day for the Pittsburgh Steelers. I guess there is no better way to describe it. I wanted to pull for them this year, I wanted to, but I just couldn't.

- **Did Jim Brown have a positive influence on the players after he left?**

When I was playing, he didn't. I think he was into movies then, and he was really distanced from the Browns. I never really even met him. I think in these last years in forming the new team and getting the team back, etcetera, I think he would have had more influence in Cleveland now than he did then.

- **What were your feelings when the Cleveland Browns left Cleveland?**

I was very heartsick and it took me a long time to get over it. I never got down on Art Modell like some did. I think he made a mistake. I think he did a lot for the city and think they could have done a little bit more for him and the team to keep them there. I don't know any of the ins and outs. When you live 1,200 miles away and don't get the paper every day, you don't know the details. I had respect for Mr. Modell. He treated me good the whole time I was there. I respected him as an owner, and I think he tried to get the players in that it took to win. He certainly had some good coaches. Forrest Gregg, Nick Skorich, and Blanton Collier were great coaches. They've had good coaches. I don't know what went wrong when he left. I still respect him.

- **Who was your nemesis? Who did you have the most trouble with?**

All of them! Bob Trumpy, the tight end for the Cincinnati Bengals; the great tight end who gave me more trouble than other tight ends. I had very little trouble with guys blocking me. Those guys didn't give me any trouble, but Bob Trumpy gave me more trouble on the hook block. He had a left-handed stance, and he could loosen his body, move his feet without moving his body, or something. John Garlington and I both had trouble with him. Blanton Collier studied films of him and told me, "You have got your feet wrong." I don't remember all the details of it now, but he was one of the players that gave me a tremendous amount of trouble. There were some backs like Jim Kiick, he was a great receiver out of the backfield. Jess Phillips from Cincinnati Bengals could run great patterns out of the backfield that I had a hard time with. Larry Brown from the Washington Redskins was a good receiver. But it was Bob who gave me trouble in the tight end position.

- **Cleveland Browns have the distinction of being labeled with several negative results: Red Right 88, the Bottle Throwing Incident, The Drive, The Fumble, and the Rudd Penalty. What was your involvement in these games and what do you think of these labeling?**

It is sad that you have a great year and one play defines your career, but I guess that is the nature of the game. That is what makes it such a great game. You can have a great year personally and one play, like Jackie Smith's, when he dropped the pass, is always remembered. He was one of the greater tight ends that ever played yet he is remembered by that one single play. If they talk about me, it would be the Monday Night interception. The local people told me that they saw a few games. Fans didn't see many games here in Clinton. It is not like it is now as you can get every game on Sunday television. But they remember Franco Harris pushing me into the end zone after hitting him on about the two-yard line. They remember that. That is what I am remembered for more than I am the Monday Night interception or any other play I made over an eleven year career. It is sad but that is the way it is. That is the nature of the game. I remember the Fumble. I remember the Rudd Penalty. Those things stick out in my mind. Ernest Byner going into the end zone and fumbling the football. Those things stick out. As an ex-player watching the game now, I am no different than any other fan. Those were great football players and it is a shame that they are diminished over one play. That is the nature of our game that makes it great. The team that wins the Super Bowl is the team the people remember.

- **How does it feel to be called the original Monday Night Football star?**

It feels good, to be honest with you, because that was the turnaround of my career. I had played in numerous games before, but never as a starter. I didn't even start that game. Dale Lindsay was the starter. I believed a lot, but I had never been the starter or classified as a starter. It was like, here I am, this player that is supposed to be too slow to do everything but, yet, I could make the plays and nobody could explain it. It was like I was a whole different player from that one play on. You know it was the interception that transformed my career. I was the player they could believe in and rely on to make plays all the time. It was just an ordinary play. I can't remember whether it was Emerson Boozer or Matt Snell who was running option pattern out of the backfield. I had him covered. Jack Gregory was rushing Namath. He threw the ball. I think he tried to throw it into the ground because I had the back covered and I dove for it. It was like it stuck in my hand. I was lying on the ground, I said to myself, "Look what I've got here." I remember Namath not even attempting to come at me. John Garlington was coming across making a block and somebody else was taking somebody else out. Before I knew it, I was in the end zone. I spiked the ball. It was a horrible spike, but I got to spike the ball in the end zone. I was so excited and everybody else was so excited for me. I think they had seen me labor all the time. To beat Namath in that kind of game, in the first Monday Night football game was incredible. People don't realize how Monday Night football wasn't accepted. My folks had to go fifty miles to find a station that carried the game. The local affiliate chose not to run the game. My mother and family drove to Hamlin and rented a hotel room where they could get it out of New Orleans. There were a few other people who could get a New Orleans station from here and they watched it. In fact, people called the manager and told them they were going to have these people ejected from the hotel because they were disturbing the hotel guests. The manager called my mother and she said, "If your son had just intercepted a pass on Monday Night football, what would you do?" She said, "I would be doing the same thing, go ahead!" It was not that Monday Night was an instant success, but I think instantly it was a success to have that kind of game and 87,000 people are there to watch it. It captured the nation. The rest is history! I still have the first Monday Night Football interception ball.

- **What kind of parental influence did you have?**

I had wonderful parental influence. My father died when I was nineteen years old. In fact, he played at LSU and then became a farmer. He was a big supporter of the local high school team and of us. He drove me to Baton Rouge to lift weights with Alvin Roy when I was eight or nine years old. They never discouraged me, though my mother told me in the last fifteen or so years that she used to worry about what kind of devastating affect this was going to have on me when I couldn't play in the NFL. She knew it was my dream and it was my life. They knew I wouldn't be able to play at that level. When I signed my college scholarship, I weighed 162 pounds. It wasn't really probable to think that I could play. When I signed with the Browns, I weighed 215 pounds. I ultimately played as high as 235 pounds, but normal playing weight was 225 to 228 pounds, which is plenty heavy enough. I was one of the few in those days that had trained with weights so I was much stronger than a lot of people in my position. I had been a dairy farmer and lifted weights with a professional trainer since I was nine. I had the kind of training that could help me, but nobody knew of this or the heart that I had. My parents worried that it was going to destroy me, but they didn't discourage me. They encouraged me to go on and work at it and work at it and work at it. My father watched the game on a Saturday and died on a Wednesday. He was at the game with the doctor holding his I.V. so he could watch the game. He was an avid fan, and they traveled all over in high school and college. They were great supporters. I had a brother who played college football with me, he was also an encouragement. He was older than me, but we played on the same team in college. He was a big encouragement to me.

- **What disease did your father have?**

Acute Leukemia.

- **Do you still feel like you are a part of the Browns organization?**

I do and, obviously, they do too because they invited me to the Countdown to '99. They included me in everything even though I left. The only time I left them in heart was the two years I played with the Chiefs. One year we killed them and the next year they killed us. It is hard to get a lot of gratification in beating the Browns. But, I was a true Chief when I was in Kansas City. I am close friends with Gregory and Dale Lindsay. My son signed with the Bears, but didn't make it. That was in 1999. My allegiance is right here though and I hope they count me as part of the family. I intend on taking them up on this invitation they have with the Browns alumni for every home game. My two daughters were too young to remember the Browns. They just want to go back and see a game in the worst kind of way. They went to interview for the Browns. In fact, my daughter went to the Countdown for '99. I don't know the new owners but the Browns are it for me. In fact, I am wearing a Cleveland Browns hat as we speak. I am just a fan now. I am just like you are. I have the NFL experience and the Browns experience under my belt and nobody can take that away. The Browns organization was wonderful to me. They gave me an opportunity to prove what I could do, when I could do it, and they let me do it. And I showed them that I could.

- **Are Cleveland Browns fans the best in the NFL?**

In my opinion they are. They are so good. They were just good people. We were friends with a lot of them. It wasn't just that they were cheering on the sidelines and paying our way, they were friends to a lot of us off the field. A lot of us were just down-to-earth, good-old-boys that just happened to be in the experience of being there. Enjoying what had already been set before us by Jim Brown, Marion Motley, Otto Graham, and all those people that went to the stadium before us. To me, it is unbelievable that my name is in that list of people that played for the Browns. It is just incredible to me to be in that list with such great players in history.

- **Where was the hardest place to play when you were playing?**

I would have to say the Steelers were tough. It was a hard place to play with the Steelers. When Cincinnati came into the league in the 70's, with the natural rivalry and the way the stadium built, with the fans so close to the field it was tough. With the Browns, the only place you were close to the field was in the Dawg Pound, in the old stadium. Even though our fans had to overcome so much by being so far away, they did. To play places like that, where the stadium was right up on you, was difficult. The Astrodome was tough, but they didn't have that big of a crowd when they first went into the AFC. In those early championship years, we went into Baltimore, that was tough. Minnesota was a tough place to play because of the ice and snow. All of them were tough for me, I guess. The Giants Stadium in New York where the Yankees played, that was a thrill for me to just walk out there, where Mickey Mantle, Babe Ruth, Joe DiMaggio, and people like that played. Just a thrill. To go out and touch the grass in the center field. It was a thrill a minute! It was like that for me with baseball and even the names in football that were there before us. To be able to be on the same fields as these celebrities was exciting. Even playing on the old baseball fields with the infields was exciting. To be in a stadium where Whitey Ford or some of these great players had been was great. Bud and Sam McDowell and players like that meant something to me. It is how I am put together. I played against Walter Payton. He wasn't that famous at that time but to remember having played against him, hit him, and tackled him is something that I will remember until I pass on to the next life. That is kind of the same way I played the game.

- **What can you tell us about the rookie hazing you guys performed?**

That was quite an ordeal. They made you sing, they made you put on skits, they made you do all kinds of crazy things. I don't think they let them do it like that anymore.

- **What is one of the funniest stories of your NFL experience?**

When I first played with Ray Nitschke, I went in the game the first time and I was snapping the punt to Gary Collins at the end of the field. Ray Nitschke was a household name, he played with the Super Bowl Champions the Green Bay Packers. Well, I get over the ball, and I am thinking this ball is three times bigger than the hole between my legs. It was like, I can't get this ball through my legs. I looked back and it looked like Gary Collins was standing up in the bleachers. He needs to move up. I can't get this big old ball back that far. Nitschke was jumping in and out of the line. As a rookie, it was frightening. If they had the film of that archive, they can see that I snapped the punt and kind of lunged and cringed and put my hand in front of my head thinking he was just going to kill me. He was a monster from what I had seen on T.V. Now he is over me and this game was on national television as a pre-season game, but he didn't hit me! I lunged and he didn't hit me. I took off to cover the punt. I hit either Herb Adler or Willie Wood, I don't remember which one, at full speed thinking that everybody back home was going to see his helmet go one way and the ball go one way. I'm kind of rolling over to take my accolades and everybody else thought I was going to kill him. They stopped, just slowed down. I took off and got beyond the wall and he went seventy yards. I gave him my best shot. It was hilarious. After thinking all those things went through my mind, it wasn't hilarious that he scored, because I figured I would get cut because I didn't make the tackle. Those guys know the first man down is supposed to take the shot and everybody else is supposed to be there to finish him off. Blanton didn't chew me out. In fact, he encouraged me for getting the punt back there and everything because he knew it was a nervous moment.

- **What was the saddest thing that ever happened while you played?**

The loss to the Baltimore Colts. The year that we went down to the Jets. They were 13-1 and we were 12-2, but their one loss was against us; we beat them thirty-something to six. We were sitting there on that Saturday when Kansas City was playing the Jets. I vividly remember we were talking about who we were going to play in the Super Bowl. Did we want to play the Jets or did we want to play the Chiefs? We lost sight of the Colts because we had already beaten them thirty-something to six. They beat us 38-0 and in the NFL Championship game they beat us 32-0.

- **Should players of today be more fan conscious?**

Yes and no; I know that is a politician's answer, but I think you have to be conscious of the people who are paying to see a game. I believe we have accountability to the fans in the way we conduct ourselves. Though we can say we are an American, and are free to do anything we want to, when you are in the limelight, you have a responsibility to present yourself as a role model for young people. We have an accountability to these people who are paying us millions of dollars to perform and to conduct ourselves in a manner that is worthy of the NFL. That was what it was originally meant to be. I don't think anyone should lose sight of that. I don't want to get into politics, but I think we see that in today's country. It is that we take all the privileges, but yet we don't want any responsibility. As American people, we have to be responsible and the NFL players who are the greatest players in the world have some responsibility and accountability to the fans, to the young people, and even to the owners. I am talking about people's morals, that they have accountability in the language that is used. People can read lips. I would say the NFL has a responsibility to say it will never happen again with what happened in the Super Bowl with Janet Jackson. I didn't see it, so I don't really know firsthand, but I have heard enough about it. I am saying we have accountability and have a responsibility to the fans, because they are actually the owners. In a sense, they are paying the bills. You can never be too big for the people who pay your bills. The guys I played with were just neat, and I think they were good to the fans. They were down-to-earth, down home, I know you and you know me. We just happened to be the ones out there playing and they happened to be the ones out here watching. It was a community and, yes, we protected ourselves. We didn't throw ourselves around or throw ourselves out there to the dogs, but when we beat Dallas in 1968 in the Eastern Conference Championship, they mauled us and they tore our chinstraps off; they took the parkas off of our backs. We lost all kinds of equipment. It was not that they were trying to do this, they just lost it. I was scared. They flooded the field, like you see in the college games. We couldn't find the dugout. We couldn't work our way through the people. That was some excitement, but there was some fear involved in it, too. We were going somewhere else the next week to play where it was cold, and they made us appeal to the fans in the newspaper. We were trying to get back the parkas that cost $1500 each. The fans sent them back to us.

- **What do you do for a living?**

I am a dairy farmer; I milk cows for a living. I'm not a big dairy as dairies go. I milk a hundred and five head, and have milked as many as two-hundred head. We actually do the milking and they pick the milk up. Haulers take it to a processing plant and process it. I don't have anything to do with the processing, just on the cow-milking end of it. I did that while I was playing for the Browns. I did it before I played for the Browns and when I retired, I sold my part of that dairy to my brother and built my own dairy. I have been doing it here for twenty-six years. I built the dairy and developed this land while I was playing football, however, I am getting out of the dairy business on April 26, 2007. That will be my last cow milking. The dairy business has really gone sour in the south. The hurricanes did us in pretty significantly. I don't know what I am going to do after that. Maybe I will do beef cows or I have a hay business that I do. We start at three a.m. and milk twice a day, and I work all day long. That is why I haven't been to Cleveland, because I am a hands-on worker on this farm. I still own and operate this dairy and I have about nine-hundred acres of land. I think when I played with the Browns, I had two-thousand acres, but it was a family business. I am separate from that. I have my own property. I have been a farmer my entire life but I have also helped coach at a private school.

- **What kind of hobbies do you have now?**

I like to snow ski, but I haven't done it in five or six years. I've had surgeries on my knees and I have to have one on my shoulder pretty soon. I still enjoy watching high school football games, college games, and that kind of stuff. I enjoy my family; I'm a family man. I do lay preaching through the church. Do some speaking engagements and stuff like that. I am mainly just a family, working man. That is all. I enjoy it.

- **Were there any other negatives that happened while you were playing?**

It was a good experience for me but there were some guys like John Matuszak who played for the Chiefs. There was a tremendous physical depression to see this man who had this talent get messed up with drugs and things. Those were sad things to me and I guess you would say negative. You would see a person that had so much talent, but yet let it get away from him.

- **Were drugs a problem while you were playing?**

I didn't know it. I found out when I went to the Chiefs. I said in front of a younger player, "One good thing about this place is there are no drugs here." He laughed and said, "You don't run where we run." He didn't mean that he was taking drugs, because he didn't. He was saying "You are a family man, you are a Christian. You aren't out with the people, so you don't know what is going on." As far as I was concerned, there wasn't any. However, I understand there was some I didn't know about. I don't know how bad it is now as there are some wonderful people in the NFL; fine men who are standing up for what the NFL was meant to be and what it was all about, so I wouldn't want to put any negative slant on it. But I've been told it is real, that it is there.

- **Was the Christian Athlete's Society a part of the Browns when you were there, or is that something more prevalent on the field now?**

Actually, the whole movement began with Don Shinnick, from the Colts, and Bill Glass, from the Cleveland Browns. It began when they started getting speakers. In fact, in 1970, they had the Pro Athlete Outreach Conference, which is where God saved me. There were about forty of us there, and it has blossomed from that initial forty-athlete conference to now where they have several conferences. It has grown into baseball and basketball. It began with Don and Bill Glass then we took over the reins from there and carried on over the years. Norm Evans, who played for the Miami Dolphins in 1972, is the President of the Pro Athletes Outreach Event in the NFL, and he was in our era. It has mushroomed from there. It has gone into every major sport. There are wonderful stories of people brought from the degraded ways of life to salvation and walking with the Lord. It has transformed lives. If I had to say, the highlight of everything for me was that, because it put everything into perspective. Before, it would have been about me and something I would have done. After that, it was not about me, it was about the Lord. That was a wonderful part of it. To be a Christian is more than saying, "Lord, Lord, am I practicing these things? I am a sinner, but is this my lifestyle I practice? Is this what flows out of me or is it curse words? Am I pointing to Jesus? He is my Lord, he is my ruler, and it does mean something in my life." I think NFL players have the responsibility that if they profess Christ, and are going to point up to God or Jesus, then let's see that coincides with what is in their lives. To me, that is my responsibility as a believer. Do I stumble and fall? Yes. Do I have to repent and go back to the people and say I failed? Yes. It is my responsibility to make sure that if I am attaching my name to Jesus, then I have to live as a Christian. It didn't begin like that, but that was the way it finished out and I am very thankful.

- **What did you get out of your NFL experience?**

I got the thrill of a lifetime! I don't know how I could say it better. A dream fulfilled, a lifetime worth of memories, salvation from the Lord, friendships that are lasting because they are built on the fact we were in the trenches together. You get some semblance to what it is like to be on the battlefield, to help somebody you fought side-by-side with, watching the other persons flank, doing your job. If I had to say something negative about today's NFL, it would be the lack of being a team. It seems like you have twenty-two individuals and a coach that can pull it together and make them believe they are a team. You have to believe in one another and play like the goal at the end is greater than the money. To be able to say, "I've played in the Super Bowl," is greater than me personally getting the million dollars. The coaches that can convince their players of that are the ones that win. I think it is a negative in the NFL today. We had that when we were playing. We may not have won, but we cried together and lost together and won together. No matter what we did, there was no individual. Though we had great superstars, they were just like us. I have tremendous memories of things like that. I don't have a bitter feeling toward one coach. Not one that I felt did me wrong or anything like that. It was just a wonderful, thrilling experience.

Andrews posing with his grandchildren while holding
the first Monday Night Football game interception ball

			Defense					Total	
William "Billy" Andrews									
Linebacker 1967-1977									
Southeastern Louisiana									
Season	Team	Game	Int	Yds	Avg	TD	Fumbles	Points	
1972	CLE	14	3	64	21.3	0	0	0	
1973	CLE	11	1	36	36	0	2	0	
1974	CLE	14	8	105	13.1	0	1	6	
1976	CLE	14	7	73	10.4	0	1	0	
1977	CLE	14	6	107	17.8	1	1	6	
1978	CLE	16	10	200	20	0	0	0	
1979	CLE	16	5	125	25	1	0	6	
1980	CLE	16	2	42	21	0	1	0	
1981	CLE	13	3	68	22.7	0	0	0	
Career		128	45	820	18.2	2	6	18	

Season	Team(s)	Punt Ret.				Kick Ret.			
		PR	Yds	Avg	TD	KR	Yds	Avg	TD
1972	CLE	15	61	4.1	0				
1973	CLE	9	51	5.7	0				
1974	CLE	21	173	8.2	0				
1980	CLE					1	-1	-1	0
Career		45	285	6.3	0	1	-1	-1	0

Season	Team(s)	Other Stats							
1974	CLE	1 TD/Fum Rec							

Andrews running back an interception against the New England Patriots, Nov 27, 1971

SOURCE: CHICAGO BEARS

10

Rudy Kuechenberg

Rudy Kuechenberg has the type of finesse a lot of players in his era have. Not afraid to go out on the field and leave it all there, his ability may not have been the best, but his knowledge of the game and how it should have been played is right where it should have been. There were better players on the field, but none with the heart and courage that "Big Rudy" had. He has a brother that has been nominated to the Hall of Fame for several years in a row. He also has a strong opinion about the game and how it should be played. The Kuechenberg brothers have a lot in common. They have that fighting spirit to play the game as hard and for as long as it takes. Many have watched Bob Kuechenberg play with the Miami Dolphins and his exuberance for the game. He never let up. He played with what some may call a "rage." He fulfilled his contract by playing hard and was never willing to give up, even if the team probably wouldn't have finished on top that day.

- **You were in Chicago and came to Cleveland. Was it any different walking on the field in Cleveland than on the field in Chicago?**

I was so good, four teams wanted me, tee-hee. I actually went from the Bears, to the Redskins, the day Lombardi died. I was at his funeral, the Browns, and the Packers all in the same season.

- **Was it any different walking on the field in Cleveland than it was on any of the other fields you have been on?**

Well, you've got to understand I was a free agent. I had been with the Bears five years and it sort of got to be like my home, old Wrigley Field. I did like Wrigley Field because the fans were real close. Cleveland, I was really hoping they would keep me and the honest truth is, I played three games there and the last game was against my brother in Miami. We beat them 28-0. It was the first time me and Bob ever played on the same field. We played right across from each other on special teams. He had to block me.

- **How did that go?**

Oh, I've always been the older brother and I've got to say that sucker clipped me. I let him kick and everything. Anyhow, we won 28-0. We had Paul Warfield and Bob Matheson and the next year Miami got them. I pulled a hamstring in that game and I didn't even know what a pulled hamstring was. I told my wife in Gary, Indiana...I said, "Hey, I'm three games in; that makes a year toward my pension. Come on out on the Greyhound Bus." Long story short, they treated me for a pulled hamstring. In the Saturday practice the following week, we were playing Detroit in Cleveland and Coach Blanton Collier walked up next to me after practice—I couldn't sprint—he walked up to me and said, "We've released you from the team." That was a total shock. I had my wife coming on the bus Friday and Saturday morning they cut me. I said, "You can't do that, you at least have to give me time to heal." He said, "Let me go talk to the trainer." I forgot who the trainer was but the coach and trainer went in the back room and when they came out, the trainer said to me, "What do you mean you have a pulled hamstring? You don't have a pulled hamstring." Okay, those are not very good memories for Cleveland. Yeah, and then Art Model said to me, "You don't have a job. You were begging for a job when we picked you up and we gave you a break. You're just like the rest, just trying to get a free ride." That was the end of my deal at Cleveland. I stayed in my hotel and watched the game on TV. Dave Robinson, a linebacker for Green Bay, pulled a hamstring. I called Monday morning, called Green Bay and everybody to see if they needed a linebacker and Green Bay said, "We'll pay your way up here and take a look." I went to Green Bay, dropped my wife off in Gary, Indiana, which is right on the way, went up there, and my hamstring wasn't torn bad enough that I couldn't play. I got well. They put me on their Cab (Taxi) squad and activated me the day I played against my old teammates the Chicago Bears.

- **What was it like to play against the Bears?**

I had to play against my old roommate Dick Butkus, who was in the "Wedge" on kickoffs. I was always crazy on special teams. I was always the Wedge-buster. It was tremendous. I remember before that game in Green Bay, Lambeau, that stadium did give me a sense of being in a sacred place. I played the greatest game I ever played against the Bears because I had to prove that they should have not cut me. I dove over the Wedge, which was Dick Butkus, and came right down like a bomb on Cecil Turner, who had tied Travis Williams from Green Bay for four touchdowns on the kickoffs. In the pregame warm-up, I heard the announcer say, "Scratch number so-and-so and add Rudy Kuechenberg, number fifty-nine." By the end of the game, the whole stadium gave me a standing ovation, which was really gratifying. Nitschke went to a restaurant that he had been going for thirteen years and then he came to practice, the third day of practice, and he said, "You sucker," he said, "I've been going there for thirteen years and they wouldn't serve me my dinner until I signed your fan club." Nitschke was a great guy. Did you see him in the movie, "The Longest Yard?" He'd punch his head in the wall. That wasn't acting, that's just the way he is.

- **What did you think when the Browns left Cleveland?**

Oh, it was unforgivable. I like your Dawg Pound. I like your Dawgs. I had no respect for the owner, Art Modell, for what he did on the hamstring thing.

- **Are Cleveland Browns fans good? Are they the best in the NFL?**

Yeah. The Cleveland Browns fans, they could lose ten years in a row but, just like the Bears, once a Bear fan, always a Bear fan. In 1969, the year before I came to Cleveland, my brother was on the perfect season, '72 Dolphins team. When we go to golf outings, he signs things like "Bob Kuechenberg, Perfect Season." I sign the golf celebrity outings writing, "Rudy Kuechenberg, 1969 Bears, Almost Perfect Season." We had one win and thirteen losses. We almost had the reverse-perfect season. Bear fans are pretty much that way every place you go. They are loyal fans. I was in awe when I played in a preseason game as a Bear and got to be in Lou Groza's locker. I thought that was sacred. I was real proud to use his locker that day!

- **You yourself have respect for the players that played before you. Do you think players are like that today?**

I think it's all about money. I do want to say the year I got in the league, I wanted to tackle Jim Brown one time. That's the year he quit. I tackled Jimmy Taylor who was, to me, second only to the "Great Jim Brown!" Jim Brown was all alone. He was a halfback and the fullback in one body. I wanted to say I tackled Jim Brown one time, or tried to, or got run over and I didn't get to do that. I've often wondered.

- **How good was Walter Payton?**

Oh, I was with Gale Sayers and Walter Payton. When Walter's running at you, you see three of them coming at you and he's setting you up. You never know if he's going to go left or right or run you over. He sees people down field with his great peripheral vision like nobody I've ever seen. Walter Payton, I have total respect for him. He's an overachiever with that little body and keeps going full speed. I know Gale Sayers was great. I was there the day we carried Gale off on the stretcher. In fact, I was one of the guys that carried him off. I'm in that movie "Brian's Song," Number 59, the guy in the back right part of the stretcher. That was a sad day. Gale never did recover after.

- **Did Gale and Brian Piccolo really work together that hard?**

Yeah, that movie was very close to it. I wasn't a Brian fan because I was a linebacker and he was an in-between. He was the number one leading rusher in college at Wake Forest. He wasn't any good in the Pros. They actually kept an extra fullback that year and kept one less linebacker in 1965. That made me go to the Taxi Squad for a whole year. They tried to make it a backfield with Gale and Brian as fullback and halfback and that did not work. You need a fullback that can block and run.

- **Brian didn't block that well?**

He wasn't big enough, sort of like Tom Mattie. He would always know his plays but he wasn't fast, wasn't quick. There's a county park here, Brian Piccolo Park here in Fort Lauderdale. He's from Saint Thomas Aquinas, which is a great high school football team. I honestly hate to ruin the movie. He was just an average football player and they couldn't find a spot for him.

- **The movie played him off as an average football player, didn't it?**

See, they tried to let him be the second halfback and there was just a large gap between him and Gale. They came up with the idea of putting him at fullback and that was a disaster.

- **Was that a tough time for the team? When Brian was sick?**

Yeah. You see, Chicago is only about thirty miles from my hometown, Hobart, right outside of Gary, Indiana. I've always been a loner and I would actually live in Hobart and drive to Wrigley Field everyday for practice. I don't say I'm cocky. I'm just not a phony and I just didn't go running with a bunch of people I don't know or respect.

- **So, you are somewhat of a loner?**

Yeah, coming up I was a free agent. Tremendous odds to overcome to get on a team and so much luck to have to go down to the semi-pros and then find your way back up. That's sort of the life I had. The main reason I got to the Bears was for when the Cowboys cut me, one of our scrub quarterbacks was on the phone, and I said, "Hey, Zeek, what's up?" He said, "Oh, I just got cut. I'm going back to my Philadelphia Bulldogs." I said "I think they are bringing me in to cut me right now. Ask your coach if they need a linebacker." When I came out of Coach Landry's room, I said, "Yeah, Zeek, I got cut. Did you ask your coach if I could come for a tryout?" He said, "Yeah, he will pay your way out here." I went and the coach was Babe Demanchez. I made All-Continental League for him as middle linebacker. In the off-season, I go back to the Cowboys for another tryout. Babe gets hired as an assistant coach with the Bears. The Cowboys cut me again on the last day of the preseason because one of their linebackers, Jerry Tubbs, came out of retirement. That's how I got to the Bears. By that luck, stroke of God, or whatever it is. But I did have a call from Kansas City Chiefs too that year.

- **You said you were a roommate of Dick Butkus?**

Yes. I was his roommate, and here is a funny story. The air conditioner had broke and I'm teaching him how to play chess. There's nothing to do at training camp. It took me two years to paint my chess set with a toothpick when I was with the Cowboys. I'm teaching Dick how to play chess in our room with the doors open because the air conditioner was broke. The sportswriters saw that and came in to get an interview. I'm just showing Dick how to play chess and the next day the Chicago paper said, "Not only is Dick Butkus an affluent linebacker, he's a tremendous chess player. He handily beats his roommate Rudy Kuechenberg." Now, that's funny. Here's another one. The kid in the room right next to me was a defensive tackle from Tennessee named Dick Evey. He was an overachiever. He was real quick but wasn't big, just a sweet person. I had an Eddie Arnold album. I love country music and play guitar. I played country and old rock-n-roll and every night before he'd go to bed, he'd come in my room and say, "Rudy would you play that song, *Cattle Call*, from Eddie Arnold for me? It reminds me of my Tennessee home." Here's this big lineman you think is going to eat you alive and he's a real tenderhearted ,sweet guy. That was pretty cool. Ernie Kellermann was one of your players but he was a rookie with me at Dallas. We both got cut from Dallas and he came to you guys and stuck and he's a very nice guy, too…from a little college in Ohio, I think. Yeah. He's a sweet guy. He was a quarterback in college and made it as a defensive back. That's unusual for that to happen.

- **How is it some players are good in college but can't cut it in the Pros?**

That's a good example of what I just said about Brian Piccolo. He led the nation in rushing but he was in a conference, you know, if he had been in the Big 10 or something! So, that has a lot to do with it.

- **When did you decide you wanted to be a professional player?**

When I was in grade school, I'd play in the gravel street out front. I played football. I didn't care about baseball. We'd play touch football. I got a picture of Harlan Hill, of course; Gary, Indiana, we were Chicago Fans. I had a bubble gum card of Harlan Hill and I would look at that thing for an hour at a time and fantasize myself being in his football card pose.

- **Are you pretty much just a football player or did you play all sports?**

I was a boxer in college. Won the Indiana Golden Glove. I would want to say '63. Novice Division. I was a CYO boxer in seventh and eighth grade. I worked on a farm. We had eight acres and a horse, some cows, but Dad wouldn't let me play any other sport. He said I had to work. By the time my brother came along, he got to play all the sports. Dad realized he got a lot of attention in the mills when he was an ironworker. "Hey, is that your boy playing there?" By the time my brother came up, he got whatever he wanted.

- **Did you and your brother play a lot of pickup games growing up?**

Well, the problem was, when he was getting into high school, I had just got in to college. When he got into the Pros, I would call him the week before to tell him the scouting report on the guy he was going to be playing across from. Sort of give him the low down. It wasn't until I was a Cleveland Brown that we played each other. Our mother and father came down for it and it was sweet. He was blocking me pretty good and I got by him one time. I was gearing up to make the tackle and somebody ran over the back of me. It was him. The ref didn't call a penalty. He said I had my head in the front. Right now, I'm looking at a picture that I had made at that game. We're outside the Miami Stadium and it's a picture of me and my mother between me and Bob and it says, "Once upon a time in 1970, brother versus brother and mother in the hot Miami sun." You can tell by the grin, if you're wondering who won, and I've got a big grin on my face. I never let him forget that.

- **What kind of parental influence did you have?**

I had a father who had a real good work ethic. He was an ironworker. A red-iron ironworker. Do you know what ironworkers do? He was one who would hang by his toes and he's like the Hall of Fame in the American Bridge. I mean he's well respected…a great ironworker who he taught me great work ethics. "Whatever you're going to do, do it well," he'd say. He raised nine kids, seven girls, me, and Bob. I highly respect him for that. He didn't hang out in the bars. I had a great high school football coach. His name was Russ Deal. He was the captain of Indiana Hoosiers in 1945 when they won the Big 10. He was a great influence on my life, too.

"ALL MY LIFE, I WANNA BE A BRICKIE, WORK, WORK, WORK"

- **What is a Brickie?**

A Brickie? Isn't that neat we're the only team in the country that has a nickname like that. Our little town was built around a brickyard. There's a big clay pit right by our farm and that's how they got to be called the Brickie's because there was a brickyard in our town.

- **Can you still remember your fight song?**

Oh, our team will shine tonight
Our team will shine
Oh, our team will shine tonight
Our team will shine
Oh, our team will shine tonight
Our team will shine
When the sun goes down
And the moon comes up
Our team will shine -- go team go
Oh, when the Hobart Brickies
Fall in line
We're gonna win this game
Another time
And for that dear old school
We love so well

And for that old ball team
We'll yell and yell and yell
We're gonna fight, fight, fight
For every score
We're gonna win this game and
Win some more
We're gonna roll those (opponent) on the
Side, on the side -- Ro-o-oll, Hey!

I play guitar when I go home on the Fourth of July. Yeah, I play guitar but do you know what a gut bucket is? A washtub? We've got washboards and spoons and tambourines we pass out to the whole couple hundred people and of course the first things we do is get up and sing our fight song.

- **Did you have to sing it when you were a rookie?**

Yeah.

- **Did you do your high school or college song?**

I didn't even know my college song. I think did a little skit and poured water down Jerry Rhome's pants, that's what I did.

- **What was Tom Landry like?**

Landry was a real religious, fair man. That's a tough job looking someone in the eye and saying your career is over, goodbye. I have total respect for him. He was a religious man and I was pretty wild at the time. Even think I got in trouble for sneaking out the window during training camp. But I have total respect for him, even though he cut me twice.

- **He didn't seem to get a fair shake when he got let go. It just didn't seem like that was a good deal.**

No. I don't know the specifics of it, but I know I have total respect for him. See, you know who makes your good coaches—the guys that were stars like Bart Starr and the linebacker for Detroit. It's not them. It's your scrubs that are reading the playbook to make the team…like Don Shula, Tom Landry and Ara Parseghian! Oh, I loved him, Ara Parseghian. I have total respect for him. He recruited me for Northwestern and I loved that man so much.

- **How many years did he coach at Northwestern?**

He was at Northwestern before he went to Notre Dame. They recruited me and the halfback on my high school team. I loved him and I went to Indiana University. Every time we'd play them I would play a great game just for him. I would actually go out to the hotel where they were going to spend the night and watch him get out of the bus. My senior year, he coached me in the North/South All-Star Game in Miami. That's when my brother got his scholarship for Notre Dame. That day. I had the greatest college game of my life. I broke Roger Staubach's ribs. They carried him off. I ran an interception for sixty some yards to steal the North/South record. I made a touchdown on the interception. In the elevator after the game, Coach Parseghian said to me, "Rudy, you've got a brother, Bob Kuechenberg, coming out." I said, "Yeah, Coach, they've got him playing in the wrong position. He's not an end, he's got a big heart and he's tough." Bob got a full ride right there. We play tennis a couple times a month down here.

- **Oh, does he live close to you?**

Yeah. We live about seven or eight miles apart.

- **When were you born?**

In 1943, in Gary, Indiana.

- **Tell us about the World League.**

I think it was 1973. I played with the Browns in 1970, I laid out in '72, when that World League formed and Paul Warfield and Larry Czonka went. They (Paul and Larry) told my brother, "Don't pay no attention to the figures you're going to see." They went to Canada for the Toronto Rifles and, long story short, they signed the contract. They called Bob and said it was real money, so Bob played out his option with the Dolphins down here. Bob was only making $33,000.00 as a Super Bowl Dolphin. That Continental League gave him something like a $90,000.00 bonus just to play out his option. I had come out of retirement…Butkus called me and said he was part owner of Jacksonville Sharks and he would like me to come to his team so, once I found Chicago had a team, I said, "Heck, I want to make a comeback in Chicago." When I left the Bears, they put a bad article in the paper. It said Rudy was tough against the run but he couldn't cover the pass, but when I went to that World League, I lead the team in interceptions. Now, Butkus wasn't too good at interceptions either, was he?

- **He kind of had hands of stone, didn't he?**

Yeah, I guess. But, anyhow, me and Virgil Carter, and we had one of your buddies, the back Kelly, Leroy Kelly….

- **Leroy Kelly?**

Yeah. He came to the Chicago Fire. Another one of the Browns' halfbacks was with us, too. Leroy was washed up when I was in Cleveland. You know I wanted to say, because I thought he was great, but he was over the hill when I got there. I can't say who's better, Butkus or Nitschke…Nitschke was over the hill when I got up there, too.

- **Did Brian Duncan play with you?**

No, it was Cyril Pinder.

- **Who?**

Cyril Pinder.... He played for "Da Bears." Cyril Pinder, oh, he was an ex-Chicago Bear and he had questionable knees. Leroy Kelly came to our Chicago Fire. The story is we won our first five games. Virgil Carter was our quarterback. He was the "chicken bleep," remember? He was a starter and had said something bad about George Halas. He said he was chicken shit, and the next thing he was traded to Cincinnati.

- **Who was your favorite team growing up?**

Oh, the Bears, because I was from Chicago, theologically.

- **Who's your favorite player?**

My favorite player? You know, when I was in college, I was a tight end and my number was 89 and my hero was Mike Ditka. When I got to the Bears, I went and told him, "You're my hero." I respected him. And Ditka loved me because of the way I'd play on the special teams. One word to describe Ditka as a player: Intense. He'd catch a little ten-yard hook pass, and instead of running for the wide open end zone, he'd just run towards somebody from the other team and start whacking them with a forearm. I loved the way he played and the intensity of it. Then he coached un-coachable people. You know, now days, you can't do what he did. He got lucky. He didn't learn anything in Chicago and got traded to the Philadelphia Eagles, but by the time the season started, he was with the Cowboys and Tom Landry really taught him. My theory is football was a chess game and there are two guys that changed it. Let me say that again. Football is a chess game. And Landry and Shula invented the man in motion. All this stuff to make you have to think and catch you right in between changing the defense as they snapped the ball. Ditka owes a lot of his greatness to Landry. Ditka and George Halas. It was Coach Halas' last year and he was all crippled. He ended up going to England and getting a hip transplant. The trainer would drive him around in a golf cart on the field. Poor old Halas, he'd be standing there cussing us out and he didn't know it, but he was falling over backwards. He fell over backwards, still cussing us out, and he retired the next year.

- **Did good players teach you? Or did they kind of shun you off to keep their position?**

Most were selfish and not wanting to show you the little trick because the old saying is, as a Pro, "If you go to take a leak, when you come back somebodys got your job." I'm sort of trying to say two things. Most of them admit it's everybody for themselves, unless you're a guaranteed. If you're a Butkus or a Sayers or something, you know you're not getting cut. My roommate Butkus would tell me things he knew I didn't know. When I was in college, I was a defensive end and a tight end for Indiana. I actually didn't know how to play linebacker. My first year with Dallas, they put me in the middle. Jerry Tubbs was a linebacker, a real nice man. Leroy Jordon was the middle linebacker and then it was open for anybody else. Laundry said, "You're in there as middle linebacker." But I don't know what to do. I don't know how to back off or nothing. I decided that center Dave Menders is going to snap that ball and, if I'm going to make a mistake, I want to make an aggressive one. Every time he would snap that ball, I would blast up under his chin with my forearm. When I got cut about ten days later, he was in the office. He said, "I really hate to say this, but I'm glad they cut you because you were beating the shit out of me." I actually learned how to play middle linebacker with the Philadelphia Bulldogs in the Continental League. Those were some good stories for a free agent you know. You get a lot more interesting stories from people where everything wasn't roses.

- **Your stories are great because they come from a different light.**

I was going to have my NFL story written, even had the perfect title for it.

- **What was that?**

If I was going to do my NFL thing, the name of my book would have been "The Average Bear."

- **That is a great title.**

It is, isn't it? "The Average Bear...."

- **Have you ever thought about writing? You've got some great stuff.**

Yeah. My brother has a friend, but I don't think we'll ever do it though.

- **Bob wrote a book didn't he?**

No.

- **Didn't somebody write a book on him?**

This guy that wants to do "My Average Bear" did a thing on our high school and the Pros, but I don't think it's even been published yet. My brother is a very impulsive guy. Bob would study his plays and he would study the films of the guy he was going to cover. I told Bob, "When you're playing Bob Lilly in the Super Bowl, he's going to eat you up. It's okay, though, because he eats everybody up." Bob Lilly, what a great guy he was, too. I have total respect for him as a human being and a football player. The second year they go to the Super Bowl, my brother Bob ate Lilly up. My brother wasn't that big, 275 pounds and 6'3. I mean he was always a weightlifting champ of all the teams in high school and college. He really studied the game, too! He didn't like Larry Little who was just a big fast overpowering person. He didn't learn any techniques; he was just raw talent. When all that stuff started fading, he didn't stick around like my brother did because Bob learned all these techniques. Bob also was a center on the team for snapping punts. That usually keeps you three or four more years, too.

- **You said Lilly gave your brother a hard time. Who was the person that gave you the hardest time?**

Well, I've got to tell you, I very seldom started. I was only on the special teams and I didn't start until the year we won one game and lost thirteen in 1969.

- **But was there anybody that gave you trouble when you were playing?**

No. I only started one year, then it was back on the special teams for me as far as in the NFL. Today, they send somebody to the Pro Bowl from the special teams. I just went and played the game. Somebody's got to bust that wedge. All these black guys can run much faster than me, but they were waiting for me to bust the wedge. That's what I had to do to make the team. I loved it and I loved my dad's work ethic. On the suicide squad, you go bust the wedge, that's how I made the team. I don't think I would've made the team if I hadn't done that. But, if there is anyone, I've got to say that the guy that gave me the most trouble, the hardest guy I ever had to tackle, that I had to do five days a week in practice, was Gale Sayers. He was the greatest. I never played against Jim Brown because he quit. Yeah, I ran him out of the league…tell everybody that.

- **He was afraid to face you.**

Yeah. I did tackle Jimmy Taylor and he ran right over me and drug me about five more yards. You guys had a good tight end, too…Milt Morin. Oh, the respect for that man. He was a tough tight end.

- **Do the Browns still make you feel like you're a part of the team? Do you get invites back to the games or anything?**

No. Nor to the NFL golf outings or the homecomings. Wait. You know what, that's not true. They did and I never responded. The good part of playing on so many teams you get invited to the golf outings everywhere. Everywhere. So, now that I'm retired, I'm going to pick up on that. My brother played in three or four down here. Bob's had them a lot.

- **Where was the hardest place for you to play because of the fans?**

Let me see, that's a good question. There were no indoor stadiums then. Well, I want to tell you, you aren't going to like the answer. It's Ohio State.

- **You played there?**

Yeah, when I was at Indiana, we went to that huge stadium. That's where I noticed the roaring crowd. You couldn't even call the defense or nothing because of the crowd distraction. Does that qualify for an honest answer?

- **Sure does.**

That was the biggest place I knew for the crowd roar. But the most terrible place I had to play was that cold Minnesota, up there before the indoor stadium. God, was that cold up there.

- **Guys have mentioned that Soldier Field was not the best field.**

No, it wasn't. Here's a story. It's colder playing football in Soldier Field than it is in Green Bay just because, up in Green Bay, the snow is powdery and dry, and in Chicago, that wind coming all across that lake from Canada. It is definitely colder and nastier in Chicago, even though it was ten degrees difference. I left Cleveland and said, "Holy cow, I'm going to Green Bay. That's got to be cold," and it wasn't as bad as I thought. I just got called to go to Wrigley field and I said, "I've got to go there."

- **Cleveland was cold, too. How did you get to Cleveland?**

How did I get there? I got cut. Every Monday, I would call every team and say, "Anybody get hurt?" I forgot who got hurt on your team, but they brought me over and I got activated until I pulled that hamstring then you know what happened there. But every Monday, I would call every team. When I ended up in Green Bay, I got a standing ovation. I'm all set. I've got a team to play on the next year then they fired the coach. They hired that one from Notre Dame…I forget his name. Who was the coach at Notre Dame after Parseghian was in there?

- **Dan Devine.**

Yeah. He was the coach at Green Bay and he made me go to Atlanta to a doctor that worked on Bart Starr, Cassius Clay, to get relief for my pulled hamstring. I went down there and the doctor said, "You have no problem. Just don't make him run the sprints for the first week." Well, my first day of practice as a Green Bay Packer, they wouldn't let me on the bus to practice until I signed a release. I read it and said, "I can't sign either one of these." He said, "Step aside and read them, or you can't get on the bus." It said if I pulled my hamstring, they can cut me and release me.

- **Several players have been in your type of situation. They cut them at the last minute, just so they wouldn't be picked up by somebody else.**

Yeah. They play games. That's what happened to me. I was with the Redskins. They cut one of their linebackers. If somebody claimed them, they can pull them back. That's what they did, pulled them back off waivers, then they tried to get that team to trade for him. They cut me, then I got on the phone every Monday, and then the year with Dan Devine, that happened again. Every Monday I'd be on the phone and it turns out that Atlanta Falcons, Norm Van Brocklin, called me like with six games to go in the season. He said, "We're going to be in Cincinnati. I'd like to have you down here and I'll take a look at you." I drove to Cincinnati and met Norm Van Brocklin. They gave me a $10,000.00 contact to play the last six games on their taxi squad.

- **What's the biggest contract you ever got?**

$22,500.00 with the Bears. When I was making $22,500.00, Butkus was making like $40,000.00. My brother, in the Super Bowl, was $33,500.00, then he got $90,000.00 to play out his option. He said "I'd like to stay with the Dolphins, but if you don't give me a good raise I'm going to put myself up for free agent bidding." He went from a $30,000.00 contract to the highest paid lineman in the history of football at that time. I want to say $125,000.00. He got $90,000.00 out of the World Football League and they owed me $50,000.00. I made All Pro middle linebacker and they only paid me $17,000.00 of it.

- **What is the funniest story of your NFL experience?**

Well, you had to do five years to get a pension. I'm an Atlanta Falcon; you've got to at least sit on the bench for three games to make it for one year. That's what happened to me. Three games left and they activated me and our last game of the season we're going to New Orleans. This is a great story and it's true. I felt Norm Van Brocklin was an alcoholic by the time I met him and, because we were losing, he would have us do live scrimmages. When your team loses, the coaches raise hell on everybody. We're going to New Orleans to play the last game of the season and he said, "All you guys got your shit packed." He said, "This is the most important game in your life because a lot of you guys aren't going to be here next year." We go down there and I'm only playing on the special teams and I'm kicking ass on special teams. I bust a wedge and am seeing double but I didn't go to the trainer. I thought, "Well, heck, I'll just play that way because I'm not playing linebacker." I didn't even report it. I'm seeing like two of everything. I'm trying to tackle a guy and I see two guys about ten feet apart. Later on in the game, I go through the wedge and it's me and the ball carrier. I didn't know which one to dive for. I am going full speed. I thought, "I'll just dive right between them and spread my arms as wide as I can," and that's exactly what I did. But I never touched anything. I never saw the game film either but was obligated to go to the Falcons the following year. Guess what, they sent me my release. "Don't even come to camp" and I know it was because of that play on that game film. I would've loved to see that film.

- **Did you ever ask them for it?**

No. I never even explained to them what happened. That last game got me my pension and, boy, when my pension notification came in, I took two hours opening it. I put a six-pack on the couch and I opened the envelope just a little bit, and take a swig of beer, because I knew what I had to go through to get that.

- **Are you part of the coalition or whatever it is to help change the pension plan for the players?**

No, I don't know much about that. I go to a few of the outings. I only get $1,250.00 a month, but it's a lot more than the guys before me got.

- **What was the saddest thing that happened while you were playing?**

Gale Sayers. Yeah, Gale Sayers getting wiped out. It was a guy named Herman Alexander from the 49ers, and he cried after the game. He didn't do it on purpose. It used to be, if you find out somebody's got a bad leg, that's the one you go for. I mean, that was part of the game. When Gale got it, Herman Alexander was real sad in the interview later, saying "I'm sorry, Gale," and everybody respected him so, definitely that.

- **What was the most memorable game in your career?**

A college All-Star game down here in Miami. If not that, then for the NFL, my game at Lombardi Field against the Bears, with my standing ovation.

- **That would be a memorable one.**

Yeah. When I heard the announcer saying, "Scratch number so and so and add number fifty-nine." Then later, everybody got up and gave me a standing ovation. I never knew what the heck that was, so definitely that.

- **Did the injuries you've had affect your career?**

Well, let me say it's the opposite, because I wasn't a starter and that's why I don't have no bad knees or neck. I got a broken nose a hundred times, but not being a starter like my brother—he had every kind of broken thing in his career and was just tough. So, that was one of the advantages of, I mean, I woke up in Saint Louis on the bench and it was just like I woke up from being in bed. I woke up and thought, "What the hell am I doing here…. Holy Christ…." I got, you know, busting the wedges, I got concussions quite often. I loved playing the game. I actually want to say, when I played my first game in the NFL, in the real game, not a pre-season, I told God, "Thank you, Lord, for letting me make it. I hope I have a long life, but if not, you have fulfilled my dream. Thank you for letting me fulfill my dream."

- **Are players worth their salary? Should they be more fan conscious?**

I don't even like football now days. I mean, it's all about commercial. They've changed the rules. You can't touch an offensive receiver but one time in five yards. Football players making a lot of money, that's all about commercial. I think everyone in history would tell you "No, the new guys don't deserve what they're making," but it's probably jealousy.

- **What do you think is the best rivalry?**

The Bears is definitely Green Bay. The Bears is always Green Bay and I think Cleveland was always Pittsburgh. Pittsburgh always has them with the Eagles.

- **What do you do after you retired from football?**

I've been a fireman twenty-five years down here for the City Hollywood, Florida. What I did for ten years, I had an advertising specialty business, which was pens and calendars and key chains. You know, I'd sell the car dealers their license plates and key rings and hats and shirts and jackets. Bobbie Green, our punter with the Bears, did that and he got me in it and I stayed in it for years. I'm actually still in it, but I'm not active.

- **So, you're a firefighter?**

I just retired twenty-four years last year. Yeah, I went from special teams in the NFL to a firefighter.

Kuechenberg (standing middle) as a Florida Firefighter

- **Where are you at now?**

Hollywood, Florida. You don't know what a tiller man is…?

- **No, I don't.**

You know that big, long ladder truck, where somebody drives the back? That's a tiller man . I was real good; real proud of being a good tiller man.

- **A firefighter is just a very honorable occupation.**

Oh, yeah. Since 9/11…yeah.

- **"Teamwork is the fuel that allows common people to produce uncommon results."**

You know as a fireman, we're supposed to be out there in the street with a boot. I'm so against that. I said, "We don't belong out in the street; we're a hazard to the drivers," and there were more than a couple near collisions several times. But, boy, since 9/11, people were dumping money in our boots, you know, and I really think we're overplaying it. It's just a job. You're supposed to do your job, whatever it is.

- **What are your hobbies?**

My hobbies are, when I'm not going through this terrible pain of the divorce, me and my brother, I play tennis and I play golf and, man, my big thing I love is guitar. I play country music and old rock-n-roll and I love the old sing-along's like, "You are my Sunshine," "You Get a Line and I'll Get a Pole Honey, Hey Honey, You Get a Line and I'll Get a Pole."

- **You know my favorite song.... I mean, I'm not a big country and western fan, but my favorite is Tennessee Ernie Fords *Sixteen Tons*.**

"People say a man is made out of mud." E minor, A minor, C7; I can't read music. That's the hell of it. I had a guy in the band who got me a trumpet. I'd drive around town about three a.m. in the morning and play *dah dah dah dah dah dah* (insinuating playing charge on the trumpet). Then I would play taps. Oh, those good ole' days!

- **What did you get out of your NFL experience?**

Oh, just like on that first day I made it, I said, "Thank you, Lord, for letting me make it." You know for years I would look at Harlan Hill's photograph — but here's a great story. The Bears were in Wrigley Field, but they can't get in there right at the start because the Cubs were there. Me and Butkus, who was driving, come out of this college to get in his car and all the kids swarmed. "Mr. Butkus sign this!" One kid kept looking at me then looking at his card. "Is this you?" he said. "Would you sign it?" I said, "Holy cow, I'm on a bubblegum card, that's me on that bubblegum card." The rest of them swarmed, Butkus and I say to the kid, "Hey. buddy, can I give you a dollar for that card?" He gave it to me and took off running. He comes back five minutes later. "Hey, I've got three more, do you want to buy these?" he said. Heck with the getting my autograph, he could make some money.

- **That's the first entrepreneur of the autograph-signing business?**

Yeah. You know, it's funny. Probably twice a week, I get a letter from somebody somewhere with my bubblegum card in it, and I sign it. They say, "Will you please?" and I actually send a big eight-by-ten glossy. If I think they're sincere, I put it in a big envelope. I got one from Mount Satibachi in Japan last year. On the envelope, it was written in Japanese. That was crazy. When I think they are sincere, I go over and above, and I sent my picture and I got a picture of my brother I send, and he sent me back a nice long letter like you did. I feel good when I do that.

- **Is there anything else you would like to say?**

Yeah. My brother says it's so great. Me and my brother…we weren't big enough and we weren't fast enough and we weren't strong enough, but we were too dumb to know it and we made it anyhow. I don't mean the dumb part, but that's exactly right. Brothers that go through trials together are tougher. I've got one brother. It's all right for us to beat up on each other, but don't let anybody try to get in between us.

Rudy Kuechenberg									
Linebacker/Defensive End 1967-71									
Indiana University									
Season	Team	Games	Defense				Fumbles	Total	
			INT	Yds	Avg	TD		Points	
1967	CHI	14	0	0	0	0	0	0	
1968	CHI	14	0	0	0	0	0	0	
1969	CHI	14	0	0	0	0	0	0	
1970	CLE/GB	9	0	0	0	0	0	0	
	CLE	3	0	0	0	0	0	0	
	GB	6	0	0	0	0	0	0	
1971	ATL	3	0	0	0	0	0	0	
Career		54	0	0	0	0	0	0	
Season	Team)	Punt Ret.				Kick Ret.			
		PR	Yds	Avg	TD	KR	Yds	Avg	TD
1967	CHI					1	0	0	0
1968	CHI					1	0	0	0
1969	CHI					1	0	0	0
Career		0	0	0	0	3	0	0	0

Promotional pose for the Chicago Bears

LINEMEN PLAY. TOO!

Seems like Fran & Dan & Joe Montan',
They're gettin' all the glory, & all the cheerin' from the stands!
All the cheerleaders really love em', & the fans they're goin' nuts,
But no one gives a dirty damn 'bout us linemen here, really bustin' our butts.

In Dallas they've got Emmit & Irving, & Troy's their main man.
They're all on "Prime Time" there, & all across the land,
But who can name the men in the trenches, the men there on the line?
Seems we've all been long forgotten, long before our time!

Now Young & Rice are really famous, up there in ol' San Fran,'
Their names are in the papers there, & all across the land.
But no one cares 'bout us big linemen here, tottin' triple chins.
You'll see a few teeth missin', too, if you see us grin.

It seems the stars are gettin' all the glory, as we give our grunts & groans
Cuz' we do all the dirty work down in the trenches, and we're breakin' lots of
bones.
Don't the fans know us linemen, damn it, we're playin' too!
We've got broken bones to prove it, man, & we're damn sure black & blue!

We grunt & groan, & we waller' in the mud.
We give & take fierce forearms, that hit you with a thud!
They announce the star's names, when they score their big TD's.
The last time I heard my name called, was for a "Holdin' Penalty!"

Right there on national TV, the ref pointed his finger right at me,
And told the whole damn world, that "That'll be fifteen"!
My coach, he pulled me out, & he said I was to blame,
He said it's all my fault, that we had lost the game!

He said I must stop holdin', & I ain't even holdin' my own,
And if I do it one more time, He's sendin' me straight home.
My wife, she left the stands early, & flagged herself a cab.
She told me my name's "Mud," & I really played real bad!

My Mamma called collect, & cussed me a blue streak!
She said she's gonna change her name, if I hold again next week!
I said, "Mom, don't change your name now, cuz' I've just changed mine.
Just call me 'Triple-chinned, teeth-missin', broken-boned,
Gruntin' & groanin', black & blued, Hand-holdin' Mr. Mud' from the line!"

Rudy Kuechenberg
December 12th, 1995

THE BOY & THE PEACH TREE

Look at the boy, amidst the orchard,
Gazing upward, past that limb.
He's spied a bright, ripe shinning peach,
He wished, would fall to him.

Now he's been standing there, for quite awhile,
As any fool can see,
For on the ground, in scattered file,
Lie peaches, he could reach.

But he doesn't care, & he'll still try,
To grasp, that luscious peach.
But oh, he wished, that he could fly,
For it's not within his reach.

Then soon he'll learn, it's all in vain,
And he'll reach, upon the ground,
To soothe, his aching hunger pains,
With peaches, fallin' down.

For what's meant to be, is meant to be,
And it's true too with, that damned old tree,
So from the ground, he grasped a peach,
Not so good, but in his reach.

Rudy Kuechenberg
May 10th, 1963

The two poems featured here were graciously contributed to this book by Rudy Kuechenberg who had the following to say about his original compositions:

On *Linemen*: "I was a linebacker, got some glory, and had my name called whenever I made a tackle, but my Great brother, Bob, was a lineman, and those poor guys don't get any credit at all, and it just doesn't seem fair that that is the way it is. This poem is a brief moment of pleasure in the life of a *Lineman*, and I have to say my brother, Bob, was the BEST!"

The Boy & The Peach Tree: "This is one of my very favorite poems! It's about striving for the one special thing you want in life! Sometimes, we achieve these goals; sometimes we have to settle for something less, and not as good as our original goals!"

Thanks, Rudy!!

11

Don Cockroft

Don Cockroft, one of the finest place kickers in the NFL, spent nine of his thirteen years as a double-duty kicker. As a punter in 188 games, he launched 651 balls into the air for a 40.1-yard average. During that nine-year career of doing both duties, he only had nine punts blocked. And no one since Don's 1976 season has been a full-time punter and kicker on any NFL team. Not many even realize his punting capabilities because of his sure-footed place-kicking accuracy—that and fans remembering plays where Don saved the game. Ninety-five percent of his point after attempts have gone through the uprights and Don accumulated 1,080 points in his years as a Brown. Many people recognize Don by a play he didn't even get to partake. Red Right 88 has been drilled into the Cleveland Browns fans minds since January 4, 1981. The temperature was a dismal four degrees and a decision was made by Sam Rutigliano to have Brian Sipe pass the ball to get closer to the end zone. The ball was intercepted, leaving the score 14-12, with the Browns in the rear. However, instead of possibly advancing on to Super Bowl XV, Don never got that chance to put the Browns into that situation by kicking the field goal for the three points and winning it fifteen-fourteen.

- **What was it like to walk on to the field for the first time as a Brown?**

[Laughs] There are two memories of a beating that come to mind. One was a game at the stadium, the last pre-season game my second year when I made the team. We happened to be playing the Green Bay Packers, the World Champs. Growing up, as a quarterback in high school, Bart Starr was my idol. To think, "Here I am in Cleveland Stadium, eighty-plus thousand fans at a pre-season game and we are playing the world champion Packers." I guess I will never forget the feeling I had standing on the side, looking across the field and seeing Bart Starr, Jim Taylor, Vince Lombardi. Do you know what I am saying? It is just one of those special things. I guess, though, the first time I suited up for the Browns was at the Canton Hall of Fame game. It was my rookie season and I was at the All-Star game in Chicago, so I did not even join the team until the first pre-season game for the Browns that year. My introduction was in the lockerroom prior to that game. I laugh because during the game I met Lou Groza for the first time. I knew of his records and history. I was trying to make conversation with him and we were out kicking extra points in a pre-game warm up. Back then, the goal posts were on the goal line so it was a ten-yard kick to make an extra point. You really had to kick it badly to miss the extra point. I was trying to make conversation with him and I said, "Lou, it's kind of hard to miss these, isn't it?" Well, he didn't want to talk, but said, "Yeah, son, it is hard, but you can miss them." Bottom line is, well, we scored and I went out to kick my first extra point ever for the Cleveland Browns and I would I like to blame the holder or the six-inch grass, but it was a perfect on-side kick. I didn't even come close. What was funny, though, was when I came off the field and Groza was smiling ear-to-ear and he said, "Well, son, you can miss them." That was my first experience as a Browns player.

- **When you made the team, you were put on what they call the "taxi squad." Did Lou Groza help you when you were coming up?**

Well, my first year…. You may not know this but I am a Christian and I believe God has a plan for our lives. I think God orchestrates a lot of things in our lives we are unaware of and wonder if possibly that wasn't part of God's plan for my life, when I didn't make it that first year. To answer your question, I was hurt (injured). I hurt my knee and was put on injured reserve and about ready to have a chance to make the team about the second week of the season. Lou was having a tough time. I got into a car wreck and screwed up my back. It was a miserable year. Did Lou help? I say this with kindness. He was a very proud individual, still could kick the football, still wanted to kick the football, and I learned more from Lou by watching than by talking to him. During that year, I was on the taxi squad and Lou kicked for his twenty-first season. Then Blanton Collier did something real wise. When I finally made the team my second year in 1968, he named Lou as a special coach to me. Lou worked with me for a couple of years. I credit a lot of my success to what he taught me.

- **When did you decide you wanted to be a professional football player?**

When I was a junior in college while at Adams State. My career average in punting was forty-four-plus yards for four years. My junior year, I was fourth or fifth in the nation with this average, and there were a few scouts who were looking at other players who began to look at me. My senior year, I led the nation with a forty-eight-yard average and was number one in the country. Certainly, people were talking to me and the reality of professional football sank in as something that might be a real possibility.

- **Is there any significance behind the number '0?'**

Well, yes. When I went to Adams State, I was a walk-on, and when I played in high school, I was the starting quarterback, starting middle linebacker. I did all the kicking from seventh grade on. Basketball was my favorite sport. I was probably a better basketball player than football and I ran track. At Adams State, I was a walk-on and my goal at Adams was to make the varsity team as a freshman. If I didn't do that, I seriously doubted that I would have continued to play because they promised me a scholarship if I made their team. But, I did make their team as a freshman. They gave me #32, which I wasn't too enamored by, but it was the number I got. I played some defensive back and did the kicking; had a really strong year. Then my sophomore year, I came back and they were handing me this jersey with a #0 on it. I said, "Coach, I don't want to wear the number zero." He said, "Well, Don, it's not zero, it's an 'O' (oh)''." There was a ballplayer there that was pretty famous named David O'Choa prior to me; I believe he was a running back. Well, he wanted zero or 'O' for O'Choa, so coach, Don McKillabee, gave me the zero. I told him I didn't want it, but he said, "Hey, you'll make this famous someday." As it turned out, they ended up calling me Donnie O from then on. I have to laugh because of what the coach had said and now that is retired at Adams State.

- **The name "Donnie O" didn't follow you into the Pros?**

[Laughs] No—but when I was picked to kick in the College All-Star Game and I forget the guy's name, but he was a coach for the All-Stars when we played Green Bay. When it came time to hand out jerseys and he saw this zero, he said, "There ain't no player of mine gonna wear a zero, get a real number." I tried to explain that I didn't care what number I wore, but that is what my number had been throughout my college career. When I came to the Pros, I just took the ol' #12 that they gave me and was happy.

- **Who inspired you to be a professional football player?**

I really can't say anyone inspired me. I didn't dream about it or think about it. I knew I was a pretty good athlete, but it just happened for me. I thank God; he kind of had it in his plans. If you go back to my youth and to my athleticism as a young man, my time at Adams State College, and to think I had a chance to play professionally. To all the things that happened between the North-South Shrine game in Miami, which I know was the reason the Browns drafted me. I ended up kicking a couple of decent field goals. I can't say anyone particularly inspired me, other than God and maybe my Mom who was always there by my side. She was the one I played hard for.

- **What type of parental influence did you have?**

I had excellent parental influence. My father was killed when I was three, so I didn't know him, but my step-dad was excellent. We were raised on a farm in Colorado; five boys, I was the middle. The things I am most thankful for are that we had to work and work hard. We had chores every day. Mom and Dad wanted us to participate in athletics but we had to get our chores done. I look back on my mom and dad and I just thank God for my mom because she loved me so much and she was always there. Dad taught me how to work. I find this ironic, that during my senior year in high school we were visiting my grandparents in Nebraska during Thanksgiving. The Browns were playing Detroit. We were watching them on television and, of course, I am in high school with no aspirations of Pro football. We were watching the game on an old black and white television. Lou had just kicked a field goal. My Dad looked at me and said, "If you could only have that old man teach you how to kick, I think you could be all right." Lord knows that happened years later, but Mom and Dad taught me how to work, how to appreciate things. Nothing was ever given to me. If you wanted something, you worked for it. I actually see that lacking so much in today's youth and it is a shame. Plus, the spiritual aspect my parents brought into my life, I am forever grateful. We grew up in a very strong, bible-preaching church. We were there every Sunday morning, Sunday night, Wednesday night. We learned at a young age there is a greater power here in this world. I am not ashamed or embarrassed by my faith, but I know I am a long way from being the man God wants me to be. At the same time, I know without a doubt my relationship through Jesus Christ, my belief, my faith. I can give you a specific example of a scripture shared with me by Monte Clark my second year. I can tell you, as God is my judge, if Monte hadn't shared this particular scripture with me, at that particular time, I don't believe I would have ever made the Browns team. The story is, basically, I came here in '67. I was in a car wreck and messed up my knee and didn't make the team. I knew I could kick further than Lou, but I couldn't get it through the upright. That was my problem [laughs], but I was failing and I signed a two-year contract. That meant I spent the year on the taxi squad watching Lou and I got a second chance to come back in 1968. Again, I am going through the same problems. Physical and mental problems that were bothering me as far as getting the ball through the uprights. I am at Hiram College and, literally, I don't know if it was *The Press* or *The Plain Dealer,* but they had put in their headlines "Browns waste their third-round draft choice on Cockroft." I was not doing very well. After a practice at Hiram, Monte Clark came to my room, stood in the doorway, and said, "Don, do you believe in the Bible?" Well, he knew I believed in the Bible, so then he told me to read *Proverbs,* Chapter 3: Verses 5 and 6. Then he walked down the hall. Well, it says something very simple, *"Trust in the Lord with all of your heart. Lean not unto your own understanding but in all of your ways acknowledge Him; acknowledge God and He will direct your life."* Well, I believed in the Bible, I believed in Christ…so, I got up, shut my door, and got down on my knees, and all I said was, "Lord, help me to trust you more." I had been so anxious, so worried, because I was missing field goals, that I just couldn't do what God had given me the talent to do. I had anxiety and pressure. I don't know if it was a miracle, but I do know this, from that day on if I missed or if I screwed up, I just remembered those verses in my heart and in my mind for me it gave me peace. I made the team and I fooled them for fourteen years before they realized I couldn't kick…. [laughs]

- **Who was your favorite team growing up?**

Well, I had two, the Colts and the Green Bay Packers, because of Johnny Unitas and Bart Starr. I actually have met Bart through our Fellowship of Christian Athletes events. But, one of the greatest things that ever happened, was that my mom, she died a young woman, was fifty-six or fifty-seven years

124

old, of cancer. Well, she loved Johnny Unitas. I remember in 1969 or 1970 and we were playing the Colts in Cleveland. I thought, "I have to get my mom here." So, I flew her to Ohio to go to the game and see Johnny play. The night before the game, I knew where they were staying, and I said, "Mom, you need to stay downtown. I know where the Colts are staying so let's go downtown and eat and we will go to the hotel." Lo and behold—Johnny Unitas walks by and I went out of my element and walked up to him and introduced myself. I told him, "My mom loves you and she came all the way from Colorado to see the game." My mom then got a chance to meet and talk to him. It is one of the greatest things I ever did for my mom.

- **What was it like to play for Blanton Collier?**

I thank the good Lord that Blanton was here when I got here. Blanton, of all the coaches I had, was my favorite, without question. The reason was that he was an older man when I got here and was like a father. I knew he cared about me. "Don Cockroft." He cared about me, my family, and every player on that team, above and beyond the ability to play. He wanted the best for you because you were you and God gave you the talent. He was a great teacher. I have all the love, respect, and admiration in the world for Blanton.

- **Did he learn a lot from Paul Brown?**

Well, I am sure he did. I got here after Paul and I am sure he did.

- **What was Nick Skorich like to play for?**

I think I had my best years with Nick as coach. I don't know if it was because of him, but I liked Nick. I don't know if a lot of players had respect for him and maybe he didn't carry the authority he should have carried. But I'm not going to say anything bad about him. Sure, maybe wasn't the greatest coach in the world, but like I said, I had some really great years with Nick.

- **What was Forrest Gregg like to play for?**

Forrest went from a coach that understood to a coach you didn't know, whether you won or lost the game. I respect Forrest and like him, but his first year with the Browns was a terrible year. I respected and admired him for the way he handled the situation. I really did. Next year, we started and we lost in Baltimore to the Colts. We are on a three-week, pre-season journey. We go from Nebraska to Oklahoma, and it is 110-115 degrees when we lose to Baltimore. I think Forrest's approach to coaching and the team changed forever. We lost to them then he got on the players really heavy. In Oklahoma, we were in pads all week long and the day before the game. He just really beat us in the ground. We ended up kicking Atlanta's rear end. I think from then on, Forrest kept that sort of demeanor as far a coaching for the rest of his career with the Browns. I do respect him; he just had a different style.

- **What was it like to play for Dick Modzelewski?**

I only played for him in one game. I was hoping he would have been the head coach and had come back the next season. I think he would have been a Blanton Collier-type coach—maybe not as far as teaching, but the players would have respected him.

- **What was it like to play for Sam Rutigliano?**

Well, obviously, he was my last coach and he and I share a lot together in our faith and belief. I think he made the biggest mistake in the world when he called "Right 88" [laughs], but I respect him. He has a tremendous faith. Sam wouldn't let you get to know him like Blanton did, but that is how he got the job done. I am a very personable person and I want to know who I am working with. You often hear when a team starts to play well, they had bought into the coach's plan or vision and they believe it.

- **Who was your college coach? What type of influence did he have?**

When I was in high school in Fountain, CO, Adams College said, "We will give you a scholarship if you come over here and make our team." At that time, Darrell Mudra was the coach and he had like a 45-5 record at Adams. He was a great coach. That summer, he went to North Dakota to coach, so Adams got a new coach named Don McKillum. He came in and was a true gentleman. He worked us real hard, but was very fair and great to play for. I actually started my senior year as a defensive back and, fortunately, I got hurt and that is when my punting started to pick up. I have very fond memories of him at Adams State.

- **Who did you enjoy playing with while at Cleveland?**

Oh, well [laughs], every year was a little different, but I liked the years we won! Each year you look at the game and team differently as you grow and mature. Coming in as a young person, there was Bill Glass, Monte Clark, Dick Schafrath and John Wooten, Frank Ryan, Leroy Kelly. That was a whole different personality as those guys moved on and left. Brian Sipe, Clay Matthews and Ozzie, Dave Logan, they were all great. My closest friends though were probably none that were recognized. Probably my best friend ever was Reese Morrison, who backed up Leroy Kelly. Tom Beutler, linebacker from Toledo, Billy Andrews, those were some real close guys.

- **Did any previous players, such as Jim Brown, have a positive influence when you were playing?**

Well, they didn't have a negative influence, but I don't know if they had an influence. There has always been talk about the veterans getting close and tight with the current Browns team, but when the veterans were around I never really gave it a thought. I was there to do a job and I always played against myself.

- **Was your kicking career a job?**

I never thought about it as a formal job, but it was a job. I tell people, even though I enjoyed my career, I thank God for everything. I think I could have enjoyed it more had I had a different mindset. By that, I mean, I competed against myself, and to this day, I don't think anyone kicks as much as I did. A few years ago, I was down at the Browns camp and one of the kickers told me he didn't kick at all on Fridays, very little on Thursdays. I asked him why, and he said his leg gets tired by the end of the season. I told him he had to be kidding me. I kicked a lot [laughs]. I worked hard like I did, though, out of fear of failure. That isn't a bad thing, but you don't want to run your life or your career on that. You want to transpose that fear of failure into confidence so you can enjoy what you do a lot more. There is healthy respect for fear of failure, but your entire career should not be based on fear.

- **Your religious beliefs are very firm.**

I'm a Christian. Religion is man's effort to find God. All religion is man's effort to find God. Christianity is God's effort to find man through his Son, Jesus Christ. There is a difference between Christianity and Religion.

- **You are a very proud man and any field goal you missed, you were sad about it. Is that the way you lived—like the way you played?**

Well, I am going to go back to the word "proud." My dad always said, "Son, always be thankful and humble." I hope that for the majority of my career, I was able to be thankful for what happened and the good things I was able to accomplish and that, hopefully, I remained humble through it. Proud, yes. As I tell young people, "Take great pride in what you are doing." In other words, do your very best, but don't be so full of pride. The one game you referred to in your comments earlier was the most memorable game in my entire athletic career. Not only in high school or college, but also Pro, when I missed a field goal with two minutes left to go, which would have beaten the Pittsburgh Steelers. I would like to preface that by saying I had already kicked three field goals in that mud and I had hardly missed any field goals all year. I kicked a fifty-seven yarder that year and, yet, I miss the most important field goal of my life at that time. As a believer, I asked God why, and jokingly said to Him, "You could have moved the goal post, you could have done something." I missed it by about a half inch. The point I am trying to make is it was one of those moments I was so anxious to see the ball go through as I went to kick it, I pulled my head up too quick and pulled my foot just enough. At that time, I thought life ended. That was such an important kick and I missed it. Billy Andrews came over, when I got to the bench and said, "Don, get your chin up; we are going to get the ball back and we are going to get you a second chance." That was after one of my other co-players chewed me out. As you know, we did get the ball back. I kept my head down and drilled it through the uprights and won. It was the greatest thrill of my professional career. I'm not sure how to answer your question. There are trials, tribulations, and disappointments in life just like in the game of football. I guess my philosophy in life is you can't let yourself get too low during the bad times and don't get too high during the good…try to have a stable life.

- **What were your feelings when Cleveland went to Baltimore?**

At the time, I was living in Colorado, but I came back. I was working for a company based here in Ohio, so I came back on occasion. I guess the simplest way to put it is, every time I flew into Cleveland, I didn't even have to go to the stadium. It was like somebody burnt my house down. It was a very empty feeling that part of Cleveland and part of my history was gone.

- **ESPN made the statement last year that Ohio State vs. Michigan and Cleveland vs. Pittsburgh are the two greatest rivalries in sports today. What is your opinion?**

Well, I'm not going to argue with them [laughs]. Everyone thought when Paul Brown went to Cincinnati that the Browns/Bengals would be the greatest rivalry, and it is in-state, but nothing compares to the hate and dislike for the Steelers and vice versa [laughs]. It is a great rivalry. As players, you still respect them, but you want to beat their butts so bad. I don't think it is animosity at all between the players, it is just the way it is. You want to win that one. Unfortunately, we never could beat Pittsburgh [laughs].

- **Who was your nemesis on the field?**

Well, Ted Hendricks blocked a couple and, after I retired, he sent me a picture of one he blocked. I guess he wanted me to keep that memory. Bubba Smith blocked a couple. He was a big man and got up in the middle. I was a little bit slower when punting.

- **Did you ever encounter any negatives as a player?**

Well, I didn't focus on it. If you play with guys though five, six years, and all of sudden they were gone, that was hard, but eventually we all have to leave the game. The 1980 Cardiac Kids, that was a team; that was a team of players. Obviously, the following year they let at least three of us go and that was three major cogs in the wheel. I say this humbly, but they kept a kid they should have never kept as a kicker and he hurt them badly the following year. That same year, I think, Charlie Hall who was a great leader for the Browns and Jerry Sherk, was released. We were all released that same year. I am sorry, I may have been kind of quiet, but people still had a lot of confidence in me and my ability to not miss when the game was on the line. You take that away and you take Jerry out of the picture, a great football player and leader, and Charlie Hall…when you start losing some of your close friends and you are not going to play ball with them anymore, that is a negative, but it is part of game.

- **Were you released from the Browns organization?**

Yes. When people ask me when I retired, I tell them I didn't retire. I was fired. There has only been one player in Cleveland Browns history who retired and that was Jim Brown. The rest of us were fired. [laughs]

- **Cleveland Browns fans have been labeled negatively with games such Red Right 88. What is your experience and thoughts?**

Well, they are Browns fans and only Browns fans. Some, who do watch the Browns, and watch with intensity, will concur. Overall, they happen and they aren't going to go away. Even after twenty-five years, every place I go to speak or meet somebody new, without question, ninety-five percent of the time I am asked, "Why didn't we kick?" Red Right 88. I wish I had an opportunity, but they are part of the game and the history. It was miserably cold and I told Brian get it on the right hash mark, whatever you do. The wind was blowing right to left and field was frozen. Kicking from the left hash, I would be kicking into the wind. I could kick it badly from the right hash and it would still go through the uprights. Obviously, we didn't get that chance, but people don't understand. Sam called the play, he told Brian to throw it into Lake Erie if no one was wide open. What people don't know is that year, I was not one-hundred percent physically. I played the entire season with a torn cartilage in my left knee. If I bent my knee too far, the cartilage would lock and I couldn't straighten my leg out. I also had two herniated discs. I had five epidurals to get through the season. For what it is worth, I was not a hundred percent. I had missed a couple of kicks on that end of the field in the early part of game so it was not a given. I don't care how close we were . Sam knew that and I knew he wanted to give Brian an opportunity. My job is not to question the coach. My job is to go out and make the kick when I am called to kick it. I wish I had been given the opportunity, but life goes on. It would have been a great opportunity, but it is a great story in life. I use it. I use my second-chance story that I got in Pittsburgh to share more important things in life than a football game. We don't always get a second chance. We got to make the best of what we have today.

- **Do you still feel like you're part of the Browns organization?**

Yes—sure. I will always be a Cleveland Brown.

- **Do you talk to the players today?**

No, not at all. I am working and making a living, I am not involved.

- **Talk to us about the "Water Bowl."**

Adams had a pretty good team my senior year, so we were picked to play in that bowl game. I don't know if I kicked any field goals, but I punted well and we beat them. They were twenty-five pounds. a man advantage against us. It was a big bowl game, probably five hundred people there…. [laughs]

- **Are the Browns Fans the best in the NFL?**

They are great fans. They are great, great fans and deserve a winning team. There are probably more Browns Backers in the world than any other team. You can't go anywhere in this country without finding a Browns fan. Denver has some great fans, Pittsburgh has great fans, everyone has great fans, but the Browns are some of the greatest in the world.

- **Do you think the Browns would have been back if not for the fans?**

No. I do not think they would have been reestablished there if it had not been for the fans.

- **Where was the hardest place to play because of opposing fans?**

Oh, Pittsburgh was pretty nasty. They had signs hanging around after that game where I got the second chance. They love me, but it made me work harder.

- **What is the funniest story of your NFL experience?**

There's some stories [laughs]...lots of stories. I guess, well, guys always used to get on my case about being too serious. I was always honed in to the moment. One of the funniest things is the extra point I missed, as I described earlier, that was totally embarrassing. Another time we were playing the Bengals, Ray Guy was one of the greatest punters for the Raiders. Well, we were down in Cincinnati and the Raiders were playing somebody on Saturday. I noticed before Ray punted, he would do a simulation punt where he would swing his leg up high to get loose. I'm thinking, "Maybe I am going to do that tomorrow when we play the Bengals. Maybe I'm not quite loose enough." We are playing and I am going out to punt. Well, I swung my leg up high and my left foot went out from under me [laughs] and I landed down on my butt. I thought, "Boy, if I get up real quick, no one is going to see me." I ended up with a standing ovation from 63,000 Bengals' fans.

- **What is the saddest story of your NFL experience?**

Well, there were two injuries to players, and one of the very saddest stories to me is when Jerry Sherk got that staph infection. I remember going to the hospital and his knee was bigger than a basketball and we had thoughts of maybe his life was over. He did come back from that, but it was never quite the same. The second was when Greg Pruitt got his knee hurt. He wasn't quite the same when he came back. Another is Walter Johnson, we were up in Minnesota, and he nearly lost his fingers because it was so cold. He was injured and was shot up with Novocain so he could play. When he put his fingers down on the ground, he couldn't feel the cold. I also remember a coach we had, named Howard N. "Sonny" Keys. This guy could snap a football like noone I had ever seen in my life, so I worked with him on punting and field goals. He was a center that played for Philadelphia Eagles for five years. I remember one day, someone said he wouldn't be with us, that he had cancer, and it seemed like two weeks later he was gone.

- **Are players today worth their salaries and should they be more fan conscious?**

Well, when you look at who are the highest paid individuals in our country, it is entertainers and that is what the football players are. Entertainers. We pay to go watch them play or watch them on TV. Are they worth it? No. Do they deserve it? Yes, because we are willing to pay to watch them play. But I also believe they should be more fan conscious. Not just today's athlete, but all athletes. We owe it to the fans to appreciate them. We do what we can for our communities because we are given a privilege and opportunity in a very select group in our society, the Pro athlete. So, yes, today and forever, those players, who never took into account the importance of the fans and their responsibility to influence and do good for the betterment of the fans, have failed. The hardest part is, I can't do all the requests I receive. I need to make a living and would like to have a life where I can go to every one of these tournaments, meet people, have a free dinner and a good time, and help in the charity efforts, but I just can't do them all. I think one of the greatest misconceptions is that people think because I played professional football, I live the life of Riley and have all the money I would ever need. That is so far from the truth for me and a lot of other players.

- **What kind of hazing occurred when you were a rookie?**

Nothing serious—they gave you grief, a hard time. We had to sing every night and do something for the veterans, like carry their shoulder pads out to practice. We had to sit at the back of the bus. The greatest, though is the turkey story. That could range from a drive around the block to only find out there are no turkeys to a sixty-five-mile jaunt on your day off to pick up fictional turkeys for Thanksgiving.

- **What made you so unique during your NFL career?**

I believe I was the last full-time, double-duty kicker in the NFL. For nine years I punted, kicked off, kicked field goals. If there is any uniqueness about my career that would be it—I was the last one to do it.

"I live and die with the Cleveland Browns every year..."
— *Henry Aaron*

Don Cockroft kicking a field goal against the Houston Oilers on Sept 19, 1971

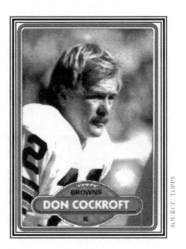

Don Cockroft						
Kicker/Punter 1968-1980						
Adams State						
Season	Team	Games	Punting			
			Punts	Yds	Avg	Blk
1968	CLE	14	61	2,297	37.7	0
1969	CLE	14	57	2,138	37.5	0
1970	CLE	14	71	3,023	42.6	0
1971	CLE	14	62	2,508	40.5	0
1972	CLE	14	81	3,498	43.2	0
1973	CLE	14	82	3,321	40.5	0
1974	CLE	14	90	3,643	40.5	0
1975	CLE	14	82	3,317	40.5	0
1976	CLE	14	64	2,487	38.9	0
1977	CLE	14	1	30	30	0
1978	CLE	16	0	0	0	0
1979	CLE	16	0	0	0	0
1980	CLE	16	0	0	0	0
Career		188	651	26,262	40.3	0

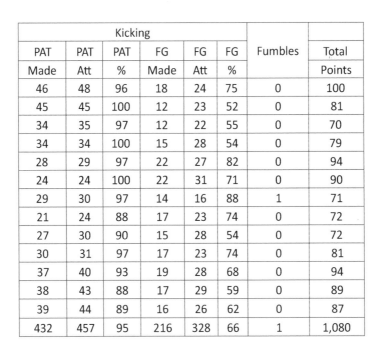

Kicking						Fumbles	Total
PAT	PAT	PAT	FG	FG	FG		
Made	Att	%	Made	Att	%		Points
46	48	96	18	24	75	0	100
45	45	100	12	23	52	0	81
34	35	97	12	22	55	0	70
34	34	100	15	28	54	0	79
28	29	97	22	27	82	0	94
24	24	100	22	31	71	0	90
29	30	97	14	16	88	1	71
21	24	88	17	23	74	0	72
27	30	90	15	28	54	0	72
30	31	97	17	23	74	0	81
37	40	93	19	28	68	0	94
38	43	88	17	29	59	0	89
39	44	89	16	26	62	0	87
432	457	95	216	328	66	1	1,080

SOURCE: CAMMETT

12

Bo Scott

Bo Scott is man of few words, but they are powerful, well-defined words. He didn't go into detail with his answers. Short and to the point answers were Bo's manner of speaking. After spending his years at Ohio State, he opted to spend four years with the Ottawa Rough Riders in the Canadian Football League. "It went really well," he said. "I made the all-star team and we went to the Grey Cup in two of the four years I was there. We won one and lost one." His rights were still owned by the Cleveland Browns and the Oakland Raiders of the American Football League. "Several NFL teams contacted me," he said. "I thought I was headed for the Raiders when the Browns contacted me. It worked out and I played six years with the Browns before retiring." Bo was primarily a blocking back for Leroy Kelly. "I told Leroy (my blocking) is how he got to the Hall of Fame," Scott said. "Being his running mate was special. I enjoyed being able to play with Paul Warfield and Leroy Kelly, both Hall of Fame players." *(Quotes were drawn from an article written by Fred Greetham on the Cleveland Browns website titled "Where Are They Now? Bo Scott.")*

- **What was it like to walk on to the field the very first time as a Brown?**

    Exciting! Sometimes words can't describe it, but it was a fantastic feeling.

- **When did you decide that you wanted to be a professional athlete?**

    Way back when I was in junior high school. I played football and football was a big part of my life. I had an older brother who went on to college and to play a couple years of professional football. I just loved football, I was from Pennsylvania and the Pittsburgh Steelers was our team. I was from a little town called Connellsville, Pennsylvania, fifty miles south of Pittsburgh.

- **Was there any one person that inspired you to play?**

    Probably my brother, Wilbert. He went to Indiana. He played for Pittsburgh, then Philadelphia, and ended up in the Canadian League with Montréal. Wally Scheryer was a big influence. He coached little league football back in Connellsville. He was the one that put a uniform on me for the first time when I was seven years old.

- **What kind of parental influence did you have?**

Real good; my mother and father both liked sports. Both told us to always give your best. My mother loved sports and always encouraged us in school. They were always at our games, very supportive. When we played in high school, they were there every Friday night. Then they came out to Ohio State a few times. They also saw me play as a Cleveland Brown.

- **Who was your favorite team growing up?**

Pittsburgh—because that is what we saw back then. You know, in the 50's, you didn't have the television coverage that you have today. It was like you saw your local teams, so our family was Steelers fans. My brother also played for the Steelers. My mother and father were big football fans. When I came to Ohio State, then I became a Browns fan, because I loved Jim Brown.

- **Were you a Pirates fan also?**

Not as much as I used to be. I was more of a fan during the era of Roberto Clemente, Dick Groat, and those guys. I was a big Brooklyn Dodgers fan because of Jackie Robinson.

- **Who was your high school coach; what kind of influence did he have?**

I played quarterback in high school and in my junior year I got a new coach. He came to me and said he was going to switch me. As a quarterback, I was the best runner on the team. He moved me to running back and that is how I ended up being a running back. I started playing quarterback in the fourth grade. Moving me might have been a blessing. I don't know how far I would have gone as a quarterback. I was a pretty good quarterback, but I don't know if I would have been as good of a quarterback as I was a running back in high school.

- **Tell us about Woody Hayes?**

Woody was a heck of a coach, but I guess a lot of people don't know that he was one heck of an individual, a great human being. That was the thing that I liked about Woody, he was just a fantastic individual. Woody was the type of person you liked him or you didn't like him. There was no in between with Woody. He didn't take any bull crap from anybody. A lot of this stuff these guys are doing today—no way! If he liked you and he was on your bandwagon, you were fine. If he didn't like you, it was almost like he put you in the closet. It was all based on your attitude and effort.

- **When he struck the guy from Syracuse, would he have done the same thing to one of his own players if they had acted the same way?**

Woody was really an intense person on the field as most can probably remember. I think when that guy tackled him, going down the sideline, I think Woody was just so high-intensity that he just lost it. To say that he would have done that to his own player, well, his own players would not have been in that position.

- **What kind of an influence did he have on you? Did he help you get in the Pros?**

Yes, he did. The things he would tell you; not only about football but just about life. I can't think of aby one big quote he would say, but it was always encouragement beyond the football game itself. It is about school, about what you are going to do with yourself after football. Woody had been in contact with a lot of players once they left college. That was another good thing about him.

- **What was it like to play for Blanton Collier?**

I always felt he was a good person to play for. Blanton was mild-mannered; he wasn't the guy who would go around screaming. I've heard him say very few profane words. You just didn't hear him go around hollering and screaming and cussing. He didn't do that and he treated you as men. I will always respect him for that. He was one of the few coaches I played for that didn't go around hollering and screaming, but he treated you as men and respected you as well.

- **How about Nick Skorich?**

Nick was a little bit different than Blanton. He didn't do a whole lot of screaming. Nick was a nice guy, and he was kind of on the quiet side. I think that he followed into Blanton's mold. From working under Blanton and seeing how Blanton treated his guys. Nick kind of fell into that same mold.

- **What players did you enjoy playing with?**

All of them.

- **Who were the team leaders at that time?**

Leroy Kelly, Bill Nelson, Gary Collins, and Jim Houston.

- **What were your feelings when the Cleveland Browns left Cleveland and went to Baltimore?**

I was angry, but I wasn't so much angry at Modell as I was the city of Cleveland. I felt that Cleveland could have prevented that from happening.

- **Ohio State/Michigan, Cleveland Browns/Pittsburg Steelers have been chosen as the two best sports rivalries; tell me about your experience with both of them?**

Ohio State/Michigan, there is nothing like it. I think it is the number one rivalry in all of college football. I think it has even spread across the country. There have been a lot of people who don't know that much about Ohio State/Michigan, but they know about their rivalry game. In Ohio, Michigan is regarded as "the team up north." Woody would start working on the gameplan for Michigan during spring practice. Sports are a funny thing. On any given day, someone can beat someone. I look at it that as who is the best at that time. I always say the team that won that day was the best team. I can't tell on paper who is the best team. That is why they say you've got to play the game. The team that wins is the better team that particular day.

- **Tell us about the Cleveland/Pittsburgh rivalry.**

It is not getting the buildup that it has over the years. I remember when Pittsburgh wasn't winning, in the 1960's, but still it was that rival game, especially between the fans and the cities. Still at that Pittsburgh/Cleveland, some of the hype is not there because, well, on the Browns side, I would say, they are not winning. When Pittsburgh comes here, almost a fourth of the stadium is Pittsburgh fans. You always got fired up for that game.

- **What was it like playing against Paul Brown?**

To me it was interesting. I remember one year he gave me a compliment in one game we played. I really appreciated that. Another game I scored three touchdowns and caught this little short pass. I was able to get away from four different tacklers; he gave me the compliment about that run. It was a broken play. I was blocking and I heard Bill Nelson holler my name. I turned around and he threw it to me.

- **Who was your nemesis on the field? Who gave you the most trouble?**

I'm not sure. I remember when I first started and we played Green Bay, Ray Nitschke was and Dick Butkus from Chicago. Both could hit hard.

- **Do you still feel like you are a part of the Browns organization?**

Yeah, probably a little more with the older Browns than the newer ones.

- **Do they still contact you?**

Yeah, they have a person, Dino Lucarelli, who (was) the coordinator in charge of the alumni. It was his responsibility to get a hold of the different alumni for functions in different parts of Ohio.

- **Are Cleveland fans the best in the NFL?**

Yeah, people in northern Ohio love their football. In the state of Ohio, they love their football, period. I think Browns fans are the best fans in professional football. The Browns have the largest fan club in football in the Browns Backers Worldwide.

- **Is Romeo Crennel a good coach?**

I don't know; he had so many players hurt and it usually takes three years to get your personnel in place. I feel he needs more time.

- **Do you think Charlie Frye is the quarterback of the future?**

I was a Charlie Frye supporter for a long time. Now I don't think he is the quarterback of the future for the Browns.

- **Did you send Joe Jones two years in a row to get the turkey?**

All the veterans used to do that with rookies.

- **What are some of your funny stories from the NFL?**

It wasn't me, but I remember a year we were out playing in Oakland, we were beating Oakland. I had one of my better runs out there. I remember one time Jack Tatum hit Frank Fitz and Frank wouldn't get up off the ground. He crawled on all fours to the sidelines. I remember when Greg Pruitt came to Cleveland; we were in the locker room. I told Greg to hold on to my shirttail and, "I'll take you on to stardom!!!"

- **What is the saddest experience during your NFL career?**

When they traded Paul Warfield. That was a shocker when they traded him to Miami. When that happened, I was thinking anybody could go.

- **What was your most memorable game?**

The game with Cincinnati. We were playing in Cincinnati and we were behind and we came back to win it. That day I scored three touchdowns. Also, 1969-1970, the years that we played Dallas for the Conference Championship. We went out to Dallas and pretty well manhandled them. We won our conference and went to play Minnesota, which was the last year for the National Football League. We played them for the championship and we lost. The only thing I can remember about that day was it was the coldest game I ever played in. In Minnesota that day, it was eight below zero. Walter Johnson got frostbitten hands that day. Minnesota beat us and they went on to play Kansas City in the Super Bowl.

- **Are players worth their salary? Should they be more fan conscious?**

Football is football; they play the game the same way they played when I was in the game. You don't have the team concept and you don't have loyalty anymore. Are these guys worth five million, seven million dollars in one year when other guys were making seveteen thousand a year doing the same job? I just don't know. That is the market and that is the way it goes. I think the owners did all that. I think a lot of the salaries, in any sport, are because the owners put it there.

- **What is your job today?**

I'm retired.

- **What did you do?**

I worked with juvenile delinquents. I was in administration; Assistant Director for the Franklin County Juvenile Detention Center. I worked with kids for thirty years.

- **What are your hobbies today?**

I like golf. I like photography.

- **Are you still involved in sports any; do you still go, play and watch?**

Oh, yeah. I have grandkids playing all kinds of sports. I've have a granddaughter at University of Akron playing basketball. I've got four grandsons playing football. They keep me going. I still attend Browns and Buckeyes games.

- **What did you get out of your NFL experience?**

One thing it is the fact that knowing I did something I dreamed of doing; a dream that came true. It was something that you look back and you did something that thousands of others who played football and didn't make it to the professional ranks. They would love to have accomplished the goal or have the opportunity I got in the NFL.

Bo Scott											
Running Back 1969-1974											
The Ohio State											
			Rushing				Receiving				Tot
Year	Tm	Gm	Rsh	Yds	Aug	TD	Rec	Yds	Avg	TD	Fm	Pts
1969	CLE	13	44	157	3.6	0	6	25	4.2	0	1	0
1970	CLE	13	151	625	4.1	7	40	351	8.8	4	4	66
1971	CLE	14	179	606	3.4	9	30	233	7.8	1	4	60
1972	CLE	12	123	571	4.6	2	23	172	7.5	0	2	12
1973	CLE	7	34	79	2.3	0	6	23	3.8	1	0	6
1974	CLE	14	23	86	3.7	0	7	22	3.1	0	0	0
Career		73	554	2,124	3.8	18	112	826	7.4	6	11	144

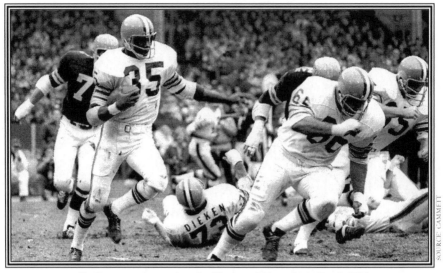

Bo Scott running against the Cincinnati Bengals on Dec 5, 1971
with Gene Hickerson leading the way

Bo Scott at a speaking engagement in Marietta, Ohio,
at the River Rats Browns Backers Celebrity Golf Outing

13

Joe Jones

Dick Modzelewski classified Joe "Turkey" Jones as one of the best defensive ends he ever coached and that says a lot considering he was in the business for twenty-two years. Joe had the tools of the trade. Being 6'6"and weighing 250 pounds, speed, size, and agility were the skills he possessed that inspired Jim Houston and Walter Johnson. These two players saw greatness in this young player and taught him the refined skills of a defensive lineman. His fingers today show the wear and tear of his ten years in the NFL. This is the consequence of him "Head Slapping" the offensive lineman then blowing by them into the backfield. He studied Deacon Jones before he came to the Browns and, in his career, Joe was often compared to Deacon. The 1970 Associated Press Small College All-American teammember was an instant success in the ranks of the Browns. Now Joe works with many charities all across the country. Golf tournaments are a favorite, as he picked up the game early in the twenty-first century. Infamy followed Joe during his career, from his ferocious hit on Terry Bradshaw to the reason he was labeled "Turkey." His daughter has followed in his footsteps by attending Tennessee State University.

- **What was it like to walk on the field the very first time as a Cleveland Brown's player?**

I was elated when they called me then drafted me in the second round, second pick, in 1970. I was in the cafeteria eating my lunch when the guys called. Back then, we didn't sit around and sweat the draft out. I was very happy. My dad and mom were happy. I have an older brother, Charlie Taylor, who played professional football. It was very elating.

- **What was the first game like?**

I didn't have any questions about my skills and God-given ability. I was coming out of the south, going up north, and it was the first time I ever witnessed black snow from the steel mills. The climate was a lot different from what I grew up in. It was very exciting. I was like a kid in a candy store.

- **When did you decide that you wanted to be a professional athlete?**

I did not decide. In the 1960's, I did not have any kind of inkling about the draft, except for what I knew from my oldest brother. I did not base my own selfish spirit on becoming a Pro football player. The truth is, I was a basketball player. Basketball was my best sport. The Dallas Chaperelles came out to my high school in the early 60's and asked my parents and coaches about me. My mom said I was not mature enough to go off to the arena. My scholarship was in basketball at Arizona State University, behind my brother as a basketball player. Matter a fact, I went there and lived with my brother.

- **How did you get to Tennessee State?**

I'm from a small town, Grand Prairie, Texas, and all my coach's parents were from either Tennessee or Mississippi. My biology teacher, Mr. Randolph Jackson, had a friend, Coach Shannon Little, that he was very tight with from Tennessee State. Back in those days, the black community had friends, relatives, or coaches in the area of Tennessee and Mississippi. They made friends or they were a part of the fraternity. Coaches came to Texas to go to college and recruit. They kept in touch with each other. My brother had bought my mother a restaurant and that was where the meeting place was. Like I said, Mr. Jackson made contact with Coach Little, who was the recruiter for Tennessee State. They made contact with Shannon Little, and he came to Dallas and picked me up. We went to Sherman, Texas, to pick up my roommate and my best friend, Vernon Holland, that played for the Cincinnati Bengals as an offensive tackle.

- **Was your biology teacher the person who inspired you to play?**

No, I have three brothers and five sisters, and my stepfather, which is my dad, was athletic himself. He was a custodian at Grand Prairie State Bank, and he inspired me. Of course, my oldest brother Charlie Taylor (Pro Football Hall of Famer) was my inspiration. We had a gentleman, Mr. R.B. Clark, and he owned a grocery store in our neighborhood and that is how my brother and I made contact with Arizona State. He was the only Caucasian man in the neighborhood and he was a sports fan. I am thankful we had that connection.

- **What kind of parental influence did you have?**

We had a gas station and all of us children helped with the business. My mom even helped with peeling potatoes in the restaurant. I have sixteen aunts and uncles, a whole host of nieces and nephews, cousins. My family were educators and very strict. My dad was in the Army in World War II, so he was a disciplinarian. I grew up on a farm that my grandpa owned. He had about four hundred acres. We had cows, hogs, and corn. I was a blessed to grow up on the farm because of the work ethics my grandfather taught me. My aunt had a barbershop and everybody came to get their hair cut. I was very fortunate growing up the way I did, and I wouldn't take anything for how I grew up. There are two different cultures, climates, and environments with people from down south and up north. My dad was a master mechanic and he was deacon of the church. But, I didn't know that John F. Kennedy came through our little small town, nor did I know the Ku Klux Klan came into our little town.

- **Who was your favorite team growing up?**

Washington Redskins, because my brother was drafted there in 1964.

- **Who was your favorite player?**

Once I got knowledge of what was going on in the world, Deacon Jones was my favorite player.

- **Was he your role model at the time, too?**

I tried to pattern myself after him, because he had the head slap and that was what I was brought into the league doing. It was legal then. He was fast and very athletic and had a God-given ability. Therefore, I focused on him.

- **Who was your high school coach? What kind of influence did he have?**

My coach was Randolph Reed. My position coach was Reggie Brown; he stood 'bout 6' 6" and was at least 280 or 290 pounds easily. He came from Sherman, Texas. Also, my principal, David Daniel, was a very educated man and earned his Master's Degree. I had some very influential coaches as far as teaching me about life and sports. Boston Grant was primarily the track coach, but when you grew up back then all the coaches helped each other. Randolph Reed was the head coach of the football and basketball team. Reggie Brown was his assistant coach, and also Mr. Jackson. They all came to Grand Prairie, which is a black community between Dallas and Fort Worth, and this was before integration. I had been talking to my high school coaches in the late 80's, and they told me that back in the 50's, they could not coach at the white schools. We stayed on one side of the tracks and the white people stayed on the other. It was an experience. I have a lot of respect for my high school coaches. Growing up in a black community before integration, you didn't get to venture into other areas. I grew up in a close-knit community where you respected the pastors of your church, you also respected the teachers. Your neighbors would look after you and tell if you would get into trouble. That was from their days of coming up through their mother and father through slavery, and I am intertwined with that.

- **Who was your college coach? what influence did he have on you?**

My college coach was Joe Gilliam, Sr., and he had a great influence on me. He was a military man and genius. John Meredith was also a head coach. They were both a great influence on me. They took a country boy and made him out to be a man.

- **Tell us about Blanton Collier?**

I played for Blanton one year, when he was at the end of his tenure with the Browns. I really respected him. He was an old-school coach and very creative. I wasn't mature enough to understand the politics and the management part of the professional football game. The head coach is only as good as his assistant. If a head coach is afraid to bring people around them that have just as much knowledge as they do, then their business is going to sink. I understand human nature now much more than when I was that age. Some head coaches are control freaks and they have inferiority complexes with another genius around them. The coach is only good as the players. I wish I could have played under him for a little longer than I did.

- **What was it like to play for Nick Skorich?**

Nick Skorich was the offensive coordinator. Everybody cannot be a head coach. The head coach has to be very creative and a politician.

- **What was it like to play for Forrest Gregg?**

Forrest was a different animal. I did not care for him too much. Like I said, everybody cannot be a head coach. He came from under Vince Lombardi. I know I cannot treat my child the same way how I grew up but sometimes people don't know how to change with the world. The team did not buy into what he was trying to do so that made it very difficult for him to relate to us.

- **What was it like to play for Dick Modzelewski?**

MoJo was a great man. I respected him tremendously. I spoke to him about a month ago and played a trick on him. I pretended like I was a reporter to get him to answer my questions. He took me from young adulthood to manhood. He was a small, as far as height, and I think he was a Napoleon-complex in a funny way. Coming out of college, I had a great technique coach, Junior Coffee; we called him "Old Buddy." He was a kinesiology professor. So, I learned a lot about techniques, like what is entailed in muscle movement. He was also a technique coach. He would actually get out on the field and show us what he wanted us to do. He was very creative and had the best defensive line Cleveland ever had with me, Jack Gregory, Walter Johnson, and Jerry Sherk. MoJo was a hell of a coach, but not only from a coach's standpoint. If we went on a trip, he would take us out to dinner. He told us a lot of Polish jokes. He was willing to get down on our level. He demanded a lot, and that was because we were so God-gifted with our talent. He wanted us to reach our full potential. He was an awesome man.

- **Do you think that with the coaching staff being close to the players, it created a positive image and made the players want to win?**

Absolutely. In the old school, I came up under Fritz Howard was the defensive coordinator, Eddie Uleski, Bob Dowler, Nick Skorich who were from the Blanton Collier days. When I got to Cleveland, I was a young immature guy, but ran like a deer. Jim Houston was playing defensive end. He was a great, great man. He had been in the league for a few years. I was coming out of college and I wanted to play. Jim Houston and Walter Johnson took me under their wings and they became my mentors. Once an athlete comes out of college and was an all-American, they think they can conquer the world. However, there is a process at each level. You have to wait your turn when you get to the Pro ranks. The Pro's are a step above college. College is not as strenuous as the Pro ranks. They took me aside and accepted me into their world. They were part of my maturity. I give kudos to Dick Schafrath. You see, when you are very talented and you are a humble person, you draw good people to you. They see a quality in you that turns them on. I didn't know Dick Schafrath from the man in the moon; he was an offensive tackle for the Cleveland Browns. But, after practice, he would take me aside and practice with me, going over pass rushes. I didn't know at the time he was making me better. He saw something in me that would make him better. I was fast and agile. He took me and trained me with him to make both of us better. I really respect him for that.

- **What was it like to play for Sam Rutigliano?**

Sam came from New England, but he was polished and articulate. There was an educated coach. He had what it took to be a head coach. He was an administrator, politician, babysitter, psychologist, and psychiatrist. I'm sorry I only played or him for two years. I liked his mental preparation for a game and as a person.

- **Who did you really like to play with on the Cleveland Browns team?**

When I got drafted, the Browns were coming out of the championship years. I enjoyed the whole team. I admired all the guys, but I really admired Bill Nelson. I was very disappointed Art Modell or Nick Skorich did not hire him to tutor Mike Phipps. Modell was a nice guy, and he took care of me and his team. He was a businessman, and I did not understand why the Cleveland Browns did not have a Hall of Fame ring in Cleveland Stadium.

- **What were your feelings when the Cleveland Browns left?**

When I first came to Cleveland, the people had their babies dressed in Browns paraphernalia and it hurt me to see politics destroy that particular history. I understand it was a business decision, but it hurt me more for the fans there. That was their entertainment and is what they grew up with, the Cleveland Indians and the Cleveland Browns.

- **Tell us about your thoughts on the Pittsburgh/Cleveland rivalry.**

Pittsburgh Steelers and the Cleveland Browns was what we would call "Turnpike Rivalry." When we would play Pittsburgh, our team would play a game during the week preparing for them. A lady who was in her nineties' gave me a book that came from Ireland and I read it. I understood the steel mills, Bethlehem Steel, up in Pittsburgh that is a coal mine. I witnessed the fans coming to the stadium with overalls and their hard hats on. I don't know why that started from Rooney to Modell, but when we played Pittsburgh, it was a "Turnpike Rivalry." I am pretty sure that was bragging rights to the fans from Pittsburgh and Cleveland. The sons of the Rooney family were more visionary than Modell, because Modell was married to Pat Modell who was an actress. They had two young sons who grew up and got into the business at a later date. The Rooney sons took direct interest in their club. I respect the Rooney family very much. We should not forget the history with the Cleveland Browns and the Cincinnati Bengals. Paul Brown left the Cleveland Browns and bought his own team. Paul Brown was another visionary person. He was a genius. I put him in the category with George Allen, Tom Landry, and Art Rooney, Sr. He had a vision and won championships. He had a vision far beyond what Art Modell was involved in. In Pittsburgh, Art Rooney Sr. is gone, and in Cincinnati, Paul Brown is gone. In Cincinnati, Paul's vision, which was his club and whatever that process was, is still there. On the other hand, in Cleveland, Modell got his money and gone.

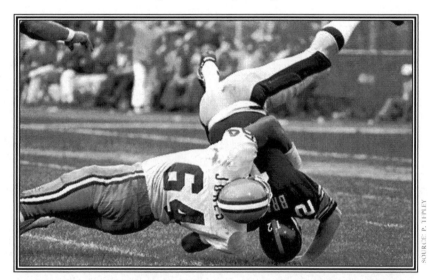

Joe Jones's historical tackle of Pittsburgh Steelers Quarterback Terry Bradshaw

- **You sacked Terry Bradshaw.**

During the course of playing Pittsburgh, the coaches would get uptight. They would pump us up for those games. The whole team would be wired up. It was the first time that the NFL had seen a play like that. During the game in Cleveland, I rushed Bradshaw and beat the offensive tackle, John Brown. My momentum and Terry's movements caused me to pick him up and tackle him to the ground, where he landed on his head where he laid on the ground and started convulsing. Afterward, I had to stay at a different hotel than the team because they felt I needed a security guard. Even though it was a great play, I was eventually fined by the NFL. Art Modell did give me my money back at the end of the year. I went to the locker room after the game to see Terry. I told Terry that I was sorry, that was just the heat of the game, and he understood. But his wife, professional skater Jo Jo Starbuck, saw it differently. She had two security guards with her and she was very unhappy with me. After what had happened with that play, I received some very encouraging letters.

- **Talk to us about your touchdown with the Browns in 1976.**

Scoring a touchdown is one of the greatest experiences in life.

- **Who gave you the most trouble in your career?**

When you get to the professional ranks, every player is as good and if not better than you. They are Pros. As far as running backs, Rocky Bleier gave me the most trouble. He was a military man, and the training that he went through in the military remained with him. Roger Staubach had been in the Naval Academy. I would hit him with everything I had, but he would get right back up and play. Larry Czonka in Miami was a big man and he had that All-Pro line in front of him. Czonka would run over you and mow you down. He would make you reach for oxygen! When I played against Johnny Unitas with Baltimore, he would run three straight traps at me. His intentions were to tire me and slow me down. On one play, he separated my shoulder. Bob Greasy, Johnny Unitas, Fran Tarkington, Joe Namath were an extension of the head coach. They were the coaches on the field playing. They knew how to run and control an offense to get the best use out of it. I used to play against Fran Tarkenton. He would get the ball and take off running, which meant I would have to chase him. He would run running plays right at you. Walter Payton was a load, too. O.J. Simpson would run all over the field. Dan Dierdorf and Conrad Dobler put me in the hospital. They would chew chewing tobacco, and to get you out of your mental game they would spit it on your head, because once you get a professional ballplayer off his concentration, you've got him for the whole day. I would have my work cut out for me against Bob Brown, who played for the Philadelphia Eagles. He felt like Mr. Atlas because he weighed 300 pounds. He was a tough player.

- **Do you still feel like part of the Cleveland Browns organization?**

I feel like the memories and the people, the fans and the ballplayers. Yes, I am still a part of them.

- **Do you think the Cleveland Brown fans are the best in the NFL?**

Obviously, they have a strong tradition and the knowledge of the game. Once I was in the league, it surprised me that the Browns fans were so very loyal all over the United States. We used to go to training camp in Pal Alto and we had a great following on the West Coast. It was amazing what a tradition the Browns had. I would say the fans are very knowledgeable in their support of the Browns and the game.

- **How did you score your six points?**

I think we played the Saints. I know Walter Johnson scored a touchdown because I batted the ball down from Archie Manning. I don't know if that was the same game that I scored a touchdown in.

- **What was your most memorable game?**

I have many memorable games. I have forgotten what year it was but my most memorable game was against the New Orleans Saints. It was a very enlightened game for me, because the defensive line was clicking on all cylinders. I had a beautiful game against them. Of course, the Bradshaw hit was a real brawl of a game. The preparation we had that week rolled over into that Sunday game.

- **How did you get your nickname "Turkey?"**

I have had that nickname since high school; several actually. In high school, I was pretty good in track. The coach would make me run with the sprinters. I ran the low and high hurdles, shot put, discus, and high jump. My teammates would call me "Greyhound," "Runs like a deer." I don't know specifically why they called me "Turkey," but it has stuck throughout the years. When I played professionally, the veterans would play an initiation game on us. Dick Schafrath, whom I really admired, would give you a map to nowhere to get a turkey. I couldn't find the particular farm for these turkeys so I had to call back to the training facility to find out where I was supposed to go. They would then say I was the "Turkey." The nickname stuck then because it had a meaning behind it. I actually did that twice, I was a double turkey. In training camp, we had to do sketches and sing school songs and it was pretty interesting. We had a lot of tricks played on us in training camp, players would even tape the doors up and you couldn't get out. They used to have a young man come around with a bullhorn to wake you up at six a.m. It would startle you and you would get up hysterical, and then you couldn't get out your door because of the tape. They would put little matches between your toes and light them. It was good clean fun.

- **Are players worth their salary? Should they be more fan conscious?**

Yes, they are worth every penny they can get. The world, society, and technology changes and they are worth the money they make. The league has totally changed, and I understand that from a business standpoint. If things stay the same, it would be very boring. I think the league is doing the best they can as far as the rule changes. It is just like a father raising a child. He cannot raise his child the same way his father raised him. You have this "now" generation, and the coaches and the system have to adjust to it the best they can. George Allen, Paul Brown, Hank Schram, Tom Landry were ahead of their time back in the 1960's and 1970's. They were very creative, and that is what made them great coaches. I also think the ballplayers are very fan conscious. They have to be because that is the market. It is a must to mature and change with the society. The guys of the era of today and from yesterday's era love to play football. Football players do not make the rules for corporations. In 1970, Dick Butkus was involved with the NFL PA. He was the president of the alumni association in Chicago. In 1970, I played in the All-Star game in Chicago. Dick came and spoke to us because there was number one and number two draft choices at the time. He said that we would strike. He explained to us that the players in the 1950's and 1960's did not have a pension. They were trying to make a statement for us to think about retirement for the older players. We did think about retirement. As a businessman, you have to also change your paradigm and understand the players of today. We were more fan conscious of children and adults alike. We were closer to the fans, because it hadn't gotten widespread yet. We see younger owners coming into the league. It was a different time and there was a different work ethic in the older league during the Modell and Rooney era. When the market is open and you have these players making the kind of money they make, you are going to wake up the beast in people. The market wants the players who are household names. However, you still have a lot of good guys in the league.

- **What was the saddest thing that happened during your career?**

I cannot pick out one thing. Modell flew us to Gatlinburg, Tennessee, and that was the first time I ever faced racism. It was in the mid 1970's, in Gatlinburg, Tennessee. I can remember it distinctly. Gatlinburg was like a resort area and they had an amusement park. They flew us in and said they would give us the red carpet treatment. Some fellow players and I went out exploring but we were not welcome on the strip. That was definitely the saddest moment in my career.

- **Why didn't you play in 1972?**

I got hurt in an exhibition game at Ohio State that resulted in knee surgery. My roommate at the time, Brendan Holland, got drafted by the Cincinnati Bengals as offensive tackle and I got drafted with the Cleveland Browns. Of course, he played right offensive tackle and I played left defensive end. He threw a crab block on me and, being a young player, I didn't use my gymnastic training on it. I tried jump out up under his crab lock and tore my knee out. There was a defensive end from the Denver Broncos, Rich Jackson, which Cleveland traded for. He came into Cleveland and I got operated on in September. I was running full speed by December. Rich was a weight fanatic and my rehabilitation was very educational because of him.

- **Tell us about your charity organization.**

I support different charities. One of my favorites is the Child Abuse Prevention Center in Dallas. Also, since my father-in-law passed away with prostate cancer, that is one charity I am involved with. I plan a Wednesday's Child golf event every year. I am good friend with the founder of the Wednesday's Child organization. It is a chiropractic organization that is all over the United States that is similar to the Make-a-Wish Foundation. They support primarily underprivileged children with education needs, clothing, and special desires of the child. We do a big golfing event in Dallas, Texas, to help support that organization.

- **Did you play with Charlie Hall?**

Oh, yes! He is an awesome gentleman. I would say he did not get his kudos. Every year he would come into training camp in excellent shape; he would run for days. Charlie was very consistent, and I really enjoyed backing him up. He was a workhorse. He is in Houston now and is a family man. I'm surprised his name is not brought up in the Legends of the Browns.

- **Do you do any other kind of work now?**

I just retired from American Airlines about a year and a half ago. I'm playing golf and attending my charity events.

- **What are your hobbies?**

Golf and fishing. I have been fishing since I was a kid because my mom liked to fish. I fish for freshwater fish. I just started playing golf three years ago and I've met some of the nicest people on the golf course. The friendships and the people I run into on the golf course make it a joy to play golf. I golf with a lot of business people who recognize me on the golf course. I am enjoying the fruits of my labor now.

- **What did you get out of your NFL experience?**

Professional sports threw me into the world at an immature age. It was a fast life. The camaraderie, the friendship that I formed through my teammates and the players I played against allows me to be anywhere in the United States and still have a home. There are alumni associations in every city and town in the United States. I always call up the NFL alumni before I go to a city, and the people welcome me by offering me housing, dining, etc.

Here we go, Brownies! Here we go!

Joe Jones								
Defensive End 1970-1980								
Tennessee State								
Season	Team	Games	Defense				Fumbles	Total
			INT	Yds	Avg	TD		Points
1970	CLE	14	0	0	0	0	0	0
1971	CLE	14	0	0	0	0	0	0
1973	CLE	14	0	0	0	0	0	0
1974	PHI	14	0	0	0	0	0	0
1975	PHI/CLE	13	0	0	0	0	0	0
	PHI	*7*	*0*	*0*	*0*	*0*	*0*	*0*
	CLE	*6*	*0*	*0*	*0*	*0*	*0*	*0*
1976	CLE	14	0	0	0	0	0	6
1977	CLE	14	1	0	0	0	0	0
1978	CLE	14	0	0	0	0	0	0
1979	WAS	16	0	0	0	0	0	0
1980	WAS	7	0	0	0	0	0	0
Career		134	1	0	0	0	0	6

Joe "Turkey" Jones and his Foursome

This picture has been included as a tribute to one of the golfers pictured here. Lou Petronio and his father played together just to give his father a good time with Browns players. Also in the foursome were Brooks Espy and Jim Sneider. Two weeks after the tournament, Lou passed away with a massive heart attack.

14

Doug Dieken

Doug has been classified by his peers as <u>THE</u> leader of the team. Just about every player donning the uniform during his playing years also referred to him as the leader. And while many players say they helped lead the team by actions, "Number 73" took those actions on the field to the management as the Cleveland Browns players union representative. Doug explained how many a time he went nose to nose with Art Modell and other management to fight for players' rights. Rights that the players of years past didn't have, and the rights and privileges which those players deserve that Doug still struggles to attain. The only time Dieken wasn't on the field or in the booth as a colorful commentator on a Browns radio broadcast was the three miserable years after the team was taken to Baltimore. This tight end converted to left tackle was elected to the Pro Bowl in 1980 and was later inducted into the Cleveland Browns Legends in 2006. In 1982, he received the NFL's highest humanitarian award, The Byron "Whizzer" White Award.

- **What was it like to walk on the field the first time as a Cleveland Brown player?**

That was so long ago, I can't hardly remember. I was kind of fortunate because I caught the tail end of the '64 championship guys. A lot of the guys had been on that team were still on there. You had Gary Collins, Leroy Kelly, Gene Hickerson, Dick Schafrath, and Jim Houston. I guess as a rookie, you think about getting out there and, hopefully, playing and doing some good. When you get a chance to walk into a huddle and are looking around and here is a guy, Gene Hickerson, that belongs in the Hall of Fame (since this interview Gene was elected to the Hall of Fame in 2007) and Leroy Kelly that is in the Hall of Fame. Then you've got Gary Collins who is your hero from when he caught his three touchdown passes. It sends a tingle through your spine. Unfortunately, the guy on the other side was Claude Humphrey so the tingle didn't last too long.

- **When did you decide you were going to be a professional player?**

Probably the day they drafted me. Back then, you didn't have the access to ESPN or three networks carrying the games and things like that. I played in college, but I didn't play for a real good team in college. We (Illinois) were on probation all four years I was there, so we took our lumps. You couldn't play as a freshman, but on the varsity, I think we were 1-9, 0-10, and 3-7, so it was not a pretty thing. I fared well as a receiver, and I played in the Blue/Gray Game and in the Senior Bowl. Then there weren't quite as many bowl games like there are today. I got a phone call one night, the first day of the draft, back then I think there were like seventeen rounds. Nick Skorich called up and said, "The Browns just drafted you in the sixth round as an offensive tackle." I said, "Nick who?" I remembered the head coach being Blanton Collier. He said, "Nick Skorich," and I said, "Is there any chance I can play tight end?" He says, "Well, we will see when you get here." When I got here for rookie camp, and they gave me #73, I knew my little "we'll see" was very short lived.

- **Being a sixth round draft choice, how did it affect your play?**

It didn't affect it. I guess I knew that having been a tight end and getting drafted at a position I had never played, it was kind of a borderline reach to some extent on their behalf. I figured make the best of it and see how it comes out. It is all about timing and you know right place, right time, and I was fortunate Dick Schafrath was in his thirteenth year. Prior to mini-camp or to training camp, he had gotten in some deal where he jogged from Wooster up to Cleveland for a promotional deal to get use of a Chevrolet from an auto dealer named George Lamb for a year. If you never ran that kind of distance, it can beat your legs up. By the time Shaf came to the training camp, his legs were pretty well shot. I was in the right place at the right time.

- **Who inspired you to play ball?**

No one really, it was one of those things. I actually thought I was going to be a basketball player. I had a brother who was 6' 9" and the basketball coach told me if I wanted to go out for basketball, he wanted me to go out for either cross-country or football first because when he got you for the basketball season, you were in shape. I wasn't about to go out for cross-country, so I figured I would try football. Back then, you didn't have any Pee-Wee Football or any youth football. Most of the guys had their first real exposure, other than pickup games out in the yard. So, you know, they started me, and I went the whole gambit. I went from guard to end, quarterback back to wide receiver. It was a crapshoot of where I was going to end up.

- **Who was your college coach?**

Jim Valek.

- **What kind of influence did he have on your playing?**

It was one of those things where you are sitting there going, "Okay, what did I get myself into now. We've got all these restrictions against us and this probably won't be a real fun four years," but it turned out to be a good time. Jim Valek was a straight arrow. He was a guy who didn't just sit there and let us feel sorry for ourselves because we were on probation. We just tried to make the most of it. We took our lumps on many a Saturday afternoon but, in the end, we showed some people that we had more character than most the people around.

- **How many college teams recruited you?**

Boy, I told my high school coach I didn't want to go real far. So, I talked to the big ten schools that were interested and so I went to Purdue. I went to Michigan. I went to Northwestern. I might have gone to Iowa, but that is about it. I kind of kept it at that, but both my parents were Illinois graduates. So, you know, I was getting a free trip.

- **Why did you shy away from Ohio State; was there a reason?**

They never recruited me, but when both your parents are Illinois graduates and you as a kid grow up watching Dick Butkus, it isn't a real tough decision.

- **Where was your hometown?**

Streator, about one hundred miles north of Champagne and about a hundred miles southwest of Chicago.

- **What kind of parental influence did you have?**

Very supportive. My parents made every game I played in high school and college. My dad was one of those guys that you really never please. It was always, "You can always do a little better." He was from the school of hard work. I always tell the story of when I got drafted by the Browns he told me, "Well, if you ever make it." That was 1971 when he said, "If you ever make All Pro or the Pro Bowl, I will give you a hundred dollars." Well, my dad never congratulated me on anything I did. But, finally, in 1980, I made the Pro Bowl. I got all fired up. I was going to call him and tell him he owed me some money. I get home and call him and I say, "Hey, Dad." "What?" I say, "You owe me a hundred bucks." "What for?" "I made the Pro Bowl." I think, okay, here it comes. He is finally going to say congratulations. But he goes, "Think you will make it again next year?" It is kind of hard, but it is also like when you think you've got it done, you can always do a little better. My dad died at sixty-nine, my mom was seventy. They passed ten days apart.

- **What was it like to play for Nick Skorich?**

It was like any football coach. You have no idea what the Pro game is like. Back then, it wasn't real professional. I mean it was, you came to training camp. Training camp could go for like six to eight weeks before you even played an exhibition game. You came there to get in shape. The season

154

started and you played six exhibition games. What they would do is they would play their regulars quite a bit for the idea they wanted to get you in shape. Nick was a good man. He was a nice man. Prior to that, he might have been the defensive line coach or some kind of coach. He was an honest, square guy to play for. Some of the other older guys, like Gene Hickerson, knew him from when he was assistant coach. Then you get a different kind of relationship. They liked to give Nick a hard time about stuff, but he was a fair guy. I remember my rookie year, during training camp, they called me to his office. I figured I was getting cut, so I went with my playbook. He said, "No, we aren't cutting you. We want to keep you, but we want to put you on cab squad for two exhibition games." Since we had a wide receiver my rookie year, we took in the fourth round Paul Staroba. He said, "We figure if we put him on the squad, somebody will claim him. We figure since you are making a move from tight end to offensive tackle, nobody will claim you." So, they put me on waivers. They were going to put me on the cab squad for a couple of weeks, then bring me up when the season started. They thought I could play better special teams than Staroba. Turned out when they put me on waivers, Miami claimed me and they ended up telling Miami if they didn't withdraw the claim, they were going to pull me off the waiver wire. Miami said, "We'll, let you slide on this one." I was on the cab squad for the last two exhibitions. Then, when the regular season started, they moved me up and next thing you know, I was covering kicks and on the punt return and punt team. I really didn't get any regular snaps until maybe the sixth, seventh game of the season. The right tackle got hurt, Bob McKay, and you only had forty guys back then. I had never played a right tackle in my life. So, I had to go in. It was pretty exciting when you get to play in your first regular season Pro game and, like I said, you see Gary Collins, Gene Hickerson, Leroy and Bill Nelson—and Schafrath was there, too. Then all of the sudden they break the huddle and you go to the line of scrimmage and you see this guy Claude Humphrey, you know he has made a living killing quarterbacks. This is your first guy you are playing against. It was an eye-opening experience.

- **Tell us a little bit more about Gene Hickerson.**

Gene was one of those guys that was a little bit of a natural. He was built to play offensive guard in the NFL. He was about 6'3", 248 pounds. Well, he never looked 6'3" to me. Depending on how many scotch and waters he had, he might have been. Gene was just amazing. The guy, he had a natural physique to being, pulling, and he was sure to hit you. My first year, we had a new offensive line coach by the name of Ray Perasta and Gene was probably in his thirteenth year at that point in time. Ray is trying to get Gene to change, and Gene is the epitome of an anvil head. He was as stubborn as a mule. Gene was not about to change. He would motivate himself because he would get pissed at Ray. The guy could run with the running backs. You watch Jim Brown, I mean here is this guy running right alongside and keeping up and it's Gene Hickerson. He has such a low center of gravity, if he centered in on somebody, he wasn't going to miss them. When Gene retired, Jim Brown was the number one all-time leading rusher and Leroy Kelly was number three or four. Jim Brown was a beast among beasts. Leroy didn't have the physical tools such as Jim Brown. So, obviously, somebody along the way was helping him. None of those guys that were on that offensive line were ever put into the Hall of Fame. Gene to me was the cream of the crop. Hell, they drafted Pete Adams in the first round and Pete couldn't beat out Gene. Gene was special. He was textbook. If you watched him pull, if you watched him pass block, he held his own.

- **There was a drive to try to get him into the Hall of Fame.** *(Hickerson was elected to the Pro Football Hall of Fame with the Class of 2007)*

That I don't know. Unfortunately, you know what happens is that these people vote on the Hall of Fame, people write them and tell them how stupid they are for not putting Gene in. They take it personal and it works against them. It's a shame because it shouldn't be that way. Gene has the credentials that would merit getting into the Hall of Fame. The Hall of Fame has become a little bit of a political animal. You see guys that want to get in and they've got a press guide on their careers that are maybe two inches thick. Gene ain't going to do that. As a rookie, if he would go someplace, Gene would always pick up the tab. It took me about four or five times, but on Friday nights, he would have this party for his birthday. Finally, I realized his birthday wasn't until February. This happened all during the season. He wanted somebody to go drink with him. Gene was one of those kinds of characters. I talked to Joe Greene about him. Joe Greene says "I played him my rookie year and he schooled me unmercifully." They have a couple of Hall of Famers that address the selection committee. A couple of guys that played against Gene. Both endorsed Gene. Then it got political because some sportswriter endorsed Hank Stram, then you know Hank went in and Gene didn't.

- **What was it like to play for Forrest Gregg?**

Probably like playing for Vince Lombardi. I think he has been exposed to a coach that's had a lot of success and, obviously, Forrest did with Lombardi. You are going to copy that style and what's made him successful. Forrest was pretty tough and to him it was a personal thing. He wanted a tough football team. I remember after I was playing for Forrest for about three or four years, I picked up a Lombardi book and started to read it. I'm reading his quotes and said, "I've heard this." Forrest was a tough guy. He copied the grass drills that Lombardi did and, in a lot ways, the way the Packers did. He coached offensive line the year before he became the head coach, so he knew all of us on the offensive line. He probably knew us too well, because when he took over, he decided to have curfews on not only on Saturday night before the game but on Thursday and Friday. He and his wife would drive around and to see if your car was at your condo or your house. Back then, you didn't have the cell phones. If he didn't see your car, he would go to the payphone and would call your apartment. He had his phone list with him. If you weren't there, you would get fined for not being in your house on a Thursday or Friday evening. When he got let go, I went over to see him and I said to him, "What was with the curfews on Thursday and Friday?" He said, "When I was the assistant line coach, I used to sit there and listen to you guys talk about what you did the night before." He said, "I knew if I ever became the head coach, I was going to make sure you weren't doing it." I got along with Forrest well. In fact, I had not seen Forrest probably fifteen years and we were down in Cincinnati last year playing the Bengals. I was talking to Marvin Lewis and I asked if Forrest ever came around. He said, "He is going to be at the game today. He is going to be at Mike Brown's stadium suite." So, I went up to Mike Brown's suite. I asked the guy outside, "Has Forrest Gregg gone by here yet?" He said, "No...well, wait a second, here he comes." Forrest walked by, he looked at me, and said, "I know you." I said, "You damn well better, Forrest." He said, "Come on down, I want you to say hello to Barbara." He was a tough guy and that's the way he wanted to play football. That's the way he learned it from Lombardi. He had some success, but I think for some reason he and the ownership didn't get along. They let him go and I thought we were taking off and going in the right direction.

- **Then Dick Modzelewski took over for part of the season.**

He coached one game in Seattle in 1977. Mo was a great guy. One of the real good guys. He gave a pre-game speech that was as good as any you'll ever get. We went out and, unfortunately, didn't win. Everybody wanted to play for Mo because he was such a good guy; had always been a player and understood where players were. Unfortunately, we weren't too good then.

- **How was Sam Rutigliano to work with?**

Sam was kind of like night and day in regards to Forrest. Forrest, we talked about the Thursday-Friday curfew. Sam would let you stay at home the night before the game. He enjoyed it. Sam had his little clichés. He had a good coaching staff. He was a fun guy to play for, because he wasn't a screamer and a yeller. It is typical with a lot of organizations you go from one type of coach to another. Obviously, Forrest was a hard-nosed guy that would scream and yell at you and tell you that you suck, whereas Sam was a guy that tried to motivate you in a different way. He was fun to play for. He was a player's coach. We had a lot of success with him.

- **What was it like to play for Marty Schottenheimer?**

I only had a half a year with Marty. As far as I was concerned, that was a half-year too long. Marty was all about Marty. He did some things that, for a guy who had played the game.... Well, you need to show the players the proper respect and freedom like men. You don't backstab them for your own sake. That's Marty. He finds the right scenario and jumps on it. He is what he is. He is a bit of a carpetbagger coach. He's made a lot of money in the game. He has won quite a few games, but it's the same old story that when it gets to crunch time, he always seems to come up a little short.

- **He wasn't a head coach, but what about Lindy Infante?**

Lindy came after I retired. Lindy was a good guy; I liked him. Lindy was a guy that knew his offense, and knew how to use it. He had a quarterback in Bernie Kosar that obviously knew how to operate it. Lindy was a good guy.

- **Back to MoJo just for a second. A couple of your other players said MoJo didn't get a fair shake and he should have been the head coach instead of bringing in Sam. What is your thought about that?**

I could see why. The guy that just died had ties with Sam from the past. He wanted his guy in there. He didn't want to get into hiring from within. Like I said, Mo's pre-game speech was as inspirational as any I've ever had. He was a guy you wanted to play for. You trusted and respected Mo. He was good people.

- **What players did you enjoy playing with?**

Obviously, Gene Hickerson was one. Jerry Shirk was one of the great. Clarence Scott was a super guy. Clarence was one of the, as they say, "silky smooth." He just had a way about him. He had his own style and he was a good football player. Clarence and I came out of the same draft class. We had Charlie Hall who was a great guy, but all the guys for the most part on the offensive line were. Robert Jackson, a guy that didn't even get drafted out of Duke and became a starter. Cody Risien, he was like a son, because he came about the middle of my career. He played guard next to me for about a year. After he got his feet wet, they moved him to tackle on the other side. Henry Shepherd was like Charlie Manson; he was totally off the wall, but he was one of the fun guys to be around. Tom DeLeone was a second generation of Hickerson as far as being an anvil head. Tom was feisty guy. One year, he went through an unbelievable thing with his wife passing away during the season. Lost her to cancer. Everybody in that group had their own personality. Then, of course, you had Ozzie Newsome and Brian Sipe. Brian was a guy who got bashed by management and turned around and stuck it up their butt. You know, everybody talks about Sipe, what a great season he had in 1980. Sipe was one tough son-of-a-bitch. When he got hit, he didn't bitch. He just picked himself up and went back. That's true of a lot of people. Greg Pruitt was a great athlete. Dave Logan was one of the really more competitive people. Logan got drafted in all three major sports professionally. He was drafted in baseball, basketball, and football. Dave could play some basketball. Then you had Mike Pruitt. On a defensive side, Henry Bradley was a beast all of his own. You had Lyle Alzado who was a very interesting human being, depending on which day it was.

- **Was his death due to steroid abuse?**

Well, I don't know. Unfortunately, I am afraid he is the only guy that knows what he put in his body. I had him for a roommate for a year and a half. I think, all of a sudden, he started appreciating me. Even Bill Cowher; I mean Bill was there for three or four years. He was a good guy, fun to be with. Clinton Burrell was one of the nicest people I've ever met. He came out of LSU, and had a rap as being a troublemaker. I don't think I've ever met a finer gentleman than Clinton Burrell. Curtis Weathers was one of the really good guys. There were a lot of good people that came through.

- **Tell us about Paul Warfield.**

Paul was just a very talented athlete that was very methodical in how he approached anything. Paul wanted to know why everything worked this way or that. If you talk to Paul, you know you can take a ten-second answer and turn it into a forty-second answer. He gets into some things and he gets going and it is like, "Okay, he needs a Cliff note for this one." He was an unbelievable athlete. He was so fluent and everything like that. He is a class act and super guy.

- **What kind of a leadership role did you take?**

I guess I was one that led by being there. I played in every game for fourteen years. A big part of leadership is dependability. You can't help the team if you aren't on the field. I was able to play for a long period of time and played every game. I wasn't a guy that was going to stand up and give a team speech. I felt when a guy stood up in front of the team and started talking, he is really saying, "the problem is not me, it is you guys." I'm not from that school. I think we are all in it together and if things aren't going well, it is because of what we are doing collectively, not as individuals. I guess that was my sense of leadership. They finally came in with the off-season weight program in probably 1979. The guy they brought in as strength coach was Dave Redding. Dave used to tell me, "You are the key. You are the older guy. If you don't buy into my program, I won't be able to sell it to the others." I was going to have a real tough sell. You know guys were going to follow whatever cue you gave them. I spent more time in that weight room than anybody. I would like to think I did my part. I was a union rep and we had the strike. I figured if things went south, you wanted someone that had the balls to tell management what you thought. I wasn't intimidated by the ownership or management.

- **It's been said that, as a rookie, you had to sing.**

I never sang one. First, I can't sing and have no rhythm. We would go down to the tavern outside of Huron or Freedom Inn, or to Garrettsville, and to have cocktails. We would show up about the time dinner was over. By the time we got there, everybody had left. I never sang, it was kind of an amazing thing. By the same token, I never made other guys sing either, because I never did. I found other ways to screw with rookies. You just pull practical jokes on them. Send them somewhere there was going to be a team party and they find it wasn't a team party, it was something else. There is another guy that came along toward the end of my career. He was one of the great guys, Dave Puzzuoli. Dave was, "I guess you start looking for safer guys to play with." Puzzuoli was one of them. I mean Puzz was a good guy and a good football player. The last time I checked, he was in Strongsville,

Ohio. It is funny because as close as we were, and he was one of those guys that you kind of took under your wing because he was a lot of fun. He is one of those guys that distanced himself from football. He had his own life.

- **Did Jim Brown or any other players have an influence on the team?**

To be honest, Jim Brown never came around when I was playing. I happened to meet him in Las Vegas at a union meeting once; I'm going to say that was '82. That was the only time I ever met Jim Brown. I don't think it wasn't until Bill Belichick was around that the organization reopened their arms to Jim. He might have been in town for events, but nothing like today. Bellichick was the guy that kind of opened that door and got back into the situation where he was involved. Then the team left. He did do some work for Baltimore. When the team came back, Randy Savage had been adamant about the history of the team. He grew up watching it and obviously knew what Jim Brown meant to football. Jim was not only a Cleveland Brown, but the greatest at his position. Randy has made sure he is part of the organization.

- **That is a positive thing. How do players feel about it?**

Players like to be around those who have been there and done that. They don't want you to tell them how it used to be. They want you to understand their position and listen to their bitches. Listening goes with the territory. A lot of guys want to tell how they used to do it. Well, these new guys could give a shit less about how they used to do it. They're in their own world and they are playing their game and rightfully so. You know, time marches on.

- **What were your feelings when the Browns went to Baltimore?**

I never thought it would happen. You thought, when push came to shove, Art Modell would cut a deal and everybody would be happy. When it happened, it wasn't like somebody punched you in the stomach—no, they went a little lower. Anytime you do something where so few profit and so many get hurt by it, that ain't right. I think Modell's inability to get into the Hall of Fame is a reflection of the facts. People support you. They are loyal to you and, granted, there are other things involved in what happened. It wasn't just Modell. We would be kidding ourselves if we sat here and said it was all Modell. I think it was some bad estate planning and some bad investments. It was bad business sense that got him a jackpot and it was a jackpot. It is like it had to happen, because if it hadn't of happened, he wouldn't have the money to play the game today. Yeah, he won a Super Bowl in Baltimore, but he didn't win a Super Bowl until of all of a sudden he had some cash. He had some money to pay the bonuses and incentives. There were a lot of things, the mayor and the politics of it, that led the team to Baltimore. I guess if you are going to assign blame, you blame David Modell, more so than Art.

- **Ohio State/Michigan and Cleveland/Pittsburgh were chosen by Football Analysis as the two best rivalries in sports. What is your experience with Pittsburgh/Cleveland games?**

Unfortunately, my experiences with Pittsburgh games were when Pittsburgh was in their prime. When they were the king of the mountain with the four Super Bowl wins. They had a hell of a run. I think out of that steel-curtain defense, ten out of the eleven guys on that defense at one point or another played in a Pro bowl. That is a pretty talented defense. Then you go on the offensive side and they had a ton more over there. Both wide receivers, the quarterback, the running back, and the center are all Hall of Famers. It was a talented football team, there is no doubt about it. Even as talented as they were, I don't think we ever played a game where we thought we couldn't win. We didn't have any luck at Three Rivers, but we had one game taken away from us in '79 when their kick return guy, Larry Anderson, fumbled a ball and the referee said the ground caused the fumble. The guy tripped over his own feet. The ground can't cause the fumble if it is your own guy. We should have gotten the ball. Anyhow, they got the ball back and Terry Bradshaw throws some flea flicker to Benny Cunningham and they win. Out of the fourteen years I was here, we beat them five or six times at Municipal Stadium. Those were special games because they are your archrivals and it meant a lot to the fans. If you got that done, you were king of the mountain for at least another week. Do I like the Pittsburgh Steelers? No. Do I respect them? Yeah, because they play tough, hardnosed football. People say, "Who do you like in the Super Bowl?" I like the Steelers. Why? Because that is the way they play the game of football. It hurts to see them win in some ways, knowing we don't have any wins. But by the same token, you would rather see a tough team win, rather than some team full of pussies.

- **Do you still feel like you are a part of the Browns Organization?**

Not really. I'm considered a media guy now. A media guy is perceived as something else. It is not like you can walk in the building and go anywhere you want. You play by the rules. You talk about Clarence Scott; I often thought, you take Clarence Scott, myself, and Charlie Hall, I think between the three of us we never missed a game. You are getting a pretty good bang for your buck when you get that. Yeah, it's because I work for the media, but in my own mind, I don't. I go in the locker room and try to become friends with the young kids. You talk to them, try to relatie to them. You have been there and you know what it feels like to get your butt kicked. You also know what it feels like when you win and things are going well. The players, they are your friends, and the last thing you want to see are your friends lose. It is not fun when they don't win. The kid that left and went with Marty Shottenheimer of all people, Aaron Shea, was like a second son. I played ball with his dad. When he bought a house, he had me walk through his house for the inspection to help him out. A lot of these guys are good guys. You know them as people not as just numbers with helmets.

- **Was the player you were talking about Ben Taylor?**

No, but Ben is another one. Ben is about the nicest kid you are going to meet. Whether you are playing or you are in the media or whatever. Some of these kids you get to really like them and it is sad to see them go. One guy was Courtney Brown. I have never met a player that was more respected in a locker room than Courtney. Andra Davis, a linebacker, he looked up to him like he was his dad. Courtney was a pure, professional, gentleman football player who had some bad luck with injuries. Tim Couch was one tough guy. I've been around quarterbacks and, when things aren't going right, you know it is somebody else's fault. Tim never pointed a finger; he just got the shit knocked out of him and kept coming back for more because he just wanted to compete. I have a lot of respect for Tim. People say he was a butt however they never invested anything in the offense when he was here. That year they went to the playoffs, I think he was the starting quarterback in eight of those games before he finally got dinged. Butch Davis then started playing the game of musical quarterbacks. That is how a lot of them buy time.

- **Are players worth their salaries? Should they be more fan conscious?**

I don't know of anybody playing the game that is worth their salary but if the money is being made by the people that are getting the crap beat out of them, then they should get their share. I never begrudge a guy that wants to earn his money. I begrudge a guy who just wants to make the money. There are a lot of guys on the football team that want to earn their money. There are guys like Brant Boyer. He was basically a backup linebacker but was a good guy in the locker room. The kid they got from Minnesota, Brian Russell, the same way. I hear people dog him, saying he is not a good tackler. Well, these people don't see what this kid does with the younger kids in the locker room. He is helping them with everything. He understands the game. He is like our coach in there. Daylen McCutcheon is a great kid; just a super, super guy. Daylen has taken his lumps for his entire career, but he doesn't bitch and complain and point his finger. He just comes out and says, "Let's see if we can't get better." Andra Davis or Orpheus Roye. Orpheus doesn't say 'boo' to no one but he comes and plays every Sunday. That is the one thing that I think that Phil Savage and Romeo Crennel have put back on the table. You're not just a football player; you are a professional that plays football.

- **How was Lewis Sanders when he played?**

He was a talented kid, but had some injury problems. Unfortunately, that is the bugaboo of the game. We talked about dependability; however, if you get hurt a lot, then all of a sudden you get stereotyped as injury prone. Aaron Shea was a classic example of that. He brought a lot of enthusiasm, a lot of things to the table. Coaches played him out of position for a couple years, putting him in the backfield. He was getting his shoulders beat up. Then all of a sudden, here comes contract time and you see how many games he missed. You look at it and go, "Well, that's a black mark." I thought differently. I saw a kid who was great on special teams that was played out of position and got his shoulders banged around because they thought he was an H-back. He wasn't an H-back. He was an offside tight end. (*Note: An H-back is a power back, also called a wing back or a slot back. It was devised by Joe Gibbs with the Washington Redskins. The position isn't commonly used in the NFL but was reintroduced by Butch Davis, Cleveland coach 2001-04.*)

- **Who was your nemesis? Who gave you the most trouble?**

I would have to say probably Elvin Bethea down in Houston. He finally went in the Hall of Fame.... One of the writers here, Tony Grossi, I always promoted him to Tony, and they finally got the guy in. I played him twice a year for probably thirteen years, so whether the Oilers were up by two touchdowns or if they are down by three, you always knew he was going to bring game. He played hard, regardless of what the score was. Those are the guys you respect. I get along with Jack Lambert. A lot of people thought Jack was a strange duck, but Jack and I always got along because Jack played the same way. You might not be in the Hall of Fame, you might not have a bunch of Pro Bowls or a Super Bowl, or at least you like to think you got the respect of the guys you played against because of how you played. You played to win; you played as hard as you could for as long as you could.

- **You've got respect for a guy who played like you did then?**

I've got respect for guys that brought it. Joe Klecko, with the Jets. Here is a guy, talk about Pro Bowl people, Joe was a guy that made the Pro Bowl at three different positions: defensive tackle, nose tackle, and defensive end. Joe was a guy that, when you played him, was so damn strong he could pick you up. The whole time he was picking you up and sitting you down, he was smiling. He was a challenge, but was a classy one. Leroy Selmon with Tampa Bay. Leroy was exactly like Courtney Brown. He had immense talent but was a true gentleman. You knew when you played him, you weren't going to get a cheap shot, you weren't going to get into a fight; you were just going to have sixty tough minutes.

- **You were the only player in Cleveland Brown's history to recover a fumble, score a touchdown, block a punt, and score a safety. Is it the ultimate dream of a lineman to score a touchdown?**

Yeah, but I never considered myself a lineman. I considered myself as a guy Nick Skorich was playing out of position. Ironically, my last real game as a tight end was a Senior Bowl and my receivers coach in that game was Sam Rutigliano. I told Sam if he had kept me where I belonged, he would still be coaching. He thought Ozzie Newsome was better. I said, "Did you ever see Ozzie drop a pass?" He said, "Yeah." "Did you ever see me drop one?" He said, "No."' I said, "Well, then I rest my case!"

- **You had a touchdown.**

It was supposed to be a little swing pass to Matt Barr. I got so wide open, even Paul McDonald couldn't miss me. It was against the Oilers and we were down at the time. I don't come from the school of major celebrations and I had already caught a touchdown in an exhibition game a few years earlier. But things happen so fast and you enjoy it. It was like putting your money where your mouth is because I had been saying "I can play tight end all along." Hell, when I left Illinois, I was the second all-time leading receiver there. I kept reminding people of my ability, but they wouldn't listen. That gave me the chance to justify what I had been saying.

- **How did you score your safety?**

Bobby Walden the punter from Pittsburgh fumbled a snap and Clarence Scott tackled him. I think they figured Clarence might have another chance to do it again and I wouldn't. So, they gave me credit for the safety.

- **Where did you block your punt?**

Against Atlanta my rookie year. We didn't even have a punt block on. I was supposed to hold up the full back and the full back looked the other way. The next thing I know, I had a football coming into my hands. So, I blocked it. Bo Cornell, who was one of my roommates, was a second round pick my rookie year, picked it up and I still give him shit for not being able to score with it. I did all the dirty work and he didn't make it.

- **What was it like to go to the Pro Bowl in 1980?**

It was a great thrill. I can honestly say it wasn't my best year. I had sprained my knee against the Bears, about halfway through the season. I had to play with a knee brace most of the season. I had a better year the year before. The Pro Bowl is for offensive lineman. Do you win and did you have a thousand-yard rusher? It wasn't until 1980 we won the division, so that was how it worked out for me.

- **Are Cleveland Browns fans the best in the NFL?**

I think so. There are a lot of good fans. I've got a lot of respect for the people up in Green Bay, too. Granted, we don't have the best weather, but those people are sitting out there in snowstorms every Sunday. I think the Browns fans have been loyal. They got their hearts ripped out, but they didn't sit on their hands. They did something about it and they got their football back. We were talking about the Steelers; yeah, I don't like them, but like I said, I respect them. One of the reasons you respect them is because, when we didn't have a football team, the guy that said "Let's get a franchise back in Cleveland" was Mr. Dan Rooney (*the owner and chairman of the Pittsburgh Steelers. He is also the son of Art Rooney, founder and original owner of the Steelers*). He was a big advocate for the Browns fans and wanted to get a team back in Cleveland. He knew how much that rivalry meant. He was a big part of it. He was a classy, classy man.

- **Where was the hardest place to play because of the fans?**

The Astrodome was a hard place because the field was hard, the lighting was terrible, and people would smoke in the stadiums and the smoke would seem to come down. If that was the eighth wonder of the world, I would only want to see the first seven. That place was bad news. They would have a rodeo there on a Friday night then would flatten out the field and put the

164

Astroturf down. Then you could go play a game. Well, you can't flatten the dirt down that smooth. There were places all over the field you could step on and it would be like stepping in a hole and you would pull your knee out. Keith Wright did that down there one year; didn't get hit or anything. It was in pre-game warm ups, stepped in one of those pockmarks that was caused by the unevenness of the dirt and blew his knee out. That place claimed some victims. We didn't play out in Oakland too much, but that place was kind of a dungeon. Three Rivers, since we never won there in the fourteen years I went there, you would have to put up there with tough places to play.

- **That is pretty hard for you guys to swallow isn't it?**

Yeah. One time, when Mike Phipps was quarterback, we had a twenty-point lead and still managed to botch it up. The one that really gets you is the one where Larry Anderson fumbled the ball. Little be it for me to remember a referee, but Freddy Winans blew the call. That was, like I said, '79; he did not do another one of our games until 1984. The third down pass was incomplete, but they called me for a holding penalty. Obviously, the Steelers declined it. The next time we went back on the field, I walked up to him, I told him, "Well, you blew that call, just like you blew the one in 1979!" I think he was a little surprised somebody remembered it. I had been looking for him for four or five years, just to say something to him. It is one thing if you aren't good enough or the other team is better, but when a referee makes a bad call and it costs you the game, that pisses you off a little bit.

- **What is one of your funny stories from your NFL experience?**

That would be a tough one. Just playing next to Hickerson would be a few funny stories. Gene did what he wanted to do. When they ran a stunt for the guard to pick up the first guy that was in the stunt, which was our kind of a rule, Gene kept blowing it. He would take the first guy and he would pass them on to me, then he would grab the second guy and I would have to try and figure out who I was supposed to take. Finally, we were playing out in Oakland and I remember I got mad at him. I said, "Old man, it is guard first man!" He looked at me and shook his little finger, "No, no, no, no, it is guard first choice." That was Gene. Gene did what Gene wanted to do. There was a coach when I came here by the name of Richie McCabe. He played for the Redskins and Steelers. He was a good guy. He got hurt one year and wouldn't take a check because he couldn't play. Anyhow, we were playing the Oilers. We were up by maybe two or three touchdowns and the game was in the fourth quarter. We were just running the clock down. You are trying to get the game over with and move on. Richie was standing on the sidelines. He is yelling at Elvin Bethea, who I was playing against. He is saying, "Bethea you suck; you don't belong in this league if you can't beat Dieken." I'm sitting there going, "Ritchie, shut up. This guy is just beating on my head because he is pissed at you." I guess one of the classic ones is a M.O. (nickname of Dick Modzelewski, offensive line coach of the Browns) story. We played the Patriots, must have been when Forrest Gregg was the head coach. Before we got to the stadium, we would go out on the field to check it out, then go back and get dressed. Well, Dick Modzelewski was the defensive line coach then and Mo was out on the field. He had on a blue windbreaker that was his jacket for the trip. The referees usually come out and check the field before the game, too. He saw one of the referees, walked up to the referee and said, "Hey, I want you to watch number seventy-three. He holds every play." Of course, he is talking about Hog Hannah, John Hannah. The ref saw the blue windbreaker and figured he was from New England and was complaining about me. I ended up with about three holding penalties in the first half. Later, I find out what had happened. We come in at halftime, we had a quarterback coach, Dick Wood, who had played with several NFL teams. He gives this speech about what we have to do in the second half. He says, "And we gotta quit getting these holding penalties. Dieken, you've got two or three already." He said, "If you can't block them, I don't know what we are going to do." I say, "Hey, Dick, here is my helmet; do you think you could do better?" Little did I know. I thought they were terrible calls and they were but he only reason I was getting them was because Mo had complained.

- **What was the saddest thing that ever happened while you played?**

I had a brother die during the '82 season; that was about the saddest thing that personally happened to me. Other than that, I think when Tom DeLeone lost his wife. That was a pretty tough one. The offensive line, I don't think it matters what team they are with, but they are probably the one group that is the closest on the team. Tom was one of the guys and his wife had cancer. She had taken a turn for the worse, maybe a week before, and we had played down in Tampa. They asked Brian Sipe and myself if we would go with Tom to New York to see his wife at Sloan Kettering. So, we went up there with him and that was tough. To take a guy up to see his wife who is dying. We came back and the next week played the Oilers. Before the game, she passed away. Her wish was for Tom to play so he played. It was tough and after the game, I said, "How are you getting home?" He said, "I'm driving." I said, "No you aren't. I will drive you." He was as stubborn as Hickerson but I talked him into letting me drive him home. I drove him home and we get to his house. They didn't have any children but Tom had a dog. Jimmers was like a kid to him. We get home and found out somebody had shot the dog. Tom and I go up and down the neighborhood asking anybody if they had shot the dog and I'm just hoping nobody says yes. In Tom's state of mind, he wasn't a very happy camper. That was, other than the personal loss of my own brother, that was the toughest.

- **What is the difference between players today and your era?**

I think they are much more health conscious. Today, it is a transient world. Free agency gives them the ability to move. It is not like you get to a team and say, "This is my team for life. This is my team unless somebody else offers me more money," and you can't begrudge them for it because the career expectancy of a football player is four years. Those big paydays don't come very often. We played in an era where you got a signing bonus when you were a rookie and that was the end of the signing bonuses. Today, every time you renegotiate, or renegotiate within your own contract, the signing bonus is a way to beat the salary cap. I guess they have cleaned the game up to where they have made it safer for the players. Hell, today you not only would get the penalty for it, you would also get a fine from the league. People say, "Do you begrudge these guys making all this money today?" I say, "Well, considering the amount of fines I would have ended up with, I would have been making about the same, so it really doesn't matter."

- **What did you get out of your NFL experience?**

Two bad knees, bad back, bad shoulders. I got an opportunity to work with a bunch of great guys. You start with your rookie class, because those are the guys you come in with and those are the guys, hopefully, you stick around with for a long period of time. I go back to Clarence and Charlie Hall. I think I said Clarence might have played twelve or thirteen years and Charlie played eleven or twelve and I played fourteen. Between the three of us, I don't think we ever missed a game. Football is a game of dependability. That class might not have been as spectacular as when they drafted Ozzie Newsome and Clay Matthews but as far as getting their monies worth out of us, I've got a feeling that it might rank up with there with the best of them.

- **The linemen do not get the recognition many believe they should get.**

Nobody did anything for recognition. It was your job. When I started, I had an off-season job. I guess it was Lyle Alzado who kind of exposed us to the era of shameless self-promotion. They just enjoyed playing and the challenge from week to week. With Cody Risien, it was like we would keep track of how many guys we could put down on the ground on a Sunday afternoon by chopping them out. We had our own little kangaroo court where we would keep track and see who the winner was each week. It was a fun game and I think back then a lot of things were different. Guys would go out after every practice. We would always stop and have beers together on the way home. That was just the way it was. It was truly a game for the most part as opposed to being a job like it is now. I think the off-season programs came in about in the middle of my career. At one point, you went to training camp to get into shape and, today, with the off-season programs, the guys are ready by the time they get to training camp. They've got the whole offense in for the season. Players are in shape because they have been in an off-season program. It was a different back in the old days. Neither one is better or worse. I guess you like to see the guys do as well as they can financially, as long as they are looking to earn it and not just make it. If they can find a way to keep guys from getting hurt, that is good too. You watch one of those old NFL film things and the runner would be going to run out of bounds. That didn't mean you couldn't tackle him in the old days. That is when some of the best shots would be delivered. Today, there would be flags and fines. It was more like an alley fight then. Now it is pretty sophisticated.

- **Would you say that there was more of a comradarie between the players back when you played?**

No, I think it was because our time wasn't consumed so much by football. Today, these guys are over there seven in the morning until six at night. Back then, we would be done at three-thirty or four. We would have our three or four beers and our burgers and we would be on our way home. Back then, they didn't have a cafeteria where they fed the guys' lunch every day. We would take our lunch. Every week one of the guys on the offensive line would make the sandwiches for the offensive line for the entire week. You just hoped it was a married guy, because then you would get condiments. You would get tomatoes, lettuce. If it was a single guy, you got two pieces of bread and a bunch of meat.

- **What are your hobbies today?**

Mostly golf. My knees are such that I quit playing softball when I turned forty-nine. We won a State Tournament. We had a good team and, all of a sudden, we were playing twenty year olds. It got to the point my knees weren't functioning well enough. I've got a couple of younger kids and we do a lot of jet skiing. As far as hobbies, I would have to say golf is the one I am most addicted to. It is a way of competing. I used to play racquetball, but one of the guys I used to play with had a heart attack and died on the court. That kind of put a damper on that game. Golf is a gentleman's game.

- **How was it being the player rep for the Browns in the Union?**

It was kind of frustrating because you knew the money was there but, for the most part, you had no leverage. Even after the strike was over, there was no hold to help the players. I voted to end the strike. I thought the guys who had played before weren't getting the compensation they deserved, like Lou Groza, Otto Graham, and people like that. For a long time they didn't even have those people included in the pensions. It was a crying shame, but if there is money to be spread.... It is a game of tradition. A lot of the people are a part of that tradition, people were playing way before we played. I thought they should have had something in the package that helped them out a little more. There was a guy that stood up and said, "The heck with those guys, what about me?" Unfortunately, that is the attitude some people have. You see them on television, you hear them on television, and you know he likes to talk about himself and think about himself.

- **Rumor is you had words with Modell while being the player rep?**

I used to tell him that the NFL was going to go to pay-per-view television and he said never. Well, shit, what do you got now when you've got these NFL packages? This is paid television. Maybe he didn't see the big picture, but that was the thing. The guy that is the player rep is the guy that is going to piss the management off the most. That didn't bother me. I got no problem standing up for the guys I play with, as opposed to picking the management side of being twisted. It wasn't until free agency came in that all the sudden you started finding some holes in those front pants pockets and some of the change started to fall out. You look back, say, "Hey, it was part of my life. I did it." I like to think I was there every week and move on.

- **What is the Doug Dieken Foundation?**

Like I said, my younger brother passed away in 1982. He was mentally retarded so I've been involved with the Special Olympics since 1971. I started them up back in my hometown. When I got out here, guys used to go to the Special Olympics with me, and I guess when I retired I got involved with the kind of inner-city Special Olympics and realized those kids have some rough deals. We started having golf tournaments for the Special Olympics and would raise money and send it down to Columbus. They would take their twenty-five percent out and would send you the rest back. You sit there and say, "Wait a second, these people here in northeast Ohio are the people that are giving us the money. Why are we letting somebody else have twenty-five percent?" So, we set up a foundation with the idea the money we raised here would stay here. What we do is, we don't give them money, per se, where we raise $35,000 and we hand them a check for $35,000. What we do is we raise $35,000; we say, "Give us an invoice for what you need and we will pay it." In doing so, you shop that invoice so these people who are donating money get the best bang for their dollar. That is the philosophy of this business. We are there to help the kids, but we aren't going to just give the money away we raise. We are going to try to maximize the dollar as much as we can.

- **Is there any way we can help with that in the future?**

We used to do something with the hockey team (Cleveland Barons). We have a golf tournament every year. We raise money and are able to buy the physicals for the athletes. That is one of the things we do. A lot of the money goes to transportation because public schools are locked into contracts. If you want a bus, you get the bus for four hours, not just for one or two. I had a meeting with the Browns a while back. Randy Lerner, his number one objective of charity work right now is disadvantaged kids. Hopefully, we can piggyback off of something they do and make it work. You can't force it, but Randy has always been a big supporter of it, and I think we have got it in good shape. It is something you would like to get some of the active ballplayers involved with because I think the exposure to seeing these kids is a humbling experience. It is something special. It is not about winning or losing. It is about the opportunity to do it. I think the Special Olympics are great. When I started them in Illinois, I went around to all of the schools he participated in Special Olympics at that first year. I was going around shaking hands in a town about thirty miles away, and we drove back and my brother had his jacket on. I thought he had got a chill or something but he wanted to see some friends of ours who owned a restaurant. So, we went over there and he asked for the lady who owned it and she came out.

He unzipped his jacket and he had his four ribbons, you know. It was the first time he got a chance to be Paul Dieken. He is no longer Doug Dieken's little brother. It was an opportunity. I still say it is a great thing. Those kids are special. They are a hoot to be around and watch. It is probably the purest form of sports you can find.

"We went from Pete Franklin having funeral services for us on his radio show to being the toast of the town...."
— **Doug Dieken on the Kardiac Kids, 1979-80**

Doug Dieken				
Tackle 1971-1984				
Illinois				
Season	Team	Games	Other Stats	Total Points
1971	CLE	14		2
1972	CLE	14		
1973	CLE	14		
1974	CLE	14		
1975	CLE	14		
1976	CLE	14		
1977	CLE	14		
1978	CLE	16		
1979	CLE	16		
1980	CLE	16		
1981	CLE	16		
1982	CLE	9		
1983	CLE	16	Rec:1/14yds,TD	6
1984	CLE	16		0
Career		203		8

The Browns are back!

Cleveland Browns Tight End Doug Dieken scoring his only
NFL touchdown from quarterback Paul McDonald

Joe Jones & Doug Dieken

15

Thom Darden

Talk about the Ohio State versus Michigan football rivalry and Thom Darden is your man. He had a bird's eye view of the Woody Hayes emotional fury. On November 21, 1971, Thom intercepted an Ohio State pass late in the game that set Woody Hayes off as he clearly thought it should have been a pass interference call on Thom. Woody destroyed several sideline items and Jerry Markbreit evoked two fifteen-yard unsportsmanlike penalties on Mr. Hayes. It was Thom's second interception of the game, an interception that ESPN chose as one of the Top 100 Interceptions in College Football. Born in Sandusky, Ohio, Thom was recruited by six of the Big Ten teams, holding several Michigan records and gathering an All-American Honor in 1971 before going on to the Cleveland Browns. With the Browns, he began collecting honors as he did in Michigan. Thom was a 1978 Pro Bowl selection, All-Pro three years, NFL Interception Return Yards leader (1978), and the Interception leader the same year. Records he still holds as a Brown are Career Interceptions (45), Single Season Interceptions (10), and Career Interception Yards (820). Now a Cedar Rapids resident, Thom took a big interest in Maurice Clarett's bid to enter the NFL Draft. Another large interest of Thom was when, in 1998, the NFL was taking bids for the new team—as he was a member of one of the six groups bidding for the rights to the team.

- **What was it like to walk on the field for the first time as a Brown?**

How many years ago was that? My first opening day game at home was against the New York Giants, 1972. I had a bad ankle sprain in pre-season and, I can't remember what games they were, but like two games into the pre-season I hurt my ankle. So, I was really having difficulty with that...it was a chronic problem. When I came out on that field, opening day, 80,000 people in Cleveland Municipal Stadium, chills went up and down my spine. It was an unbelievable experience. I proceeded to get welcomed to the NFL by...well, they (the Giants) had this play where they faked the ball, like they were going to run a halfback off tackle. A tight end fake, like he was blocking down. So, my read was, when I see the tight end block down, I come up. Well, he slipped out and scored a touchdown on me and I was so embarrassed. Wait, excuse me, that was the Packers. Yeah, it was the Packers and the

Packers weren't that good then. In 1972, and that's when I got fooled by that play...and that play never beat me again because I was just embarrassed.

- **When did you decide you wanted to be a professional football player?**

I didn't decide until my senior year in college because, all throughout my high school and collegiate career, people kept telling me I wasn't big enough, I wasn't fast enough, and when people tell you something over and over again, you start believing it. Then when I got to my senior year, I was up in Ann Arbor in the summer working and working out, Bo Schembechler called me in and he said, "Look, you've got to have a great year this year," my Senior year. He said, "You're going to be an All-American and you'll be drafted high in the National Football League." I said, "What?" You know, I hadn't even thought about that and then it finally hit me that, if you play well, you could get an opportunity to play in the National Football League.

- **Who inspired you to play? Anybody or did it just come natural?**

You've got to remember back in those days—I'm from a little small town called Sandusky, Ohio—all we had to do back in those days, we didn't have computers or any of that stuff today, all we had to do was play sports. I'd get up in the morning and there would be guys come to my place, because I lived in the projects. My place was like the center. Guys would meet there and then we'd go. We played basketball, baseball, and football. That's all we did. I was a pretty good baseball player. Actually had my first article in the paper when I was seven because I pitched a game with either hand.

- **With either hand?**

Yeah. In my little community and the Elyria Chronicle, I'll never forget this, did an article...they came over to our little place and did an article of me throwing the ball left-handed and right-handed.

- **That's something you don't really hear of.**

Football was not my first choice either because I was a better basketball player. But I wasn't quite good enough to play with guys like Austin Carr and some of those guys. That's when I knew I'd never make it on the level they played on because in college I had an opportunity to come out when Johnny Orr was a coach at Michigan. He asked me to come up and play basketball and Bo wouldn't let me because at that time. You didn't have... well, Rex Kern tried it at Ohio State...but you didn't have too many guys play two sports back then, so I felt I could've played professional basketball, but I wasn't quite sure. I wasn't quite as sure with my talent in basketball as I was in football. All my coaches kept telling me, "You keep playing the way you're playing and you're going to be able to play on this level." So, I just focused on the fact that it was my best opportunity to get a scholarship to play football in college and that it was going to be my best opportunity to make a living out of my town.

- **How many people recruited you?**

Not many.... Oh, you mean recruited me in high school? I got recruited by most people. All the Big Ten teams, a couple teams down in Texas, all the Mid-American Teams, that was about it, I guess.

- **What made you decide on Michigan then?**

A couple things. One my father had a love affair with Michigan, so we would watch. At that time in Sandusky, the Big Ten basketball games were broadcast in our area. So, Rick Mount, Campy Russell. I remember those Big Ten basketball players like Havelcheck, Lucas, Siegfried, and my father liked Michigan for some reason. So, when they started the recruiting process, Bump Elliott came to my house. Well, at first Woody came.... When Woody would talk about football he'd get fired up, he'd start frothing at the mouth, and he started talking about war and football a time or two and he started cursing.... You just don't curse in my father's house, so my father said, "You can go anywhere you want to go, but you're not going to Ohio State." Then, Bump Elliott comes in and he was just the suave, debonair-type guy. He was suave and my mother fell in love with Bump Elliott. So, a couple things, my father's love for Michigan, my mother fell in love with Bump Elliott, then I make my visit up there and it is such a beautiful campus and, at the time, there weren't many black football players there. There were only like four scholarship black athletes on the team and they were trying to get more black football players and so we had ten.... Yeah, I think there were ten of us...and that is when this whole renaissance of Michigan football started happening.

- **Ann Arbor sounds like a great place.**

But don't just drive through here. If you can, go down and just spend an afternoon, go down to the stadium...that was one of the other things that got me, man, was when I made my visit there. As a recruit, they would take you down to the locker room. You'd wait outside and then when the team would go down on the field and you'd come behind them. When I came down on the field, they were going through pre-game warm-up. I looked up from the tunnel on the other side and there wasn't too many people in there, so (the administrators) who were responsible for you, they'd walk you around and introduce you to people and stuff.... So, by the time I got over to my seat on the side, the place was full with 100,000 people. I mean it was breathtaking, you know, just how quickly that place filled up and how huge that place was and I was saying, "Man.... I thought I was doing something when I played in front of 10,000 people in high school," which for a high school game is not bad, but, when I saw that, it just took my breath away.

- **Who was your favorite team growing up?**

My favorite team was the Browns. My father would take me and, when I was a kid, you could go up and sit in the bleachers for two or three dollars. But, my father would take me up to a game and I'd watch Jim Brown and also there was a Saturday game that they played against the Steelers. John Henry Johnson and Jim Brown; man, every kid in our neighborhood wanted to be Jim Brown, except for me.... I didn't want to be Jim Brown.

- **Why not?**

Because I never wanted to run the football because you attracted too many people, you know, and I was just a little skinny guy.

- **So, the players on the Browns team your favorite then too?**

Well, you know, I loved all the Browns players. When I played with the Browns, we had a traveling basketball team during off-season and they did the same thing when those guys were playing and they came to Sandusky and played the Globetrotters. Jim Brown wasn't with them, but Ernie Greene....

- **What kind of parental influence did you have while growing up?**

I was very fortunate. My father played sports. He was a very good baseball player and they had a traveling softball team. You know back in the '50's and '60's, blacks were not allowed to participate in the mainstream, so he had a team of guys that were great athletes. They played softball and they played basketball. They actually went to the American Softball Association (ASA) World Championship and played an Indian team from Fort Comp, Texas. They lost 5-4, but they had a good team, and I was the bat boy. Then when my father's basketball team would come in, my father would have the basketball team and I'd be the ball boy for the basketball team. My father was just always there for me. My parents went to every Big Ten city. Every Big Ten city, plus Hawaii.... Did they come to Hawaii? No, I don't think they came to Hawaii...they came to the Rose Bowl. My parents just supported me throughout my entire athletic career. I don't have that single-parent-family thing going on like a lot of guys have today. I had both of my parents there. They supported me, they watched over my academics, they punished me, they made me toe the line, they kept my feet on the ground. I never had a hero outside of my family. My hero was my family.

- **Do you think that the father should be the first role model?**

There's no doubt about it. Just like now, my father is up in his eighties.... He's a minister, always was a very religious man. He wasn't a Minister when I was growing up, but he was like the guy that everybody looked to when they were trying to get something done. My father never had a lot of money; but he had integrity, he had honesty, he had compassion. So, whoever it was, whether it was an alcoholic in the family or outside the family, whether it was a person that couldn't read or write, he always helped them. That's what I saw every day.

- **You've mentioned Bo Schembechler already. Is there anything else you'd like to say about him?**

I didn't necessarily like the guy when I was there because he worked you to death, but when you get away from there, you start realizing how strong this guy is and how much like a father he was to you. I mean all of my dedication.... Not all of it, because I got a lot of my dedication in high school too because the staff that I had at Sandusky High school. Most of those guys went on to become college coaches. There was a group of those guys that were very successful coaches.

- **Who were they?**

Guys like Mike Currence, who went on to coach at Massillon High school. Well, Earl Bruce had just left, Bob Seaman who ended up coaching at Wichita State when they had that plane accident. Bob Reublin who ended up coaching at Bowling Green. Milan Vooletich who used to be on the Iowa staff here, he was my secondary coach.... I'm trying to think of who else that I remember that went to college. But, we had a staff of guys, that's why we were No. 1 in Ohio my sophomore year, No. 3 my junior year, and No. 5 my senior year.

- **Pretty good records in the State of Ohio because the State of Ohio is tough, tough football. Tell us about Forrest Gregg.**

Forrest Gregg, that was an interesting time period for, at the time, I was the player rep because nobody else wanted to be the rep. It was by default. I'll never forget it as long as I live. We went to Stillwater, OK, in the dead of Summer...I mean that was the time when everybody was putting in artificial turf because artificial turf was the new thing and, man, we were there for a week. There were no kids on campus. This was at Oklahoma State in Stillwater. We were in a dorm.... Well, first we flew in to Lincoln, Nebraska. We played the Baltimore Colts in a pre-season game in Lincoln, Nebraska. I think this was 1974 or '75. It was the year I got hurt.

- **1975 was the year that you have no record of playing.**

That's when it was...the summer of 1975, or maybe it was 1974, I can't remember exactly, but it was summer, at training camp, and Forrest Gregg worked us like mules. We get into the game against Baltimore (first exhibition game) and we played like crap. So, we fly into or we bused—I can't remember—into Stillwater, OK, and got on the bus and he announces that because we played so poorly, that we were going to be practicing the next day and we hadn't had a day off.... First of all, there was no collective bargaining agreement at that time and so all of these guys, Walter Johnson, some of the older guys, were saying, "Come on, Thom, you're our player rep, give us a day off. Give us a day off." So, I go in and Forrest, he was hot. He was so mad because we got beat by the Colts in our first exhibition game. I went over to him and said, "Coach, we haven't had a day off in seven or eight days (something like that).... Can't we just get a day off?" He said, "The way you guys played, you don't deserve a day off. You're not getting a day off, and that's that." I said, "Now wait a minute, according to the collective bargaining...." He said, "Don't even mention to me anything

176

about a 'collective bargaining agreement.' You guys are gonna" well, I can't say what he said, but "you guys are going to get out on that field tomorrow." I said, "Well, can't we sit down and talk about it?" He said, "About that, Mister, we can't talk." Okay, now I know what kind of guy I'm up against.

- **So, he was real hard-nosed?**

Yeah, he was very hard-nosed.

- **But did he know his game?**

Well, you know Forrest knew the lines. You see, that was why, from my perspective—I'm an old man now, I can probably say this—you can't have a guy in my mind who only knows one position of the game. I mean, I look at a guy like Don Shula. Shula coached both sides of the ball. He's one of the rare guys that played defense but learned the offensive game. See, Forrest didn't know much about the defensive side of the ball. That's when, in my mind, you need to surround yourself with guys that can handle it and give them the authority and the ability to assist in putting game plans together in the area that you don't have the expertise. When Forrest was a coach, we always played well early in the season, but when you look back (and I think I can say this safely), when he was a coach, and I can't remember the years that he was a coach, like 1974 or '75....

- **Forrest was a coach from 1975 through 1977.**

Yes, then Sam came in and 1979 was my best year ever. I flourished. I started coming into my own when Forrest came there because I knew what I was doing. I knew the system. I felt comfortable. I was in the best shape I had ever been in my life because I came off of that knee injury and went up to Michigan and coached during the off season and worked out everyday day hard...tried to rehabilitate for a year.... I went to school that year. I went back to school at Cleveland State...took some business courses.

- **Tell us about Dick Modzelewski?**

Dick was my man. He was my man. See, that's the thing that you appreciate when you get to that level is how the guys that respect you as a man as long as you did what you were supposed to do. He was the guy.... He was the guy and I was really sad that he never really truly got an opportunity to be the head coach that he probably could have been.

- **How about Sam?**

Sam is the consummate salesman. Sam could sell an Eskimo an igloo. I tell you what, Sam knew his stuff. Sam was a guy that had experience on both sides of the ball and I'll never forget how there would be times at practice when he would come out and talk to the secondary tell the secondary things that they should be doing. I was impressed with that. To me, a head coach is a guy who is supposed to be able to know what he has to know and get that point across on paper the X's and O's. He's also the guy that can fire up a guy and get him to run through a brick wall and Sam had the ability to do both of those. That was one of the things that I really appreciated about Sam.

- **What players did you enjoy playing with?**

In the secondary, Clarence Scott was my guy. I mean Clarence Scott was the essence of a football player. Ernie Kellermann was a smart player...I'm trying to think of who else sticks out in my mind. Well, obviously watching Walter Johnson throw people around was always fun from my vantage point, back there in the rocking chair, like I did it for a few years.

- **Being a first round draft choice...how did that affect your play?**

Well, I thought I had more to prove, especially back in that time. I had a pretty decent signing bonus, but your base salary wasn't much...and you had like a bull's eye on your back because you're the first round pick. And with the Browns way of thinking, before Ozzie and Clay Matthews, Clarence and I were the only first round picks that ever made All-Pro, I think. For many years in Browns history, because the Browns had trouble after those guys.... You know, when I first came here, you know the Leroy Kellys', the Gene Hickersons', the Bill Nelsons'...Jimmy Houston, those guys were coming off of the '64 championship team. They were on their way out and the Browns didn't have success with a lot of their top picks during that period. So, watching Clarence, who was an All-Pro as a corner back, and I came a year after Clarence, but anyway, there was pressure to make sure that you were successful because they were expecting you to come in and play right away. All it did was make me work that much harder.

- **Who were the team leaders at that time?**

When I first came in, you mean? Walter Johnson, Gene Hickerson, Bill Nelson, you know we got Warfield back in 1974, I think it was. Dieken, well, Dieken wasn't really a leader until later.... We had Bob Babich for a couple years as our middle linebacker....

- **You're forgetting one. A lot of your Pro fellow players have said that you were a leader on the field. They classified a leader as someone that set an example and did the things that they had to do and they said that you were the one that did that.**

Well, I don't know about that, but, wow, I appreciate it.

- **Well, that's your players speaking about you.**

And, you know, that's all that matters because when it comes down to it, the guys that lay down their lives every Sunday with you.... Man, you know, I hate to say it but there were times when there were some guys, you know, when times got thick...fourth quarter.... You're tired and you're losing by a touchdown, or six points or something, and there were some guys that

178

would just welter away. Fortunately, we didn't have a lot of those types of guys, but throughout my career, we had a couple of guys like that. I knew that we had guys, you know, all I can comment is on our defensive because that was obviously what I played and we would get into the huddle and say, "Look, we've got to come up with a turnover. We've got to figure out how to get a stop here. We got to get a sack, we've got to get something." That's the way you would talk in the huddle. And that gets you inspired because you know that the guys are trying to create things, make things happen. We always used to have like a game, like Jerry Sherk, myself, Mack Mitchell, planning, "Okay, who's going to get this, who's going to make the sack, I'm going to get in first...." You know, that was the thing.

- **What was it like to have a song written about the team?**

Oh, you mean the Kardiac Kids? That was pretty wild. I tell my kids about that and they just start laughing. That whole season was like a dream. We won six games in the fourth quarter on miraculous-type turnarounds. Somebody always came up with a big play and you don't have those kinds of seasons too often. We only had one like that.

The Kardiac Kids and the Twelve Days of Christmas
(Elliot, Walter, & Bennett)

On the 12th Day of Christmas Art Model gave to me...
The Brown's in the playoffs
Dave Logan leaping
Doug Dieken blocking
DeLeone a'hikin'
Kardiac Kids a'Winnin'
Darden interceptin'
Newsome a'catchin'
BOTH THE PRUITTS' MOVES...
Alzado attacking
Brian Sipe a'passin'
Don Cockroft Kickin'
On a Rutigliano Super Bowl team!

- **You guys had such a terrific year and were called the Kardiac Kids as you won on last-second plays and stuff like that, but they never named those. How come every time there was a Browns play that was negative, it was named and shown on ESPN a hundred times a week? The Drive, The Fumble, Red Right 88, the Bottle Throwing Incident, the Rudd Penalty.... Everything is negatively named for the Browns. The Kardiac Kids, like you said, won six games on last-second plays. Why didn't they name any of those?**

Well, I think the biggest thing is that Cleveland has one of the richest histories in the National Football League. I think people like to see like the Lions, the Bears, the Browns, the Steelers.... Steelers have always been pretty competitive. The Browns have had their ups and their downs. I think people like having Cleveland down for some reason. It's just like the city...when I was playing and would go to other cities for banquets or whatever, they always had to mention the fact that the Cuyahoga River caught on fire. Or that Mayor Perk declined an offer to the White House because he had a bowling tournament or something, you know. They always had the negative things about Cleveland. That's just a thing from my position, a historical perspective of Cleveland.

- **That's a great explanation. Anyway, ESPN has made the statement that Ohio State/Michigan is the best college rivalry in sports and Cleveland/Pittsburgh is the best pro-rivalry in sports. You've got kind of a little bit of an insight on both of them.**

You know what? I never think about this until the two games happen. For one, I've never won a game in Three Rivers Stadium in ten years because they were such a good football team and we just seemed to not be able.... I mean, there were some questionable calls in some of the cases but, generally speaking, they outplayed us. But we always played them pretty tough in Cleveland. There would always be more fights in the stands than there were on the field but now, as an older person, that rivalry between Ohio State and Michigan, there is none like it. You can talk about UCLA/USC, Auburn/Alabama, you can talk about some of those other rivalries that they talk about, just from a pure emotional perspective there's nothing that compares to the Ohio State/Michigan game, whether it's in Columbus or if it's in Ann Arbor. I have to admit, generally speaking, the people in Ann Arbor handle themselves a lot better than the people in Columbus. My junior year we went to Columbus and lost the game. One of my roommates had a knee problem and wasn't playing so he drove his car down and he had a University of Michigan sticker in the back window of his car. They tipped the car over because he had that University of Michigan sticker in his back window.

- **How about Pittsburgh and Cleveland?**

Oh, Pittsburgh/Cleveland. You throw out all the records, you throw all the whining and complaining, and you strap up because there's going to be hitting. Lots of hitting. Ron Bolton knocked Lynn Swann's teeth out in one of the games. Joe Jones picks up Terry.... I mean, I'm standing right behind him when this happens, and he picked up Terry Bradshaw and dumped him right on his head and he flopped around like a turkey. Man, I thought the guy was hurt or something you know. You can always look at some play in one of those games that was just an unbelievable play. Like I said, Ron Bolton knocking Lynn Swann's two front teeth out.

- **In my opinion, he needed it.**

I loved every minute of it.

- **Tell me about when Lynn Swann was at Mario Lemieux's golf tournament and had several kids standing around him begging for an autograph and he just blew them off.**

Yeah, that's the kind of guy he is. I've never liked him. Nope, never will. And, I certainly wouldn't vote for him that's for sure.

- **What are your feelings when the Browns went to Baltimore?**

I was still in Cleveland at the time and working on one of the committees, the Dome committee, trying to get a dome stadium there from the other people in the community. I realized there was a problem between Modell and Mike White, so something had to give you know. I didn't feel as strongly as a lot of people, those that felt that Mr. Modell was a traitor and all that kind of stuff. I knew it was a business decision. That the thing that is always the most difficult in the world of sports is separating the humanity standpoint side of it from the business side of it. And, when you're in it, unfortunately, you don't get a chance to feel good about the business side because a lot of times things were done from a business perspective that was contradictory to a humanity perspective. So, in looking at it, I knew it was tough on the guys on the team and it was tough on the coaches and their families, but from a business perspective, because he couldn't work it out with the city to get what he felt he needed to have to compete in those times…. Let's face it, when I played, they had just started getting into luxury suites. But, they didn't have the type of luxury suites they have today. And, it still is a place where the owners don't have to share the revenue with the players. So, from a business perspective, you want as many of those as you possibly can get. And, you know, the city wasn't willing to work something out on the land and the construction, so he really didn't have a choice. The thing that I didn't understand was why the two of them couldn't sit down and work that out for the benefit of Cleveland and that's where I left it. Because, to me, it was two egos and Cleveland was not in any serious financial problem. We had come out of the back door of that situation and I just felt that problems were just between the two of them not being able to work it out. But I was glad and grateful that they kept the colors of the team, the name, the records, the trophies, all of that stuff, in Cleveland.

- **Do you think the fans will ever understand the business side?**

No, the fans don't really care, generally speaking, and you know, that was the one thing that I learned about Cleveland, and one of the things that I actually loved about Cleveland. Nick Skorich said to me, he said to all of us actually, when I first came to Cleveland, "This town is above the ground when you win on Sunday and they're below the ground when you lose on Sunday." He said, "The fortunes of this town rise and fall during football season with you guys," and "'It's easier to deal with this city when you win than when you lose." Oh, man, I enjoyed playing with guys like Frank

Pitts, Leroy Kelly, Ben Davis, Mike Howell—well, Mike Howell had his own issues—Fair Hooker, Gene Hickerson, Jim Houston, who else can I think of?

- **Gene Hickerson; what a character.**

All of those guys, they were like—they were the ones, especially Walter Johnson, Jerry Shirk, he was a few years older than me—those guys taught me how to be a Pro. How to give back to the City, how to handle yourself, enjoy yourself, how to prepare yourself. I mean those guys, they were Pros because they had won a championship and they knew the good parts and the bad parts of winning. They knew the bad parts of losing, too. So, yeah, I enjoyed my time with those guys.

- **Did they also teach you respect on the field?**

Well, you see, that's the thing. The thing that they all imparted to me was to act like you've done this before. If you intercept a pass and you're supposed to jump up and sing hallelujah...run it for a touchdown, then you're doing something. It's your job to get the ball back for your offense. And, you're doing your job. So, from my perspective that's what you're getting paid for. I, as a defensive back, was getting paid to stop that offense from proceeding down the field and scoring. Whether I made tackles, or whether I made interceptions, that was what I was supposed to do. And, they used to say, "Look, act like you've done this before. Don't act like this is something special, because this is what you're paid to do."

- **Do you still feel like you're a part of the Cleveland Browns organization?**

You always feel like you're a part of an organization. I mean, I still have friends in the organization. Dino Lucarelli is a good friend of mine. That guy has always treated me with the utmost of respect and he's always taken care of me. I will go to my grave looking upon him as a good friend.

- **Are Cleveland Browns fans the best in the NFL?**

Well, let me just say this. I don't think there are any fans that live and die with their team as much as the Cleveland Browns fans live and die with their team. I mean, it is amazing to me, just amazing to me, that I can still go places and they have a Cleveland Browns support club.

- **Browns Backers worldwide?**

Yes, Browns Backers. Man, they are something. That is always, I guess now, being an old man, that you still feel a part of it because the fans know who you are and they still love the Browns and anything that has to do with the Browns. They treat you like they love you and that makes...it has such an impact on how you feel.

- **What was the hardest place to play because of the opposing fans?**

The hardest place to play? Well, let me see….

- **Mike Babb said it was Houston because the field sucked.**

Mike's got a good point because we played in the Astro Dome. I'll never forget how Dan Pastorini threw a long pass that was headed for Kenny Burrough and I go up to try to intercept his pass…. I think it was Clarence and myself. He, myself, and Kenny, we got tangled up, my feet went up from under me and I landed on my hip. And, like a fool, I didn't wear hip pads. I wore knee pads and thigh pads. I didn't wear hip pads and I had a deeply contused hip…. That thing swelled up to almost the point I couldn't put my pants on and they brought me back and put me in the hospital for like three or four days so I could get the swelling down and stuff. That was how hard that stadium field was. It was the worst thing I'd ever played on. Plus, you know, the Astro's played there as well, so they tried to fill in the baseball area with patches…and they had creases in the turf…so, you could be running, and if you hit second base and there was one of those creases, you'd trip over that crease. I mean, it was just horrible.

- **Not to bring up bad memories, but tell me about the Bengal's game in 1980.**

See, to me, that wasn't a bad memory. That was a great memory, actually, because number one, we won the game, and we won the Central Division.

- **But, you were kind of labeled at that game. Tell us about that hit.**

Yeah, I was labeled, wasn't I? I was labeled a "dirty player" because of that hit and I'll go to my grave saying it was a clean hit. We were face to face; it wasn't like he had his back to me. It wasn't like I hit him illegally; we were face to face. You see, at the position that I played, you had to make a decision quickly, because if you waited, it would pass you by and the next thing you know there's a touchdown against you. So, you either had to make the decision now and react and do it, or lose it. And, I couldn't decide to try to shoot to get the ball. I didn't think I had enough room at the time to get between him to get the ball but, I got to jar the ball loose from him, so I went up when he went up and I hit him right in the face and it just so happened that he swallowed his tongue. Thank God, they came out and pulled his tongue out so he could breathe, but I don't think it was a dirty play.

- **The receiver coming across the middle is still the most vulnerable. But, the man knows you're there; that players are going to come after him.**

When I came up, people knew that they were going to get hit if they were a wide receiver, which is why I chose to be a defensive back instead. You know, I was a receiver in high school. When I went to college my freshman year, I played receiver and defensive back and then went to the platoon where you play specialized…. You know, where you played one position. We were taught from high school to college to Pro that the best way to deter someone from trying to catch a ball in your area is to smack their head off. "Separate the ball from the player," that was the way we were trained. We were trained to knock the ball out. If you couldn't intercept it, next take the guys head off because then he wouldn't want to come back in your area to catch a pass. So, if you're trained that way, that's the way you're going to execute.

- **Because Cincinnati fans still don't like you. But you were never a dirty player. One play doesn't designate a man's career.**

I got fined. I went to New York and sat in with the commissioner.

- **Was that Pete Rozelle at the time?**

Pete Rozelle, yes. I got fined for it. He said...I mean, he read and quoted to me the article and infractions of the bylaws of the NFL, that I was against and, you know, I listened then I said, "Well, Commissioner Rozelle," I said, "I'll tell you what, I don't think it was a bad hit...we were face to face...and I'd do it again if the situation occurred."

- **How many interceptions for touchdowns did you have?**

I know I had one against the Cowboys, one against the Patriots, one against.... I thought I had four, maybe I only had three, I don't know.

- **Do you remember them?**

Well, I remember when I picked up a fumble against the Patriots and ran it in. Of course I remember Dallas on Monday Night TV—Monday Night Football. Roger Staubach came in with, I don't know, a couple hundred passes in a row without an interception. I had a radio show at the time and I interviewed Howard Cosell for my radio show, and Cosell and I were talking and he said, "Well, what do you think about Staubach's interceptions?" I said, "Well, Howard, I'm going to tell you this. I'm going to intercept a pass Monday Night and run it in for a touchdown," and lo and behold, I got the opportunity to do that. That was just unbelievable to me.

- **Do you think that's part of the reason why you had said earlier that nobody really wanted to see Cleveland succeed or they always had a negative for the city? The Browns don't ever get a break by an announcer either, especially Cosell when he was around.**

I liked him. You know, most people didn't like him. He was always arrogant and he was always, like you say, "negative." But I liked the guy; the guy was a bright guy.

- **Maybe he just didn't know football.**

No, I don't think he knew football either. He was engaging. He could talk for hours about all the issues that were going on in the world. I spent an hour with him, maybe it was a little more, he was a nice guy to me.

- **Have you been back for a while?**

The last time I was there...I went in for the United Way Browns Alumni Golf Outing last year, I guess. I didn't go to a game this year.

- **What was one of the funniest things that ever happened on the field when you were playing?**

Well, I can remember Brian Sipe having to go to the bathroom one time. You know, that was always kind of difficult. And, if I remember correctly, he didn't quite make it. Yeah. Ask him about that one. One of the weirdest things is that Monday Night game.... I don't remember what wide receiver, I don't know if it was Drew Pearson or Butch Johnson. It was somebody that threw up on the sidelines on the Monday Night game. He was running a route. I thought it was kind of strange. But, I'll tell you one of the funniest things that ever happened.... It was my rookie year. Can't remember if it was my rookie or my second year. We were playing the Bears and a guy came out of the stands in Cleveland and was running on the field and Dick Butkus just clotheslined the guy. That was the wildest thing that I've ever seen.

- **How come Butkus gets mentioned every time we talk about the Bears.**

Because he was the Bears, as far as I'm concerned, because they weren't that good then. But, man, he was so tough. The guy had bad knees but he just kept playing. He played his heart out every time he stepped on the field. See, to me, that is the epitome of a football player. A guy had blood coming down his nose, arm pads taped up.... I mean, he just looked like he was ready to hit somebody. That's what a football player to me is all about.

- **Who was the player that gave you the most trouble during your years?**

Isaac Curtis. He just literally gave us fits all the time because we had not seen speed like that in our division. Swann and Stallworth were good receivers; they didn't have burning speed. Isaac Curtis had burning speed. That guy would always catch a touchdown pass against us in Cincinnati. Not so much in Cleveland, but in Cincinnati. See, he comes to mind immediately. Warfield gave us fits! You know, I looked back on this, we played the Dolphins during that undefeated season they had and we had them beat down in Miami in the playoff game.

- **Paul said it was the only game that they should've lost.**

They should've lost that game. Mike Phipps threw six interceptions and we still had them beat in the fourth quarter but lost it when Paul ran his famous post corner move on Ben Davis. We had the perfect coverage for it. Billy Andrews.... We had a defensive coverage called Seven Web where we would have the outside linebacker on that side go out. He was supposed to jam the wide receiver. But he didn't jam the receiver, then Ben was covering him...and I slide over and pick up the tight end and Billy Andrews was supposed to give him outside help.... Davis was inside of Warfield.... So, he

185

made us pull his corner. Andrews gets an interference call on him...they get the ball down there then and the next thing you know they ran the ball and Jim Kiick, who at that time, you know, he was just a hardnosed running back. He and I hit each other at the goal line. I'll never forget that either. They scored. They beat us 20-14...but we should've won that game.

- **What was the saddest thing that ever happened during your career?**

Probably when I got hurt. It was an exhibition game against the Eagles and I was back returning a punt and there was a guy down on the outside running. I looked up and saw that it was a rookie. I had a teammate running with him stride for stride, so I figured he would probably either push him by me or at least screen him. I tried to catch the ball; the guy hit me before the ball got to me. No, I'm sorry, the ball hit me and slid down my gut and as I reached down to pick it up, another guy hit me with his helmet right on my knee. I heard this "pop" in my left knee. I recovered the ball and I got up and I went to the sidelines. They could swing my leg from the knee down to my foot. It didn't really hurt that bad but just seeing that they could swing my leg like that scared me. So, that was probably the worst thing that happened to me, but one of the most frightening things was in my first year. When, Brian Slidell, who was part of that older team, took the pile in one of our games and one of his cleats got caught in the turf and the pile bent him back.... Man, you just heard this scream. He broke his hip. That was a frightening experience.

- **How far did you have to go to get the turkey?**

I got out of that.

- **How did you get out of that?**

See, I was friends with those guys before the season started. My first wife was from Cleveland. I came and lived in Cleveland right after I left or before I even...well, when I signed my contract, I came. And, when I came to Cleveland and got an apartment, I was interacting with those guys. So, I don't know if it was Ben Davis, Leroy Kelly, or Walter Johnson, I can't remember but one of them had told me that it was a hoax. So, I didn't do it and I got out of that.

- **What was the most memorable game?**

Well, the one that sticks out is that minus-thirty-six degrees Froze Bowl that we played against the Raiders. That one sticks out because we had the game won and could have been on our way to an AFC Championship game in San Diego where it was a lot warmer, but things didn't work out that way. That Monday Night game was a memorable game because we won the game. Cowboys were supposed to be that good; I had a great game that game. I always had good games against the Raiders. I think I intercepted more passes on Kenny Stabler, with the exception of maybe Bradshaw. Nothing else really stands out.

186

- **Are players worth their salary? Should they be more fan conscious?**

Well, you know, obviously there is more money involved than when we played, through television contracts alone. They cover their obligation for the year so, because the revenues that are generated by the game and the ancillary things that go on with the game, players are entitled to their piece.

- **Where's your piece now that you're retired?**

In the retirement? Well, our retirement isn't the best in the world but, you know, at least it's a retirement. I mean, they're working on it and getting a lot better known obviously because they've got more money. We didn't have great representation during those years, in my mind, to the point where like baseball got those great retirement packages. But, we finally got like a 401K, I guess. They didn't have that when I played. I think one of the problems that you have when you start making the kind of money these guys are making is that they are disassociated from the fans. See, we didn't make too much more than most of the guys that were working so you kind of related to the steelworkers and other people that worked for a living in the City of Cleveland. We used to drink beer with a lot of those guys.

- **Should they be?**

I think that's part of the game. I think part of the game is interacting with the fans. And, I think that guys before me and the guys in my era relished that...looked upon it as a responsibility.

- **Should there be a better retirement system for older players?**

Well, you've got to remember again, you know, we were the first back in the '70's...see pre-1949, those guys didn't have any pension. They didn't have anything. We were the first to contribute to a pension, to include those guys. There's no way that these guys shouldn't be putting money into the pot to help those guys as well. And, with all the money that's being made, it is inexcusable that guys don't have a decent pension.

- **What is your job today?**

Today, I'm in the financial services business. I help business people who are looking for capital to expand their business or refinance their plants or looking to acquire other businesses. I help people with ideas and, hopefully, dreams to own their own business or to set up their own business. I have in my mind the greatest job on earth because I get paid for helping people.

- **Is it your own company or do you work with somebody?**

You know, I worked in the securities business for a while in Cleveland and that's what got me out here. I came to work for a company named Aegon, which is a big Netherlands Finance Company. I started working for them and, in 1998, I opened up my own business.

- **How many kids do you have?**

She has two, I have two, and we have two.

- **Are they all sports minded?**

Actually, my eleven-year-old daughter is the only athlete who I believe has the intensity inside of her to want to put forth the effort to do what it takes to get it done. The other ones, they liked it, but they didn't want to sacrifice to become good at it. My wife and I laugh because my wife, she's a Catholic, she played high school basketball...she was a jock herself. And, out of the six, we kept saying, "Are we going to ever have an athlete?" She's trying out now for a traveling basketball team. They do a good job on the local level of getting the kids the fundamentals. I mean these kids go to Florida, they go to Las Vegas to play in tournaments and stuff...it's pretty good.

- **What did you get out of your NFL experience?**

What did I get out of it? Probably the biggest thing I got out of it, I think, was the ability to interact with people. Being in the National Football League allowed me the opportunity to meet all kinds of people. You have to have compassion for people and I think having that exposure to all kinds of people made me see the good and the not so good in people. I find that when it comes to sports, for whatever reason, it brings out the best in people. And that's the thing I think I will cherish for the rest of my life. I meet somebody and they say you're the Thom Darden that played for the Cleveland Browns... immediately, it's a positive thing. We go into a conversation about Jim Brown, or my career, or who was the best player, or do you remember that game when they played? Even here in the State of Iowa, I was coming in off the plane one time and this young lady who is the President of the local Brown's Chapter in Waterloo, Iowa, sixty miles north of here...she starts talking to me and we just struck up a conversation and she knew a lot of statistics about the Browns and she was just saying, "It's just a pleasure to meet you." You know, that just makes you feel good. So, thankfully, the idea that what you did for a living makes you feel a part of a lot of people's lives. It is such a great thing.

"Repetition is learning." — *Paul Brown*

Thom Darden								
Defensive Back 1972-1981								
Michigan								
Season	Team(s)	Games	Defense				Fumbles	Total
			INT	Yds	Avg	TD		Points
1972	CLE	14	3	64	21.3	0	0	0
1973	CLE	11	1	36	36	0	2	0
1974	CLE	14	8	105	13.1	0	1	6
1976	CLE	14	7	73	10.4	0	1	0
1977	CLE	14	6	107	17.8	1	1	6
1978	CLE	16	10	200	20	0	0	0
1979	CLE	16	5	125	25	1	0	6
1980	CLE	16	2	42	21	0	1	0
1981	CLE	13	3	68	22.7	0	0	0
Career		128	45	820	18.2	2	6	18

"He was a consummate free safety.
He could play center field like Duke Snider or Willie Mays.
He made the big plays, the big tackle."
— Sam Rutigliano on Thom Darden

Darden interception against the Buffalo Bills

16

SOURCE: CAMMETT

Greg Pruitt

This five-time Pro-Bowl player was told from high school through the professional ranks he was too small, that "You are going to be small compared to the giants on the field." But after showing his strength and speed at the University of Oklahoma, he played. Pruitt was an All-American 1971 and 1972. He ranks third among Sooners in career all-purpose yards. Pruitt attained 3,122 rushing yards, 491 receiving yards, 139 yards on punt returns, and 679 yards returning kickoffs. Pruitt scored forty-one career touchdowns as a Sooner. He was All Big 8 in '71 and '72. Greg still holds the school record for most yards in a game with 294 against Kansas State in 1971. Pruitt also had the record at one time for all-purpose running yards in a game (374), season (1,970), and career (5,784). His 9.41 yards per rushing attempt in 1971 is an NCAA record. He was third in the Heisman voting in 1971 and second in 1972. He was elected the NCAA 1972 Football Player of the Year by the Pigskin Club of Washington, D.C. He rushed for 1,665 yards as a junior, but was injured with three games left in his senior year and was denied a second straight 1,000-yards season by sixty-two yards. Up to that point, Steve Owens was the only conference player in history to accomplish that record. Nick Skorich kept him from the field, not wanting to give him the chance for which he drove himself. His agility and determination in Cleveland got him close to the field, yet butting heads with Nick still didn't get him on the field full time. A coaching change with the Browns gave him the chance to prove himself—and that he did. In 1975, '76, and '77, Greg rushed for 1,000 yards or more during those three years. What was it that drove Greg to rush for an average of 4.8 yards per carry? Coaching, motivation, self-desire? Only Greg really knows; but Forrest Gregg was pleased with his effort. However, it wasn't enough to save the coaches job. Mastermind Sam Rutigliano came to Cleveland to initiate another winning season. The injured Pruitt was then relinquished to kickoff and punt returns. Even though he received a Super Bowl ring with the Los Angeles Raiders, his heart and home are still in Cleveland. In 1999, he was inducted to the College Football Hall of Fame.

- **What was it like the first time you walked on the field for the Cleveland Browns as a player?**

Well, like a dream come true. There were a lot of Pro teams I watched and, of course, everybody knew Jim Brown. We used to pull straws to see who would be Jim Brown in our sandlot football games after watching the games on Sundays. When I got drafted by the Browns, my first thought was "I get to play where Jim Brown played...." He was one of my idols. To step out on the field he had played on; there are no other fans like the Cleveland fans. It was a lot of hard work and a lot of dreams come true.

- **When did you decide you were going to be a Pro football player?**

Well, I played every sport. I just liked sports, period. It just so happened that, coming out of high school, the opportunity to continue to play in college came through football.

- **Was there any other sport you would like to have played?**

Looking back, I was a pretty good baseball player and maybe, if I could go back and make a choice, I might choose baseball.

- **Do you follow the Indians? Do you have another team you follow?**

I follow all the teams here. I am real excited about the Cavaliers and LeBron James.

- **Have you met LeBron?**

Yes, I met him once.

- **Is he as down to earth as they seem to think he is?**

Yes, he is a good kid. He's a good player. He says all the right things. He comes out of a tough situation and has overcome that. He seems to know where he wants to be and he seems to know how to get there.

- **Do you see what you were at his age?**

The money was a lot different and with more money, the more pressure there is to play. I am sure he feels the pressure. You have to get in a comfort zone and I tried to train myself to be able to function when the pressure was on. Most people don't want it at that time. That's the time I want it.

- **What inspired you to be a professional football player? Was there an individual or an event?**

I would say it started out watching professional football on television and then playing in my neighborhood. We organized the teams ourselves. Different streets would have a team and we would play against each other. After watching the Sunday game, or even a college game, that would fire us up and we would get together and play. We would imitate the people we just saw.

- **When you got to the Pro levels, did the imitation of other players still take effect, or did you have your own style and method at that point?**

Oh, I had my own style. I think like everybody else, you talk confident when you are in front the press and you say a lot things; like a duck, you're floating around real smooth on top but you're paddling like hell on the bottom. I used the same thing in high school. Then I would say, "I can't believe I said that."

- **Where were you born and grow up?**

I was born in Houston, Texas. I went to B.C. Elmo High School, which is now Forest Brook High School. They tore it down and built a new school.

- **What were your high school playing days like?**

Up until my senior year, I was a quarterback at high school then I was switched to wide receiver. As a result, I got a scholarship offer to play at Oklahoma. My high school coach was like a father to most of the players and we respected him a lot. He was almost like a little dictator. Whatever he said was right and whatever we said was wrong. He said "jump" and we'd say "How high?" He did all right by us because he knew better than we did. I found out there were underclassman that Division 1 schools were after. He became very good friends with an offensive line coach, which was the recruiter for Oklahoma, by the name of Bill Michaels. Bill Michaels wanted this junior linebacker whose name was Gene Settlers to make the team. The coach cut a deal with him that if he would give me the opportunity to make Oklahoma's football team, he would make sure that Gene Settlers went to Oklahoma. Most of the players did what the coach said, except Gene Settlers went to UCLA. But, by that time, I had established myself at Oklahoma.

- **Did you have tough games at Nebraska?**

I've got to admit there were some good rivalries there. When I was there, we were always challenging for the National Championship.

- **What players did you enjoy playing with as a Pro?**

When I was with the Browns, I became very good friends with Ben Davis. Ben had been in the league quite a long time, maybe five, six, seven years. He took me under his wing and tried to teach me to do the right thing. Prior to me coming here, he was the shortest guy on the team. He was half an inch taller than me and he made sure everybody knew it. Officially, that was passed on to me. The perks of being a rookie.

- **Was there a lot of hazing as a rookie?**

Yes, they made you sing your school song. They'd wake you up and make you go to the store early in the morning and get bubble gum. Crap like that.

- **Who was the guy you had the most trouble with in a game?**

That's a tough one. I can't think of one specific guy but, if I had to say.... Do you remember Lemar Parrish? He would be one, and then it would be Reggie Williams, the linebacker from Cincinnati, is another one. But I would say Lemar Parrish more than anybody because Lemar just wouldn't shut up. He would just talk, talk, talk all the time. He would make it a point to come out in pre-game while warming up, saying, "Hey, hey, Pruitt, you better look out. It's going to be a rough day for you today. I will personally see to that." And all that crap. I'll tell you a true story. I had to look back over the fence. I can't remember what team we played, but I threw an option pass for a touchdown. The very next week we played the Bengals. Pre-game, here come Lemar Parrish, "Pruitt, if you throw that pass you threw last week, it's going to be a touchdown, but it will be a touchdown the other way." So, after Glouster Richardson, my wide receiver, when they called the option play, I said, "Go opposite. Lemar came down and told me he was going to jump that play." We were in what we called a flag panel, where the side that I sprint out to, the receiver is on that side (he runs to the middle flag and then he runs to the flag). Lemar knew that, so I told Glouster to go to the middle of the field and take three steps and then go to the opposite side then. Lemar jumps, we are going to be in the other way. I ran out and go opposite and Lemar jumped that pass and I threw it the other way. You could hear him cursing. He had plenty to say after the game, "That's all right. Yeah, that's all right. Wait till the next game." I said, "You've got to wait to the next year, Lemar. This was the last game of the year."

- **What did your parents have to say about you playing ball?**

Funny you asked that. When I was playing football, I wasn't a very big guy. I asked my mom if I could play football and she told me no. I wasn't going out there and get hurt in no way. I tried to explain to her—in fact, me and my mom, I could tease her all the time because I went into this spiel of how I wanted to go to college, but I knew she couldn't afford to send me and if I played football, I'd probably get a scholarship and she wouldn't have to pay. All of this was crap. I was just trying to get her to say okay for me to play football. My mom was a beautician, so I knew Saturdays were her busiest day. She told me under no circumstances could I play. I waited until Saturday and I waited for the shop to be full of people. Then I went in and told her I've got this paper I want you to sign, because you had to have insurance to play football. She was so busy she didn't look at it and signed it and told me to get out, you know, "I'm busy." Go get home with that. I thought I got away with it but I had another paper they wanted me to get signed too, so I had to go back. She caught me then and said, "If you get hurt, don't you even come running to me." In high school, I played football and my mom didn't watch me play until I was a senior. Her customers would tell her how good I was as a player. The first game my mom came to see me play, I got hit and cracked three ribs. I'm lying on the field in all this pain and I look up and my mom had jumped the fence and ran out onto the field and stopped the football game. For the rest of the year, my teammates teased me like no tomorrow. "Don't hit Pruitt; if you do you better make sure his momma isn't around because she will come out and get you."

- **What did you get from your high school coach?**

Wendell Mosley was my high school coach. I got confidence from him learning the game. I was fortunate for Coach Mosley and, when I went to college, Coach Switzer was the offensive coordinator. Chuck Fairbanks was the head coach. Switzer was the kind of coach where you float along, even numbers to the right and odd numbers to the left; zero in the middle; one through five, go left; two, four, six, eight, the fullback is the three back; and the halfback is a two back. When you call Twenty-Five Trap, you knew it was the two back going into the five hole. And that is as far as we went. But, they were different; they insisted you knew the defensive fronts, the shifts, knew the defensive pass, defensives, so you could position or knew where guys were. You could make the play more effective by knowing where everybody was. When I learned that, I was a better player because I was ready for guys, because I knew where they were coming from.

- **Your first Pro coach was Nick Skorich. What did he teach you?**

Nick and I didn't get along too good because Nick was not very tall. I wasn't very tall either, but I was taller than Nick. He used to walk and look up at me and tell me I wasn't big enough to play. I wanted to start, but he wouldn't start me because he didn't think I was big enough to be a starter. Pete Eddy was the general manager here for a while, but he told my agent after he left here, "I went to the press on Nick Skorich because I couldn't play and I shouldn't have done that. I kind of went out of what we call 'The Circle.'" The last game, when Nick found out he was going to lose his job, we played Houston in Houston. It was the last game of the season. He told me, "You've been hollering about how you can play, how you're big enough to play, and now you're going to get a chance to play." He played me and I had almost four hundred offensive yards. It was too late for him, but if he had realized it earlier, maybe I might have helped save his job.

- **What was it like to play for Sam Rutigliano?**

I would say of all the coaches, Sam understood my ability better than any. Unfortunately for Sam, I got hurt. He wanted to throw the ball to me out of the backfield. Being part of the pass defensive, running out of the backfield, that's how Sam wanted to use me. He wanted me to run and kick off.

- **How did you get hurt and how did it affect the rest of your career?**

Well, it probably cost me a lot of things in Pro football. I cost me a lot of yards. Every day in training, once I got hurt, we can't move a passing team and I didn't run the ball very much anymore. I was a receiver out of the backfield. In fact, when I came back, I ended up catching sixty-five passes.

- **When you came back after the injury, Mike came in and took over the backfield and you started catching a lot more passes at that point.**

I didn't agree with that. They were trying to protect me because I used to get into it with Sam. They don't play touch football when they throw it to you. They tackled me just as hard, no matter how I get the ball. I don't understand why, if I am going to be out there, why can't do everything I used to do? I wouldn't be out there if I didn't think I could do it. But as a result of that injury, eventually, I ended up with the Raiders. I went to the Raiders as a back for reception. I didn't catch one pass.

- **You hold the record for a Raiders ninety-seven yard kickoff return.**

I went out there as a kickoff and ball-return specialist. When I went to Oakland, it was Marcus Allen's rookie year.

- **What was it like playing with him?**

Well, you don't get to play a lot. Oh, Marcus was a good guy. He was a rookie. I used to get on Marcus' butt. He would walk around there and play like he was the guy. I told him Marcus, "Whatever you would have done, I've already done it." He was a rookie. You had to treat him like a rookie. I don't care what he did, what he brings there, he's still a rookie.

- **What was your influence with Jim Brown?**

Jim was my idol. Jim is who got me interested in football, in the style, and how to dominate as a football player. Jim and I are two running backs playing with the same team, but there were things I couldn't do that Jim Brown could do, but I also felt that I could do things Jim Brown couldn't do.

- **Do you still have a good friendship with him now?**

Yes, I play golf with him and he's just as competitive as ever.

- **You were classified as one of the very best in the Browns organization. Is that something you are very proud of?**

Yes, I am. I am fortunate but, because of my injury, I think I could have challenged for second all-time rushing total yards. With 5496 yards, that is listed as the fourth. What it caused me in terms, you look at the carries; there are guys who have a lot more carries than what I had. As a result, being hurt and not getting the opportunity after the injury.

- **I read two different articles; one had you had second in the Heisman voting, the other had you as third. What were you really?**

I was both. My junior year, I was third, and my senior year, I was runner-up. Pat Sullivan from Auburn was elected in 1971 and Johnny Roger from Nebraska received the award in 1972.

- **Has your Heisman status brought you any fame?**

It helped me get into the College Hall of Fame. I made High School Hall of Fame, College Hall of Fame, and I've been nominated in the Pros, but don't know if that will ever happen. I have almost 14,000 yards combined in my career but the way it breaks down you have to have a dominate number in one category. I don't know if I will ever get nominated again or if it will ever happen. *(Greg made the long list of nominations in 2009 for the Pro Football Hall of Fame, but did not make the cut to twenty-five.)*

- **What's it like to have that Super Bowl Ring?**

There are a lot of great players who never got the opportunity but I'm not one of them. I am so happy for that. I got it late in my career, so I know how hard it was to accomplish. There are a lot of rookies that play in the Super Bowl and don't realize what they accomplished and how tough a feat it is.

- **What were your feelings when the Browns left Cleveland?**

First, I thought it was just a ploy. You know, a lot of teams are always threatening to move when they are trying to get something from a city. I thought that was all it was. When they moved, I was desolate. I was in shock. I really didn't believe it happened. I had people ask me as if maybe I had some insight information on it and I told them, "Oh, this is just a ploy." Then, when it happened, I said, "Well, I didn't know. I am just as shocked as you are." My grandfather always said, "You can find some good in any tragedy," and the good in this tragedy is we found out what kind of fans we really had. I qualify myself by saying I played with the Raiders and the Raiders went from Oakland to L.A. I'm from Houston, the Oilers went from Houston to Tennessee, and the Browns went from Cleveland to Baltimore. But when the Browns left here, the people put up such a fight they literally made it difficult for teams to move from one city to another without some kind of compensation to their team. No other team move had any kind of compensation to those cities. They left those fans, no matter how and where they supported them. Now, you have to match money and there are things you have to do as a result of the effort the fans put up when the Browns went to Baltimore.

- **Did Art Modell get a fair shake?**

I think he got used a little bit, maybe by Lerner. I don't know what the situation had been with Lerner, but I think he was in deep debt to him and Lerner kind of gave him a way out. I believe if Art had the chance again, you couldn't make him do it for anything. It literally changed his life. I don't think he could even come close to the repercussions he feels as a result of moving Cleveland to Baltimore. When I was drafted, I was not a part of Cleveland plans to draft me. I was a player that Art had paid particular attention to and liked as a player. He stepped in and made the decision to draft me. He took a large part in the draft process.

- **Sportswriters have stated that Ohio State Buckeyes and Michigan and the Cleveland Browns and Pittsburgh Steelers are the biggest rivalries in sports today. What is your experience with these games?**

Well, I'll tell you this, when I was a rookie, we played against Pittsburgh, and I had played in big rivalries in Nebraska against Oklahoma, Oklahoma/Texas, Oklahoma State/Oklahoma, and I would have to say that is a bigger rivalry. When you can't challenge a rivalry in college as a Pro team, that's a pretty big rivalry.

- **Were there any real negatives to playing football?**

I can't really think of any. I think, to me, it is part of the game. You never think, as a player, "I came here the second line draft team" and you go into camp and then they cut people because they have over a hundred people and need to cut down to fifty-three or forty-seven. Whatever it was, and I never was a part of that process. Then I got traded to the Raiders and all of a sudden I got to experience what so many other players had experienced for the nine years I was with the Browns. I can't say that's a negative, it's a part of the game. You never think you are going to be traded or cut. Then when it happens to you, you aren't prepared for it. I wasn't. I was very disappointed and, actually, I was not going to play anymore. Just retire. The running back coach, Jim Garrett, came to a softball game I was playing in during the off-season. He had called me a number of times but I'd ignored his calls. He found out where I was playing and came out on the field in the middle of the game and stopped the game. He told me he wasn't going to leave until I promised I would talk to him. I said okay. I don't think he believed me, so he waited until the game was over and followed me to his house. When I got to his house, he picked up the phone, dialed a number and it was Al Davis. I talked to Al and Al is kind of like a sports encyclopedia. I mean, he knows about everybody in football. He started to tell me stuff that I had done in high school and how he wanted me to come out and play for him. Regardless of what Cleveland thought, he didn't think I was through as a football player. I agreed to go to the Raiders. Depending on how well I did with the Raiders, because it was a conditional draft pick, the Raiders would give up a draft pick to the Browns. So, my first conversation with Al Davis when I walked in and he wants to know physically how I was and if I had any problems. I told him I had some problems with my back and I said it was more nagging. I could play; I just had to get treatment on it constantly. He said, "Okay." He then said, "You are here on a conditional draft pick, meaning how well you play will depend on what kind of pick I give the Browns." He said, "I think you are a very good player." He said, "I'm not going to be stupid like the Browns. If I play you very much, give them the lowest pick I can give them and then you can play." The first year, I didn't play very much and they ended up giving the Browns a third round draft pick for me—and the next year, I went to the Pro Bowl.

- **How was the Pro Bowl? What was it like?**

It was in Hawaii. That can't be bad.

- **What's it like playing with the Best of the Best?**

You know, I'm kind of torn. Even when the Raiders come to town to play the Browns now, I stay home because I'm torn in between. I have a lot of great memories there. I like Cleveland as a home, and I appreciate what the Raiders did for me. I had over 10,000 yards in the league but not one with the Raiders and I sat in their camp just like a lot of guys that sat in camp and I never realized the pressure I was about to go through. But, I knew I had two choices: One was to quit and go home, and the other was to make the best effort I could. If it didn't work out, I would not have any doubts for the rest of my life wondering if I had done this or it I could have made a difference. I gave it my best effort and it worked out for me.

- **Browns fans have been labeled with certain plays and a lot of them were season ending—Red Right 88, the Drive, the Fumble, the Bottle Throwing Incident, the Rudd penalty. What things happened while you were playing that were changing moments on the field?**

Well, I was there for Red Right 88. We shouldn't have lost that game. If we lost it because Cockroft had missed his fourth field goal, it would have been easier to swallow because you're supposed to play smart football. We risked the whole game for four points we didn't need to win the game. That's not smart football. When you lose like that, it is a bitter pill. I will say I know Brian Sipe won a lot of games for us that we thought were lost, but you still can't get away from smart football. The next team would expect you to play smart football when you're in field goal range and you're not just trying to position the ball to kick a field goal and go home. So, under those circumstances, yes, you might catch them thinking one thing and, maybe, if you can catch them on a pass, then fine. But, if that man isn't absolutely wide open, you don't throw the ball. You just don't do it. But, again, I have to say, I understood also, how he felt. He got us out of the jaws of defeat a lot of times. So, it happens; I know he wanted to win just as much as we wanted to win.

- **Cleveland fans have been labeled by the bottle-throwing incident in the game against Jacksonville. What do you think about that game?**

I have been in games against the Houston Oilers when the fans threw dog biscuits and whatever out of that Dawg Pound where they actually had to take the game to the other end of the field to continue it.

- **So, you're saying that other fans are like that also.**

There are some teams you hate to go play. You want that to be true at home when you play, too. You don't want people coming in here and feeling comfortable when they are playing us. The fans are very good at not letting them be comfortable.

- **You played in Oakland and they have been classified as second.**

No, I never got the chance to see the Oakland fans. I played with the L.A. Raiders and we had to look back sometimes to see if they were there. They were like being in the town square, a meeting place. They were just good background.

- **Who are the worst fans in the NFL?**

I would have to say the L.A. fans are up there. I came from Cleveland and went to the Raiders. If I had come from someplace else, maybe that wouldn't have been something that stuck out to maybe another player, but I knew what I was used to. I wasn't getting what I was used to.

- **Who were the leaders on your team when you were there?**

Sipe, Doug Dieken, Ozzie Newsome, Dave Logan, Tom DeLeone, probably Thom Darden, Ron Bolton. We had a bunch of guys that took on the leadership role. I think that was what made us so good.

- **How long after you were there did you become a leader?**

I did a lot of talking on the field. I didn't do a lot of talking off the field. I let my plays speak for me. I think you can lead by example. So, in that regard, by example, by play, probably right away.

- **What is the difference between the professional football players of today and the professional football players when you were playing?**

One big difference is money. They play for a lot more money and with more money comes a lot more pressure. Football, unlike all the other sports, is not a guaranteed contract. So, the guys with representation, agents, they are advised not to play when they are still hurt. And the reason they don't play is not because they are not tough or anything but because there is a lot of money involved. When you don't have a guaranteed contract, if you go out there and get hurt, you are going to lose the rest of the money on your contract. So, agents guarantee that the players make sure they are completely healed before they go out and play. I think that people who are watching the game kind of think those players are not as tough as they were when we played. I think that's the one big factor.

- **Was there more drive to play when it wasn't as money-oriented?**

I think so. I think there was more pride. The money wasn't a factor. The guys didn't have to worry about this or that pertaining to money. Now, it's all to the highest bidder. Why am I playing the game? To become the best football player I can play. I think that's a part of it, but I also think it's to make as much money as I can make. I think one of the biggest differences, too, is because of salary caps and team, because of money players don't play in one pot very long.

- **Are agents a good thing for the NFL?**

I think some agents are very good for players and some agents are just trying to get a reputation. They can sacrifice a player that way. I think that in some situations you have guys that need to be in camp when the team invests a lot of money. A player expects to get some kind of return. Not just football, in everything. Everybody looks for a return on their money. I think when these players get picked number one and they negotiate and can't come to terms, I think something else should be done. Maybe if a guy comes in and he's not signed a contract, they sign another contract, something in place, so he is practicing. So, if he gets hurt, he's protected in some way. It is not smart for a guy to come in and play and not be under contract and have a chance of getting hurt and all is for naught. I think from an owner's perspective, they want a return on their money when they draft a guy first like that. They expect him to come right in and make an impact. He can't make an impact at home. He can't make an impact if he doesn't know the plays.

- **What's "The Circle?"**

It means that, during the course of the season, whatever problems you have between coaches and players and players and players is supposed to stay within the walls of that practice facility. That's like if we have a problem and I go to the media, I went outside "The Circle."

- **What kind of hobbies do you have now?**

I like to hunt and I like to fish. I like to shoot pool. I love golf. I have been salmon fishing for the last three years. The first time I ever salmon fished was with a Browns Backer named Marvin. He was the president of the Browns Backers of Fostoria. I went turkey hunting with Ron in Newark. I go deer hunting every year with Ron.

- **What did you get out of your years as a professional football player?**

I met a lot of great friends as teammates and as fans. You know what Curt Gowdy always said, "The thrill of victory and the agony of defeat." It helped me in life. I look back and see the things I accomplished and I accomplished them through hard work. There is no easy way you came to appreciate things more when you work for them than when they are given to you.

My grandfather used to tell me, "You can always find good in tragedy: you just have to look for it." The tragedy for me was God shorted me two inches. I despised that; but it was the motivation that I needed to help me play. I had to learn how to use size as an advantage. —Greg Pruitt

Greg Pruitt											
Running Back 1973-1984											
Oklahoma											
			Rushing				Receiving				Tot
Yr	Tm	Gm	Rush	Yds	Avg	TD	Rec	Yds	Avg	TD	Fm	Pts
'73	CLE	13	61	369	6	4	9	110	12.2	1	7	30
'74	CLE	14	126	540	4.3	3	21	274	13	1	10	30
'75	CLE	14	217	1067	4.9	8	44	299	6.8	1	10	54
'76	CLE	14	209	1000	4.8	4	45	341	7.6	1	7	30
'77	CLE	14	236	1086	4.6	3	37	471	12.7	1	8	24
'78	CLE	12	176	960	5.5	3	38	292	7.7	2	12	30
'79	CLE	6	62	233	3.8	0	14	155	11.1	1	1	6
'80	CLE	16	40	117	2.9	0	50	444	8.9	5	1	30
'81	CLE	15	31	124	4	0	65	636	9.8	4	3	24
'82	LAI	9	4	22	5.5	0	2	29	14.5	1	5	6
'83	LAI	16	26	154	5.9	2	1	6	6	0	10	18
'84	LAI	15	8	0	0	0	2	12	6	0	9	0
Career		158	1196	5672	4.7	27	328	3069	9.4	18	83	282

Greg Pruitt playing against the Houston Oilers on Oct 21, 1973

17

Cleo Miller

Recognition for him and other players like him that cleaned out many a defensive lineman to make a hole for the star player to run through for glory is what Cleo Miller would like to see. He spent nine years as a fullback for the Kansas City Chiefs and the Cleveland Browns. He understood his position on the field was a tool for players to reach for the end zone with. He loved playing the game and loved carrying the ball, but he knew his role. Cleo taught other players in the backfield as well as on the offensive line, letting his fellow offensive players know what was expected from them on the field. He looked at it as a teaching exercise and realizes it wouldn't be allowed on any team today. "Team" was emphasized pre-1972, where Cleo is convinced that the game changed forever due to free agency and overzealous agents. Players pre-1982 played the game out of love of the sport. Many players had an off-season job as the money wasn't good enough to sustain them year round. When free agency came about, driving up the price for a player to come to another team, bidding for a player was like bidding for a piece of beef at a livestock auction. The better the beef, the more the price was driven up. Cleo enjoyed his tenure in the NFL, however, he believes he could have done more if given the chance.

- **You started in Kansas City. 1974. Were you drafted by them?**

  No, I wasn't. I was a free agent. I walked on and said, "I want to play."

- **How'd you get to the Browns?**

  The Kansas City Chiefs released me and I was a free agent again so I walked on with the Cleveland Browns, who picked me up off of waivers for a hundred dollars. During my first season [with the Chiefs], Hank Stram was the coach and he called me his "secret weapon." He told me before the end of the year was over that I would be starting, which I did in two or three games before the season was over. Coach Stram was then going to move me to the fullback position the following year and have Woody Green as the star halfback, but they fired Stram after the season. They brought in Paul Wiggins who called all the players and told them I was going to be starting fullback. In training camp, I got hurt twice. I ended up with a hip pointer and was off for a few weeks. After they cut the guy [who hit me], he told me the coaches had set me up and had him do it because we didn't have pads on. So, I wasn't able to play because of the injury. By the time I had healed, the full season had started. We had lost two games and I thought I could have actually helped the team win. I would go in after each game and talk to Coach Wiggins about playing. He said, "Fine. All you need is to play with is enthusiasm. You're going to play next week." But, after, he told me that his offensive coordinator Bob Schnelker said I wasn't going to play. So, it's going back and forth and I lost a little respect for Paul at the time. Finally, I got to play and we won a game. He jumped off the handle at me and said I couldn't let him feel wonderful one damned day, that I spoiled it. Before I knew it, I'd lit into him and told him he'd spoiled every day since he had been there. Didn't say exactly those words, but…(chuckling)…I was a young guy, in my second year, and back then you had to really get yourself established in the National Football League before you'd go anywhere. I learned a valuable lesson because I gave them an ultimatum. I told them to "trade me, play me, or put me on waivers." I didn't care which one, but they needed to do it, and the sooner the better. Unfortunately, they ended up blackballing me to a certain degree. I went from practicing at running back to doing the dummy plays for the practice squad. I moved out to wide receiver position, but the coaches were not communicating directions to me. After the seventh game of the season, the team pretty much had their team set and was not trading anybody. Before the season was over, Paul told me he'd tried to trade me to a team but nobody wanted to give up anything so he was going to release me. I said, "Fine, when are you going to do it?" He said, "We already did." I said, "You already did it and I didn't even know it?" At that time, I was only living five minutes from the stadium in Kansas City. When I got there, nobody was there. They were all gone; everybody had cleared out. The only person there was the equipment guy. As soon as I got back home, my phone was ringing off the hook. One of the calls was from Hank Stram's staff. He found out about my release. If I had listened to him, I might have been in the backfield with Walter Payton. Hank tried to get me to go to the Chicago Bears, but there was revenge in my eyes and Walt Corey, the linebacker coach at Cleveland had called. Cleveland was the only team playing against Kansas City left on the schedule for the year. I wanted to go to a team playing against KC to show them they had made a mistake. That's how I wound up in Cleveland.

- **What was it like to walk on the field as a Brown for the first time?**

Well, actually, and try to understand, it was almost a letdown to walk into the Browns Stadium as I was coming from Arrowhead Stadium, where they had Astroturf and modern "everything." It wasn't great coming to Municipal Stadium, which had a grass field and bad facilities. It was an old stadium, with cramped locker rooms. I thought, "Do they still have teams like this in the NFL working under these field conditions?" I stayed here though, grew to know it, to understand the tradition. I feel very proud of being here because they accepted me as a part of the family. It was my home.

- **When did you decide that you wanted to be a Pro football player?**

It's weird, I guess I really didn't decide; the people in the neighborhood decided for me. I was a little kid, somewhere around the age of twelve, thirteen years old, and I was playing with the guys sixteen, seventeen years old in the neighborhood. I was quick, a little stout, and guys couldn't catch me. I was a tough little rascal. One of the guys named me after a great defensive back that used to play for the Detroit Lions, Dick "Night Train" Lane. In those days, I was playing defense as opposed to running the ball. I would tackle the guys and prevent them from advancing the football. Then when they'd try to kick me, I'd run out of the way to where they couldn't catch me. So, they gave me that name and it followed me all the way through high school to Duke College. It went from Dick "Night Train" Lane to "Night Train" Lane to "Night Train" to "Night," until I got into to professional football.

- **Who inspired you to play football?**

It had to be the older guys I was playing against in the community. They're the ones that put it in my mind that I could go out and one day become a professional athlete.

- **Did any of them go on to do anything?**

No, I think I was the only guy to play high school and college ball and go on to play professionally.

- **What are they doing now? Do you have contact with any of them still?**

They were older guys so some are retired and some have passed away. When I go back, I try to get in touch with some of them.

- **Where was your hometown?**

Pine Bluff, Arkansas.

- **What kind of parental influence did you have?**

My father left my mother when I was about two or three years old, so I did not grow up with a "father figure." The coaches were that to me. My mother did all she could and still does. She did domestic work as we were growing up. I guess a lot of her ways are instilled in me; she taught me to move forward, to go farther, and to try to excel in life, as did my coaches.

- **Who was your college coach? How did he influence your future?**

Well, actually, I would say that my high school coaches were the ones who influenced my future more than college coaches. One was Roosevelt West, who was an offensive coordinator, and then Ollie Dyer, who was a defense guy. Both of them took me under their wing. I quit school when I was in the eighth grade and they came and got me. They instilled in me more

204

important things in life than football. They told me, "I *may* get a chance to play one day but maybe not, however, if I got an education I would always have that to lean on."

- **What was it like to play for Forrest Gregg?**

Forrest! You know, I truly identify with Forrest. I loved playing for him. While people said he had a bad attitude and was a mean guy, he was actually the type of guy who wanted to win. I had a lot of respect for him because he didn't care who you were; as long as you did the job, you played. If you didn't do the job, or didn't do what he said, he didn't want you on the football field and he would put somebody else out there. He didn't care if you were a free agent or the number one draft choice, he told you exactly where he came from. You can respect a coach when he tells you exactly where he's coming from.

- **Did his playing days influence you?**

I didn't know anything about his playing days and I didn't really know anything about Forrest Gregg until I got to the Cleveland Browns.

- **Dick Modzelewski. Did you learn anything from him? What kind of coach was he?**

Dick Modzelewski, we called him Mo; we became good friends, along with George Sefcik, who was the running back coach. Mo was the defensive coach and very knowledgeable about what he did and about the game. We had this little thing, where we would walk up to each other and saluted, a sense of respect for each other. We would hit each other on the forehead and I would tell him how short he was. I said, "How'd you shrink?" I actually thought that he should have been the head coach after they got rid of Forrest Gregg. He was there for one game, but didn't get the break to go on to be the head coach. I thought he should have been because he had a lot to offer as well as experience in the game.

- **What was it like to play for Sam Rutigliano?**

Sam was the politician in professional football. He would be the one that took a lot of gambles and relied on his players to do a lot of things. Because of that, people called him the Riverboat Gambler, but it really wasn't him gambling—it was the players. They were telling him what type of plays they thought would work and that's pretty much what he did. The bottom line is, guys had incentive clauses inside their contracts and they were trying to get as much money as they could. They wanted to go out and do things for Sam and try to win. Also, there was chemistry among all the players and Sam happened to be in the situation where he relied on his players heavily to make various plays.

- **What players did you enjoy playing with?**

Well, I can't say there was ever a guy I did *not* enjoy playing with. The one thing you have to understand is that once you are on a team, you become a team player. I think I was the only running back that would go to the meetings for offensive linesmen to find out exactly what they were doing. They considered me the sixth offensive lineman. If they missed something, I was there to pick it up. I was also the guy that tried to keep the peace among the running backs. Greg was in there saying, "I'm the Pruitt," while Mike was talking about how he was "the Pruitt," but somebody has to take a lesser role, so that is what I did. When I was in the backfield with Greg, I knew I wasn't going to be the starter and that is why I moved over to a fullback position. I guess during my tenure with the Browns, I was the only one on the team that could move from the halfback to the fullback without missing a beat. I played all my high school and college career as a halfback. Not until I got in National Football League did I move over into the fullback position.

- **You, Greg Pruitt, and Mike Pruitt were such a feared backfield; was it because all of you could do it all? Greg could break, they had you as a great blocker, and could come right through the line and just run forever. Is that what made you guys so good in your times?**

Well, no actually, I didn't play that much with Mike because both of us played the same position. The only time I was on the field with Mike was if somebody got hurt. It is funny, Paul Brown was the first one that made the statement, "When the two Pruitt's are in the backfield together, we know exactly what's going to happen, but when Miller and Pruitt are in the backfield, we don't know what's going to happen." When opponents started keying on Greg, I would run the ball down their throat. If they keyed too much on me, Greg would run the ball down their throat. I would block for Greg and open up the way or I would catch the ball. They couldn't key in on Greg because I would kill them. Mike Pruitt though never did a whole bunch of blocking. Put him in the backfield and he ran the ball. Greg also did very little blocking. But, when you had our combination of players in the backfield, they're not selfish. This is what made Greg and me so good because I wasn't selfish. I would help him because we lived together for seven years and it makes you feel good when your peers respect you. When we played against Houston, they said, "We don't know what's wrong with your coach, but we're glad you're not playing." Greg Bingham, I met him years later, said, "You know, our playbook had written in it to not hurt #43 because #30 is sitting on the bench and he's better." It makes you feel good, but it also makes you feel bad at the same time. That is when I understood the dynamics of what was happening. See, Mike Pruitt was the number one draft choice and I was a free agent. What does management do? Here I am making $70,000 a year and he is making $200,000 a year. Who should be "sold" to the public? Who do you put out there [on the field]?

- **Money has made a difference all along.**

Money makes a difference in a lot of cases. If you look at the situation with the Browns right now, they went through all these running backs and then get the guy from Detroit (Reuben Droughns). He came here and replaced William Green and Suggs, but he wasn't a number one draft choice. He was drafted, but he wasn't the number one draft choice. When I came along, I wasn't a number one draft choice, but a free agent. As a free agent, I had to play three times as hard as the guy drafted just to prove myself.

- **What kind of leadership role did you take on the team?**

When you're not selfish and you're a team player, you try to support [your teammates] and you try to do as much as you can to keep the team together. That's what I tried to do. I tried to pick up the slack, help keep somebody up to speed that didn't know what was going on. If they didn't know a play, they'd come to me. I'd let them know, I talked to them. I'm on the sideline and I see different things. I tell them what's happening out there on the football field so they can make the team and themselves better.

- **So you were more of a 'lead by example' than a boisterous type?**

I could be boisterous, but I didn't feel being boisterous got the point across. You could do rah rah this, blah blah that, but some guys take the position that you're trying to be a showboat. But, if you pull a guy over to the side, sit down and talk to him, that's being a team player. You show him where his mistakes are and tell him what he's doing wrong, that's more the type guy that I was. Regardless of what your problems are, your problems are our problems. I remember Hank Stram had this saying over the top of his door which was, "What you see here, what you hear here, what you say here, let it stay here when you leave here." That was the attitude I had. Whatever happened with us as a team, it was our problem. It was something we had to deal with, something we had to fix, and it stayed there. Do not take it outside the clubhouse. That bolstered us from that standpoint.

- **Did Jim Brown and previous players have a positive influence?**

Well, when you have guys of that magnitude, you know you can't but have a positive experience. Even though people talked about the Dallas Cowboys being America's team, it was proven when the Cleveland Browns left [Cleveland] that the Browns truly were America's team. They had the rich tradition and the history nobody could touch. True enough, the Browns have not won a Super Bowl but they were the flagship of the fleet back in the day and have won more championships than any other team even today. They had twelve consecutive championships. They may not have been a Super Bowl, but it was the equivalent to the Super Bowl in that day and time. You can't help but admire the Marion Motleys', the Jim Browns', the Otto Grahams', the nature of the Paul Warfields', and the beat goes on.

- **Things changed in 1982. The reason being?**

The reason being is that is when all the money changed. They had free agency where players can move from one team to another and big money came into the game. That was the beginning and I would venture to guess it really became evident six, seven, eight years ago when agents no longer represented players, but they represented National Football League. Agents began representing the upper office and coaches as well as players. Plus, agents now have a bigger hold on players, or at least a hold on what happens *to* a player now. They influence them [the players] in all kinds of ways. Years ago, an agent would never let a player sit out; they would have been playing.

- **What were your feelings when the Browns left Cleveland?**

I had mixed feelings because I had loyalty to both parties. I had loyalty to Art Modell for the simple fact that he was a player's owner, but he happened to make some bad decisions along the way. I was sort of torn, "Do I support Art Modell or do I support trying to get a team back here in Cleveland?" As a result, I did a little bit of work for both by being a co-chair for the Save Our Browns Committee. I was a part of that to keep the Cleveland Browns name and traditions in Cleveland. Whenever I was given the opportunity or chance to speak, I never badmouthed Art Modell. I never bashed him, for the simple fact he was a businessman. He made a decision based on what was best for his family. If you cannot do that in this day and age, what can you do? Your family is the most important thing. If he had stayed in Cleveland and something happened to him, his family would have to sell the team and would not have been financially sound. Can you imagine the pressure to be put in a situation like that [for your family] because of a poor decision?

- **Do you think Art got a fair shake?**

I don't think Art got a fair shake because he didn't do this [move] all by himself. I actually think Art Modell should be in the Hall of Fame. Who else has done more for owners and the National Football League than Art Modell in terms of negotiating contracts and different things of that nature to advance the quality of football? He worked contracts with the television networks to put more football on television. Yeah, you might say that Art Modell and Paul Brown fell out, but in business, you can't keep a person forever. You have to make decisions and whatever decision you make you have to live with; you don't look back. It may have been a bad decision at that time, but I truly think Art really wanted to win. He wanted a championship in Cleveland. He wanted to win a Super Bowl here. It was a poor decision he basically made during that time and when I say "decision," I mean, in terms of who he hired to handle various things for him.

- **Do you think Bill Bellichick is a different coach now than he was in Cleveland?**

He was a Parcell disciple; he had a lot of the ways of Parcell and still has some today. He grew through experiences he had here in Cleveland. For one, Bellichick stopped the older players from coming into the locker room.

208

It used to be tradition for older players to come around the team and talk to them about the history and tradition on what it was to be a Cleveland Brown. That changed with Bellichick and, ultimately, it was one of his downfalls in the Cleveland area.

- **He used to work his guys hard but he's changed that philosophy also.**

Yes—that is part of learning. The more you're in, the more you find out what's going to make you a better coach and get the guys to do things for you. Bellichick couldn't have worked guys any harder than Forrest Gregg. As a matter of fact, one of Forrest Gregg's downfalls with the Browns was not believing and having faith in his players. He used to have the coaches and their wives call up players at night and find out if they were home. If they weren't, he tried to find them. I'm sure he changed and learned a lot when he left the Browns and went to the Cincinnati Bengals. It's part of the maturing process going from one era to another and one year to another.

- **So, is every day a learning experience as you're playing?**

It's always a learning experience in the National Football League. You can't ever take anything for granted and you always have to be honing your skills, keeping yourself in tip-top condition to go out and perform to the best of your abilities. The lights eventually do go out on the football field, so you have to make hay while the sun shines. If you don't go out and give as much as you can and do the things that you need to do to keep your body in tip-top condition, you have a problem. That's when you don't keep your position.

- **Were drugs a problem back when you were playing?**

Drugs have always been a problem but it wasn't as prevalent, in terms of what they're doing today. There has always been one form or another of a "fashion drug" but the NFL is really trying to crack down. There is no place for it. Some guys have false hope or insecurity in terms of using drugs. It makes them think they can do a whole bunch more than what they normally should be able to do. Guys look for competitive edges in the NFL the same as in any competitive sport. Fortunately, I grew up in a time when the hard drugs weren't as prevalent.

- **Cleveland vs. Pittsburgh and Ohio State vs. Michigan. These were the two biggest rivalries in sports. What are your thoughts about this?**

I can't say much about Ohio State and Michigan as I never really followed them much because it wasn't my alma mater and I didn't play against either one of those teams in college. In terms of the Steelers and the Browns, they have great tradition and history. That rivalry may have been more between the fans, as opposed to the players. Players go out there and realize it is competitive and they have to do certain things to win, it is just the competitive nature of an athlete. Once they step off the football field though, players are getting together and laughing and having fun. Football players realize it's a job and it's something we have to do. Fans take it to another level. For example, if you went to Pittsburgh for a game and had Ohio plates, your automobile might be junked, and vice versa, if you came to Cleveland. People have gotten into fistfights if you say bad words about the Browns or if you say something bad about the Steelers. That's just how it goes down with the fans. I have fun with it today, I really do. I look at someone and say, "I'm a die-hard Cleveland Browns fan; there are no ifs, ands or buts about it because it was one of the teams that gave me a livelihood for a long period of time." But, when I see fans today, I have a way of smoothing that situation out. I simply tell people, "You know, the Steelers and the Bengals are nothing but stepchildren to the Browns. We have no problem with them because they are our stepchildren." When they ask, "Why?" I simply tell them, "Well, you know the Bengals came about because of Paul Brown and he was the first coach in the Cleveland area and he took the tradition and some of the Browns history to Cincinnati." Then, I talk about the Steelers and they could identify a little bit by what I had said about the Bengals. But, then they say, "Well, what did that have to do with the Steelers?" I tell them, "It's simple—the Steelers couldn't play football until the Browns went there and taught them how to play. If memory serves me correctly, who was Chuck Noll? A former Cleveland Brown. Who is Bill Cowher? A former Cleveland Brown." This statement gives them something to ponder.

- **Do you have a good Pittsburgh story?**

Well, no, I don't have anything from that standpoint. I was just going out there and trying to get into the game and perform to the best of my ability.

- **Did you encounter any negatives when you were playing?**

Oh, you'll always have negative talk, so you have to have a thick skin on the field. People have a right to say whatever they want as long as they don't put their hands on you. They have a right to voice their opinions but when they cross that boundary—like fans jumping on the football field—and enter my world, they are out of line and they better be prepared to accept the consequences. You don't often see a player going in the bleachers trying to get a fan. When they do, they're wrong. Regardless of what is said and done, they are wrong. And vice versa, the fan has a right to say what he wants, but he doesn't have a right to throw stuff down on the field at the players.

- **Cleveland has the distinction of being labeled with many negative games: Red Right 88, The Drive, The Fumble, the Bottle Throwing Game, the Rudd Penalty. What were your involvements in any of these games and what are your comments about them?**

I was involved in Red Right 88 but not any of the others you mentioned. For Red Right 88, I was standing on the sideline and Sam called me to go block for Mike Pruitt. I was going out onto the field and, all of a sudden, I'm hearing the players being called back to change from a running play to a pass play. To me, it didn't make sense because all we needed was a field goal to win, but you try not to second-guess anything that happened out on the field. Clearly, in situations like that, you don't throw the ball into an area of coverage. Mike Haynes intercepted the ball and there went our chance to go to the Super Bowl. You feel awful sick and frustrated while thinking of all you could have done to make a difference. You're riding high and say, "Oh, yeah, this is the year we're going to get our Super Bowl!" Then all of a sudden, it's taken away by one small interception and you go from a real high to a real low real fast.

- **Did you have to go through any hazing?**

The closest I ever got to a hazing was in my rookie year with the Kansas City Chiefs. A fight broke out on the football field between the Chiefs and the Raiders. As a matter of fact, the bench cleared except for me. I was sitting there thinking, "It doesn't matter. Why am I going to go out there and fight these guys? It does not make any sense." There was a defensive tackle on the team by the name of Marvin Upshaw. He looked up and saw me sitting on the bench, so he quit fighting and came right up to where I was and he told me, and I won't use the word that he said, but in essence he told me, "Let me tell you one thing, rookie, the next time a fight happens on the football field, you better be the first one to go out there or I'm going to kick your butt every damn practice until I get tired." That was a lesson I learned. I'm fortunate enough to have only been in one brawl after that and I got fined for it. I think it was the New England team, where a defensive guy had an offensive lineman down on the ground beating him. With the sound of Marvin's voice in my mind, I took off on a dead run. My fist was small enough to go through the facemask of the other defense end's helmet and when I hit him, he turned flips and the official saw it. He threw a flag and put me out of the game. Fortunately, it was close to the end of the game when the brawl happened and we had already won. When Forrest Gregg was coming to the sideline, he said, "Look, let me tell you something. I like what you did." He said, "I'm going to pay your fine for you this time. But I better not ever see you do it again because we may need you." Those are the things that you have to think about when a situation like that occurs.

- **Do you still feel like you're part of the Browns organization?**

I do. I like to think so because I was there and was a part of that rich tradition and history. The Browns are the only organization that opened their arms to retired players, regardless of what level you played. They say, "Hey, come back and be a part." As a matter of fact, they will give you two complementary tickets to come and be a part of what they do. I use that example because the Chiefs don't even recognize that you were part of the organization unless you played three years. That's where I started my career and was there a year and a half but I've never been invited to any function whatsoever on their behalf. Never have they called me to say, "You're a part of this organization or this family."

- **Do you have any influence on the game today?**

No, I don't think I do. If you're there on a regular basis and you're out there to talk to the players, maybe. Some may listen but they're going to do what they need to do because they dance to a different beat.

- **Are Cleveland Browns fans the best in the NFL?**

One of the things I said when I was one of the co-chairs and saw people from all over the world coming to be a part of the organization was that Cleveland not only had the best fans, but they are the heartbeat of the Browns. They are the ones that make the Cleveland Browns go. Players do have a lot of respect for the fans because they are what made us.

- **What was the hardest place to play in the NFL?**

Well, conditions were very bad when we played in Philadelphia because the field was hard and the turf was bad. Any time you're on a rival's field and the bleachers or the stands are so close to the field, it's going to hard hearing. Like at Cincinnati, it was very hard to hear when they had that old stadium. The hardest thing is when you're at rival team's stadium. It's also hard to hear in Pittsburgh, Houston, and Detroit. Those are hard places to play because of the loud noises.

- **Have any funny stories from your NFL experience?**

Well, I could tell funny stories—football related or not—but one thing the fans may not know is you become friends with the players. Sometimes, though, when you don't know each other too well, you're really competitive. Well, we were in Stillwater, Oklahoma one year, and Claude Humphrey, who used to play for the Philadelphia Eagles, was going to the Atlanta Falcons. We'd done a football clinic together about a year before and we became pretty good friends. So, we get a chance to play against each other during the pre-season and Claude comes in and he's huffin' and puffin' and he's fightin' around Barry Darrow, trying to get into Brian Sipe's head. Keep in mind, during that time, the chop block and other risky blocks were legal. So, when he came through the line, he did not see me because I came up behind. I must have been on the outside and came back in…anyway, as he was getting ready to tackle Brian, I stepped right in front of him and said, "Boo!" just like that. He stopped right in his tracks. He stopped trying to fight with the offensive tackle and he said, "Thank you, man. Thank you, man," then he turned around and walked back to the other side.

- **What's the saddest thing that ever happened when you were playing?**

The saddest thing I saw happen when I was playing may have been the Darryl Stingley situation. *(Daryl died in April of 2007. He was left a Quadriplegic from a hit on the field.)* He got hit by Jack Tatum; you never want to see any guys get hurt or maimed. That puts a different perspective on the game in itself. It's a situation where you're career could end in a minute, in a split second. You realize you're there on borrowed time and you get as much as you can out of the game. It is important to do your job and do it in the best

212

way you can, in a clean and professional way. At the end of the day, you can look back and say you gave it your all, you did it the best you know how, and you did it clean.

- **Any difference between the players now and those from your era?**

The difference between the players today and yesterday is money. I don't feel like the love or the sincerity for the game is there. It's strictly business for pay today, as opposed to loving the game. I guess that would be the biggest difference in my opinion. You had big guys back then and you had guys that were fast. Players now have taken it to another level. You have defensive guys who are quick or even faster and you have more players who have a lot of skills players in my day didn't have. And that's expected. But I don't think it is true love as it is more of a business decision.

- **Are players worth their salaries?**

I think some players are worth the money they get, but I've always said that the salary situation was backward. When I say players are worth what they get, I believe a player needs to get out there and prove himself. You have too many guys that are coming directly into the game today and, never having played a down, make millions of dollars. I don't fault the players, I fault management. I fault them for the fact they have allowed this thing to happen; it has gotten out of hand. They've let agents come in and rule the game. Agents represent players, they represent coaches, they represent general managers, and their only concern is money. They're not really concerned about the players, it is strictly business. The mentality of an attorney is not the mentality of a professional football player. It's a business. Get as much as you can and forget about the rest.

- **Are agents a good thing for the NFL?**

At one point in time, it was a good thing. They're good for some players, but they can be detrimental to others. I've been on both sides because I have had agents represent me, and I've gone in and represented myself. It's easier for an agent to go in and sit down with management, because management curses and swears at the agent, and he [the agent] walks out at the end of the day. But, when you do that as a player/agent, you are in there negotiating your contracts, and it will have a direct effect on how the player reacts on that football field. The player doesn't need that "negative energy" as he plays.

- **Do you have any hobbies?**

Love playing golf and I love to bowl. I used to fish, but I haven't gotten back into it. I now get involved with some charitable things, because of having come from a very poor family on the welfare system you have a tendency to look back and hope, wish, and pray you can make somebody's life a little bit better than what yours was. I get pleasure out of stuff like that.

- **What are you doing for a living, right now?**

I'm a sales consultant for a furniture store, but I'm getting ready to do something I think is going to be different and unique. I've had the opportunity, with three other guys, to create a company called Global Builders and Developers. We're going to have a chance to right some of the wrong in Texas, Louisiana, Mississippi, and Florida areas after these horrendous hurricanes. We have a housing unit that will stand up to level-five hurricane resistances.

- **You started to go into a conversation about lack of recognition by teams of the players that were in the organization.**

No, I had mentioned the fact they are recognizing so many players in so many different ways. There are guys that have been on the team who are very big contributors to the team. They are responsible for other guys getting the awards for doing the things they've done, but those players go unrecognized. A lot of times, they're not accepted and never get the opportunity of being recognized while they are alive, and some never will. Categories never come up where they get recognized. I think about that circle of friends, the Hall of Fame the Browns have. You know, the Leroy Kelleys', the Jim Browns', the Gregg Pruitts', or the Mike Pruitts' could not have gotten where they were if it had not been for those offensive linemen or those running backs in the backfield blocking for them. I'm not trying to toot my horn, but I am standing up for the Ernie Greenes', the guys who actually went out there and performed. You don't hear anything about these guys.

- **What did you get out of your NFL experience?**

I got an opportunity to do something guys would give their right arm and probably left leg to do. That's to be involved with a fraternity such as the National Football League. I made a lot of good contacts, met a lot of good people, and I am able to go back in and say I was a part of this. It helped me grow. It helped me mature and look at life a lot differently than what I would have had I not had the opportunity to play the game.

"A winner never whines." — *Paul Brown*

Cleo Miller												
Running Back 1974-1982												
Arkansas - Pine Bluff												
			Rushing				Receiving					Tot
Yr	Tm	Game	Rush	Yds	Avg	TD	Rec	Yds	Avg	TD	Fm	Pts
'74	KC	14	40	183	5	0	14	149	11	0	4	0
'75	—	11	13	23	2	0	2	20	10	0	2	0
	KC	*6*	*7*	*20*	*3*	*0*	*0*	*0*	*0*	*0*	*1*	*0*
	CLE	*5*	*6*	*3*	*1*	*1*	*2*	*20*	*10*	*0*	*1*	*6*
'76	CLE	12	153	613	4	4	16	145	9.1	0	8	24
'77	CLE	14	163	756	5	4	41	291	7.1	1	5	30
'78	CLE	15	89	336	4	1	20	152	7.6	0	2	6
'79	CLE	16	39	213	6	1	26	251	9.7	0	1	6
'80	CLE	16	28	139	5	3	2	8	4	0	2	18
'81	CLE	12	52	165	3	2	16	139	8.7	0	0	12
'82	LAI	5	16	61	4	0	3	20	6.7	0	1	0
Career		115	593	2492	4	#	140	1175	8.4	1	25	102

SOURCE: C. MILLER

Cleo Miller playing at Municipal Stadium

18

Dick Ambrose

Preparation is a word Dick Ambrose took to heart. He not only prepared himself for his weekly duties as a linebacker for the Cleveland Browns, but he also prepared for a life after football. Was it something that happened on the field, or was it his mental attitude to be groomed for his livelihood after football? A year before he broke his leg on the playing field, he enrolled and started taking law classes. This happened during the same time of the strike-shortened season of 1982. Dick had to reduce his workload when the dispute was settled, but continued working hard in his studies. "Bam Bam" is the nickname given to him by his gridiron gang, after the character in the Flintstones, because of the violent banging collisions he caused on the field. Being prepared for classes was something else Dick did at Cleveland Marshall School of Law as he graduated Magna Cum Laude in 1987. Dick joined the Law Firm of McDonald Hopkins. He also practiced with Chriszt McGarry Co. and Nicola Gudbranson and Cooper before being asked to serve as Cuyahoga County Court of Common Pleas since 2004. He successfully defended his seat in 2006. Bam Bam is a regular at Browns Backers Worldwide functions around the Cleveland area, where he has resided for over thirty years.

- **What was it like to walk on the field the first time as a Cleveland Browns player?**

I remember the day; it was an intra-squad scrimmage in August, 1975, or it could have been July because of the long pre-season we had then. I felt in awe, somewhat, because the scrimmage occurred at Cleveland Stadium. We came out on the field and got introduced. They let the fans in for free, so there was a little bit of a crowd. It was my first time in the stadium. It reminded me a lot of Yankee Stadium, because I had grown up in New York. I had been in Yankee Stadium several times and found out it was built by the same architect that built Municipal Stadium. I was impressed, and remember the guy that got the biggest ovation when he was introduced was Blanton Collier. He was like a consultant at the time; he wasn't really coaching.

- **When did you decide that you wanted to be a Pro football player?**

Probably when I was in the fifth or sixth grade. I had two older brothers who had played football in high school. My dad was a big fan and we would always watch the NFL. I was a Dallas Cowboys fan back then and remember the Ice Bowl in Green Bay with Green Bay and Dallas. Green Bay won when Bart Starr snuck over for a touchdown. That was a game I would remember and was so upset by that, that I wanted to play football some day and beat the Green Bay Packers. That was one of those boyhood dreams, but as time went on I got involved in sports and playing football, I enjoyed it. I continued on and played in the youth tackle league in New Rochelle, New York. I also played at my grade school, Holy Family Grammar School, in New York in seventh and eighth grade and then onto high school at Iona Prep. My coach there was Rudy Agustin. He never told me I had talent and even had a conversation one time with me in my senior year and told me that a lot of the college scouts who had come by were saying I was too small to play at Big Ten schools. He thought I should start looking at the Ivy Leagues and smaller schools. I settled on Virginia because it was the only school that offered me a scholarship. I accepted their offer not even knowing that Virginia was considered an Ivy League school, a public Ivy League School. They played Division I football and played in the Atlantic Coast Conference, so the competition was good. It was quite a challenge, because we never had a good team when I was there. I ended up being All Conference my junior and senior year. Freshmen were not eligible in 1971, when I started there. I started on the varsity my sophomore/junior/senior years at Virginia. I played fullback my freshman year, defensive line my sophomore year, and was converted to linebacker my junior and senior year.

- **Was there any one person who inspired you to play football?**

It would be a combination of factors, really. My two older brothers, Tom and Mike, were instrumental in instilling in me the desire to play. Then I had coaches all along the way that seemed to encourage me. I still remember my coach at Holy Family, Harold McEvoy. He was a fire chief who volunteered and helped out at the school. One time, he told me he was going to get me a scholarship to high school. They had such things then, but I didn't get one. I took it as an acknowledgement he thought I had some talent and so I continued on. I went to Iona Prep, who had a tradition of football and excellence in sports. They encouraged excellence in sports and also in academics. Problems occur if you encourage one and not the other.

- **What kind of parental influence did you have?**

My mom was always supportive in terms of us playing sports. Mom would make us meals when we were late for dinner because of workouts. My dad always went to every game. He watched a lot of sports on television. They were both supportive of my being involved with athletics.

- **Where were you born?**

New Rochelle, New York.

- **Was there a player you role-modeled after?**

I always did like the linebackers. I liked Dick Butkus, Ray Nitschke, Tommy Nobis. Those were the guys that I kind of emulated and wanted to be like.

- **Did you meet any guys like that when you were growing up?**

I did meet Nitschke in later years at a player's association meeting. It was right before a Hall of Fame game and they were having a player's association meeting and I am sitting with my wife. He asked my wife to pass him the pretzels at the end of the row. She leaned over and said, "Say please." I told her, "That is Ray Nitschke, he will kill you. He is the meanest linebacker that ever played football." After that, he always made it a big joke because she handed him the pretzels and he said, "Thank you, Mrs. Ambrose." Every time I saw him at one of those meetings, again he would ask me where my wife was.

- **Who was your college coach? What kind of an influence did he have?**

The guy that recruited me to the University of Virginia was my position coach for defensive line, Al Groh, who is now the head coach at Virginia (2009 season). After my sophomore year, he left Virginia and went to North Carolina. He ended up with the New York Jets. He was with the Browns for a little bit after I retired. He is now back at Virginia. He had a good work ethic and philosophy. He worked us hard but respected us. His mantra was to work to get a little bit better every day. I still remember that, and it is still one of those things I hold on to. The head coach there during my senior year was Sonny Randall. Sonny was not your model coach. He was too emotional and lost it a couple of times with his players. The players ended up not respecting him and he had a very short tenure of two years. It was certainly a learning experience every day in college and the Pros.

- **What was it like to play for Forrest Gregg?**

That was very interesting, probably the toughest training camp I ever had in my life that first year in 1975. Fortunately, for me, I was probably in the best shape of my life. I had stayed down at Virginia the summer before my first training camp and worked out. I basically did three workouts a day on my own before I got to training camp. I was in shape for training camp, but Forrest surprised a lot of veterans with his grueling workouts. We would go out in full pads both sessions and hit both sessions every day. We would do ninety to a hundred grass drills before practice. The guys were exhausted. We did so much hitting. That is when I got that nickname, Bam Bam. We would hit so often, I broke three sets of shoulder pads. The veterans were trying to label people with nicknames and Dennis Wirgowski, a defensive end, named me Bam Bam. Somebody had actually suggested they call me Barney Rubble, but Dennis said Bam Bam. It was a good nickname.

- **What was it like playing for Dick Modzelewski?**

He was a great guy. I enjoyed playing for Mo, because he kept it simple and very basic. He focused on technique and doing the job. He was always a no-nonsense guy who had a good rapport with the players and earned their respect. It was a pleasure.

- **What was it like playing for Sam Rutigliano?**

He was a guy I respected and felt like he was interested in every player on the team and in helping them become the best player they could be. He lived by his philosophy. He wasn't just a bunch of words. He meant what he said and he carried it out. He always kept level-headed and calm. Sometimes you get coaches that lose it when things start to go south during the season, and they tend to put more pressure on the players and the players end up screwing up more. They yell more and it turns into a downward spiral, but Sam always had a way of keeping us level-headed. If you look back through the records, he kind of built slowly. He didn't get rid of a bunch of guys when he took over the team, but the next year he did make major changes and we had a major turn-around in terms of the record. We improved the following year and we had the year in 1980 because of all of the slow building he did.

- **Did you see a lot of Paul Brownisms on the team?**

I think it would have been more, but Forrest wanted to install his own system. There were anecdotal things about Paul Brown from the trainers and the equipment people. It didn't seem anything from a coaching perspective came through because Blanton was out of it by that time. Rich McCabe was the defensive coordinator when I first started. He had come from Buffalo, so I don't think there was much Paul Brown influence from that standpoint either. At least, I didn't see it.

- **Do you see a difference between coaches that were players and turned coaches from coaches that were only coaches and never played?**

Yes. It is hard to paint it with a broad brush. The only generalization I could make is that some of those who were players and who weren't really stars seemed to end up being better coaches than the coaches that were stars as players. Maybe it is because the guys that didn't have a lot of talent tried to get by on their brains. The guys that had a lot of talent just got by and didn't get into the strategy. Jim Shofner had a way about him. He was a very calm guy and steadying, which is the kind of influence you need with a quarterback. You need a guy who is part psychiatrist and part coach because it is such a mental game for those guys.

- **What players did you enjoy playing with?**

I enjoyed playing with Clay Matthews, my roommate for seven years. He made the game a lot of fun. Jerry Shirk was a good guy I played with in the early days. He was really a hard worker and didn't have the speed these guys have today, but he was always around the ball. Guys like Doug Dieken and Robert Jackson. I hung around them a lot in my formative years and made it for a great experience and a lot of fun. As you look back over time, you remember the people more than you do the plays. A lot of the offensive lineman I got along with, despite the fact we were going against each other in practice all the time. There was a mutual respect. You have to know what speed you are going in practice and who you are going against. I would go about the same speed so people would expect that. You would get disappointed if you rammed into somebody too hard during a practice drill. We always had a lot of good times with guys like Clinton Burell, Lawrence Johnson, and Clarence Scott. Scott would always come to the games with his big fedora, dressed to the nines.

- **Did any prior players before you have a positive influence?**

Yes. I say it is a lot different now than it used to be, because in the past guys would come into the locker room; Ernie Kellermann, Lou Groza, Dante Lavelli, Marion Motley. If you didn't know them as a rookie you would ask, "Who are those guys?" They would tell you who it was. "Oh, yeah, his pictures were up on the wall," "…he is a Hall of Famer." So, the players did have a positive influence. I don't know why, but they seem to shy away from those interactions these days. It is a more restricted access. That's probably just the function of the age we live in. There are some players who would not give you a minute of time, because they would say, "You are an old guy, and what do you know?"

- **Sports people have said that Ohio State/Michigan and Cleveland/ Pittsburgh are the two best rivalries in sports. What do you say?**

It is a great rivalry. I remember the first Browns/Steelers game I played in was when we played the Steelers at Cleveland Stadium in 1975. That was the game that "Mean" Joe Green kicked Bob McKay where the sun doesn't shine and there was a semi-bench clearing brawl. Tom DeLeone and Gary Paris got ejected from the game and fined. Green got ejected and fined not quite as much as the others got fined because he was Joe Green. They ran the score up on us and I remember Forrest Gregg yelling at Joe Gilliam because they put him in towards the end of the game. He threw a bomb in the fourth quarter, up by twenty points, and Jerry Shirk hit him just as he threw the ball. Gilliam was lying down in obvious pain. Forrest yelled, "I hope you die!" There was definitely something going on with this rivalry. Of course, the media, newspapers, and radio played it up big time. Every time we would go there, it would be a huge deal.

- **Did being a twelfth round draft choice affect your play?**

Only on draft day. I was disappointed but, once I got here, I figured my job is to do the best I can for this team and go one-hundred percent all of the time. I didn't think that much about it, even when they had other guys pegged in the depth chart higher than me. It was mainly based on a draft position, but after a week, I realized the team wasn't going to focus on that board, they were going to focus on performance. That is why coming to the Browns was a good thing for me because it was Forrest's first year and nobody's job was secure. The Browns had a new coach in a new year, with a crappy year the year before. Everybody's job was in jeopardy, so there wasn't any pecking order they paid attention to. I was told I would go by the fifth round then the fifth came and went. I would have been okay if I had been drafted the first day, but it went well into the second day before I got drafted.

- **Who was your nemesis on the field?**

Probably the toughest guy I played against was Mike Webster because we played a 4-3 head up on the center. If it was a drive block or similar play, he would usually win because he was like a bull. He had arms like my legs and was a very powerful guy.

- **What were your feelings when the Browns went to Baltimore?**

First, I couldn't believe the Browns would actually leave. My association with the Browns obviously began as a player. The only thing I knew about Cleveland when I came to town was the Cleveland Browns. When the Browns left, it was like there was something philosophically wrong here. It just can't be, this team is the town and the town is this team. I was stunned! I was at the last game against Cincinnati when everybody knew they were leaving. Art Modell had already made the announcement. It seemed like the countdown to the end of that game was like the countdown to New Year's Eve, except there wasn't going to be a next year.

- **Bill Cowher was on the team, did you see any coaching ability in him?**

I think looking back I can because he always did pay very close attention to the schemes and what the other team was doing. We always had a test we would take on Friday before the game and he always either got a hundred percent, or close to it. In those tests, we would draw up the other teams' favorite plays. I think he was a student of the game even back then.

- **Did you compete against him for a position?**

The way I recall it, we really weren't in direct competition with each other. I know he seemed to be playing more behind Robert L. Jackson and we did actually both start the Monday Night game against Chicago in 1980. We never really competed against each other.

- **Did you encounter any negatives while you were playing?**

I didn't like it when we would lose and there would be dissension on the team with guys pointing fingers at each other. Those things seemed to break up the harmony and unity. It would be disheartening. There were little flare ups from time to time, when there would be little cliques of players.

- **Cleveland Browns fans have the distinction of being labeled with several negatives: Red Right 88, The Drive, The Fumble, the Bottle Throwing Incident, the Rudd Penalty. What were your involvements?**

Obviously, a game is more than just one play or one event, but that is what people recall. I recall where I was and what I was doing when the pass was thrown in Red Right 88. I look more or less at the whole game and think about the missed opportunities. What I could have done better? Was there anything I could have done to change that outcome? In the end, you realize what is done is done. It's, where do you go from here? It's an experience to get that close, but unless you concentrate one hundred percent and not let up for one second then it may not be your time. The ball can bounce the other way and you lose the game, but there is always tomorrow.

- **Do those types of plays make a team stronger or do they hurt them?**

It depends on the team. Yes, it can make a team stronger if everybody views it the same and comes back with the same resolve. We lost a game in Minnesota on a last second catch by Ahmad Rashad, but everybody was focused. Everybody was disappointed and upset we lost that game, but everybody was focused. They knew we had a chance to redeem ourselves next weekend. So, we quickly and collectively put that disappointment aside and focused on what was yet to come. That was the key to beating Cincinnati for the division title that year. We were all on the same page and focused before we ever got back to Cleveland.

- **Are Cleveland Brown fans the best in the NFL?**

You can say that in every city but I talked to Andra Davis the other day and he said the fans here just feel different. They are really great fans. I told him they are. They will love you, win or lose, as long as they know you are making an effort and giving it your best. Obviously, they prefer you to win, but they like guys that work hard, try hard, and respect the game. They are knowledgeable fans in that regard. There may be twenty percent of the fans that will jump on the bandwagon and they will be the same twenty percent that will be on your back when you don't do well. The majority, though, are solid fans. I shouldn't say other cities wouldn't have similar fans. I would say they wouldn't have them in the same proportion. I think there are more here. Other cities will have more "fair weather" fans.

- **Where was the hardest place to play because of opposing fans?**

It was probably the King Dome in Seattle, because it was so loud. In the early days, the Seahawks were an expansion team and we had nothing to gain, but everything to lose, by playing them. There was nothing I liked about it. I hated their uniforms, they wore black shoes, and they looked like robots running around. The place was loud and, if they did anything good the fans went crazy, which made you feel even worse that you let an expansion team get a first down or anything like that. It just got you into a mental funk.

- **What is the funniest story of your NFL experience?**

During the Raiders game in January, 1981, Jerry Shirk had been hurt because he had a staph infection. He had picked up photography as a hobby, so he had all of these new cameras and a press pass. He was going up and down the sidelines taking pictures. He was hanging around the bench talking to us. I came off the field after one series and grabbed a cup of Gatorade that was basically frozen because it was so cold. It wasn't that I was so thirsty, but I needed something to wet my whistle. I took a sip then tossed the rest back over my shoulder then I was going to crumble the cup and throw it on the ground. I tossed the liquid over my shoulder and I heard, "Hey," and I turned around and it was Jerry Shirk standing right behind me. I had thrown Gatorade all over the cameras hanging around his neck. The Gatorade froze almost instantaneously on his cameras. I said, "Oh, sorry, Jerry."

- **What is the saddest thing that happened to you on the field?**

I remember spraining my ankle in Houston, 1976, and something felt really weird. It was a really severe sprain. I stepped into a dip in the end zone. They used to have rodeos at the Astrodome and the field was not level in some areas. I had to hobble off the field. It happened in the first half. I spent the rest of the second half in the locker room soaking my ankle. It was distressed, wondering how bad is this, what is going to happen, is this going to end my career...? It was only my second season. I don't necessarily say that was sad, like somebody dying. Actually, the saddest part of my career was when I broke my leg in 1983 and had surgery on it in 1984. It got infected and I missed all of 1984. I was trying to come back in 1985 and was still in a lot of pain. I came to the realization that my career might be over. I was sad to come to that realization.

- **What was the most memorable game during your career in your mind?**

Other than Red Right 88, I think the Monday Night game against the Dallas Cowboys in 1979. We were both 3-0 coming into the game or 4-0, but we were both undefeated. It was a huge game. I remember driving into the stadium that night from home and everybody was talking about it on the radio. It was almost on every station you tuned in. Everybody was psyched; it seemed like the whole town was pumped for the game. The game began and we jumped out to a two-touchdown lead. My best recollection was sitting on the sideline, after a defensive series, the offense is out on the field. I was catching my breath and looking up. In the players that were standing up there was a gap, and I could see a pass play was underway. Ozzie Newsome was running down field while looking up. It was a forty-yard pass and he was looking back over his shoulder. All of a sudden, the crowd became a little bit hushed because the ball was in the air and they were waiting in anticipation. He had two steps on Cliff Harris, and I could see right through this little gap, the ball just nestled right down into his hands and he stepped across the goal line. The place exploded. It was one of the greatest thrills I can remember from a crowd at Cleveland Stadium.

- **How did you break your leg? How did it affect your career?**

It effectively ended my career. It happened in the sixth game of the regular season in 1983. It was a pass play. We were playing the New York Jets and Bruce Harper, running back for the Jets, had caught a little toss over the middle. I was coming in on the tackle and Clay Matthews was coming in on the tackle from the side. I hit him high and Clay hit him low, but Clay's body also came in against my left leg, which was planted firmly. Basically, the force of him coming into my leg pivoted my whole body over the top of him but my leg stayed in the ground. So, my body acted like a wedge and broke the fibula in my left leg. I didn't hear anything snap, but I could feel my ankle inside the tape puff up immediately. The tape felt like it was so tight on my ankle, all of a sudden, and before it had felt comfortable. I knew something was wrong. I had to be helped off the field. I don't think I could have hopped off on one leg. They x-rayed it and didn't see a break right away. They moved the x-ray up higher and found a break. I thought I would have surgery and they would fix it. They had done that a couple other times with other players. They decided not to operate, but decided to set it in a cast and see if it would heal by itself; which it did. That may have been an error because had they opened it up and done some internal fixation instead of using a cast, it would have healed quicker. By immobilizing the leg for a long time, it allowed bone spurs to form and it screwed up the ankle. I had to have another surgery to get rid of the bone spurs and that is what got infected. I believe if I would have had surgery right after the break, I would have avoided the other surgery and not had an infection. I would have probably been able to play in 1984. Instead, I missed all of 1984 and by the time I tried to come back a year later in 1985, I was still having a lot of pain in my ankle. I really couldn't move at all. I would be hard pressed to be competitive in a touch football game, let alone play professionally. The problem was, when I had the infection in the ankle, it had eaten away all of the cartilage in the joint. So, I basically had bone rubbing on bone and it was excruciatingly painful every day with every step. I eventually did have to have that joint fused. They took a bone from my hip and put it in my ankle and screwed it together, and let it all grow together. I don't have a working ankle joint, but I don't have the level of pain I had back then.

- **What kind of hazing went on when you were a rookie?**

We had to sing; we had to put on a rookie show. The rookie show usually happened the last day or the next to last day of training camp. We had to put on a show for the veterans. We had to make up skits that would make fun of coaches or of players, etc. I thought we did a pretty good job. We made fun of Dick Modzelewski, Walt Corey, and Mike Phipps, who was the quarterback then. I remember that skit because Henry Hynosky from Temple was Mike Phipps. He imitated Mike Phipps by taking antiperspirant and spraying it on the side of his head, which would make it look like he had gray streaks in his hair, because Phipps did. They had all of these guys pretending like they were in the desert dying for water and they are crawling toward this glass of water on the table and Hynosky comes in and is pretending he is Phipps. He walks over top of all of these players and walks on top of their backs. He walks over to the glass of water on the table, then takes a comb out of his back pocket, dips it in the water, and combs his hair.

- **Are players worth their salary? Should they be more fan conscious?**

I think they should be more fan conscious. That makes more sense from a PR standpoint. When you have teams that aren't as successful as they would like to be, it is better to have a type of connection with the fans where they know you from a personal meeting or face-to-face. They carry a different opinion of you in that regard and it helps. When you win, they are even happier for you as they are for the team. As far as the salaries go, everything is relative. Like I said, we made a lot more than guys like Lou Groza and Marion Motley, but it was all relative considering the economy in the rest of the country. I always felt if the owners only knew I would play this game for half the salary, but I wouldn't let them know that. I don't know if there are many guys these days you could say that about. Would they still be playing the game if you cut their pay in half? There are guys that don't seem to put the team first. There are a lot of guys out there that think the letter "I" is in "team." I think it is the hype the league gets overall now from the media. The whole world seems to be so celebrity conscious. Sports figures have always been celebrities, like one step down from a Hollywood movie star. In some cases, maybe even greater than a Hollywood star, but there is that whole idol-worship thing that is just rampant. I think it is a bad thing, because it is part of our culture emphasizes a rapid rise, rags to riches, but without any work to get there. We focus on the end result, and everybody forgets what it takes to accomplish something like a career in the NFL. We still live in a country where you need to earn a living and earn your position.

- **Would Tim Couch, who didn't interact with the fans, have been a better player if he had been more fan conscious?**

If they were more fan conscious, more involved with the fans, then even a bad performance sometimes would be forgiven. I know a lot of the times fans don't know everything going on, they couldn't possibly know the level of preparation a player has to have, or what he was supposed to be looking for when fans see a guy out of position. You have to understand that as a player and realize all the fans don't know it really wasn't your guy that scored that touchdown. You can't get mad at them for that. You've got to understand that it is part of being mature. Some guys aren't mature and they are still looking at this like everybody owes them a living and nobody should criticize them, or how dare they criticize them. The player says they (the fan) don't know anything, and I don't need to get close to them because they don't know anything. A lot of fans know a lot more than you think they know. They just want to be a part of it.

- **Is the game today like it was when you played?**

I watched the Browns/Eagles game from the sideline ten years after I had retired. Coach Bill Belichick let two alumni players stand on the sidelines each home game. Lou Groza and myself were chosen for the Eagles game. I couldn't believe after ten years of not standing on the sideline how violent the game is. How fast it is and how severe some of the collisions are. It was almost to the point where I was incredulous I had ever played this game. I thought the difference between even a normal guy being in shape and being able to go out there and do that was night and day. Anybody from the general public who thinks they can play because they are in shape is still not even close to being in football shape. Nobody knows how hard players work out, how long they work out. After that first week of camp, you would be ready to quit because every muscle in your body would be sore. You cannot work out and get used to hitting. You can't do anything to condition yourself for the collisions. It is a world of difference and it is something difficult.

- **Do you still feel like you are part of the Browns Organization?**

Yes, and that is because I think the Browns make an effort to keep us involved. The fans will always want to remember you. The fans will not let you forget. They know the past and the experiences that were part of your life because it was part of their life, too. It was an enjoyable part of my life. It was a labor of love.

- **What is your job today and how do you prepare for it?**

I am the judge of the General Division of the Court of Common Pleas in Cuyahoga County. That means I have countywide jurisdiction over all felony and civil cases assigned to my docket. I have a docket of probably close to five or six hundred civil and criminal cases and an additional three to four hundred foreclosure cases, which are handled separately. It is a treadmill every time I go into work in the morning because we follow the airline overbooking policy. We have five cases set for trial and we have ten to fifteen cases set for pre-trial on any one given day. It is a constant battle of juggling that schedule, trying to find parties that are going to plea or settle their case. Then getting a jury up and a trial going for the ones who want to have their cases heard. A lot of the preparation is quick; it is on the fly. So, it is a lot of thinking on your feet and handling things, personalities, and people on a rapid basis. It was a good pre-cursor to have a sports career and good preparation to be a defensive player, where you had to react to everything. You didn't necessarily have your whole game plan set, you had to guess what the other side was going to do, and then react to what they actually did. That is what my day is every day, but I really enjoy it. It is a challenge. I am taxed in using every ounce of legal knowledge I acquired over the seventeen years before I became a judge. I enjoy it though.

- **Do you have a law degree?**

Yes. I actually started in law school in 1982 when we went on strike. The 1982 players strike lasted fifty-seven days, and I had enrolled in law school prior to the strike. School was to prepare for what possibly could be a career-ending injury that could happen anytime. Basically, I was setting up a "Plan B" while I was still playing. I didn't know I would have to put it in place so soon. The strike happened on September 20th, and I believe the first day of classes was September 21st of the same year I had enrolled in law school and was accepted. I was in class the first day and we returned to work right before Thanksgiving. I had to drop a few classes so I wouldn't hurt my GPA. It took me longer to do it that way, but I enrolled in night school and started piecemealing back into the courses I had dropped. I eventually graduated in 1987, which was two years after I had retired from football. I went to work for a couple different law firms over a seventeen-year period. I was asked if I would want to be considered for an appointment to become a common plea judge because a judge was retiring. I said I would consider it, and all the sudden the next thing I knew I was the guy being appointed by the Governor.

- **Ever disqualified yourself from a trial due to knowing someone?**

Nothing sports-related thus far, but there have been one or two other matters I had when my old law firms were involved and I had to excuse myself from those. The one case that came up with the guy running out on the field was handled by a friend of mine, Judge Joan Synenberg, at the municipal court level. People didn't understand because they wanted him to go to prison, but the maximum you can get on a charge like that is six months in jail with a $1000 fine. It is hard to justify a jail sentence when the guy has no prior record. Judge Synenberg devised a probationary term for this guy who had gotten a lot of publicity. He couldn't watch the Super Bowl because he had to serve a three-day jail sentence over the Super Bowl weekend. He is not allowed to attend a Browns game for five years. The national media had a field day with that, asking where the punishment was in not having to attend a Browns game.

- **What did you get out of your NFL experience?**

I had a lot of good times and met a lot of great people. I learned a lot about life, because the NFL is like a microcosm of life. You learn about cooperating with people, giving an effort to achieve something positive, working together, and even the sacrifice and pain is all worthwhile when you achieve that common goal together. When you achieve a goal together, it is worth the sacrifices of ninety degrees in training camp, having your legs feel like lead, getting up at six in the morning, and all that stuff. When you are in the locker room celebrating a successful season with your teammates, it is the greatest feeling in the world.

Dick Ambrose									
Linebacker 1975-1983									
Virginia									
				Defense					Total
Season	Team	Game	Sacks	Int	Yds	Avg	TD	Fumbles	Points
1975	CLE	14		0	0	0	0	0	0
1976	CLE	10	not	0	0	0	0	0	0
1977	CLE	14	kept	0	0	0	0	0	0
1978	CLE	16		2	46	23	0	0	0
1979	CLE	15		1	0	0	0	0	0
1980	CLE	16		0	0	0	0	0	0
1981	CLE	16		1	0	0	0	0	0
1982	CLE	9		1	0	0	0	0	0
1983	CLE	6		0	0	0	0	0	0
Career		116		5	46	9.2	0	0	0

Judge Dick Ambrose walking in a parade

Bernie Kosar & Dick Ambrose

19

Clay Matthews

Defensive linebacker and offensive guard stand opposite, staring at each other over that imaginary plane called the line of scrimmage. Each prepares to explode from a position they have trained for months to defend. The offensive guard grinds his teeth, anticipating the train wreck that is about to happen in order to protect his field general. The defensive linebacker flexes his hands, tenses his body like a bull preparing to charge a matador. The linebackers target is the quarterback and the guard is in his way. The snap is called, the center perfectly positions the ball in the quarterback's hands. In unison, the offensive line crouches to form a pocket of protection to give the quarterback time to hone in on his receiver. With the quickness of a leopard and the strength of a lion, the linebacker aggressively hits his opposition, trying to maneuver himself to the backfield. As the guard is wittingly trying to anticipate the linebacker's moves, a fury of arms and legs entwine, helmets and shoulder pads clash, and each player is performs his duties as he had been trained to do his entire football career—teachings that began in Pee-Wee football and were perfected to this very day. They have seen each other on different sides of the field for a long time and have served long tenures with their respective teams. Yet, this specific time happens to be in Cleveland's Municipal Stadium, where the Cleveland Browns are taking on the Houston Oilers. The offensive guard is future Pro Football Hall of Famer for 2007 Bruce Matthews, and the defensive tackle is All Pro Linebacker Clay Matthews. It just so happens these two players are brothers who have played opposite each other since high school. Both hold records for the most games played in a career for their respective teams. Clay was nominated to the Pro Football Hall of Fame, but has never made the final cut.

- **What was it like the first time you walked onto the field as a Cleveland Browns player?**

I can't remember the first time, but it was great every time. The locker room was a fair distance away and you would come out of this long, dark, dank tunnel. Then you would come up out of the first base/dugout side. There were a few light bulbs hanging, and you would come out, and the second the fans saw those orange helmets, you would start to hear that noise, sense the energy. I remember there was one game I had the flu and thought, "There is no way I can play. I'll go in and do the best I can." Go down the tunnel, pop my head out, and all of sudden *BAM* you hear that noise and it was about twenty-one degrees. That cold wave hit me and I heard that noise. I played the whole game and felt great afterwards. Definitely the noise was one of the magical experiences of that old stadium. The transition from the locker room, it was a little small and wasn't appointed that well. You go down the tunnel. That thing smelled like you were in a swamp, but when you came out, those fans would hit you with that noise and you were ready.

- **When did you decide you wanted to be a professional football player?**

Oh, as long as I can remember. My dad played professional football; he played for the San Francisco 49ers for three years over a five-year span—two years he went into the Airborne (Airborne forces are military personnel set up to be moved by aircraft into battle zones). Playing professional football was something I wanted to do, because of him.

- **Did any one person inspire you to play football?**

Well, I would have to say it was my dad. It wasn't anything he went out of his way to do and say, "You're going to become a football player;" it was just the way he carried himself and the fact I grew up a football fan.

- **So you had a lot of good parental influence?**

Oh, yes. Really the strength of me as a player, with some people its size and speed, talent. All the things that kept me around a long time were instilled by my family, which was to be prepared, show up to work on time, bring effort, apply yourself, become professional about being a football player. Do your best all the time.

- **Isn't that the thought instilled in people at that time?**

You have that of every generation, but I certainly think it was a little more distinct at that time. Maybe that is a little old fashioned, but you still run into folks that are doing that, but it takes self-accountability to be responsible for what you do. Take the good with the bad. Just show up, show up on time, and be ready to go. It is pretty simple, but I think it works.

- **Who was your favorite team and players as you were growing up?**

It would have been the San Francisco 49ers. Since my dad played for the 49ers, I grew up a 49er fan. I pulled for them, I was a big-time fan. Favorite player? Well I don't know, I was just a fan of the game. I loved to watch it. Don't know if there was one specific player.

- **Where did you play high school football?**

I played two years in Southern California at Arcadia High School and then my senior year my family moved to Chicago and I played at New Trier East High school on the North shore of Chicago.

- **Did you have influence from both of your coaches?**

I had outstanding coaches. I was fortunate to have two long-time coaches I revered. The one I had in California, Coach Dick Salter, he coached at many high schools, specifically at Arcadia and was one of those guys who probably coached thirty years, if not more. Fabulous character, hard work type of guy, players still talk about him. Then I was fortunate when I moved to Chicago and played for Gene Jacowski, who had played in the Canadian Football League and the NFL. He was the same type of guy, an outstanding educator and coach who served young men for a long time. Both of them were not only good coaches but good men who taught their players about doing the right thing and being professional and responsible in how they approach the game. I was very lucky to have those two coaches.

- **Who was your college coach at Southern Cal?**

I had John McKay for two years and then John Robinson for two years. Those are two pretty good coaches.

- **What kind of affect did they have on your life and your play?**

The college coaches were not as instrumental but I think with what my family instilled and the high school coaches, I was pretty goal-oriented once in college. They provided a forum along with a lot of other good players to get after it, I certainly enjoyed playing there.

- **Picked in the first round; the Browns had a good year, didn't they?**

Yes, we did! We had two first-round picks that year and they were looking for a tight end and a linebacker and they took me and Ozzie Newsome. It ended up being a couple pretty sound picks for the Browns. I remember there were a lot of players who had stayed around. The team was in transition and it was a team that was playing around .500 as we built towards the 1980 team. I would like to think the draft had something to do with that.

- **What was it like playing for Sam Rutigliano?**

I really enjoyed that. He brought an enthusiasm to the game. I really had not had a coach like that. I had these quieter coaches, who played it a little closer to the cuff, and then Sam had all these jokes and sayings and created an energy about the team. It was a nice change and good to be exposed to. He certainly took a team that had been floundering around .500 and within two years put us on the edge of going to the Super Bowl. I really enjoyed him. He was a good man and did a fine job in the football department. I really enjoyed having him as my coach.

- **What was it like to have a song written about your team?**

It was great playing in Cleveland. The people in California don't know the passion the Browns fans have for that team. Generally, in that part of the country, in Cleveland, there aren't as many distractions as there are in Southern California. Since people were leaving Cleveland in the late 70's and early 80's, northeast Ohio kind of "retooled" itself from a rubber and steel industry to different types of industries. Most of the people who lived there had been there a while and their grandparents watched the Browns, their parents were Browns fans. When you come out to the Atlanta's and the Houston's and the LA's, these people had come here within one or two generations and didn't really have that same die-hard affiliation with their team. That really appreciated over time, to have a community that cared about the team that much.

- **What was it like playing for Marty Schottenheimer?**

It was good. He actually taught me a lot about defense. He was very professional, he was a more stoic coach and he certainly built that team. Sam got it up and going, then we floundered a little bit in the early to mid-80's and Marty took it and really made a good run with it through '88 and '89. We were in two AFC Championships and knew you were going to be prepared with him. We were a very professional, well-rounded organization.

- **If he would've picked an offensive coordinator, would he have stayed?**

I am not entirely sure what happened there. I know Marty felt he had done a good job, which he certainly had. I don't know if the management or ownership wanted to change a few things. They don't exactly keep us in the loop. I don't know if they wanted him to fire some people he felt had done a good job. All I have ever heard is just speculation and I have never asked.

- **He's knocked on the door of the Super Bowl several times, hasn't he?**

Well, look at Bill Cowher, it is the same thing. You don't appreciate knocking on it until you are six and ten, or seven and nine and not in the hunt.

- **What was it like playing for Bud Carson?**

Well, we had a good year in 1989. We were a mature team, and he added some new wrinkles and we got some things out of it. Unfortunately, the team was aging and the team was really in need of an overhaul. We may have gone one or two years too long and that lead to 1990, which was not a good year.

- **What was it like playing for Jim Shofner?**

I think he was around a short time. A lot of the old players were gone. Coaches were trying to find new players and they were hard to find. That was a quick turn around there.

- **How was Bill Belichick?**

As far as a talent evaluator, organization and managing the team, he was outstanding. I never had any problems with him. I thought he was an outstanding coach. He probably needed a little polishing as far as dealing with the Cleveland market. To its credit, the Cleveland market is such an interesting market. They want to be involved with the team. They want to know what is going on. Bill came from New York, which was different. He did a lot of good things as far as turning that team around. Bill has prepared New England, he got the team on course to compete for the Super Bowl for years to come. It went bad with the fans and the media as Bill wasn't media friendly. It was a tough situation. But, as far as getting his players prepared, being prepared, having an eye for talent, he was without a peer.

- **Art Modell took the Cleveland Browns out of Cleveland. What do you think about that? Was it good? Was it bad?**

There are about six sides to that question. He, to his credit, always wanted to win and was always willing to put resources towards winning. I think he would let people "in his ear" and got pulled in the wrong direction by people who perhaps did not have absolute clarity on how to win and win consistently in the NFL. But, he always wanted to win and I give him the benefit of the doubt for that. There were a lot of guys who were content to run it as a business and take their profit and move on. He was felt compelled to win, so for that alone he deserves his kudos.

- **How heartbreaking was it though to see Cleveland go to Baltimore?**

I remember I was in Atlanta at the time, when I saw it come out on a news conference. I was in the weight room. Players come and go, and know you are going to be moved and accept it. I remember thinking about all the people I ran into in Cleveland who were heartbroken. It was a tough situation. I felt for all the people who weren't involved on a day-to-day basis but who supported the Browns as all the players came and went. I remember thinking they must have been devastated and, of course, they were.

- **What players did you enjoy playing with?**

All of them. Probably the highlight is the relationships you build or had with other players. The beauty of that is you had guys brought in from all socioeconomic classes, all areas of the country and everything was based on teamwork and production. There were no political agendas. Plus, when you put guys under a little bit of pressure it forms bonds. I really enjoyed all of my teammates.

- **When you ask players from the 1960's who was a team leader, they say Jim Houston, in the 70's, Doug Dieken, and for the 80's, they say Clay Matthews. You led the defense. What made that happen?**

I wasn't one of those guys who went around trying to be a leader. I was just trying to be professional, which was the best way I found to prepare. Be professional in how you play football. Your preparation, your weight lifting, how you practice. I think when people look around and it wasn't just me, when a young guy comes in and says, "I like this job, I would like to stay in it a few years." Why does Clay Matthews play for X number of years? Or Hanford Dixon or somebody else? They look at those players and they prepare. They see they work hard on the little things they do on defense or they look at a Frank Minnifield. All of these guys had gone through that process. They come in as a bright-eyed rookie who was happy to be there and a guy who realized, although there was no guarantee, I will be here a long time. The best chance I have is to be professional and work my rear end off. I think young guys come in to camp and see that.

- **Sports announcers say Ohio State/Michigan is the greatest college rivalry and Pittsburgh/Cleveland is the greatest rivalry in professional football. Tell me about your experiences.**

Well, USC/Notre Dame isn't a bad rivalry…[laughs]…but the Pittsburgh/Cleveland game though is a tremendous game. When I went back there, they were in the midst of their four Super Bowls, now they have five, and they were "the" team. When we played in Pittsburgh, it was hostile, and when they came to Cleveland, it was hostile. A lot of times, a team becomes "America's team," like when the Steelers were winning. You would have thought there would have been some fans who converted over, but not in Northeast Ohio. Steelers came into Cleveland, it was a hostile area.

- **Who was your nemesis on the field; who gave you the most trouble?**

Oh, all of them…[laughs]…well, one guy I really respected was Earl Campbell. He came in at the same time and was a physical running back. There weren't many like him. Unfortunately, that kind of style cut his career down quickly, but he was a guy you not only had to worry about missing him, but you had to worry about him running you over.

- **Did you ever encounter any "negatives" while you were playing?**

You know, none that I can think of. There was pressure to perform or you would lose a teammate. All in all, it was a great experience. To have a job where people are interested in your product makes it exciting. Obviously, you get paid a little more than the norm, which helped a little bit.

- **You came on when players started getting paid a little bit more?**

Yes. Towards the end of my career, it started to change a little bit. It had always been more than the norm, but it was two or three times in the beginning, but in the end it was multiples. It always keeps building.

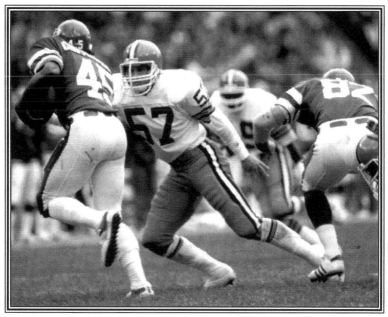

Clay Matthews getting ready to make a tackle against a New York Jets player

- **On that same topic, should players be more "fan" conscious today?**

Well, to a degree, it is part of being nice to people. With the internet, cable, you are under a microscope more than you were twenty-five years ago. So, yes, everything you do is going to end up on video. We use to have three major networks and now you have several.

- **Do you still feel like you are part of the Browns organization?**

No, but I don't feel left out either. I just feel like they are running their business. Obviously, if I go back there and walk into the stadium, I am going to have pride because I played there and I am going to pull for the team. My kids still pull for them and I still pull for them. It was a great chapter in my life, but you've got to turn the page.

- **Would you explain your family history at USC?**

Well, my dad actually went to Georgia Tech. We moved out here (California) and ended up going to USC. My brother went and my oldest son played down there, and my middle son is playing down there right now. He is on the kickoff and punt team and was on the National Championship Team, and was on the team that lost to Texas there at the end. We've enjoyed watching him play. *(In 2008, Clay Matthews Jr. was a starting linebacker for USC and played up to his father's standards all year long. He ended up playing as an All Pro for the Green Bay Packers.)*

- **You played 232 games at Cleveland, the most games played by one player. Does that mean anything to you?**

235

It seems like a lot [laughs].... I enjoyed playing them. I enjoyed competing. Getting out there, getting after it, and trying to make a few plays. It was always fun at least ninety-nine percent of the time. Every now and then you would have a bad back or something and you would have to punch your way through it, but ninety-nine percent of the time it was a blast.

- **You also have 76.5 sacks, which is a Cleveland record.**

Yes, I liked that. It was like scoring a touchdown for a defensive player.

- **You also have two touchdowns, can you tell us about those?**

Oh, yes—they were both against the Steelers [laughs].... One was when I picked up a fumble and rolled into the end zone. The other one I intercepted a pass and ran it back about thirty-five yards. One was at Pittsburgh, and the other was at Cleveland Stadium.

- **Are Cleveland Browns fans the best in the NFL?**

From my perspective, I would say yes. All the fans throughout the Northeast part of the country, you go from New England all the way down, Philadelphia, wrap it on around through Chicago, those folks definitely pull for their teams. The rest of the country had a little later growth, and there are too many other things to do in the Sun Belt. But, definitely Cleveland. You know, if you went into the grocery store on Monday, they would ask you, "Hey, what happened here during this play?" There are players, who may think that is a pain in the neck, but you go to a team that doesn't have that history, they would miss it.

- **What was it like playing against your brother for so many years?**

That was exciting, and the fact he was in our division we got to play twice a year. It always made for a great game regardless of the scores or ending.

- **What is the saddest thing to happen while you were playing?**

A player leaving was always tough. When you were a relatively young man and you have these dreams of playing and you see some leave that was always tough. That happened fast so they weren't around very long.

- **What do you do today?**

I do a little real estate developing and I am actually a coach at a local high school. I am the defensive coordinator.

- **Do you remember Lance Mehl?**

Yes. I went to a Pro Bowl with him. Actually, I have his helmet sitting right here in front of me. When you go to the Pro Bowl, what you usually do is trade helmets, and I have his Jets helmet right here. He was a good player.

- **What are your hobbies today?**

Well, I have five kids so I am involved with them, plus coaching at the high school takes a lot of time. That pretty much eats my time up right there.

- **What did you get out of your NFL experience?**

You know, it was such an exciting career and I was so blessed to play as long as I did. I've got friends across the country. I've got memories of all those games. It is just a wonderful thing.

Clay Matthews shifting positions to move towards a tackle

"He was one of the greatest players to play the game. I remember, when I came to Cleveland, some people said he would never play, that he wasn't tough enough, that he was a great athlete but not a football player. Boy, nothing could have been farther from the truth. He had a standard of performance that was excellent, and he did it for an extended period of time. That's the portrait of greatness. He's one of the top three or four guys I have ever had the privilege of coaching."

—Marty Schottenheimer on Clay Matthews

Clay Matthews									
Linebacker 1978-1996									
Southern California									
Season	Team	Games	Defense					Fum	Total
			Sacks	INT	Yds	Avg	TD		Points
1978	CLE	15		1	5	5	0	0	0
1979	CLE	16		1	30	30	0	0	0
1980	CLE	14		1	6	6	0	0	0
1981	CLE	16		2	14	7	0	0	0
1982	CLE	2	0	0	0	0	0	0	0
1983	CLE	16	6	0	0	0	0	0	0
1984	CLE	16	12	0	0	0	0	0	0
1985	CLE	14	6	0	0	0	0	0	0
1986	CLE	16	1	2	12	6	0	0	0
1987	CLE	12	2.5	3	62	20.7	1	0	6
1988	CLE	16	6	0	0	0	0	0	0
1989	CLE	16	4	1	25	25	0	1	6
1990	CLE	16	3.5	0	0	0	0	0	0
1991	CLE	15	6.5	1	35	35	0	0	0
1992	CLE	16	9	1	6	6	0	0	0
1993	CLE	16	5.5	1	10	10	0	0	0
1994	ATL	15	1	0	0	0	0	0	0
1995	ATL	16	0	2	1	0.5	0	0	0
1996	ATL	15	6.5	0	0	0	0	0	0
Career		278	69.5	16	206	12.9	1	1	12
Season	Team	Other Stats							
1989	CLE	1 TD/Fum Rec							

Topps
Riddell
BROWNS
OLB
CLAY MATTHEWS

SOURCE: TOPPS

K
Clay Matthews
Linebacker, 1978-1993
57
Excellent linebacker named to four Pro Bowls; holds franchise record for most games played (232)
K

SOURCE: HEROES DECK

SOURCE: CLEVELAND BROWNS

20

Mike Baab

Look into the eyes of Mike Singletary and you see the intensity of a linebacker in the NFL. Look into the eyes of Mike Baab and you see that same intensity in an NFL center. Singletary played in the glamour position of a stand up linebacker, and most people have seen the pictures of him roaming the secondary, anticipating the offense coming in his direction. As an offensive center, no one saw Baab's eyes, except maybe the middle linebackers playing head's up. But, if they had, they would have seen the utter determination in his eyes. Mike knew his job was to first get the ball to the quarterback in a clean, quick, but efficient manner. Yet, after accomplishing the snap, his job was to also protect his field general and then open a hole for one of his many running backs. Quarterbacks like Brian Sipe, Paul McDonald, Bernie Kosar, Gary Danielson, Doug Flutie, Steve Grogan, and Mike Pagel all received snaps from this enthusiast in the center position. And few players from his offensive position got to the man he was protecting. Most will say centers in the NFL were efficient—however, Mike only accepted excellence.

- **What was it like the first time you walked on the field as a Brown?**

Well, I'll tell you, I was very fortunate that I played at a big college so I could handle eighty to ninety thousand people. I remember some of the guys I played with had never played in front of more than two or three thousand people. The little rookies would be just totally awestruck with their tongues hanging on the ground. I remember the part I liked most about it was that my dad was an orphan raised in Ohio and that was the only game he ever got to go to. They took all the little orphan kids up to the football game and he got to go to Cleveland Stadium and watch the Browns play some thirty years before. So, that was really cool for me to go to the place where my dad had gone, and plus the fact that it was a great old barn. It was a great place to play football because you could just smell the history in there.

- **When did you decide to be a professional football player?**

Actually, I never did. I was one of the fortunate that was just good at something. I had grown up my whole life planning on being a doctor and I was always a straight a kid, the kind who behaved because I had something that I wanted to do. I remember in seventh grade, we moved into a new neighborhood and the people there all played structured team football. We just played "kill each other in the yard." All the guys said, "Come play football because girls like football players." At that point, I didn't even like girls but I figured, what the heck, it'll be fun. So, in seventh grade I started, and I stunk. Then by eighth grade I was a starter; by ninth grade, I was playing for the high school. I was just lucky to be born big and strong. I was an instinctive football player. I just knew how to do it. So, somewhere around my junior year at the University of Texas, I started getting letters. The first letter was from the Cowboys, which, of course, being raised as a Texas kid, there's no greater honor than to get a letter from the Dallas Cowboys. That was probably my junior year because I was still planning to be a doctor.

- **Where were you born and raised?**

I was born in Fort Worth, Texas, and was raised in a little town called Euless. That is right between Dallas and Fort Worth.

- **Is that why you're back in Texas now? Is that your roots?**

Oh, absolutely. The one thing I liked about living in Ohio is that they have a tremendous amount of state pride. There's not a lot of that. I've been around a lot of states and most of them are not that way. But, Ohio had a tremendous pride. Texas does, too. If you're a Texan, you're a Texan forever. You always want to get back to Texas as fast as you can. And, my family is here. My wife was born and raised in Mexico and all of her brothers and sisters have moved into Texas, as well as her parents. We came back for family. Plus, the fact that at the time we moved back in 1996-1997, Austin, Texas, was the fastest growing city in the United States. So, there were abundant opportunities.

- **Who inspired you to be a professional football player?**

Again, because I never really planned on being one and it was just something I was good at, I think probably the thing that made me think, "Oh, my gosh, maybe I could do that," was the Cowboys' players. I grew up ten minutes from Irving Stadium where the Cowboys play and every Sunday our whole family got together to go over to Granny and Granddad's home because they had what they called a "Cowboy Antenna." They blacked out everything locally, but if you had this big, huge 30-foot antenna, you could get the Cowboy games. So, my granddad had a cowboy antenna and the only color television in the family. And everybody would go and we would get there two hours early, play tackle football in the street until the game, watch till half-time, go out at half-time and play tackle football in the street, and then come back after that to watch the rest of the football game. So, I think it was from watching people like Bob Lilly, Chuck Howley, and Roger Staubach. Growing up as a little kid in Texas, there probably wasn't a better job in the world, other than governor or president, than playing for the Dallas Cowboys.

240

- **Did you meet any players when you were younger?**

I was fortunate enough to meet alot of them. I remember my dad was in the Texas Air National Guard and when I was little, probably seven or eight, I met Bob Lilly and I thought, "Oh my God, that's probably the biggest man in the history of the world." But now, I look back at it and Bob was 6' 4" or 6' 5" probably weighed 250. But, he seemed like the biggest man I had ever met.

- **What kind of parental influence did you have?**

I was born with four brothers and I think we were all born over the span of about five years. I don't think my parents understood birth control very well for a while. So, we played in the yard. Every game we played was two-on-two tackle. We played a game called "Meat Chopper," where one kid tries to run across the yard. You had three tries against all your brothers. Including my cousins, I think there were fifteen boys in our generation. So, we had some pretty good games. My parents were the kind that, no matter what it took, they went to every game. They drove me to millions of practices. They bought me my first weight set. Whatever it took, our parents did it because they really, really enjoyed watching their boys play sports. My parents still say the most fun they ever had in their lives was when I played at Texas. They could get in the car and go every Saturday and watch the football game.

- **What kind of influence did your college coaches have on you?**

Whenever you're in high school, you tend to be big enough and strong enough that you can just pretty much run over people and beat them up. I mean, technique and proper body position, things like that, really doesn't enter into it until all of a sudden you get to college and everybody else is big and strong, too. If you don't have the technique, you don't get it done. So, it's a combination of Coach Akers and then my offensive line coach. Coach Manley is about eighty-five, or I don't know how old he is now, but he's still out there kicking. He is the one who taught me about head position and body position and move your feet, the little tiny things of how you can really succeed. Take a big body, because every time I see a big huge person, they all think the same thing. They all think they can play on the offensive line. Well, they're wrong. The number one thing that makes an offensive lineman is talent. But, number two is technique. With technique, a lesser man can beat a better man all day long.

- **Who do you think is one of the best linemen in the game right now?**

Well, I really don't watch football too much, so I'm not much of a help on that. I know that the big guard who just got cut by the Cowboys was really good for a long time, Larry Allen. He is enormous, so he could play really high. He could do things the rest of us couldn't do because, if you don't weigh 360 pounds, you better drop your butt if you're going to block a 360-pound guy. So, I was really impressed with Larry Allen for a long time but I really don't watch it well enough to tell you.

- **Have you lost interest in the game since you left it?**

Oh, yes, completely. By the time I was done with football, I was done. Probably the most I ever watched football was this year (2006) because my college won the National Championship. I still didn't go to a single game. I have moved on to other things.

- **What are those other things now?**

Well, my family is number one. I have two beautiful girls, fourteen and nineteen (2007). Same wife, Lolis, I've had the whole time, which makes me unique in the world of football. I compete in a sport called Scottish Heavy Athletics. I am one of those people that when I got out of football, I lost a bunch of weight, started jogging, played basketball, and then I played racquetball. I'm a pretty obsessive person and my wife says I'm "psychotically-physically obsessed." I was fortunate enough about three or four years ago that I found this one great sport for an offensive lineman because it's about two things. It's about power and technique.

- **What year were you born?**

1959.

- **Did you ever play in any of the NFL competitions like they have today? They started right around your era.**

Well, they don't invite offensive lineman to things like that. But we did some fun stuff. I remember one time we played a touch football game against the Steelers. No, they just didn't have stuff like that for offensive linemen. We did have a traveling basketball team. We had a lot of fun with that. That was a blast.

- **And that's fun, isn't it?**

Absolutely, it's all the marvelous things that come from football, you know, being a special person, being treated special because you can knock people down, which is sort of a silly thing. But, anyway, that's the way it works. Glad it does. About the end of my career, Bernie Kosar couldn't go to the grocery store. It would turn into a mad house, things like that. That gets old in a hurry. I pretty much tried to be as patient as possible with people because I remember standing in line to get Walt Garrison's autograph one time and I remember being on the other side of the table. The only thing that ever got me was drunken adults. I mean, if some wasted guy comes up and throws his arms around you and breathes booze in your face and says, "Oh my God, I love the Cleveland Browns," I will make that person get away from me. Other than that, it was just fun, fun, fun from the beginning and anybody that complains about being a professional athlete needs to be slapped across the head a couple of times until they wake up. People are different. The team doctor for the Browns was John Bergfeld, who is a fabulous doctor.

He worked on me five times. When I won the world championship in my sport last year, the first thing I did was call Dr. Bergfeld and said, "Brother, my knees still work, my right hand you surgically repaired still works, and everything is just fine." I thanked him and we started talking and we did a little emailing back and forth, and one of the things that stuck with me was he said, "You were extremely fortunate to play when you did because the game is very different now. The players are much more self-centered and maybe it's just because there's more at stake. I don't know." But, he said there is much less camaraderie and a whole lot more "me, me, me." That's also a symptom of free agency. I mean, when I played, you were pretty much with that team unless they traded you or cut you. It's not that way anymore. Now it's, "Who's got the most money?"

- **I read where he called you a warrior. Why was that?**

Because I was too stupid to stay off the field. Big Daddy (Carl Harrison's nickname) was lying on the ground, and I tripped over him and hurt my left knee and tore my meniscus. I knew I had done it because I had done it before. But, it was one of the things that comes and goes, so I let it come and go for a long time, and then it flipped up in training camp or something happened that I can't remember, and I went and got it fixed. Well, by that time, it had been hurting me for so long that it was a relief to get it fixed because it didn't hurt any more. So, I'm out there practicing within two days, and they're making this big deal out of it, you know, the "tough Texan" and all that junk, but really if anyone has torn a meniscus, you know that arthroscopic surgery might be the best thing that's ever happened to you because it kills the pain. All of a sudden, you look really tough, but in truth, you're really relieved because the pain is gone. Danny Fike, one of my teammates is like that. Poor Danny has had two hips done and about to have a knee done.

- **What was it like to play for Sam Rutigliano?**

The best thing about Sam, I was very fortunate because I caught the "Cardiac Kids" at the tail of their careers. Sipe was there, Dieken was there, DeLeone, Reggie Rucker, Logan, the list of all those hero guys who I knew nothing about because I was playing college football in Texas and was not a football fan. When I heard I got drafted to the Browns, someone said, "What division are they in?" and I didn't know. That shows you how out of touch I can be about football. I know some people like Chris Spielman (Detroit Lions-Ohio State Linebacker) and like my buddy Bob Golic who lives and breathes football. I mean, it just seeps into their every pore. Actually, it was never that way for me. So, anyway, I remember getting drafted and then going to these guys and I did some real quick research. First of all, my dad was very pleased because I was going to Ohio. I had aunts and uncles all over the place, I was going back to his town, I spoke to his elementary school, his middle school, and his high school. Now, I got to do lots of neat things in connection with my father. But, I was just really lucky to walk in at a time when the only negative aspect was that whole "inner circle" thing that had broken out like two months before I got drafted and I remember sitting in training camp and it seemed like every other day we would have a drug counselor come in and talk to us. And they just went on and on about it, and I'm looking around like why the heck are they talking about this so much. I'm a kid from Texas and I may drink a beer, but that's about it. It's like finally, I woke up to what was going on and looked around. But the best thing about Sam, who cares about the records of football, was he created things like the "inner circle." He saved some people's lives. Sam was a good man and, in football, there are good men, but they will tell you a lie in a heartbeat to keep their job because it's the nastiest business in the world. That's just the way it is. All professional sports are like that. Who's got the gold makes the rules. That's the Golden Rule. Sam was an excellent man. I loved him. I thought he was a great guy. The only negative feeling I ever had with Sam the whole time was we were going to play "Pittspuke" and we hadn't won there in fifteen years or something like that. They had been talking trash about us in the paper, like they always did. They were sort of stupid at that kind of thing. We wanted to kill these bastards. Just before the game, Sam is giving us this speech and that's when he did the, "Guys, there are sixteen million Chinamen who don't give a damn about what happens in this football game and I just want to let you know that I love you very much." We all looked at each other like, "What?" Tell us to go out and rip their heads off. But that's the only negative thing I had with Sam and that he was just a really good, nice man. He didn't have that nasty, "let's go kill those buggers" attitude. That was not his style. Marty, though, had it in spades. Let me tell you one story about Sam. Henry Bradley was a nose guard when I got there. Henry was from the Deep South, he had a very poor education, a nice guy, played five or six years in the league, so he came out way ahead. Anyway, Henry was sitting by me in a meeting and Sam gets up in front of us and he starts quoting Socrates and Plato really trying to help us and educate us and giving us this really great English major kind of speech. I remember Henry looked at me and said, "Who be Plato? Who'd he play for?" I started laughing in the meeting and Sam, of course, calls me out. "Mike what are you laughing at?" I said, "I ain't telling," but I did. I think that meeting room laughed for ten minutes. "Who be Plato?" All I had to do was walk up to one of my teammates and say, "Who be Plato?" and they'd laugh. Good old Henry, what a great guy.

- **You made the statement one time that after you beat Pittsburgh at Pittsburgh, the best drive during the whole game had to be the bus trip out of the stadium.**

Absolutely. Well, the thing was that we had come close a couple of years before to beating those guys. They really had the Browns number for a while there. But, it was always very nip and tuck. It was just hard to win in Pittsburgh. If you remember, there were a lot of people who had a lot of trouble winning in Pittsburgh during that span. But, anyway, we got really tired of the jinx thing. So, we flew in one year, we drove buses in the next year. We tried everything we could to break the jinx. So, this year we drove the buses in. We got there, and I think we beat them in the last seconds of the game. I can't remember what it was, but we did something great and we won in the last seconds where we silenced all those stupid terrible towels and all that. It was sweet. We beat them. We broke the jinx. And it is the kind of thing where when you run off the field you can hear sixty little Browns' guys going, "Yea, yea," and a whole stadium of silence. So, that's it. We go in and we get dressed up and packed up, it takes forever for a football team to get anywhere. So, after about an hour and a half we get on our buses, which were always down in the bowels of the stadium depending which team you played. You couldn't get too close to the fans because they'll spend all their time throwing stuff and spitting at you. So, anyway, when we come driving out, all 60,000 people that had gone to the game were still there. They had lined the whole exit, all the way out where we drive to get on the highway to head back to Cleveland, and I remember seeing about, well, if there were 60,000 people, I probably saw 100,000 middle fingers and I saw about twenty-five or thirty thousand bare asses. They were throwing beer bottles at the bus; it reminded me of some of the high school games we used to have when we would go into some very, very unfriendly places. And, of course, we had to find a way to get those bus windows down so we could salute them in return. It was excellent. I still love that.

- **In the years that you were with the Browns, the Browns' fans have the bad distinction of labeling some negative results from games like Red Right 88, The Drive, The Fumble, the Bottle Throwing Incident, the Rudd Penalty.. Tell us some stories about your association with some of these things, and what you think of the others.**

Well, remember, I played in New England for two years, back when the Sullivan's owned the team. And I have been to the armpit of football. I have been to the place where the fans hate the players. They hate the team and they come there, that is the difference. In New England, the fans came to the game so they could sit in the parking lot, get as drunk as possible, and boo the hell out of the Patriots. Then, there are the Browns fans that get to the game two hours early, get as drunk as possible so they can cheer for the Browns and cry for the Browns, if they have to. That's completely the difference. I never had a single problem with the Browns' fans. I remember one year we were 1-8, just before Sam got fired, and we stunk, we were really a bad football team in many ways. Bad to watch, boring to watch, not entertaining, the whole bit, and we still had 75,000 people in the stands. How could you possibly complain about those people? There is no complaint about them. The only problem I had with Browns' fans is when they throw those stupid dog bones in the field. I saw two guys blow their knees out, and several guys popped their groin, because they stepped on a stupid dog bone. Other than that, and that's just the excess of enthusiasm, I never had a single problem with Browns' fans ever. So, what if they get fired up because they care?

- **Are they the greatest fans in the NFL?**

Yes, they have to be, if not they're really close. I remember at the end of my career, I hooked on with Kansas City for four or five games and Kansas City is just like Cleveland. They just have better weather. They care there, too. It's a classy organization.

- **What was it like to play for Marty Schottenheimer?**

Well, Marty was completely different from Sam. I never had any trouble with Art at all. A lot of things happened with Art before I got there and after I left. When we were there, everybody loved Art because they won. The one thing that Art did, if you go back and look at Browns' history from as far back as I can remember, he had vacillated enormously between choosing a players-type coach or a beast. Between a, "I'm going to kill you all to get what I want," kind of coach and then a guy who is going to be your buddy pal and be sweet to you. I can't remember who the guy was before Sam, but he was a tough ass from what I hear from people like Dieken, then we go to Sam who probably was the nicest man that was ever head coach in football and then immediately *BAM*. Marty was completely the other way. Marty is extremely intense, doesn't pull any bones, used to cut people in the film room. Oh, yes, we would watch films on Monday and he'd say, "If you don't get two tackles on special teams next week, your butt is gone." And the next week he'd stand up, he'd turn the camera on and he'd say, "So and so, how many tackles did you get?" "Two, sir." "No, you didn't. You got one. Go pack your shit." He got your attention. In my first practices with Marty, was a Wednesday practice that lasted five hours. I mean, we actually filed a claim. Deacon was our rep and we filed a claim against the league because that's abusive. They can't do that kind of stuff to us. But anyway, they did. But, the most important thing is that we all knew Marty really cared. He used to cry on Wednesday. Before Pittsburgh, that Wednesday is the game plan day and he would stand up there and he could hardly talk he was so fired up. And that was cool. We all bought into Marty big. I bought completely into Marty. I never worked harder; I never did everything right more. I assumed a leadership role on the team because Marty asked me to do and things like that. That's why he's still working. The most important thing in football and professional sports is how long can you fool them into thinking you can do and Marty has been fooling them for an awfully long time.

- **You think he is fooling them?**

No, it's just something we used to laugh about as players. We'd say, "Are you still fooling them?" "Still fooling them" into thinking you can get it done. No, I don't think Marty is fooling them. The only problem Marty has ever had is that he is conservative. On defense, he is not conservative at all, but on offense, he was always heroically conservative. The only reason the Browns team lit everyone up in the mid 80s is because we had Lindy Infante running the offense. You need two good coaches. You need a good defensive coach. Actually, you need three, including a special teams coach, and you have to have an offensive coordinator. Lindy Infante is what made Bernie Kosar and the Cleveland Browns go on the offensive. Marty made the defense go. Marty was fired because Lindy Infante left and Marty took over the reins and tried to do the things that Infante, who was an offensive genius, could do. Marty did a good job and went back to the AFC Championship game.

- **After they got rid of Schottenheimer, do you think Linde Infante should have been the head coach?**

Infante, no, he was already at Green Bay.

- **How come he wasn't successful in Green Bay?**

Because he didn't have the players. It didn't make any difference how good your coach is or how good your scheme is, if you don't have any players, it doesn't make any difference. Look at Bud Carson. When Bud was in Philadelphia, they had the scariest defense in football because they had Reggie White and a whole bunch of other screamers. Well, if you come to Cleveland in 1990, you don't have any screamers; you have the worst defense in football, even if you're running the same design.

- **What was it like to play for Bud Carson?**

I loved Bud's coaching staff because, I mean, you talk about a bunch of guys that had been around football for a long, long, long time. Dan Radocovich was an experience all to himself, but they were fabulous coaches. The problem was that he had just inherited a team. Clay and Mike Johnson and someone else, our three linebackers stayed out all training camp because Raymond Clayborn had signed for a bunch of money. That team just blew itself to death. That was also during the era when coaches weren't picking the players. The players were being picked by Mike Lombardi. To my memory, Mike Lombardi never busted anybody in the chops and drove them in the ground. I remember we came in after cut day and the coaches would say, "Well, who's here?" because they were not involved in the decisions on talent. Now you tell me if that's a stupid ass way to run a football team. That's what happened to the Browns. That's what completely happened to the Browns.

- **What is your take on Art Modell before, during, and after you played?**

Oh, every check cleared. I never had a problem with Art. Why wouldn't Art leave Cleveland? They hated his guts. They burned him in effigy. They floated balloons in front of his lodge that said, "Jump, Art, jump." Then Baltimore offers him, to my understanding, the richest deal in the history of professional sports, and what are you going to do? You're going to go. Because, what is professional sports about more than anything? Television money. Art had an opportunity to take care of his family. You have to remember Art was not that wealthy of an owner. In comparison to people like Jack and Kent Cook (owners of the Washington Redskins), he didn't have a pot to pee in. I always liked Art, especially in the beginning, before the strikes. When I first got there, Art was at practice every day. And he would come up and shake everybody's hand. Everybody knew him and you would throw your arm around him. Then we had two strikes, and he didn't like the strikes. And that's when he stopped going to practices and got distant. Then he had people like Lombardi come in and whatever. All an owner can do is pick the guy who interviews the best and hope that he made the right choice. I mean, that's a pretty big decision.

- **You talked about Radokovich, the offensive line coach who came in.**

If you do some investigation into Dan Radokovich, he was probably one of the best offensive line coaches in the history of football. He coached the Steelers during all the years when they kicked our butt and when he came in, he had a very different way of coaching football. My other great offensive line coach was Howard Mudd, who is still working in the NFL and has worked there for thirty years. Obviously, he is fooling somebody very well. But, Bad Rad said there are three ways to play football. There is the right way, the wrong way and the "Rad" way. We're all going to learn the "Rad" way. He was a tough dog. Except for Belichick, he was probably the most profane, get in your face, and make you do it right person I ever met. But, I'll tell you what. He really helped my career. When you get to your sixth or seventh year, you think you know what you're doing. And it's always good to have someone walk in and say you don't know what you're doing, or do it this way, or why don't you? What he did was take my technique and fine focused it down to the point where I didn't get beat often. 1990, we stunk as a team. We were 3-13; we were the worst team in Browns' history and I had my best year. I played great and that was just part of having the right coach at the right time. If you go back and check out "Bad Rad," he is a hell of a coach.

- **What was it like to play for Bill Belichick? What is different now?**

Well, everybody says he's grown up and has really changed, and he's eased off and not such a psychotic. We used to call him "Doom," because everything was doom with him. He could walk by you in the hall and you could feel the evil waves of chill come off him. Really, it was that way in '91. I remember our first speech with him. For two hours he told us how bad we were and then he finished it up by saying, "I worked too long and hard to get where I am to let you guys 'blank' it up. Do you understand?" We all went, "Yeah." He said, "Okay, I'll see you at 6:30 in the morning, get ready to run." And he ran our guts out for two or three hours. I mean, making the Browns football team in '91 was the hardest thing I ever did because he ran the hardest training camp. The training camp in '91 with Belichick was probably harder as far as just as running sprints, lining up and running sprints, and lining up and hitting Michael Dean Perry in the face every day in the Oklahoma drill at least ten times. He crushed us so badly; we never had any legs. We never recovered and we finished 6-10 because he crushed us. The overwhelming attitude was, "You guys are pieces of shit and if you don't do it my way, I'll bring in more. Everybody who gets cut from the Giants can come over here and take your job." That's how it was. It was really ugly. It really was. I am very glad I got picked up by the Chiefs after I got cut by the Browns because I really would have hated to have left football with it that way. Now, they say everything is different, so obviously that's why he is winning. But, it was a challenge to play for him. Both our tackles retired because they hated Belichick. Cody Risen and Ricky Bolden were two very fine, Christian young men. Great guys, and he was so profane, so in your face attack dog mentality, they both said, "Screw this, I'm out." That's why we sucked. We lost both our tackles because the head coach drove them away.

- **What players did you enjoy playing with the most?**

Well, there were a number of them. Brian Sipe had more of that stand in the huddle and raise sparks kind of person. Bernie had some of it, but not as much as Brian. Brian was this little, bad, old, barely-can-run guy, but he had a heart bigger than all of Cleveland and the guys loved him. When I got there, those guys loved Brian Sipe. He was NFL MVP two years before and they just loved him to death. I remember standing in the huddle and just being so happy to be a part of that. Ozzie Newsome was a classy guy, I always loved Ozzie. We called him "Peanut Head" because he has a little bitty head. Everyone loved Ozzie. He always had the greatest hands of anybody I have ever seen in my life. He made catches in practice you couldn't believe. Dieken was fun. Dieken taught me how to hold. He changed my career. He said if your hands stink of armpit after the game, you had a great game. Bernie, of course, was maybe the smartest player I ever played with. He was the most prepared, smartest player. I enjoyed playing with Gary Danielson because he was very smart, too. He understood football. We always had fun with Cody Risien. We were both from the Southwest Conference, and everything we did was based on what we learned from drive blocking, run blocking schools, and when we got to the Browns, they did not run block. They ran sweeps to Pruitt and they threw the ball. Then, of course, Marty came in, and we completely changed it and all we did was thunder block for a while. So, Cody and I would butt heads constantly in a huddle. Danny Fike was my buddy for years. On defense, I always respected Clay Matthews. Clay Matthews was probably one of the most professional players I ever played with. Totally prepared and totally obsessed, he taught me so much about nutrition and fitness and things that I never knew anything about. Mike Johnson was like that, too. I loved Mike Johnson. I haven't seen him in ten years, but I'd run up and hug him if I saw him tomorrow. On other teams, Anthony Munoz didn't miss a block for six years. He was the best I ever saw on the offensive line. Then on defense, there was Reggie White who was scary. Reggie took two or three people to block and if you made him mad, he could tear your whole team apart. He was impressive.

- **Who were the team leaders?**

When I first got there, it was Dieken and Sipe, one-hundred percent, and maybe Clarence Scott on the defensive. Then, after they all left in the mid-80s, on offense, it was Ozzie, but he was a very quiet leader. Ozzie was not much for talking, but he was a leader by example and then Kosar and me. That was my offensive line and then on defense, it was GoBob (Bob Golic). GoBob was a big mouth who loved football, but Clay was also a very quiet player who was not a "rah, rah" guy. Mike Johnson turned into the leader when he got there. When he started in 1986, he became the mouthy guy.

- **Bernie Kosar had a very odd throwing technique that was very slow. He wasn't the best in the backfield, but there are a lot of people who say he was one of the best quarterbacks who ever played the game. Why was he like that?**

He played with his brains. Bernie was very smart. You have to give him a lot of credit because he realized very early that a quarterback can't come to his offensive lineman and kick him in the leg and say, "You need to block better, you bastard." That's the guy that could let you get your gizzard knocked out. So, Bernie was smart enough to have me as his liaison. He'd come to me and say, "Go talk to Paul Farren. Go help Paul out." What do we have to do? Go talk to so-and-so; go do this, do that. I was more of the mouthy person so that Bernie could stand over there and stay in the esoteric world of quarterbacks and do his thing, and then I took care of the rest. Bernie was just smart enough to realize that quarterbacks can't really get in peoples' faces. You can't because your life is owed to those people.

- **That was your leadership role?**

That was me; I was the one who stood in the huddle before we went down and scored against Denver. I stood and I slapped everyone across the head and looked at them and said, "Who wants to be a damned hero? It's time. It's right in front of us. We've got one shot; we've got however many yards it was…." I'm getting goose bumps talking about it. I said, "Who wants to be a hero?" I repeated it and repeated it until they started raising their hands. I think the first one was Webster Slaughter who said, "I'll do it." Then we got the whole thing together and went down there and scored points. Bernie never even came in the huddle until we had done this.

- **You said it was your offensive line.**

Yes, that was my offensive line, and that was the role that Marty had asked me to take. He said, "I can't have my quarterback yelling at people," and I said, "You betcha." In the beginning of my career, I was very fortunate because I played with a bunch of older guys and they could be the leaders. There isn't a better leader in life than Doug Dieken. Somebody had to pick up the reins and Marty asked me to do it. I relished it, it was great.

- **You take a lot of pride in that part.**

Well, if you're going to do something, do it with everything you've got, or why the hell are you doing it?

- **You and Greg Pruitt are talking the same way.**

I don't say anything against those other schools, those are fine rivalries. I grew up a Cowboy fan, so I grew up hating the Steelers. I mean, it was easy to hate the Steelers. When I came to Cleveland, it was like, "Oh well." I already hated those bastards for years, no problem. But we had the same kind of thing with Oklahoma. If you went to OU, I don't like you. That's it, I don't like you. You're not my friend.

- **Did you and Pruitt get along well?**

Remember, I didn't play with Greg because he had been traded to the Raiders about two weeks before I ever got there. But, I know him well and I've actually gone on trips with him and it was all in the past. We didn't talk about it. Like Cody and I are some of the greatest buddies in the world, but he went to A&M and I went to Texas. We just don't talk about it.

- **Explain a little about the Pittsburgh/Cleveland rivalry at the game level.**

Pittsburgh was a little like Cleveland in that they would actually pick people and leave them there for a long time. Most teams don't do that. The thing about Pittsburgh that made it different was with Chuck Noll their attitude was I'm going to kick your butt. I'm going to line up in front of you and you know where I am going to be all day long. I'm not going to come out of a bunch of funky places, like Bill Cowher does now (Cowher retired as the Steelers head coach in 2006). He comes with all kinds of defenses and all kind of weird set-ups. But they used to line up in front of you in a three-four and they said, "Okay, here we come." I was never sorer in my whole life than after playing in Pittsburgh stadium. Number one, because their turf stunk. It was really hard, and they lined up and butted you in the nose all day long. It was very conducive to hating those buggers because you knew they were bringing it. Plus, Lambert was a jerk and the whole bit.

- **How did you feel when the Browns left and went to Baltimore?**

Well, again, I saw it coming. Everybody saw it coming. It was two rich men, Al Learner and Art Model, getting in an airplane and making plans where they could both get their teams. They could get Art to get out of Cleveland, because of the combination of everybody hating Art since he fired Paul Brown, and then he fired Bernie and then nobody liked his son, David. David had a very poor reputation around the town and he was going to be the one to run the team. So, Art pretty much knew he had to leave town. He was being run out of town. They didn't build him a stadium; they built the Indians a stadium. There were lots of things Cleveland did wrong, City Council and things like that. They had always had the Browns and they figured they would always have the Browns. They screwed this up. Why didn't Mayor White stop it? Why didn't he build them a new stadium? If they had built the new stadium, the Browns never would have left.

- **The stadium was promised two weeks after the Browns left.**

Absolutely. They managed to put together the money to build it for another team. But they screwed it up. The thing was, what did they get? They got a new owner, Al Learner, who wanted to be there, who's got great big pockets, and eventually they will start winning and nobody will ever remember about this again. It will all go away. I was there on the field the day of the last game. As a matter of fact, I was with Dick Ambrose.

- **People who hate Art have no understanding of what's going on.**

Art is the one who made the television networks pay us big bucks, which changed the face of football. Television contracts changed the face of football. It went from a sport where you didn't make very much money and you had to have a job in the off-season and when you retired like me, you go out and get a job. It's a business where now if I played ten years, I'd be retired on easy street. That's the difference.

- **Do you resent that fact?**

Oh, sure. I made more in my last year than Doug Dieken made in his thirteen. Tony Jones, who I taught how to hold, made in his last year in Denver more than I made in my eleven years. But that's how it should be. God bless them. Let them make money. I just wish I was coming out now.

- **Some may say that players in the league now aren't as good as the players from years ago.**

They're better. There's your first mistake. They are bigger, stronger, faster, they're everything. It doesn't make any difference if they have bellies hanging out, look at them move. They're better. That's the one thing I got really irritated at in Cleveland because they live so far in the past. It was the Jim Brown's and the Otto Graham's and all that stuff. And I am sure those guys were really good, but there was maybe one or two of them that could have played in today's climate. Maybe Jim could have because he was a superlative stud. He could do whatever he wanted to do. But, are you going to tell me Dick Schafrath is a better tackle than any member of my team? In his day, he was playing a bunch of white defensive ends that weighed 220. What's he going to do if he has to block Reggie? He's going to get crushed.

- **That makes you a better player because you did those things.**

Absolutely. But, if you look at the great centers of all time, Mike Webster, Dwight Stevenson, and then there's guys who played before them. I believe Gunner Gatski died this year. I don't care what era he played, people should be judged by their era, not by history, because history evolves constantly.I mean, Gunner Gatski wouldn't even make a college football team now, but when he played, and he played on ten championship teams in a row, something stupid like that. That's remarkable. Fans tend to color everything by their devotion to their team and to their devotion to the players. The guys of yesterday, none of them could play today. Not a chance. Guys even of my era probably couldn't play. We would get mauled. I couldn't play today. I'm too small. One of my godsons is playing center for the Longhorns, a championship team last year. He's 6'6" and weighs 320 pounds. When I started in football in 1982, I was 6'4" and 275, and I was the second biggest center in football. When I retired eleven years later, I was still 6'4" and 275 and I was the second smallest center in all of football.

- **Doesn't guts, determination and drive have a lot to do with giving the ability for a person to play?**

Sure, absolutely, one-hundred percent. It all still comes down to talent. Give the ball to a guy who's one-hundred percent determined and give the ball to a guy who is three seconds faster in the forty, who is going to get across the goal line first? Being an untalented person *per se*, people like me have tremendous problems with people like Eric Metcalf. Eric is extraordinarily talented, ridiculously good at what he did, run back punts. But, he was the worst blocker in football. And he was probably the worst interior runner I have ever seen. You could tackle him with two fingers. He would fumble if you hit him with three fingers. But, running back punts, he was maybe the most exciting player I ever saw. That's the difference between a slow overachiever and a kid that was born with talent dust.

- **You mentioned Jim Brown earlier. Did Jim and a lot of the older players have a positive influence on you while you were playing?**

Sam was big on this; he would bring them in all the time. The University of Texas had done that, too. We always had lots of older players that we watched as we grew up come back and talk to us. Just being around them. I remember Doug English is one of the reasons I wanted to go to Texas. I remember looking at Doug English and thinking, "Look at that big, tall, good-looking bugger making $100,000 a year. Okay, I'll do that. I'll take that." Yes, people like that were very instrumental because Cleveland is one of the towns where an extremely large portion of the players retire into the town, because they love you so much that you can make a good living.

- **Off the field?**

Absolutely, or when you retire. If you had a chance to buy insurance from Lou "The Toe" Groza, who are you going to buy it from?

- **Who was your nemesis on the field? Who was the player you had the most trouble with?**

The worst games I ever played were early in my career, of course, when you come across a stud, who would tear you up. Joe Klecko, the New York Jets nose guard, got me one year. He killed everybody that one year. I was just one of many. Then, there was a nose guard named Ken Clark who played for Philly who tore me up one game when I was learning to play. There was a guy named Kragin, Denver Bronco's nose guard, who was really hard to block. He was really smart, he moved around well, he was relentless. You had to lay on him to keep him from making a tackle. He was hard to block. Of course, any time they jumped Reggie or Howie Long down on the nose. That was hard. They would spread out and cover all the linemen and put the biggest stud of all time on your nose and they would rush your snap hand.I mean, it was a challenge. But, probably the player that I had the worst relationship with was a guy named Williams who played nose guard for Pittsburgh. He was just one of those mouthy guys and he would talk the whole game. That's not my style of players. So, we had some fun poking each other in the eyes and groin, things going on under the piles. I would look forward to playing him because I really hated him and wanted to kill him. He was one of the few guys that I tried to put in the hospital every time I played him. But, the other side was that you'd think, "Oh, God, I've got to listen to his crap for another game." Randy Gradishar got me real good one time, too. He was hard to block. He was in his tenth year All Pro and I was the rookie center. I don't think I ever touched him. He was good. I remember three or four games that stood out where I just played poorly. Once you learn how to play, you don't have games like that anymore.

- **Some of the players have talked to me that they have had a fun time with hazing. What did you think about the hazing rules as a rookie?**

We wouldn't do any of that. We didn't do any at all. Sam didn't believe in it. Remember, when I got to Cleveland, I broke every weight lifting record the first week I was there. Nobody messed with Mike. I have a demeanor, my wife says it's my "don't look at me, don't talk to me, don't speak to me" face. People don't mess with me. I'm not going to put up with it because I'm going to kill you if you do, and that was my reputation.

- **Paul Warfield said the best time he ever had was when he had one rookie who used to come in all the time and he would tell them to go to the store and get him a piece of bubble gum.**

Well, if somebody told me to do that, I'd tell them to go get it for themselves. I wasn't raised that way.

- **Did you ever encounter any negativity as a player?**

Other than the harsh realities of football,l which is show up or go home, I loved it. It was fun. You couldn't have had a better job.

- **Do you still feel like you're part of the Cleveland organization?**

I'll always be a Brown. I'm extremely proud of my years at Cleveland. I still look at Cleveland as my second home. I go there every summer to stay with Danny Fike and see my buddies. I run into Herman Fontenot every summer. There's a list of guys that I try to see when we go back, such as Reggie Langhorne and Tom Cousineau, Dave Puzzolli, and Brian Brennan.

My kids were raised with their kids. They were womb mates; our wives were all pregnant at the same time. I love Cleveland and I love the Cleveland Browns, and I am very proud of them. Am I attached to this organization in any way? Through one man, Dino Lucarelli. There are very few people like Dino. I'm connected to the Browns because of Dino. That's it. I don't know anybody else. Dino is a great guy. If he would call me tomorrow, I will run and help.

- **Do you still watch football?**

One of the impetuses for leaving Cleveland and going home was because of the Browns leaving and everything. It was time to go home and get a real job. I hated being a "has-been." I hated it bitterly, because I couldn't play anymore. I hated seeing Steve Everett wear #61 and I know they did that as an honor to me. They told me they did and I am very appreciative of that, but I hated it. I bitterly hated seeing people wear my uniform and my colors and doing my job. I still do to this day. I don't watch the Browns because that was my job. It's funny that I tell you I don't watch football but the other half of me, my wife, says you're full of "blank, blank," because the reason you don't watch football is because you can't do it anymore. Where some guys hang around the sport, that's their way of getting out of the sport. I just left. I want to play; I'm not going to watch. I don't watch sports. My kids will get mad at me because I'll make them watch playoffs because playoffs are great. I don't care what the sport is. They're laying it on the line. That's all I want to see. I watched the Olympics from front to back because it is championships. People laying it on the line and doing their best. That's what I want to watch. But, am I going to watch the Browns play whoever? I don't even know what the record was last year. I'm all done. I just finished a two-hour practice of throwing my weights and stones and log around, so I am done. Now I have kids who play sports and I'm all about teaching them how to throw the shot put and how to shoot a basketball. No, I'm done.

- **Do you have any influence on football today?**

No. Not in any way, shape or form. Nobody asks me about my opinion. A few years ago, the coach at Texas used to bring me in because I am very physically active. I'm the same size I was as a player and I'm almost the same strength that I was as a player, so I can still move around and show things. He had me come in and teach the University of Texas players how you handle offensive linemen and how you handle this type of situation and how you handle this kind of player, what would you do here, what would you do there, that kind of thing. I made them a training tape to keep them in shape in the offseason. So, that's the only impact I've ever had. It was fun. Three of them played in the Pros.

- **Would you do it if they asked you to show your tape again?**

Sure. I go there and work out all the time. They have the greatest weight room in the history of the world. The strength coach, Jeff Madden (they call him Mad Dog), is a good buddy of mine and I am always picking his brain because I want to win the World Championship again this year.

- **When is that?**

It is June 25th in Scotland. I'm still trying to figure out if it's going to be in the budget to take my family to Scotland to watch me throw rocks. I'm wondering about that one.

- **What brought you to start doing the Scottish games?**

My mom made me do it. My mom had been bugging me for twenty years to go honor our Scottish heritage. She is a genealogist and this is very important to her. She had been after me for twenty years to go out and do it. It was really funny and I laughed because here I am in the 80's wearing earrings and a mullet and all the crazy clothes we used to wear back then, but I wouldn't put on a kilt and go throw something because that wasn't macho. I was just a young stupid putz. When I retired, mom came to me and my brother and said, "You guys are going to wear kilts and you're going to go throw cabers and you're going to go throw weights and rocks and you're going to do all this stuff because if you won't, I'll disown you." So, we said, "Okay, Mom." I went to the first game and, of course, being an offensive lineman, I know everything about power and position, so it turns out I am really good at this. Anytime you are over forty and you're good at something, guess what? Stay with it. So, it's a chance to win stuff plus I like the guys. They're just like a bunch of offensive linemen, a bunch of big dummies, just like offensive linemen.

- **You said this was in Scotland?**

That's where the championship is this year. Last year it was in New Hampshire.

- **So, you go all over the country doing this?**

Yes, as much as the budget and time allows. I have been very fortunate to throw in Florida, New Hampshire, Texas, Oklahoma, Ohio, because there are games all over the United States. It's really one of these little niche things that people just don't know about because they haven't ever seen it before. It's the kind of thing you go to a Scottish Festival and you see a bunch of guys running around carrying poles and flipping them and ask, "What the heck are they doing?" One thing I am extremely proud of is that as I get older, the distances and heights and things that I throw now as a master (which means I am over forty) and in the big picture of the greatest throwers in the world, I am very average. But, as a master, I am really good. It's one of those, if you can't do better than them, outlive them. I got a couple of world records. We take a forty-two-pound weight, put a handle on it, and throw it over a bar for height. I've got the forty-five and older world record for throwing the forty-two-pound weight with one hand over the bar. I threw it nineteen feet, nine inches at Arlington last year. I have a whole bunch of second best throws of all times and stuff like that because there has been a guy named Don Stewart who is better than me. So, I'm just happy to be second. It's like when I played, Mike Stevenson was the best center that ever played and I was second, in my little ego mind. That was fine. Some people are just better. That's just the way it is.

- **I understand your wife won a contest in Ohio. What was it? When?**

She was Mrs. Ohio and went on and finished second runner-up at Mrs. USA. She should have won, of course. I was playing so it was like 1989 or 1990. Now, as a matter of fact, I am listening to her with one ear and I'm listening to you in the other ear. She has a radio show she does on women's issues here in Austin. She is finishing her first season and working on syndication.

- **What radio station?**

1370 AM, in Austin, Texas. Just a little place to start. She's a go-getter. I was an extremely fortunate person. I had to fight like a dog to get her to say yes to me. I pursued her like a mad dog for a year before she said yes.

- **When were you married?**

We were married in 1983.

- **Where was the hardest place to play?**

Philly's fans are a bunch of beasts. They are the kind of fans that would go in the bathroom and piss in a cup so they could bring it out and throw it on you. Yeah, Philadelphia, plus the field was really terrible. So, Philly, bar none, and then from there, for me as a player, it goes back to like where is the worst locker room. It was the Orange Bowl. I couldn't believe this was professional sports. It was worse than high school. It's a room with hooks on the wall. It's pitiful and there's no hot water, on and on, same stuff. Houston had the worst turf.

- **Is that the Astrodome?**

Yes, it was concrete. But, the rest of it, as far as unfriendliness and stuff like that and the booing, I didn't pay any attention to that.

- **You learned to tune that out?**

You have to focus and one of the things you have to learn in a sport like football where it's sevty-five unique events, you've got to forget about the last play and you better hyper focus on what you're doing next. Marty used to say short memory, next play, short memory, one play at a time. I learned that from him. The greatest thing in the world was going into the most unfriendly place in the world and shutting their mouths and they don't say anything and they all go home by the fourth quarter. Best thing in the world.

- **So is that the phrase, "Listen to a quiet stadium?"**

Yes. They want to go home, they're already out in the parking lot, and I'm still scoring on you.

- **What's the funniest story in your NFL experience?**

There are a lot of things I can't tell you, things that happened off the field because we were pretty rowdy and crazy for a while there. Young men tend to be that way. I remember one time we were watching film and a big Dawg Pound fan threw a tennis ball out of the stands and hit Greg Rakoczy right on top of the head perfectly, so it went straight up in the air about twenty feet, and it came down and bounced right in front of me, where I am holding the football, and it goes bounce, bounce, bounce. I remember it happening and I remember sort of ignoring it and not thinking much of it because I was hyper-focusing on whoever I had to block. But when we watched on film, it was hilarious because that tennis ball came out of the stands, hit Greg on the head and bounced up in the air, and every single football player on the field, our eyes snapped to the ball as it goes up in the air, and all twenty-two heads go up and down and as it bounces. Our heads go bounce, bounce, bounce, and we turned around and went. It was hilarious. I still look at it. We laughed for thirty minutes. Aw, this is really a dumb thing. You probably want a better story than that. I never had a better laugh in my life because it was insane to watch, and half the guys that did see it didn't remember it. They said, "I don't remember that happening," and you could see them watching the ball.

- **Does that come down to your focus factor?**

Yes, that's exactly it. We played Chicago the first game of 1977. They looked good and we almost beat them. Cody Risen had to tackle trap the Fridge (William "The Refrigerator" Perry) and the Fridge was really good in the first quarter, and then he got fat and lazy and tired and he was nothing, you killed him in the rest of game. But, in the first quarter, he was hard to block. Cody came over and stoned him. I remember looking at Cody and I could see the back of his skull. He played a really good football game. He blocked Hampton all day long, did a great job, and the next day he doesn't remember a single play. He still to this day doesn't remember anything about that game. It is a weird, morbid football humor. He shook his brains so hard, he couldn't think. I remember watching Leroy Hoard laying on the ground doing the chicken because he came out of college and never wore a neck roll and he was playing fullback and playing on special teams and you better wear a neck roll or you're going to the hospital. He kept saying, "I don't need one. I'm tough enough," and all that stuff. He ran down on the punt team and threw himself on a pile and laid on the ground and did the shiver chicken for a while because he had "nerve stung" his whole body and we laughed at him about that for a while. Our football humor tended to be very morbid. Oh, yeah, he was laying there with his leg broken, crying like a baby, that kind of thing. It was a tough game.

- **Do you have a sad story to tell?**

Oh, everybody that got cut when they were hurt because these guys would come in and, the way it worked in football was, if they got you on film in your uniform doing drills, you were cut because that meant that you were well and it didn't matter how you did in the drill. So, what we would see was some poor guy who had blown his knee out, and been recovering for a year, and we would see him come out with the trainers with his uniform on and we knew that he would be gone when we got back. That was the worst part. You never see these guys again. Some of them were guys that you had been out on the street with, because you know as well as I do, most male bonding happens in bars over beer. The guys you loved more than life itself and then they're gone. Unless you make a real effort to find them, and they may not want to be found, you lose people forever. The worst part of football was that, in my rookie year, I had seven roommates in five weeks. They got cut.

- **Were you traded from Cleveland to New England?**

Yes. I think they got a fifth round draft choice or something. Marty Schottenheimer and Howard Mudd thought that Greg Rakoczy was going to be the next greatest center in the history of football and I had also had a pretty tough year as far as injuries the year before, and I told the team how bad my knees felt. I learned later that you shut your mouth and grit your teeth and pretend you're okay .

- **Is that part of the inner circle you talked about?**

No, no, no. It was just that they made a decision to start Greg and I went to Marty and he said (God Bless Marty), "Mike, if you happen to lose your starting position, will you accept the back-up position?" I said, "Hell, no. Cut me." So, he traded me to a team that wanted me to play. I started every game for two years. They brought me back and paid me way too much.

- **How did you get back with Cleveland from there?**

Plan B, which is a free-agency thing they had then. But, it was before true free agency. They would put players on Plan B, which means that you could become essentially a free agent. The Browns paid more or I would have been a Jet. The Jets were the next team in the running.

- **How did you get back to Kansas City?**

I got cut by the Browns and then I was probably going to get picked up because I was still good enough to be a backup for somebody, but I went to Sea World and fell on a ride, trying to protect my daughter, and broke my right hand. What's the one thing a center can't do? He can't hurt his right hand. So, I'm retired and go on with my life. I'm done. Then, my hand healed really well. I was always very fortunate to heal very quickly, and Marty's center broke his foot with four games to go, and they're in the play-off hunt, so he called me out of the blue and said, "Mike, what kind of shape are you

259

in?" I said, "Actually, I just played racquetball today (January 2008). I'm in great shape." He said, "Will you play for me? My center broke his foot." I said, "How much are you going to pay me?" Well, he paid me enough and I went and played four games and into the play-off game and started every game and actually played pretty well. But, I knew I was done. I was too old and too small.

- **How come you're only listed as three games?**

I don't know, maybe I lost track. I think it was four total, because I had another year of pension out of it. You need to go four games. So, maybe it was three and then the play-off game. It was fun, I really enjoyed it. Back with Marty in Kansas City and Howard Mudd, too. Both of them made a real effort to come up and sit down with me and say, "When we traded you off four years ago, that was really stupid." Marty said, "That was probably the worst decision I ever made as a coach." That really pleased me in a weird, stupid football way. It makes me feel good. Then, Marty stood up in front of the whole team and said, "I want to tell you guys a story," and it was the first day I was brought there. I'm just a little, skinny white boy with eleven years in the league and I'm not the greatest pickup in the world, of any guys in the world, and they didn't know who I was. Marty stood up and talked about me for about twenty minutes in front of his team and, after it was over, the whole team came over and shook my hand. That's cool.

- **Who were some of the players there?**

Derek Thomas and Christian Okoye. Mudbone (Dave Craig) was the quarterback, and a whole bunch of big, white, ugly offensive linemen. The offensive line was Ault, Zott, Baab, Grunyard, and Baldinger, a bunch of big old Germans and Pols. After the first game we played, I played really well against New England, blocked my nose guard and took care of him, did my job. Marty gave me the game ball. The whole team gave me a standing ovation, which was like the coolest thing that ever happened to an offensive lineman. You don't get stuff like that. That's why I was so pleased to go out of football that way, rather than Belichick telling me I was too old, too slow, get the hell out of here.

- **What's the difference between the players today and from yesterday?**

Well, the game is a lot blacker, which is the way it is. They're better, I guess, so it's like basketball. There is a whole different style of thing going on here. It's hip-hop and it's just a different game. It's a black player's game today. When I played, it was fifty-fifty; it went both ways. We got along better. I remember the Browns' players that we had; I was just as liable to go out with Webster Slaughter as I was to go out with Danny Fike. That was the team we had. Maybe I was just fortunate to be on a team where we all loved each other. By the end of my career, it was very black and white. Plus, the players make a lot of money. I call Cody and razz him all the time and say, "Hey, did you see what that tackle signed for?" "Shut up, man." Cody would be a five-million dollar a year player now. Absolutely, and that's the difference. They make a whole bunch of money, and the more money you make the more spoiled you get. That's fine, that's the nature of the beast. These guys have been told their whole life that they're special and eventually they're going to start believing it. I don't begrudge them a thing. Good for them. Halleluiah.

- **Are players worth their salary today?**

  Absolutely, if somebody will pay it to you, you're worth it.

- **Should the player be more fan conscious?**

  They should respect and appreciate the fans, absolutely. Without the fans, you've got nothing. You can't play all the games. Television money is the vast majority of the income of football, but you're still playing in the stadium. Players should sign autographs, they should be polite. They should not be Terrell Owens. They should not.

- **Do the agents of the game make that the way it is now?**

  They had agents back then, too. No. There were bad agents when I played, too. No, no. That's the same thing. The only difference was that, remember, the professional football owners have probably the best setup going as far as kicking the shit out of the players every time the players want something because we are a bunch of stupid football players who realize that our careers could be over tomorrow and that there's always two-thousand people who want to do your job for less money. So, that's why they kick our butts in strikes. We're all about, "Where's my check? Where's my check? Where's my check? Because I could get my knee blown out tomorrow and I'm done." They change teams relentlessly because they're chasing the money. That's what you're supposed to do in professional sports. In Dante's era, it was completely different. And, of course, look at it in Dante's era, he was hideously underpaid. There are a thousand ways of looking at everything.

- **Otto Graham died broke. It's just hard to believe that, again, this may go back to the fact that the NFL didn't help take care of these people. Now it's, "What are you going to pay me?" It's hard to look at those guys like that because you do look up to them as heroes.**

  Exactly. "How much are you going to pay me?" I mean, it doesn't make any difference. Athletes are just like actors. I need to make some money because there might be a better offer and I have to take it because the shine is going to come off my butt in a hurry. And while the shine is on my butt, I need to shine it and make as much as I can. You know, it's unfortunate but people have to realize nowadays that when a quarterback like Vince Young leaves the University of Texas, the next week he's in Houston getting $100,000 for an appearance signing ninety-nine dollar apiece autographs. What do I say? Half of me is appalled, and the other half is saying, "Go, Vin."

- **What did you get out of your NFL experience as a whole?**

I get a pension, I have a boatload of memories, I have friends that will be with me until the day I die, men that I won't see for thirty years and then the next time I see them, I'm going to hug them just like it was 1985. My wife and I had a tremendous life. I was raised a poor white kid in Texas and I had a hell of a life and I've been to Europe five times and all that other stuff. There's all these things that I have done in my life because of football. More so than that, I think it's the development of you as a person. Since that time, everything that I've taken on, I went with the same attitude I had in football. I work at a car dealership and I started there as a salesperson out of boredom and a year later, I'm running it. I know how to succeed and I learned that from football.

- **Are still running the dealership? Is it your dealership?**

Sure. *(Note, later Mike did retire from the dealership to become a personal trainer.)* But, no, football players of today can afford a dealership, but the players of my era work in dealerships, so it's not mine.

- **Besides your Scottish Games, do you have any more hobbies?**

My wife and children. I've always been an avid reader. I devour books. Watching my kids do the things they do in their lives and enjoying my life with my wife and, occasionally, I will go to a Longhorn game. Other than that, again, being the psychotically-obsessed person that I am, I am obsessed with my family and my Scottish crap.

- **I want to thank you for your time. Is there aything you would like to add?**

Well, are you writing this book as something like a collection of mementos for Browns fans?

- **Basically.**

Okay then. There was not a better job in the world than being a Cleveland Browns player in the '80s. Not a better job in the world. We used to stand there on game day, Bernie and I, and because practicing sucked, they paid me for Wednesday, Thursday, and Friday, and they paid me for being sore on Monday, but I did Sunday for free. First, I did it with Sipe, and then I did it with Bernie, and we would stand there and when they would call us out and the crowd goes wild and were going to run on the field for the introduction, we would look at each other and say, "Best job in the world. I've got the best dam job in the world right now." And we appreciated it. The people who do well in life have a purpose. The people who live longest in life have a purpose. We actually have a title for the book I'm going to write some day. It's called, "You Think I'm Kidding, Don't You." I would like to. Books aren't as much fun unless you name names. Because there is nothing

Americans like better than setting a person up on a pedestal and then there's nothing they like better than kicking the pedestal out from under them. It's not as good a story unless you name names. I'm not going to name names on my buddies. I'm not going to do that. But someday, there might come out a book of fiction....

Mike Baab				
Center 1982-1992				
Texas				
Season	Team	Games	Other Stats	Total Points
1982	CLE	7		0
1983	CLE	15		0
1984	CLE	16	Fum: 1	0
1985	CLE	16	Rush: 1/0yds Fum: 1	0
1986	CLE	16		0
1987	CLE	12		0
1988	NE	15		0
1989	NE	16	Fum Rec: 1	0
1990	CLE	16		0
1991	CLE	16	Fum Rec: 1	0
1992	KC	3		0
Career		148		0

Mike Baab blocking against
the New York Jets

Mike Baab blocking against
the Pittsburgh Steelers

21

Anthony Griggs

Anthony Griggs' life evolved around his ability to extend himself out to others. If he wasn't keying on the running back coming out of the backfield, he would be keying on the person he was talking to, getting into that person's mind, and looking to find a way to help that individual. Anthony is a keynote speaker and teaches the lesson of "Life is a Sport: Train for it." While he was Director of Player Personnel for the Pittsburgh Steelers, he started the AG Foundation to help kids and young players make the right decision in life. He has a true passion for people and strives to help the people he comes in contact with to make the right decisions. Anthony has had a close relationship with Bill Cowher and played and worked in the offices of the Pittsburgh Steelers for many years.

- **What was it like to walk on the field the very first time as a Brown?**

It was pretty exciting. You hear about the Dawg Pound, you hear about the following that the Browns have with their fans, but when you walk on the field the first time, it is overwhelming. I can only tell you that because I went to Villanova University and Villanova was a small college, not known for football. They were known for basketball. We didn't have a lot of money and subsequently had to drop the football program. I went to Ohio State for my last year. I compare going into the Browns as when I first walked into an Ohio State home game. I went from a 12,000-seat stadium at Villanova to 90,000 fans in the stands, all wearing Scarlet and Grey. It was just unreal. The thing that is kind of unfortunate is there's not been a history of winning, there's been so much a history of "close."I mean, not winning the big one should I say, but so close and having great teams and great players. It was all coming together at those games. Those home games for any rookie player coming in the first time on that field it is very exciting.

- **When did you decide you wanted to be a professional football player?**

I never really decided, "Okay, I'm going to be a professional ballplayer." What I decided was that I'm going to try to maximize the opportunities that come my way. That was either going into college or I had a strike my senior year and I was only offered so many scholarships, maybe three scholarships and one of them was Villanova. I went to Villanova, by the way, because the two starting linebackers got kicked out of school for some violation and they dropped the football program after three years and having three different coaches. I went to Ohio State and switched position from an inside linebacker to an outside linebacker. So, when did I decide to become professional? When I decided to overcome the circumstances. I'm not starting here at Ohio State. They already have a team and I'm playing a position, I'll just have fun playing college football. I didn't start until I went to Ohio State, until maybe my sixth or seventh game of the season. I was still living in the dorms at Ohio State, which is unheard of for a senior. I didn't have a car until I got drafted.

Let's just take it back to Ohio State, because that was a critical year for me where football could have easily been left behind because I had to go to Ohio State summer school to get some more credits for some classes I needed. Some of the papers I had to write were actually during camp; I was in Ohio State's camp. That's when I was like "this is crazy, I can't read and write and get this stuff done. I've got practice the next morning." So, I did that, I survived and that was the first time I really started thinking I'm going to have to give up football. It was hard, football, the regime, was hard with Earl Bruce. I was in the dorms and I remember they had a draft day at Ohio State, so it was easy for them to come and test all the seniors. They were like "Okay, let's try this, you're going to run, you're going to do all these drills." "Oh, who is this guy?" "This is Anthony Griggs, he's one of the transfers from Villanova and we had four guys that transferred." They were like "Oh, okay, Anthony Griggs, I think I know his name." Then they ran me and tested me and they liked what they saw and they kept coming out and they tested me some more. I ended up being drafted in the fourth round. I'm in the dorm room my roommate answered the phone. I didn't have any big draft party. I wasn't out there promoting what round I am going to go in. I didn't have an agent. I was Joe college student. I wasn't even thinking, "Wow, I've got to get my degree now." I was just trying to survive. So, I get drafted, you go into the Pros and you know that's good for the ego. I grew up in South Jersey anyway, so I was back home. It was a big deal, Anthony Griggs got drafted by the Eagles. I was like, "This is unreal."

My mom and dad were obviously proud. It was more excitement for them to be that close because they had supported me all through the years of playing football from little leagues on. So, here I am now playing for the Eagles and my mom and dad are coming in and barbequing in the parking lot, tailgating, and everything. Being in the Pros, the first practice in the Pros, you realize not only are you playing with guys that are older, you think, "How are these guys going to be able to get around? They're like forty years old," you think they're so much older. Then you see them when they play and you're like, "Whoa, whoa." We had Frank Lemaster, Bergie I think was just finishing up, Jerry Robinson, John Bunting, Reggie White. I was like, "Wow, Ron Jaworski." I'm looking at these guys, and I'm looking at how easy they do it in practice, and in their spare time, they're not in their playbook. They're like, "Hey let's go get some drinks, let's go do this." I'm like, "I can't do it, it wasn't part of me in college," now I'm in the Pros it's a whole different mindset. I kept at it as I've got to just keep overcoming these circumstances. They don't know who I am, they don't know anything. I wasn't All American, I wasn't all Big Ten, I wasn't anything. I was on nobody's radar. They picked me to play and I always wanted to be the guy they didn't have to worry about—does he hustle, does he run, does he give effort? I never wanted to be that guy. I've been on many teams I always heard of that guy. I've always seen that guy. So, it was easy.

Now getting to the day I joined the Cleveland Browns, it was interesting because I always had to overcome things. I'm in my first year with the Eagles, they had a strike. First time the NFL football had a strike. Second year, my position coach leaves, I get another position coach. I ended up getting traded to Cleveland during the draft day. I was going out, I did a public appearance at some high school or some school. I was talking to some kids. I was coming back from there, I just wanted something to eat so I strolled into this, it was like a TGI Fridays, but some eatery place, and they were having a show there. A live draft show, not as big as they are now, but a live show. One of my teammates was there. I walked in very unassuming. I didn't say anything to anybody there, I just went in a booth and got something to eat. I'm watching the draft and they go, "Let's recap what the Eagles did today. Hey, how about that trade of Anthony Griggs to Cleveland." I'm like, that's me. I'm like "Okay, I'm traded to Cleveland." I didn't know too much about Cleveland, I didn't know all the personnel they had. I don't know if I told you, but I had always liked Ohio State. They had the high white socks and the names on the back of the uniforms, the white mouthpiece, the shiny silver helmets. I loved it. When I went there, it was like yes this is unbelievable. They didn't have to sell me too much. Nick Szabo came in to Villanova, he was the first guy I saw there. He was a defense back coach and said, "Anthony Griggs, we'd like to have you come and take a visit to Ohio State." I'm there, no problem. Got there and it's an unbelievable situation.

Now, I go to Cleveland and I know they have a guy there who I watched before, Tom Cousineau. I was a fan of his because he was a slender guy, always in shape guy, a guy sort of built like me in so many ways. He worked hard. When I got there and I saw him play I was like, "He does work hard." He lived up to everything I thought he was going to be and everything he was in college. I knew of his background in going to Canadian football. I saw him in Cleveland and now here I am. I'm competing. They had a little thing in the paper before I even went there saying "Anthony is going to Cleveland and he might have a chance to start, he might even beat Tom Cousineau out of his position...." I never really wanted to look at it as I'm beating anybody out, at least not that way. He was just a phenomenal athlete, phenomenal player, phenomenal person. I always looked up to him in a lot of ways. I think there was a sort of competitive thing he and I had that year in regards to just conditioning. Every game or so, we would always be the ones that had the most laps, him first or me first, or whatever. It wasn't like we had a vendetta against each other it's just that's the way we did it. So, here I am

I'm out there and I'm seeing him and Eddie Johnson and Frank Minnifield and Hanford Dixon, these guys are talking and that's not my game. I'm not a talker. I'm just business. I'm with this whole other mystique. Is it like you're down home and you go someplace and people hear you're a Cleveland Brown and they just roll out the red carpet out for you. They're proud of you, you're like one of theirs. That was good too, that was great.

When I was in Philadelphia, I didn't really put it all out there so to speak. I was still at home, I was still able to go to mom and dad's place, that's all I pretty much knew and go to my church, too. It was still a little different acclimation for me. So, here I am down in Cleveland, a little further from home, I packed up all my stuff in Turnersville, New Jersey, and took it to Ohio in Cleveland, like the Clampetts. I moved there, it was a great experience. The things I remember, again, overcoming circumstances. The first year, I don't think we won. I think it was the John Elway Drive. I played with Bill Cowher in Philadelphia for quite a while; he was a linebacker. I remember him coming in as rookie. He was a linebacker, he said, "Hi, I'm Bill Cowher." He was phenomenal on special teams. He and I were on the same special team. I was on the front line and he was back there in the wedge, he was one of the wedge guys. To make a long story short, I missed my block, my guy I was supposed to block ended up hitting him in the knee, and he never played another down in the NFL. I helped him get into coaching. Some people see it differently, he sees it differently, but without that little bit of divine intervention, I'm sure he wouldn't be as he is now. So, here I am doing a book interview and he's doing movies probably. He's big time. I'm in Cleveland and he was supposed to be the coach now, he had the job he was coach when I got there. He picked me up, I think from the airport, and he took me out and we had some lunch. I'm thinking in my mind, "This used to be my teammate and now he's coaching. Now he's coaching me, he's coaching me on special teams, the one I hurt on special teams...."

- **Was there any one person that inspired you to play football?**

When I was little, I loved the Pittsburgh Steelers. My dad, probably, I never saw him play. We never went out in the field and we never played or anything like that. I remember being young and I said, "I want to play." I used to watch football. I was seven or eight years old. He said, "Oh you want to play, I think they've got a team that plays in the neighborhood." They played against other parks, other neighborhoods. I was like, "Well, that would be kind of fun." So, he took me up to the field, I was like, "Wow, there they are." All of the sudden I realized, "Whoa, I don't want to do this because they're in uniform. It's a whole cohesive team and I'm an outsider and, now, dad let's just go home." He's,"No, no, no; let's just go meet the coach." The coach's name was Mr. Taylor, I'll never forget it. He was a tall guy for those days. He had a cigar butt always hanging out of his mouth, slender guy, glasses, and a guy that looked down at me the first time and said, So, you want to play football, huh, son?" "Ah, yeah," and my dad came for the first practice the next day, had to go get uniforms, and the whole time my heart is thumping. We're there, this is it. My dad brought me there and said, "Go

over there and you get your stuff, put your helmet on and go. I'll be here."
I was apprehensive and I remember I was going over there and I looked
back to see where he was. Unbeknownst to me, I found out later, he'd keep
taking a step back. My dad would take a step back and I would look over
and he'd be further away, but I didn't know he was getting further away, I
kept seeing him. Practice was going on, I'd look over he'd be there and pretty
soon he'd be behind the wall, he wouldn't be there anymore. Then I'd just
be practicing. That was my first time I really was on my own. He asked me,
"How'd you like your first day?." It was a little different, but it's the first
time you get involved with something like that. It was inspiring, my dad
said, "Hey, you like watching the game? You can do this if you want to. I'll
take you up there, but if you do it, give it all you got, have some fun." Both
mom and dad had influence on me, that's why I truly believe in the family
structure. My mother gave me a lot more of the feeling part of my personality
by helping, by assisting, by serving people. "You're no better than anybody
else," she never put me down, never. I just knew there were other people
out there that didn't have just the opportunities or weren't as fortunate.
I was blessed as I found out to have two parents that gave of themselves
unselfishly, who loved their kids and gave of themselves as much as they
could, supported me in good, bad, indifferent. They were Marva and Gerald
kids. It was my mother, my father, my sister, and I. A lot of what I went
through growing up, I was still a little shy and introverted. In some ways, I
am now, but a little older and a little more mature in knowing what I have
to do and what I want to do can be thought out. But, piece them together
and people see a lot of them in me when they talk to me, or even when they
look at me. You see them going back and forth between my dad and my
mom, so my mom influencing me was the support structure of being there
unconditionally, no matter what. It's not a situation, it's not a condition,
it's just love. We love you no matter what. That was told to me; it wasn't,
"Oh, they know I love them." No, it was told to you. Your mom and dad, no
matter if you win or lose, when you come out of that tunnel, you are a high
school player, or when you came out after the John Elway ninety-eight yard
drive or the Ernest Byner fumble. After whatever it was, and you talk to them
and they say, "Hey don't worry about it," is the greatest thing. That's a seed
that will never die. It will just be there. I look back and I think of it now. My
mom and dad have since passed away, but I still ask them for guidance. I
still feel their presence. I still their support. I really do, it's a point of my life
where I look back at football, football has done a lot of great things for me,
so many great things. I met a lot of good people and I'm fortunate enough,
not just talking to you momentarily, not even from the situation of contracts
and the business of it at all. You get around a lot of people who want the
same common goal, who are trying to make things the best they can from the
situation. You put yourself in there until you can contribute. There's not too
much else that is going to be as rewarding as that as far as outside of your
family. There really isn't.

- **Where were you born?**

I was born in Lawton, Oklahoma. Lawton, Oklahoma, on an army base. That was the last time I was there. My father was in the Army, so we moved to Europe then back to New Jersey when I was about four or five years old.

- **You said your favorite team was the Steelers. Who did you like?**

Jack Lambert was a tall, thin linebacker at that time, so for me that was perfect. That's what I was, I was a linebacker. That's the number I wanted, fifty-eight. I had fifty-eight with the Eagles and I wore it at Villanova. Franco Harris was a guy from the area, a local guy, the first person I looked at and started understanding a little more about college. I didn't understand college, I knew college football was on television. I knew there were superstars and celebrities were playing college football. I really didn't understand how these guys got there. I didn't understand the whole recruiting process. My mom and dad didn't go to college. My mom and dad were only children, so there were people around me who went to college I knew, but I still didn't understand the whole thing of it. When it was recruiting time, when schools would come and say, "We'd like you to come and make a visit," was new to me. I was learning, I didn't understand college, like a four-year ride, a five-year ride, you get a degree, and what does it all mean? Coming out of Ohio State, there were people I looked up to, athletes. I remember looking at a Kansas City team, Otis Taylor, wide receiver, the middle linebacker, can't think of his name now, I think he's since passed away, and then the Green Bay team, and the Jets, obviously Joe Namath, Johnny Unitas, Gayle Sayers, O.J. Simpson. You see them playing football in the streets, we had teams we used to play, we had great athletes that played. One girl that we played football with, her name was Cindy Stinger. Cindy Stinger was a phenomenal football player, but she was a phenomenal athlete too in high school and subsequently went to the Olympics and played handball. She is still with the Olympic team, the Olympic Committee. She works with the alumni of the Olympics. Anybody that has gone to the Olympics is an alumni. She is president of that organization. The reflected part of me sometimes is not really done too far or even too deep. It's like, "Yeah, I played football" or I did this or I've done things. It's only when people ask me questions about some of the things, like you're doing, and I can go, "Oh, I never really thought, or what did influence me, or how is it…."

- **Where did you play your high school football?**

I played at John F. Kennedy High School in. Willingboro, New Jersey.

- **Who was your coach? What kind of influence did he have on your life?**

Jim Dicicco. Back in junior high, I had a coach by the name of Pat Marino. He was a great influence on me, too. After the little league football, then after I couldn't make the weight, I was really too heavy then to play. I couldn't make the weight for like two years of playing, so I started playing in ninth grade and we went undefeated. When I went to high school, I was under Jim Dissico. Last year I watched the varsity players and was amazed at how big they were. I went through the crowd to go to the field with the varsity team. It is amazing your perspective, those cleats hitting the ground, just the whole big pad, you're like, "Oh my gosh, look at this guy running. Look how hard they run, look how hard they're hitting." Everyone knows you're playing, everyone knows who you are, we wore our jerseys to school. From your perspective, that's your world, you're doing it. Jim Dissico, I remember him. I liked high school, I wasn't a problem child, I didn't get into trouble with the law or get in trouble in school. I probably could have applied myself more, but for the most part I was just business. I was doing what I've got to do. Jim took the college recruiting pretty serious, did a lot of things for me, helped me in some ways. I was really quite introverted, I didn't even talk a lot to people. Once you did get to know me, you saw I was probably a clown in some ways. I wasn't into drinking, I wasn't into partying, go to parties, maybe I'd drink, but not to get drunk. I'm not sitting around the parking lot drinking a case of beer with my friends. I'm not that. There's a lot of things about high school and, as far as the football was concerned, again I didn't want to be that guy. It all started early. I remember going from junior high to high school, I don't know who it was, Jim Dissico or Pat Marino, saying, "You better be in shape." That was enough to get me to say, "Don't worry about me being in shape. I'm going to have to get myself in better shape than I ever was before." I'd get up really early before I'd go to school, and run around the block, or do things on my own and train on my own, and still train with the other people and even my friends. Nobody knew the things I did on my own. That's the way I approached it.

- **Who was your college coach at Villanova?**

I guess he came in a year or two before I got there. He was down to earth. I went to Villanova. My mom and my grandmother dropped me off at Villanova and drove away. "That's it, we'll see you get out of the car. We'll see you when you come home." I am up here alone. I think I cried; that was shocking. Dick Bettison was good because he kind of understood these young freshman were coming from their parents, their homes. Their parents have entrusted you to not only let them play football, getting them in shape to play football, but also to get them molded into the best citizen they can be. Catholic schools are known for being a bit more strict and Villanova was just that. He came at it from a different perspective and always made a personal note. I'm going to a bigger school right out of the box, high school had been a different situation. At a small school, you appreciate things more. I was a year behind Howie Long. He was there, across the hall from me in St. Mary's Hall. We had some fun, not that we hung out together or anything like that, but living across the hall from Howie in his college days, yeah. He's not going to say anything against me.

- **You said you were acquired by the Browns and found out just by watching television. What did you think when they traded you for Seth Joyner in that situation?**

When the Eagles got Seth Joyner? I really didn't think anything of it. I didn't know, I didn't know what they got for me. I didn't know if it was a couple of chickens and some shoestrings. "I'm going to Cleveland," I didn't think anything about it. It was just part of what happened. I wasn't married at the time. I'm on a plane tomorrow. I got home that night, when I found out I was traded, and over night I got a message from Harry Gamble, general manager. I got a message from Marty Schottenheimer's secretary telling me there was a plane ticket waiting for me when I came to Cleveland. It felt good to a point, but I downplayed it, because I knew it was still a matter of, "I think you want me, but you don't really know what I can do every day. I'm not out here trying to make the Eagles feel like they made a mistake." I don't remember what the trade was, who was involved. All I knew was, "Cleveland, here I come." I got there and after talking to Marty, he'd talk to the team in a more realistic fashion.

- **What was it like to play for Marty Schottenheimer?**

Good. He was straight. Ask the hard questions, you're going to get the hard answers. He told you what he thought. He told you what you should be thinking, and he was just fair. Marty was a great player. Marty did a weird thing for me, he did and didn't in a way. What he did for me, and it wasn't his fault that it didn't happen, what he did for me, I was finished playing football in Atlanta. I said, "I want to get into coaching, I want to be a special teams coach maybe." I drove to Mobile, Alabama, from Atlanta and I met Marty. I didn't meet him, I ran into him. They had the North/South All Star game. I met some coaches down there, they were like, "Oh, yeah, Anthony, what are you doing down here?" I saw Marty in the lobby by the hotel and I said, "Hey, Coach." He said, "Hey, Anthony, AG," everybody calls me AG. "AG, what's going on." "I'm here looking to see if I can get into coaching." He said, "Good idea, it's a good place for you to be. Anything I can do let me know." At that time Jack Pardee was a new coach of the Houston Oilers and Marty knew him and said, "Coach Pardee, come here. I want to talk to you about something real quick." He says, "Hey, I want you to meet Anthony Griggs. Anthony Griggs this is Jack Pardee the new coach of the Houston Oilers." Marty said, "Coach, if you're looking for a new coach to come into your system, Anthony Griggs I can vouch for him. He's a good player and also a good man, if he can get some stuff to you, I'd like for you to consider him." Right there, he didn't have to do it, didn't have to say anything, he could have just walked on. I never forgot that. I didn't get the job, but that meant the world to me at that time. I'm like, "How does he know, how does he get things?" He, Marty Schottenheimer, at that time was like riding the world. I think he was in Kansas City or something, in any case, he had other people around him, too. I think other coaches. So, here I am, he's introducing me as a candidate, which is unheard of. I just remember that, he never did it again. I never asked him to. There it was and that was it. That was good.

- **What was it like to play for Dick Vermeil?**

He brought that college feeling. It was good for me to go to him to get that first year under my belt. It wasn't just him, it was the college feeling; you know, winning and the team concept, the feelings. The feeling for your brothers and the people who are laying it out for you. What it means to give and sacrifice for others. It meant something. Dick Vermeil, I remember our first meeting. I am a rookie, it was one of these things, you know, you get up on the chair and Carl Harris makes you sing. You sing a fight song; of course, there is two fight songs, Villanova and Ohio State. I had the same two fight songs. I played out the whole thing. That was the first night the veterans came in. We have our big meeting, the veterans are there, and I think it lasts for three hours, with Dick Vermeil talking. He was crying about players that weren't there anymore. I was in the audience, about three rows back, in my mind going, "Oh my God, if this is what it's going to be like, I'm going to be here for three hours at a time." We're turning the pages, he'd turn the page and talk for a half an hour. He would start missing a player and start getting teared up. Here I am, all wide-eyed like a deer in the headlights, meanwhile the veterans are sinking in their seats, snickering, smiling. I'm like "I can't do that. It's not funny." It might have been funny to me, but I'm wondering if maybe Vermeil is joking and these guys are getting the joke and I'm not. Then we're at practice and he would do his best conveying his voice, especially to the assistant coaches. He would definitely get it out there and talk to the team and tell you what he's thinking. That was a big influence. It wasn't all football. "Okay, we've got to go to practice today," "Okay, we're going to have the offensive lift today," or "We're going to have that today." No, it was like he would always remind you why you're here. "This is a great opportunity for you guys," "Guys, we're in training camp now," "We're finishing training camp. Don't go out there and do anything stupid, don't do anything crazy." It was just great.

Then I had Swamp Fox, Marion Campbell, which was good because he was the defensive coordinator of the Eagles. I played under him and he liked to get after it. I look back at the players that were there, Ron Jaworski—what he's doing now, I'm not sure—Pisarcik, Harold Carmichael, Lonnie Henderson, Wood Montgomery, John Binting. I see them making their moves in businesses. Ron, I remember him having an Eagles Nest golf course in south Jersey. He had a tournament there. At that time, I didn't know much about golf, I wish I did. If I would have known then what I know now, I would have hung around him more. I would have loved to have been in the circles he was in. He's a guy you love to bounce things off of. He had a golf course—not only that, he gets along with everybody on the team. As a quarterback, I know you've got to do that, but he was genuine. It's something you see in Ron Jaworski and commentators like that. He's just a part of it. He sees me, and I don't know, I give a lot to other people, more than I give to myself, but when he sees me, it's "AG, what's going on?" He connects to me. That means more to me because I know they haven't gone too far out there because they can say "Hi, AG, what's going on? What are you doing nowadays?" They'll say little things about me like, "Don't worry about AG, AG will work, he's a worker." They could never question my work ethic.

- **Who were the team leaders?**

The team leaders were the Ron Jaworski's, the John Bunting's. I remember when we had that strike, I'm a rookie, I just came out of college, I just lived in a dorm, I didn't have a car. I'm going into a rookie meeting, "A strike? What do you mean? We're not going to play, what do you mean, we're not going to play?" "Guess what, we're not going to get paid." "Whoa. What is going on?" I got drafted in the fourth round, I got a forty thousand dollar bonus. That was more money than I ever probably saw or heard or even thought existed at that time in my life. Now we're talking strike. They listened to the veterans talking about the union, I'm like, "Wait, whoa, whoa, whoa, union?" That was a different language, you didn't understand too much of it. You really didn't understand, "We're going to go on strike and we're not going to get paid. Here's what the Players Council wants to do, here's where we're headed." What's it going to take for us to play? The leaders who took the initiative to inform us about the things going on from a business standpoint off the field. Ron Jaworski, from a leadership standpoint, on knowing his role on the team as the quarterback and what it means to be the quarterback of the Philadelphia Eagles and what it takes to do that. Quarterback position in itself is going to have a certain role in leadership, because he handles the ball, he has to make the plays when they are made up, and the momentum when there wasn't any momentum. He's got to be able to do that. He's got to control that game. You've got to have the other team fear he can. He can make something happen, just by the flick of his wrist. I think Ron was doing that. Randall Cunningham was phenomenal. I was always amazed. It's so unique, people think, "Man, you played in the NFL," and I'm like, "Yeah, I did." But, you know what was even more unique? I got a chance to see some phenomenal athletes do some phenomenal things. I never really put myself in that position like, "Hey, I play phenomenal." Clay Matthews, wow, a master, a master pass rusher, a master player. He did things to guys literally without touching them and making them fall down. Clay Matthews and Chip Banks, when we came into to the meeting to watch it on defense, highlight film, they were watching it and I was like wow look at this. Clay belongs in the Hall of Fame. There is no doubt I think he was one of the best outside linebackers I've ever seen who knew the game. He'd come up, he knew if you were leaning back, he knew if you were leaning somewhere forward, knew if he could grab you, he'd study it. He'd watch you. He got you. He's got you now. You may stop him here, you won't stop him the whole game. He'd always be prepared, be ready to go and down to earth again, joke with you, be loyal to you, workout hard. His brother Bruce, who I've met too, and his father— you can see the lineage. Bruce is phenomenal, Bruce is another unassuming guy. Clay is a great guy and, at the same time, he's a very intellectual guy, he's very much up on what's going on. He has some great ideas and great opinions on what's happening. I remember when I came to Cleveland, he would do that. Any other guy it would have been, "who are you?" arriving from New Jersey. He'd just engage in a conversation. He's not just trying to make little talk, but he is genuinely interested.

- **What were your feelings when the Browns left Cleveland?**

I said, "Someone was going to get killed. Someone is going to get hurt, someone is going to get hurt the way they did it. Modell, this is not good for you, man." It was hurtful because, first of all, I said, "Well, they're going to get another team. The City of Cleveland is not going to be sitting back, just out cold. They have too much to offer and they are going to get another team hook or crook from somewhere. Another team was going to move from another city in there or whatever." Cleveland fans, I'm telling you, they are a riot, that's what you want. They tell you, "Get another team, get a new stadium, it's all right now." Talent-wise, coaching-wise and all that, it's starting to happen. They've started to make a move. I remember I just couldn't believe it. It's like all of the sudden the President of the United States saying we're going to move the White House down to Texas. They're telling me there is no team in Cleveland. Modell did it on purpose. This is not good. As it turned out, Modell got his wrath. I know Modell can't just walk around in Cleveland right now, even when Baltimore comes to Cleveland, it's dangerous territory for anybody. Modell even being there, when I was with the Browns, and Modell wanted to come talk to the team. I'm standing there looking, "This is the owner of the team and his son. So, this is who the team is going to be turned over to. Yep, you can always tell that's the owners son." He had a stogie in his mouth, smiling. He thinks he's got it going on. It was devastating because I knew all that Cleveland had to offer as a team.

- **You were in the office with the Steelers right?**

Player development and assistant strength coach.

- **Who put you in that position?**

Bill Cowher. Bill Cowher was a great motivator. He's another engaging person. He's perfect as a coach, I've been around coaching. He took Marty Schottenheimer to another level. When I first went there, I was with Marty for a camp. When I was with the Browns, I was with Marty for three years. I was looking for another camp in Kansas City and I knew Bill was like his protégé, then I came to Pittsburgh, he did practice how he taught. That's how Marty did it, that's how he taught, that's how Marty just paused, space of words what he emphasized, what he thought was important. Bill took it to another level because of his first couple of years he was doing things as a head coach. It wasn't as much as his personality. I'm doing some things I think a head coach should be doing. Some of it is Marty Schottenheimer, because, yes, he only knows what he sees. The third year he started putting on some his personality, actually some of his feats out in the field, going out and grabbing players, getting violent. It was his personality, he started getting angry, he started a little more laughing and joking with the players. It was predictable, some certain things, but at the same time, behind the scenes, he was fair. Bill was the kind of guy that he would be open with the players. "Players what are you thinking? What do you think? I'm the coach and I'm going to make my own decision, but what are you thinking?" "Oh, you know, Coach, we've been practicing and we want to go to a movie; we never do that anymore." You think, "So, okay, maybe we'll think about that, let me think about that. Get back with me at the end of this week," and he'd want you to get back with him. My thing with him was I'd tell him, "Hey, coach, this player here is not doing too good, he's not feeling good about the way he's performing now, he's kind of like in limbo." What he's going to do? He may come to you and tell you, "I don't want to play anymore." Maybe you can let him know we recognizing he's still being evaluated. If you say something to him like, "Hey, good job on whatever, just if you give him a little recognition, I think that would be enough to pull him in." Coach would take that and do it. He would listen to the input. He made the final decision and he wanted to know why you are thinking that, why would that be the best way to approach that, or do you think we need to do it this way? I don't think he needs to approach the player, I think maybe I need to and then suggest this and do this, and the reason I'm saying that is, if you do it this way, then he's going to think this way. He's going to think it came down from you and it's coming from the head coach. It seemed to me he could quickly remember how it was as a player, how a player would feel if this was done to him. I think that's what made him unique as a head coach. Bill was able to say, "You're late to practice, all I'm looking for as a head coach is what's going on. Why are you late to this meeting? Tell me something and tell me you're not going to let it happen again." He would say, "Send him up to my office," and I would tell the player, "Coach wants to see you right now. He doesn't want you to come into the meeting while he's having a meeting. He doesn't want you to walk in there while all the players will see that you're late to this meeting. He's going to wait to talk to you, then he's going to let you go to an individual meeting." I'd always have a plan with the player, depending on the severity of what happened. If a player would be, let's say he's an hour late. He's supposed to be there at like eight o'clock in the morning or nine o'clock in the morning and he's not there, so he's not showing up. It's, "Where is he for the meeting?" Coach would say, "Tell him I want to see him in my office, tell him don't come into the meeting." Got it, okay. Now he comes in forty-five minutes later, the meeting is still going on. He's like "Okay, I'll go to the meeting." I'm, "No, no don't go to the meeting." He's like, "Aw, he's pretty mad, huh?" I said, "Yeah. You're going to get an earful." He's like, "You think so? Oh, yeah, you will, but you can buffer this now. I'm going to give you a plan, now you don't have to do it, but this is like the Taser gun or the percussion grenade, this is what it is. You can only use it one time, because if you use, it again it's not going to work. Now what you've got to do, first of all walk in his office and be distracted in your mind and 'yeah, yeah, what's up coach?' He's going to be the first one to serve it to you real quick. 'What are you doing coming late to this meeting, get in here,' something. He's going to say, 'Sit down.' As soon as he directs you to do something, tells you to sit down or asks you a question, or he says, 'What's going on?' All you have to do, now here's the concussion, you've got to throw it out there if you want to. It works good if you're married, if you have a girl, whatever. You say something to the effect, you've got to not look him in the eye, you've got to look away and look out the window, jump up out of the seat or don't sit down, or hit your hand real hard, hit one hand or pound on the desk and say 'My wife doesn't have any sense.' All you've got to do is say that, and he'll be mad, but he'll get it. He'll get it because he's a man and he's married. The first thing he's going to do is go 'Whoa' and he's going to back away from you. He's not going to come at you like a tiger anymore, he's going to back away. He knows it's something domestic and it's private and sensitive, he's going to back away. Now, if he asks another question, be distracted again, you may not even answer it. Say, 'What, Coach,' like you didn't even hear it. He'll say, 'Is something going on?' Then this is where it is, if you say there is something going once you've got him, just throw in you don't want to talk about it right now. Then comfort him, let him know 'I don't want to talk about it right now. I'm here, I apologize for being late, you don't have to worry about that again.' Don't say another word. He's going to go, 'Look, we just need you here on time, okay.' Done. He'll come at you and come at you strong if you don't throw it out there...." I say that in jest, being facetious. I don't think they would really do it, but it's a head game. If you don't do that, be prepared for what comes at you then. He's going to have you reeling. I've seen it during games, in the office, privately, but me, individually, come down to your office doesn't make a difference. At practice, alone, in person, in front of a team, the whole team, a couple of people together, whatever. It doesn't make a difference. It's like horses to the runaway carriage, when you're up there and it's running away, you've got to do a couple of things. Whoa, whoa, get a grip real quick, now. When he does that, you've got to get, you've got to pull it, so he's like, "Don't ever do that again." You can jump up and go, "Well, Coach, what do you want me to do?"

- **Tell us about your Super Bowl ring.**

I don't have a Super Bowl ring. We got the AFC Championship ring. We lost to Dallas in the Super Bowl. Remember, I told you I had all those situations before I went to Villanova, went to Cleveland and how I got treated, the John Elway Drive. I got to Pittsburgh and we're playing San Diego, we're first down at the four-yard line, we score a touchdown. It's the fourth quarter, there are two minutes to go in the game. We have four plays, the last fourth down and four, they knocked the ball down. We're not going. The very next year, now mind you it's fourth down and four, I'm on the sidelines. I've lived through the John Elway Drive, I lived through the Ernie Byner Fumble, I'm like, "Well, here we go, whatever you know, whatever happens here we go." After that game, we have the Indianapolis Colts, AFC Championship game. The last play of the game, Indianapolis has the ball, they throw a Hail Mary pass. The ref decides it's incomplete and we in the Super Bowl. Dallas runs, has its way with us. We threw an offside kick in the second half, we get the ball a minimum exchange by doing this. Neil O'Donnell throws two interceptions. Guy runs it back for touchdowns I think both times, we lose. We go to the AFC Championship again two years later. Denver Broncos, should have beat them, we lose. AFC Championship game again, I think it was the next year. I think against New England. We lose. When I am not with the Steelers, the year after I leave, they go to the Super Bowl and they win it.

- **Sports analysts have said the biggest rivalries are Ohio State/Michigan and Pittsburgh/Cleveland. What do you think?**

Having experienced it, I'd probably be biased, I'd definitely say yes. I didn't know anything about rivalries. I didn't know who Villanova's rivalry was, other than whoever we played last. When I went to Ohio State, it was evident. It was from day one. It was something like, "Don't even mention their name." The "Team up North," don't even mention it. I remember going on my visit to Ohio State, I'm like, "So this is Ohio State, wow, imagine *that*, Ohio State." Then they would just say, "No, no, no, you mean *The* Ohio State." I'd be like, "Huh? It's *The* Ohio State?" They were serious. I was like, "Whoa." Now you see every kid does like *The* LSU, but I remember "The Ohio State" and the "Team up North." We'd never mention it. Unbelievable. It doesn't matter, this is a whole new season, this is a whole new game, it's a whole different game. We played in Michigan, we played against Jim Harbaugh up there. Harbaugh and about 105,000 people. Rivalry. The whole week, every practice was like, "We're going to play a game that big." We are getting so pumped to play this game, we're going through drills, we're going through sessions and we're hearing what they're saying about us, what we need to be doing. It was uncanny. To make a long story short, we go up there and tight security, tight security. Ohio State had a walk, I always remember hearing about that. Ohio State guys take a walk every morning, which was new. They take a walk with the head coach around the hotel or in the parking lot. All this, escorts and everything, crazy. Then we're playing Michigan, big rivalry after the game, fans on the field running around. Then I go to Cleveland, about four years later, after playing with Philadelphia. In Philadelphia, our rivalry was Dallas; that was cool. It was just like a nice team, sort of more flashy. We weren't as good as Dallas at that time. We were rivals because we didn't like them, not rivals that were on the same level playing field. They were a little ahead of us in a lot of ways. Then you go to Cleveland, and we're playing Pittsburgh another rivalry. I was on the Cleveland team, we came to Pittsburgh. I guess we had never beaten them in Three Rivers Stadium for a long time, or maybe never did. One time, me being on the Cleveland Browns, we beat them. In our lockerroom you would have sworn we won the Super Bowl. It was unreal, I'm like, "What's going on?" "We beat Pittsburgh." I said, "What, what do you mean the first time?" They said, "The first time." "You mean we've been here all these years and we never won once?" I remember the first time, I told you Jack Lambert was my idol growing up. Two things I remember, one when I was in the Pros as a player, and in the Pros as administrative working with the Steelers. As a player, I remember we played the Pittsburgh Steelers and there he was, there's Jack Lambert. He's on the same field I'm on. We're playing. It was kind of surreal. Then another time, we had some function, I was around Pittsburgh, I'm around ex players, alumni players, and I met him. This guy was everything. To tell you the impact some of these players had on me when I was playing, Buck Buchanon was in Kansas City at the time, he had some function. I had a chance to meet him. I got a chance to meet Buck Buchanon. There I am I'm playing seven years and I've got a chance to meet Buck Buchanon now and he's done playing. I go, "Hi, how are you doing? I'm Anthony," and he goes, "Hi, I'm Buck Buchanon," and he wasn't even really paying attention to me. I'm like, "He doesn't even know I'm even here." He was like, looking away, says, "Hi, how are you doing?" Shake my hand. I know you want to shake my hand, here you go" and that's about it. That kind of left a bad taste in my mouth, it wasn't the best thing that I remember about Mr. Buck himself. Jack Lambert, I was looking at him going, "Yeah, you hear stories, you hear that he is a park ranger and all that. I can see where this guy would be a surly type of guy, want to get into a fight and wanted to mix it up...." I didn't like him because of that, not because of that. It's because he just played it, he played it from Kent State.

- **Who was your nemesis on the field? Who gave you the most trouble?**

What year did Barry Stevens come on the league? Eric Dickerson, that's what I'm saying. When I think of those guys, and I'm watching them, I'm in the game and you go, "Whoa, wow, wow." Then you're like, "Help me, I might bring them down." Barry Stevens without a doubt. Phenomenal and just the only person I've ever seen I could say come close to that, I know if I played against him, was Curtis Martin or the other halfback of St. Louis. Curtis Martin another guy who open field, yeah, he has skills. Eric Dickerson, watching him like, "Wow." So, you would train, like continue running, because he's got phenomenal speed and he's big. Hershel Walker. Dallas' offensive line. Washington Redskins, Sweat Hogs. Don't forget Russ Grimm was a part of those Hogs and I had to play against him and Joe Jacoby. Those guys were like, I think they were the first big line three-hundred-plus guys and I'm about 225. It was just another acclimation of it all of just being there, and it's kind of surreal, like a movie in some ways. I look at it from an alter ego standpoint at that point in my life or whatever I was doing then, how I was training, how I was thinking, how I was trying to get better, hitting on some cylinders, not hitting on all cylinders. Then you want to be a contributing player, after you contribute you want to be a starter, not just a contributor. I can be a contributor on a special team, you want to be a starter. After starter, you want to be a significant player, you want to be somebody that they count on. Then the other teams know that you're going to be a bonafide player they've got to do something with. After that, you want to be a solid player in the league, maybe an All Star player in the league that players recognize you're pretty good at that position, one of the top playing that position. After that, you want to be someone that shines in that position for the legacy. You want to be a Hall of Famer. I think I struck the point where I became a starter, I became a contributing player. I didn't take it any further. I worked probably as hard as anybody, but I don't think I took it any farther. "You know, Anthony, you could be better than what you are...." I think there was a contentedness in some of the way I worked and some of the things I did that kept me out of harm's way. Oh, yeah, I could have been better. In what ways, I don't know. You may not be any better than you are on the field because that's your own DNA showing at that point. There is no better.

- **The Cleveland Browns team has so many distinctions named after plays: Red Right 88, The Drive, The Fumble, the Bottle Throwing Incident, the Rudd Penalty, the Cross Bar. Why do we get labeled like this as the Cleveland Browns?**

I don't think it's something that's labeled as much as it's the Rodney Dangerfield of professional football. Things do happen in sports. We've had a number of situations where they've happened. It's kind of crazy we can sit here and actually name them like they have been named and, having experienced it, know there is something better to come. Unfortunately, at the time, some of the people who have been around, have lived through it, it was not their time. But the Cleveland Browns, the best days are ahead of it. The best days that they are going to have are ahead of them. I really realize a lot of things they have gone through. Not only the plays on the field. I don't think the things have happened to cause them to lose games or lose championships, lose players, when you actually lose your team the way they lost their team, the way there was no team in Cleveland. There was nothing there during that time that the NFL was having their business played. There was no team and the way they lost it and to get a team back. I get the feeling, they get the city, the fans, the atmosphere. Nothing had to be rebuilt. Tangibly the stadium, sure, but all the ingredients were there and that's why it happened. I don't know how many other teams could have lived through that. I don't know how many other teams could have done that. I don't know how many other cities would have had that happen. It had to happen in Cleveland, it had to because the energy level. It was like the big bang theory, something's going to happen, it's going to happen. It created life there, all the swirling masses were already in the air and not to have a team there...no, no. Something's going to happen. Look at it and think of all those things. Those things couldn't happen if you weren't in a position to have them happen. Cleveland has gotten close, they've had some winning teams, they've had some winning players, and some winning plays still to make that happen. At the time those things happened, I wished a lot of teams would of had those same mistakes. Look at Denver, when they lost four Super Bowls in a row and they came back and won two Super Bowls in a row. A lot of teams have done that. Look at all the AFC Championship losses that Pittsburgh has, they lost home, then they win in the Super Bowl. Green Bay for a while, they win the Super Bowl. Indianapolis Colts, they lost the AFC Championship, then they go to the Super Bowl and they win that. A lot of players are going down with their own Rodney Dangerfield plays—a lot of players, a lot of coaches have had that happen running Rodney Dangerfield plays. That's part of life. It's something you can be a schlep rock, I guess it used to be in the Flintstone's or whatever it was, you know, the bad cloud flying over your head if you want it to be. I don't think Cleveland has that. Cleveland loves to say that, you can talk about the house they may keep, but it's theirs. You can talk about the bad plays they've had, you can talk about the legacy they have, how they didn't win this big game, but it's theirs and they are proud of it. I had the unique opportunity last year to go to a Cleveland Browns game, because as an alumni you can go. It was one of the greatest experiences of my life. I never went to too many professional games. I haven't gone to too many, except as a player or as a coach or as an administrator. I went there and I was sitting in the stands being amongst it. It was a whole other element of energy created and there is a whole expectation as a fan that is expected. They know football and they expect it to be played the way it should be. There's no hiding from any of those fans in that stadium and they expect everybody who comes there, I think it's because of the Midwest blue-collar mentality, to put a fair share of energy into your work and you will be rewarded. I think Cleveland right now is at its renaissance peak of things happening, with or without the current staff or some current players that are there. It's going to happen. When Cleveland wins the Super Bowl—and it's not going to be too far off, it really won't—but when they win the Super Bowl, it might be when your book comes out, it could happen just like that.

- **Are Cleveland Brown fans really the best in the NFL?**

There are two fans I say, Pittsburgh and Cleveland. The reason that rivalry is so good is because of the fans. Not because of the players or the teams. They've had some bad teams. One team was doing a lot better than the other team, it's because of the fans. Rivalries are good because of the fans. You're not going to find two better cities, you couldn't write a better script: Rivals Cleveland and Pittsburgh. Look at that calendar when it comes out I guarantee people in the Midwest from Cleveland and Pittsburgh look to see when those games are and they schedule around them.

- **Do you still feel like you are a part of the Browns organization?**

Yeah I do, I really do. I could be more connected to it. Not just when I see the players, but also Dino Lucarelli. Memories flush (run) through my body like when I think about Baldwin Wallace, the practices there, the games, the old stadium, the old locker rooms. I look back and I go, "Wow, what a ride. That was fun." Being a part of the Cleveland Browns, even thinking about it, now there's people I met, people I saw, the things that were done, things that weren't done, it's all part of it. It was a great time and it's a great city. I still feel a part of Cleveland, I want them to win. I really do. I really want them to win. More than the Steelers, Pittsburgh is going to win, but I'd like to see them win. If it comes down to Cleveland and Pittsburgh going to a championship game to see who goes to the Super Bowl, man, it wouldn't, but I think I'd probably want Cleveland to go because they haven't. You won't see the likes of what they would do, you'll never see a parade, you'll never see anything to the likes of what the Cleveland people, the city would do. Anything anyone's ever said about Cleveland would be over. The Cleveland chip on the shoulder playing, they are going to be behind it. Right now, that's what they are doing. They play with a legacy of a chip on their shoulder. They don't get the respect. People think now, "you know you're good and everything else, but you're going to find a way to lose. You've got a good team, got some great running backs, got a great quarterback. When it comes out to the end the long and short of it, something's going to happen...."

- **What was the saddest story during your NFL experience?**

The saddest story was probably when my father passed away in '85 and playing that '86 season. That was a little bit different, going and playing and practicing and coming back to the hospital and seeing what's going on. I was at the hospital when he passed, that was a little different. I was young and immature. It is tough. Another hard part was when Eddie Johnson passed away. He was getting sick and I had known Eddie, I had talked to Eddie.

- **Tell us about Eddie "The Assassin" Johnson.**

You saw what you got. Eddie Johnson was another guy that I came there and he talked to me, very giving of his time, one that was very curious. Very intense on the field, wanted to win in the worst way. Did whatever he could to win. Off the field, no other guy is going to be as pleasant or as giving or has a bigger heart than he does. I always enjoyed him because he would at least talk, he'd engage, he'd be real, he'd be true. What I saw in the paper matched up to what he was in real life. He didn't talk to get sound bites. He liked to have fun, know what you're doing, what you're about. He was neat.

- **What about "Go Bob."**

I remember Bob Golic being at Notre Dame. I was thinking, "Man, that's a good linebacker." Then I saw him at Cleveland and thought, "Man, he's gained a lot of weight, but, man, can he move." I knew he was going to be in movies, with his personality. I was shocked he didn't get more offers because his personality was spontaneous, had a great smile, always had a great dialogue, and could take whatever you threw at him. Another guy, Clay Matthews, Clay was a little more serious. Clay could talk on a whole other level, and I don't know if "Go Bob" knew, but he's got it. We had a lot of serious people there, we had a lot of intellectual people, Dan Fike.

- **Was there any negatives while you were playing?**

No, the game has been very positive for me. It is something I look at and I'm very proud that I played. I'm very proud of the way I played it, very proud of the way I approached it. I can say with a straight conscience I gave it all. I've got as far as the training and getting ready to play this game. I know what it takes to be the best, to be a champion. I've seen great players, not just me. I wasn't a great player. I was a good player, a great human being. I look at it and I know the steps I took to get there. When the light is turned on, you that's what you've got to do, that's when you perform. When the lights off, okay you're off. The great players, players make plays during the times you've got to make it, and that's all I did. It just happened to be in Cleveland and Philadelphia and Pittsburgh. I had opportunities and I'm looking for opportunities now. Seeing which way can I utilize everything I've gone through, not just sports or in life, but what can I do to enhance anybody's position and whatever they're looking to do. Football has taught me a lot of ways and a lot of good ideas on how to handle such things. Just a great reflection, I reflect. I can't imagine putting on a helmet now and having to get used to it being tight on my forehead. I can't imagine getting running on a sweep or running up the line having to throw myself into a lineman. I can't imagine running, sprinting…I don't know the last time I did that.

- **Are players worth their salaries? Should they be more fan conscious?**

Yes and yes. The money is going to be something the market is going to control. It's not going to be something you're going to control. The monetary basis, that's something the fans can't control to a point. If the fans love the product, they're going to buy it. People are going to talk about the high cost of health care, the high cost to go to the doctor, but the reality of it is, these guys know what they are doing and you're going to get sick and you want somebody that knows what they're doing. You're going to pay for it. You will pay for it because you want to get well. I know this is entertainment and you're going to pay for it because you like the team, so when you're playing for it doesn't seem, "well, it's just a jacket," yeah, it is so the money part of it is one thing. Television people want to see something that larger than life and, unfortunately, in sports, that's what it becomes. I've seen a lot of players do a lot of things in sports. I'm looking on the field and I'm seeing these guys are incredible. I'm one of them. It was such a surreal point in my life. "Wow, we're going to come out to your house, what a game you had, you're with the Eagles, with the Browns." "Yeah, I am." Sometimes I think I even felt, like don't look at me like I'm different, don't look at me like I'm something unique. I'm just like you, flesh and blood, but the difference is by me getting in position to show my football skills. Somebody somewhere at a team somehow believed enough that I was able to do is good. I love that aspect of that whole part of being successful. And my whole thing of being successful, the first thing about being successful, I'm not even talking about training, I'm not talking about you've got to want it, you've got to really think about how you're going to get it. No, the first thing you've got to do being successful is just show up. Just show up, just be there. If you have an interview at ten, be there at ten o'clock, even if you don't have anything else, you have a chance. Here you go you might have a chance. Teams any given Sunday say you have a chance. You don't know what can happen, but for me that's what it was all about. For seven years I did that, each year it got harder and harder and each year I overcame it. So, I look for things like that in my life. I've done things like that in my life, whether it's running a marathon, whether it's doing martial arts, two different disciplines, what's next? What is it getting a Master's Degree, what's next? PhD, what's next? What can I do? I can do anything. I played professional football, my years of playing and getting developed to be anything other, anything else professionally as athletic ability goes, those days are really behind me. I'm not looking to become a professional hockey player or anything like that now. My development in that is past me. I'm not looking, but what do I really want to do now and going after that. Look at that in terms of I'm not going in for fanaticism, the whole fanaticism of being a fan of anything is a whole different exploratory situation for me because I find that so fascinating. It's such an emotional game. Any other type of entertainment you go to, you watch television, you go to performing arts, you go to a play, go to a movie, you read a book, they're putting in certain words, certain lines the act of doing certain things, certain tools they put in there to get you to feel a certain emotion. It is preconceived that they want you to feel sad at this point, they want you to feel happy right here, they want you to feel angry right here, they want you to feel terrified right here, they want you to be scared, they want you to be happy. Sports is the only one that's not written down. What you see is real emotion, what you feel is real emotion, it is not preconceived on how you're going to feel before the event happens. When you feel happy, you feel it, when you feel like your team has just lost, you feel sad, you feel it. That's why after Sunday, or whenever Super Bowl Sunday is, when all the emotion ever flows because it's real, it's the real deal. It's not like all the emotion ever flows after the Oscars are announced or the Emmy's are given out. Not like all that stuff, it's after the emotion of a game and you feel emotionally drained or you feel emotionally high, that's when people have parades and they get arrested for burning cars. They're losing control. They're out in the street. From what I've seen, you've got to have a control of that factor coupled with taking advantage of your opportunities. Being in Cleveland is a great opportunity in not only the people I met from playing football, but people I met off the field. Friends of mine, I'm still friends with, that was twenty years ago. If I'm up on a stage and doing a show, or I'm in a movie, I'm not the guy that's getting a shot, it's not a "we" thing. I'm feeling something affecting me because of how you're in the scene. I am playing the game with my team, here I'm feeling the ebb and flow after every play. That's how it is that's the game. People come to the game, "Get ready to ride this ride, here we go." If you're playing it, if you're watching it with some friends who are on the other team, be ready for ebb and flow and help them down. It's a great, great ride. I think there's something to be said that I don't think it can be captured, but people like that. Maybe it can be bottled, then sold in some way, that feeling, and they try to attach rivalries and try to attach some of the bigger hyped games, some leagues and people like that ebb and flow of natural, that sports gives them, that real emotion. Maybe we can have football all year around, arena teams, all these different arena teams coming up and we can have all these different sports leagues and make it so it's competitive. That competitive instinct, or competitive nature, what else can we have people compete where people want to watch? So, what do you have? You have the Donald Trump show, you have all these reality shows on making it, or getting the job, or competition in dancing, competition in singing. Competition, that's what it's all about. You're touching on something competition brings it out. People want to see the winner and the loser. People want to see it coming to a head. People want to see the best of the best. When those two teams take the field, if you have a team on the sidelines of a professional football game, it is a whole different level than watching it at home on your television. You're seeing, it may change your life from what you think sports is about because these guys are really going after it. They're really laying it out there. They are moving so fast, so quick, with such energy level, somebody's going to get hurt. I can say that, somebody's going to get hurt out here.

- **What are your hobbies now?**

Hobbies now, there is some entrepreneurial stuff I like to do. I like to run and keep in shape. I want to take up Aikido as my third martial art and get more proficient in it. Golfing is good, reading. I like to get into movies, not be in the movie, but be involved in help producing movies. A friend of mine who is a Villanova graduate is in the movies in New York and him and I have been collaborating on some movie gigs. Entrepreneurially, I have a program called "Life's A Sport, Train For It." It's a program I developed involving six areas of an athlete's development. Six processional parts of an athlete's development, from skills to endurance to speed to weight training, diet, and rest. They also contrast to life. I'm putting it into a program where I can help families get their son or daughter to be in the best health they can be at this point of their life, not just to be playing on the team. It is my job, it's one of my own companies I've started, my company is "Stepping Toward Success."

- **What's the AG Foundation?**

The AG Foundation is a foundation I started when I got with the Steelers that involves helping players [and] young people get better frames of reference when they make decisions. Basically helping them understand they have to make decisions, you are only as good as a reference, you are only going to make as good a decision based on the reference around you. Whatever somebody's put under your nose, whatever you might have gotten a chance to bring into your reality. Other than that, you're left with whatever you know, not what somebody's taught you or whatever. A lot of decisions players make, good, bad, indifferent, in the league, you can see they're making decisions based on what they know. Michael Vick, he made some decisions based on all he knew, not somebody saying, "Hey Mike, this's what I'm thinking. Your name is pretty big, I wouldn't do this, I wouldn't do that, but it's totally up to you…" but I would save him the consequences. That's what I see. The way you're brought up definitely has an influence on the next step. People sometimes either overemphasize the way you're brought up, or de-emphasize the way you're brought up. I think it's a little bit of both.

- **What did you get out of your NFL experience?**

I got a sense of my own, what can I do. That was something that I did. Out of all the support, out of everybody being behind me, of everybody supporting me and rallying with me, it was basically me, me and myself, just me and nobody else. That gave me some reassurance I can do some of these things on my own. I never had that before. I never did a lot of those things until I got into the Pros. It wasn't easy for me to do. Also, beyond that, it gave me a feeling you can do anything, you really can. The mind is an incredible, incredible thing that can take you to the level. I wasn't the biggest guy, I wasn't the fastest guy. I wasn't the guy that everybody said oh this guy is going to blow it up or make things happen because of his size. What I was able to do was look at it from this different perspective. I know this too will pass, no matter what the circumstances or conditions. I look better from that aspect, I saw this is going to pass, this is going to be the way it's always going to be for me. That reassurance for me to play professional football, leading up to professional football, I think I got the attitude I can overcome a lot of things if I believe and I have the faith. I wasn't always a religious person. I thought I was and always believed in God. I thought I did and always believed that He would take care of me, I thought I did. Only since looking back at it and being realistic about what football has done for me and what it's been able to give me, football has given me a better sense and a better perspective of the world, a better perspective of my own world view on what is real and what isn't real. I'll have many opportunities to do a lot of things. I've been around players, as a player, also I've been around players not in the evaluation perspective, but also as someone who is helping them in non-evaluating positions. That gave me the heads up, at least a little bit of being the first being able to say, "I know that everything people may think of me isn't true, I know a lot of the bad stuff people may think of me is true isn't always true."

One of the things I got from Coach Cowher is, "You're never as good as you think you are and you're never as bad as they think you are. It's somewhere in between. Don't take yourself too serious because it can change, it can change with the snap of the ball." What I try to look at is, and this is all from my reflective Monday morning quarterback looking back at my life, just keep moving. I never played organized basketball, but one of the things that I realized in basketball is you've got to keep moving without the ball in your hand. The ball in your hands means that you're up, you're about to make a play, you're a playmaker if you have the ball in your hands and you can make something happen. Not all of the time are you going to have the ball in your hands, and sometimes in your life things are not going to go the way you want them to. You're not always going to have the best opportunities to make something happen the way you want it to, but you still have to keep moving, even without the ball. The unique magic is when you get the ball, you'll do what you do best with it, as basketball players do. The unique things they do are based on repetition and being able to do their natural DNA stuff and that's the same way here. Football has allowed me to be able to paint, so to speak, to create my own artwork in seven years of time, a piece of art of my life, to quantify it down to playing a sport. You want to see what I'm about, watch the way I approach the game, maybe that will show you a little bit. Watch the way I play the game, that will show a little bit. Watch the way I respond to losing, watch how I respond to winning. There's a lot more that goes into it on a preparation aspect of playing professional football, I've learned some things.

Anthony Griggs								
Defensive End 1982-88								
Ohio State								
Season	Team	Games	Defense				Fumbles	Total
			INT	Yds	Avg	TD		Points
1982	PHI	9	0	0	0	0	0	0
1983	PHI	16	3	61	20.3	0	0	0
1984	PHI	16	0	0	0	0	0	0
1985	PHI	16	0	0	0	0	0	0
1986	CLE	16	0	0	0	0	0	0
1987	CLE	12	0	0	0	0	0	0
1988	CLE	5	0	0	0	0	0	0
Career		90	3	61	20.3	0	0	0

Anthony Griggs zeroing in to make a tackle against Green Bay

SOURCE: CLEVELAND BROWNS

22

Mike Pagel

Mike Pagel has been honored as one of the smartest quarterbacks who ever put on a Cleveland Browns uniform. He took over the field general's position after injuries to Bernie Kosar and Don Strock. Otto Graham, Frank Ryan, Milt Plum, Mike Phipps, Brian Sipe, as well as Bernie Kosar, were all great quarterbacks. Cleveland writers compiled information and decided that leadership skills of Mike were second only to Bernie himself. And that leadership has never failed Mike since he left the playing field in 1993. Now he is a coach and mentor to several high school and college players. He not only works with kids to make them better at the next level, but also tutors players to get them through the season. The job is a labor of love as he is now working with his son, Kellen, who just finished his school career at Strongsville High. Presently enrolled at Bowling Green, Kellen is confident in his abilities at the college level. Mike says coaching and teaching is not always a positive for his students. Sometimes a harsh reality has to be communicated to the student. As in life, as parents, we think our sons and daughters are much more gifted than they ever can be. Yet, sometimes the reality has to be explained to the player and his guardians. This ability Mike has to get that last bit of knowledge out of the player is not something all coaches possess. When we talk, he expresses himself in a concise manner, in a way that leaves no question as to what he is trying to say. Too many coaches want to teach, but the students don't understand and are left behind. That won't happen to his pupils as long as the player is capable of moving up and on. His physical talent runs in the family as his brother Karl Pagel was a Professional Baseball Player with the Chicago Cubs and the Cleveland Indians. Mike was not a one-sport athlete in Arizona either. His knowledge is not only touted to high school and college players, but has been offered to a larger audience as he has also been a commentator for television and radio.

- **What was it like to walk on the field as a Browns player the first time?**

Well, I will tell you—when the Colts were getting ready to trade me, the head coach called me in and said, "If there is anything I can do for you, let me know." One of the things that I said was, "Please, if you are going to trade me, do not trade me to Buffalo or Cleveland," because I played a number of games in Buffalo and it seemed to be always wet, always windy, always miserable. The one time I played at the Cleveland Municipal Stadium in 1983, it was late November, typical Northeast Ohio day—dreary, cold, windy, cloudy, and felt very oppressive to me. I did not want to come up and play and this be my home field. But, when I walked out onto the field for that first game—of course, it was a pre-season game and weather was a lot different— but to see those seventy-plus thousand fans in orange and brown going crazy for those orange helmets coming out onto the field, that was a GREAT feeling. There is nothing like standing in the tunnel of old Municipal Stadium, and I was always one of the last guys out of the locker room because I got claustrophobic in that tunnel. I could always feel it though—when that first helmet popped up out of that dugout—because you couldn't hear the cheer, but you would feel the energy come down that concrete hallway and just hit you with such force. It was like, "Okay, here we go—lets go," and it would take a while for all of us to get out of that tunnel, but that roar would just keep pounding you, that energy, the sound waves would keep hitting you, all the way out, until you got out onto the field and then you could hear the roar. Wow—what a way to start a game.

- **Did you get that kind of feeling while you were playing?**

When you were actually playing, no, you didn't, but for me as a quarterback, to drop back on a Monday Night game against Indianapolis in 1988, third game of the year. We had not scored a touchdown…took the opening drive down the field, and I think it was an eighteen-yard pass to Ozzie Newsome in the back right corner of the end zone. To watch Ozzie lay out, catch it, score a touchdown, and to hear that roar that came, that is why you played the game. To hear the appreciation of 75-80 thousand people.

- **When you played against the Colts in 1988, did it feel like revenge?**

No, it really didn't. It was kind of fun to get out and play against some of my former teammates. We were 1-1 at that time and it was Monday Night. It was my first start for the Browns. I was more geared to making sure I knew what I had to do and perform at a level that was needed at that time for this team. It wasn't so much of a revenge factor, but it felt good. It felt good to be able to go out and control the game from the outset, but we never really were challenged by them throughout that game. I think the final score was 23-17 or something. I don't feel like we were ever really challenged by them in that game and it felt good to come out and dominate from the opening kickoff to the end of the game. For my first start with the Browns, I think it helped our team for them to think, "Hey, third string guy, he can still play. We are going to be okay."

- **When did you decide you wanted to be a professional football player?**

[Laughs] I don't think I ever decided I wanted to be a professional football player. It kind of fell into my lap more than anything. I had a chance in high school to play the State Semi-final and Final games in Sun Devil Stadium at

Arizona State and after the semi-final, Frank Kush walked onto the field and offered me a scholarship at Arizona. I thought, "Okay, this is the way I am going to go." I actually thought I was going to be a baseball player, but being Arizona Player of the Year my senior year in high school and getting that scholarship opportunity at Arizona, I said, "Okay, I'll take that and I will go play football." Then again, my senior year at ASU, we had a very talented offense—led the nation in total offense. I had a pretty darn good year and, all of a sudden, people were saying, "Hmmm, possible late first- or early second-round draft choice...." I thought "Okay, works for me," but I was still playing baseball at the time at ASU. It came down to, where were my talents better? Higher in ranking in baseball, I was just an average player, whereas in football, my quarterback talents were near the top. It more fell into my lap than me deciding, "I'm going to be a football player."

- **Browns fans thought they had the best quarterbacks back then.**

Well, I think as a staff, we were the most talented, no question about it. Buffalo had Jim Kelly and Frank Wright, but they only had two. We had three. I think at that time—maybe not player for player, the most talented quarterbacks in the league—but as a staff, the most capable staff.

- **Was there a lot of camaraderie between you guys?**

Yes. We worked had together. It was more of a camaraderie with the whole team. It was such a pleasure to play on that team because we had forty guys that lived in Cleveland year round. It was just a natural offshoot for the quarterbacks to have a nice working relationship. We respected each other tremendously and that goes a long way.

- **Any problems with injuries due to the lack of hitting during camp?**

I've always thought that one of the problems you run into in the NFL is you notice how many quarterbacks go down early in the first two or three weeks of the season. Part of that is because you don't get enough game reps in camp—preseason games. Most starters only go, at most now, a half and you're just not getting into that flow or rhythm of getting hit because you don't get hit in practice. Then you get into a game and you might throw ten or twelve passes in a half and you're going to get hit five or six times there. Most of those are bumps and things like that, so you are not really getting hit and your body is not getting into that shape. It could be the same that is happening with this team now. You go from no hitting to, all of a sudden, full speed, full contact, getting hit on every play. That could be one reason why we have the number of injuries we do.

- **You hear some camps hit more; those seem to have fewer injuries.**

Well, there seems to be a happy medium there because I played on some teams early in my career where we hit constantly in camp and throughout the season in practice, and by mid-November, the tanks are empty. Physically, you just can't take that kind of pounding for six months and still have "gas in the tank." Whereas I have been on other teams and we hardly hit at all, and, yeah, we had energy by the end of the year, but we had a bunch of guys that were banged up because they weren't used to taking the hits. So, I think somewhere in between is where you want to be. What is that right amount of hitting? Who knows, but what coaches are deadly afraid of is their star runningback being hit in practice and destroying a shoulder or breaking a leg. If it's going to happen, let it be on the field during the game.

- **Where were you born?**

A town called Douglas, Arizona, right on the Mexican border. I lived there for about six to nine months before my mom took a job in Phoenix, Arizona. My dad was a teacher at Douglas High school. He said he could get a job in Phoenix coaching/teaching somewhere, so we moved.

- **What high school did you attend?**

I went to Phoenix Washington High School. I was Arizona Player of the Year in football. I played basketball and baseball there also.

- **How did you do during your basketball career?**

I was the starting point guard and made the At-Large All-Star Basketball Team. We had a North and a South, and then I made the At-Large team. For baseball, I started as a sophomore, was the 2nd leading hitter all three years.

- **Were you aware that you were classified as the second-best all-around athlete the Cleveland Browns ever had?**

No, I wasn't. I didn't read the article…. Well, I will have to thank my mom for writing that article. [Laughs] I always thought I was a pretty good athlete. I had the opportunity to play college-level in all three sports, football, baseball, and basketball. After I graduated, in baseball they replaced me with a guy by the name of Barry Bonds.

- **Who was your college coach?**

I had two. I had Frank Kush for two years; Darrell Rogers for two.

- **How did they influence your professional career?**

Well, Frank is from Winthrop, Pennsylviania, a small coal-mining town. He was about 155 lb. All-American nose tackle at Michigan State. He developed this tough guy attitude and, during my first two years in college, I had the talent to play at that level. I thought I knew how to work hard but he taught me how to push myself above and beyond what I ever thought I possibly could. He did it out of fear—that is how he coached. I was nineteen years old and deathly afraid of letting him down. Darrell came in the next two years and went completely one-eighty the other way. Darrell would say,

"Just relax. Go and play the game and let your abilities go." He taught me how to relax and not allow one bad play turn into two bad plays or three bad plays. They both had a very strong influence on me making it into the NFL.

- **Is it a combination of both those things that make your game better?**

Yes. Absolutely, yes. It was that work ethic and then the ability to relax and just let my abilities take care of themselves.

- **Did the work ethic improve the skill?**

Well, I knew I had the ability to play because from the time I was walking, I could throw a football. They used to tease me in college that I always threw a football harder than a baseball. In first and second grade, I was drawing up plays from scratch that worked actually. My high school and JV coach would implement the plays and they would work, too. I have always had the ability to play and understand the game. The work ethic that Frank taught me was how to push myself and not accept where I was, always push myself to a higher level. The desire to never be satisfied with where you were, he was very good at making guys push themselves to the next level.

- **What kind of parental influence did you have?**

My dad was a coach—football and baseball—in high school. My mom, unless there was another game going on with one of my brothers, never missed one of my high school games. My mom would listen to two different baseball games on separate radios almost every night.

- **What was it like to play for Marty Schottenheimer?**

Marty was a stickler on playing the game his way, he was a very conservative coach. He could not stand guys making mental mistakes, which was fine with me because I didn't like making mental mistakes at all. I didn't like making physical ones either, but mental ones are something you can control. That was something instilled in me when I was very young. My dad is the same way. For me, playing for Marty was not difficult at all.

- **Was he a stickler for getting ready for the game physically?**

He was more of a mental guy than a physical one. Having the right footwork and doing things the way the game plan dictated. Whatever position you played, you did it right every time. That was both a combination of mental and physical—he did not like busted assignments. He did not like guys doing needless or useless penalties, such as offside. He did not mind the occasional holding call because that meant you were trying, but an illegal block in the back he could not stand. He thought if you were behind the guy, let him go. Marty liked smart players.

- **What was it like playing for Bud Carsen?**

I loved Bud. He was a defensive coordinator in Baltimore when I first got into the league. Bud was a football guy one-hundred percent through and through. That is all he was. There were no "airs" about him. What Bud told you was honest and came from a football guy. His problem was he was also a defensive coordinator through and through. I am glad he got the opportunity to be a head coach, he did some great things with us in 1989, but I think in 1990, we had twenty-two or twenty-three new players on the roster, and I think Bud took the fall for that. But don't think he had a whole of say in the matter because Bud was a blood and guts, pound on them, get after them, "we are going to be very aggressive" type of coach. All of sudden, we went from a team who thought that way to a team of pure speed. In a nutshell, I enjoyed playing for Marty and Bud for different reasons.

- **How about Jim Shofner?**

Jim? Oh, he was like your best friend. Very good offensive mind. Very well respected, very knowledgeable. His problem was, he came in as an interim guy and was a very nice guy and a lot of guys took advantage of that. Plus, it was 1990, a very ugly season. "The rats were leaving the ship in a hurry...." When the wheels started coming off, there were guys stealing the lug nuts.

- **As a fourth round draft pick for Baltimore, did you expect to play?**

Actually, I did not. Going into camp that year we had two veterans: Greg Landry, who had been in the league forever, so long in fact we called him Pops, and David Humm, who was a guy that only started one game. We also drafted a quarterback that year, a guy by the name of Art Schlister out of Ohio State. Going into that camp, my chances of playing a lot were not very good, knowing how good Greg was, how good Art was…. I heard so many things about Art's abilities. He was up for Heisman, won a lot of football games. I played against him one year, but I didn't really study him, so I did not know how good or what type of player he was going into camp. I thought I would just go out and bust my tail, work as hard as I could.

- **What was your rookie song?**

Actually, we had as many, if not more, rookies on that team. Frank Kush was my first coach in the NFL—he was a rookie coach. We had two veteran coaches and the rest were rookie coaches. Frank spent that whole camp trying to make the veterans understand they had no rights because they were 2-14 the year before. So, we did not even have a rookie song. The veterans reported in the afternoon. That morning, the fourth or fifth day of camp, they cut Greg Landry. Outright cut him. It sent a signal to everyone that nobody was safe. They traded Bert Jones the morning of the draft to get the fourth pick from the Rams. The first day of practice for the veterans, Roger Carr came out in red shorts, which we were blue and white, of course, and Frank told him to go in and change his shorts. Roger refused, so Frank suspended him and within two days Roger was gone. There was not a whole lot of any hazing going on because Frank treated the veterans worse than the rookies.

- **What players did you enjoy playing with anywhere?**

Some of my favorites were Clay Matthews, Matt Barr, Pat Beach, a tight end with the Colts. We actually played against each other four years in college, went to two All-star games together, and became very good friends. I'd even thought, "Wouldn't it be cool if we got drafted by the same team...." What were the odds of that? It ended up he went in the sixth round for the Colts. He played thirteen or fourteen years as tight end and as long snapper. The long snapper kept him in the league a few years longer. I enjoyed playing with Jim Everett, quarterback for the Rams and the Saints. Harry, I had a lot of fun with him. He played wide receiver while at Stanford and we played together for a short period of time. Brian Brennan was my roommate for five years with the Browns. Dave Puzzouli was another favorite.

- **You took a big leadership role when you were playing, even when you were third string quarterback. Is that part of your nature?**

Yeah, sure. It is part of my personality. One of the things about the three of us [quarterbacks] was that there was not a lack of confidence in any of us in our own abilities. None of us could not stand to lose. We all understood how to play the game. We had some interesting meetings, especially when Marty was the offensive coordinator, because under Lindy Infante, we were allowed to voice our opinions, but Lindy had final say in everything. But, with Marty being more of a defensive guy who decided to take over the offensive coordinator position, he allowed us to have a lot of input and, boy, there were some interesting discussions. We all had our own beliefs in how we should attack our opponents and, sometimes, they were similar and, sometimes, not, so that led to some interesting discussions, to say the least.

- **What were your feelings when the Browns left and went to Baltimore?**

I was devastated, not in a personal way, but more for the Browns fans—but not just Cleveland, because I know there are some loyal fans that extend way beyond the Cleveland area. Having not won a Championship since 1964 and you are still selling the place out, you still have people that can't wait for camp to open, and they can't wait for the season opener. They live and breathe Browns football and for this team to be moved out of this area [Cleveland], the pain and suffering they created for a lot of fans in Northeast Ohio or Browns fans in general—it just devastated me.

- **Was Art Modell to blame for the whole thing?**

No. I think there is plenty of blame to go around. I don't have any specific information, but there was a lot of politics. The people in Cleveland essentially were pawns in the game. We were all sacrificed.

- **You were born, raised, played high school and college ball in Arizona, played for Baltimore, moved to Indiana, came to Cleveland, then went to L.A. to play for the Rams. Why did you move back to Cleveland?**

Well, my ex-wife was from Indianapolis, born and raised there, and she wanted to move back there but I had said, "No, it is too close to your dad, why don't we move to Phoenix?" and she said, "No, it is too far from my dad." So, we looked at L.A. and thought, "way too expensive and not a place to raise children." At the time, we said, "Why don't we stay here in Cleveland? It is a great place to raise kids. The weather isn't the greatest, but the cost of living is reasonable and we are comfortable here."

- **Ohio State vs. Michigan and Cleveland vs. Pittsburgh are two greatest rivalries in sports as stated by ESPN. What is your opinion on this?**

Well, it is hard to argue with that. You could go down to Auburn vs. Alabama and they would argue that point. Or Florida State vs. Miami , Florida State vs. Florida, Texas vs. Oklahoma...they would argue that. I could argue Arizona State vs. Arizona. There are lots of rivalries, but the passion Ohio football fans have for their teams, it creates such passion against those guys up North and those guys across the river—I can't even say their names. It just creates so much animosity and so much passion for the home team. It also creates just as much dislike for those other two teams. Now you could go over to Pittsburgh and they would say, "Cleveland isn't our biggest rival, Cincinnati is." But over the years, with the proximity and the fact that Cleveland and Pittsburgh are "sister cities," they are an extension of each other, it is like "I can beat on my brother, but no one else can." Now with Michigan and Ohio State, how many years were they the "Big 2" and everybody else in the "Big 10?" It came down to that game every year, who was going to win the conference and, therefore, the National Championship.

- **Do you believe the Cleveland Browns fans are the best in the NFL?**

Yes. Because they have not won a championship here in over forty years and they still breathe orange and brown. It has been fifteen years since we have had a good solid football team and people still love the Browns.

- **Do you still feel like you are part of the Browns organization?**

I feel like I am a part of it, but that's because the fans keep me a part of it. The Browns organization does try and some are reaching out. I get two free tickets for every game if I want them. There are some things here and there— perks we get out of it. They are starting to understand most of us don't need to be coddled or expect to be treated like royalty, but that a lot of us feel we have helped to build the fan-base here. They recognize us for who we are. The thing is, I understood a long time ago that players are not the game, the owners are not the game, television coverage is not the game, the referees are not the game—the *fans* are the game. Without the fans, there are no players. What did I say at the beginning of this? When you have seventy or eighty thousand people jump onto their feet and roar their approval—well, the way I look at it is, if you send me a card and ask for my autograph, you are giving me your approval, so I should say "thank you." How do I do this? I sign it and send it back. That is one of the rewards for being a fan.

- **Who was your nemesis on the field? Who gave you the most trouble?**

Oh, boy, Darrell Tally. He was a linebacker for Buffalo. He was the biggest thorn in my side. Every time we played Buffalo, he just always seemed to make something happen that took us right out of the game. He was the glue on that whole defense. He always seems to come out—at least when I played—and make a play that would take the game away from us.

- **Was Lance Mehl a pain?**

No, Lance was very good. The guy on that team that scared me the most was Joe Klecko. Why it wasn't Lance was because they did not blitz a whole lot, they didn't need to. They had Gastineau, Marty Lyons, Klecko...they had enough pressure. I loved playing against teams like the Jets because guys like Lance, he was a Pro's pro, knew hit job so well, you could count on him to get to the right spot. Because of that, I knew where I could throw the ball.

- **Cleveland Browns Fans have the distinction of being labeled with several negative plays. Why do you think that is?**

Well, when you haven't won a championship in forty years, it is hard to have a positive label on a team. There aren't many places that have had to struggle for as many years as Cleveland without winning a championship.

- **What was the hardest place to play because of the opposing fans?**

Well, when I played for the Colts, it was tough to play in Cleveland. But, as a Brown, Buffalo. Not as much for the fans, but because the way the wind always blows there and, even on a day that was nice, it was just hard to play on that field. If you get a thirty-forty mile per hour wind going—like it blew in that place—it made it tough to throw a football. The other place I would have to say is Chicago, Soldier Field.

- **Who was your favorite team growing up? Player?**

Minnesota and Fran Tarkenton. I liked him for two reasons, I liked his style of play and he was the classic overachiever. Wasn't very big, wasn't real strong, didn't have a big arm, but he went out there every day and competed.

- **Did you ever get a chance to meet him?**

No. I have not.

- **What is your funniest story of your NFL experience?**

Ah, man, I can't think of any.... Hmmmm, okay, well, we had a quarterback, I can't remember his name. He was huge. Not big by quarterback standards now, but he was 6'5" 240 lbs. Huge. Cannon of an arm, but didn't move around very well. He didn't make the team, out of Towson State. We were in a dorm of an all-female college in Towson, Maryland. It was a community bathroom and I come around the corner while this guy is turning on the faucet to wash his hands. The faucet broke with the water going full speed all over him. The look on his face was priceless, I can't describe it. It was between fear, astonishment, and a little bit of chest pumping knowing he broke it with just one turn. He stood there looking at me for about ten seconds and looking at this water splashing all over himself before he even did anything about it.

- **What is the saddest thing that happened during your career?**

Well, the amount of abuse Ernest Byner took for the fumble. Because the guy carried us that game, made one mistake, and took the brunt of it. But, it was also one of my proudest moments to watch a guy with the class Ernest Byner had in taking it all and never once flinching.

- **How were you acquired by Cleveland? How did you leave?**

By trade, for a tenth round draft choice and I was released.

- **Then you got to go play with the Rams as a starter?**

No, I was a backup behind Jim Everett.

- **Tell us about your Bills vs. Browns game in 1999.**

I retired in 1994 so do you mean the Browns/Bills alumni flag game at Finnegan Field? [Laughs] We did it for the fans, trying to get things going again for the fans.

- **What is the difference between NFL players today and back then?**

Oh...well, I think the game has changed a lot. When I first got out of the league, ESPN was a struggling network. You played on Sundays and you got the rare occasion to play a Monday Night game. You did not get to see the highlights of other games, they were not shown. Maybe Howard Cosell would do highlights of two or three games at half time and that is all you saw. Now with so many networks out there, so many instant replays, and so much instantaneous television that the game is played much more for the television than the sake of playing the game. That is not every player, that is just a general impression. One of the things that drives me crazy now as a quarterback is that when you threw a touchdown pass, you went to the sidelines. Let the guy who caught the ball be the center of admiration from the fans. Nowadays, when a quarterback throws a touchdown pass, he is screaming down the field to join in the celebration. You don't need to do that because if you are good, you are going to throw a touchdown pass—and you are expected to throw them—but just go to the sidelines. Get back, go to the sidelines. Be a Pro, be a gentleman. Don't run down the field. I've seen guys get beat 35-7, with three minutes to go in the game, throw a touchdown pass, and the quarterback is one of the first ones down there to jump on the receiver's back. Don't do that; be the first one to shake hands with one of the linemen or high-five the tight ends. I had a referee my rookie year, we were playing Denver. It was my second start and I hit a pass. The receiver was running down the field making some moves. The question was whether or not he was going to make it all the way and he didn't. He ended up getting tackled. But as he was running, I started to run down the field to be part of it. The referee grabbed my right arm and pulled me. He said, "Don't go running down there. You go running down there and some guy blind sides you, because it is legal you will have no recourse. You stay back here with me, we'll get up there, they will spot the ball, and I'll make sure you have time to get up there. Protect yourself. There is no rule that says you cannot touch the quarterback if he is running down the field...."

- **Are players worth their salaries? Should they be more fan conscious?**

I think they should be more fan conscious, but there are a lot of players who are. Are players overpaid? I don't think anyone is overpaid if someone is willing to pay them. I look at people who make movies, forty, fifty, sixty million per movie. Are they overpaid? They have a unique talent and if someone is willing to pay them for that talent, I don't blame anybody for getting as much as they can. Unfortunately, in our society we put such a high premium on entertainers and not as high a priority on public servants such as teachers, who have direct contact with our children on a daily basis, and those who are out there protecting us. Those people are under appreciated.

- **What are your hobbies today?**

Coaching. I don't do as much as I would like to, but I enjoy being around sports and helping kids. I go up to the high school and work with a player here and there. My wife and I also do a lot of work on our house, all the woodworking, drywall, wiring, painting, and landscaping.

- **What is your job now?**

I work for AT&T as a project manager for cellular network installations.

- **Tell us about Mike Baab.**

[Laughs heartedly] He was a character, the definition of what a football player is. Very intelligent. Loved to play the game. No knees, ankles were shot, constantly beat up, but he was out there busting his tail and left it all on the field every day. Then afterwards, he went out and lived life the same way.

- **What did you get out of your NFL experience?**

A lot of aches and pains. [Laughs] The greatest things about playing in the NFL is the camaraderie you have with guys and the people you get to meet. Just the experience of going through a season, with all the ups and downs, pluses and minuses, going through it with guys you respect.

			Passing							
			Mike Pagel							
			Quarterback 1982-1993							
			Arizona State University							
Yr	Tm	Gm	Com	Att	Comp	Yds	Yds/Att	TD	Int	Pass Rtg
'82	BAL	9	111	221	50.2	1,281	5.8	5	7	62.4
'83	BAL	15	163	328	49.7	2,353	7.17	12	17	64
'84	IND	11	114	212	53.8	1,426	6.73	8	8	71.8
'85	IND	16	199	393	50.6	2,414	6.14	14	15	65.8
'86	CLE	1	2	3	66.7	53	17.7	0	0	109.7
'87	CLE	4	0	0	0	0	0	0	0	
'88	CLE	5	71	134	53	736	5.49	3	4	64.1
'89	CLE	16	5	14	35.7	60	4.29	1	1	43.8
'90	CLE	16	69	148	46.6	819	5.53	3	8	48.2
'91	LAM	16	11	27	40.7	150	5.56	2	0	83.9
'92	LAM	16	8	20	40	99	4.95	1	2	33.1
'93	LAM	7	3	9	33.3	23	2.56	0	1	2.8
Career		132	756	1,509	50.1	9,414	6.24	49	63	63.3

Yr	Tm	Other Stats								
'85	IND	Rec: 1/6yds								

Rushing				Fum	Tot Pnts
Rush	Yds	Avg	TD		
19	82	4.3	1	9	6
54	441	8.2	0	4	0
26	149	5.7	1	4	6
25	160	6.4	2	6	12
2	0	0	0	2	0
0	0	0	0	0	0
4	1	0.3	0	0	0
2	-1	-1	0	0	0
3	-1	-0	0	3	0
0	0	0	0	0	0
1	0	0	0	1	0
0	0	0	0	0	0
136	831	6.1	4	29	24

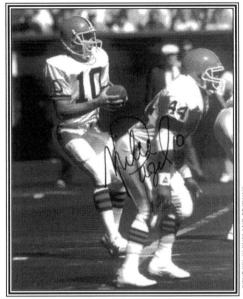

Hall of Fame running back Leroy Kelly
blocking for Mike Pagel

Mike Pagel setting and throwing a pass

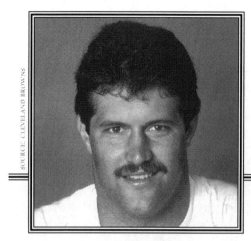

SOURCE: CLEVELAND BROWNS

23

Dan Fike

Many players show the scars of a very strenuous career. And Dan Fike is one of the hardest hit players one has ever seen. Lance Mehl had to slow his pace down dramatically due to the knee and back pain he experienced from his years at linebacker of the New York Jets. Dan has even more injuries than Lance and has gone past the phase of joint pain to joint replacement. Dan has had his knees replaced and one hip. His wrists have had damage done to them as well as his shoulder. Yet, even with his damaged body, he owns and runs "Let's Entertain Party Rental." This fits right in with what his fellow players credit to his organizational as well as mechanical skills. As Mike Baab called him, "The organized leader of the group." He and his wife run also a rescue center for cats and this athlete of the '80's deftly services his company as a laborer while still looking like he could play tomorrow.

- **How did football prepare you for the jobs that you do today?**

I don't quit. I don't like to lose. I work my tail off, which I had to do my first two years. So many times there were hundred-dollar weeks. I was sleeping on the floor at the office for a couple hours at a time at night. Get a couple hours of sleep, and get up and keep working.

- **What was it like to walk on the the field the first time as a Brown?**

I had a few games under my belt before I got to Cleveland as I played, of course, high school and college and I was drafted by the Jets in 1983. I was the last player released that year. I went home for four months before signing with the Tampa Bay Bandits (USFL) for two years. Cleveland was my first NFL team, actually, to be able to be a starter. It was really unique because I had heard so much about the Browns and about the fans, and they didn't let me down. Never let me down.

- **You were drafted by the Jets? What round?**

Tenth round.

- **You were released by them?**

I was the last player cut, the last cut day, but came real close to making it.

- **To be honest, I'm glad you didn't. Where did you go then?**

I went back home to work two jobs before signing with the Tampa Bay Bandits, part of the The United States Football League (USFL).

- **How did you get along with Browns after that?**

Well, after my first season with Tampa, a scout named Chip Falavene contacted me and asked me to come to a tryout. They'd watched me in New York and also with the USFL. He was tied in with Ernie Acorsi, who is still in the NFL. He was one of those guys who scouted for players in the USFL and brought them into Cleveland. After I worked out for Chip, he took me to meet the coaching staff. After the meeting, he said that they would be in touch. It didn't take too long to give me a call back and we worked out the details, signed the contract, and the next day I'm heading to Cleveland. It was really crazy because when I finished the USFL season, I had a grand total of thirteen days rest before beginning the next season.

- **At what point did you realize you could be a professional player?**

When I was in New York with the Jets I pretty much saw those guys who were on the squad at that time and thought, "I could play as well as they are playing" and I knew I had a shot. It just took me getting into the right situation, getting into the USFL, and getting experience. The Jets said I needed experience and playing time. Well, I wouldn't get experience and playing time if I was being cut and released. I got down to Tampa, my first camp, and I'm the third string tackle. "Well, this is not looking too good." By the time we got around to our first scrimmage, the offensive lineman coach walked up to me and asked, "Can you play left tackle," and I said, "Yeah. It's just a matter of switching stances. I know the plays." And he said, "Good. You're starting at left tackle in the scrimmage today." I said, "Okay." And I played next to a guy by the name of Fred Dean, who was one of the original "Hogs" of the Washington Redskins. After that first score and scrimmage, and on photo day, the line coach walked up to me and said, "You did real well, as well as Fred Dean. You're good. You're going to be just fine." After that, it was all downhill. Just going out there and doing my job.

- **You were just good at it?**

I was good in a lot of sports. I was good at baseball, basketball, track, football. Oh, yeah, I played four sports in high school. My high school football coach sort of forced me into giving up baseball and basketball to concentrate on track and football. Back then, I was pretty skinny and he wanted me to put some weight. If I was playing basketball, I was running it off. But, they're the ones that forced me into sticking with football.

- **What kind of parental influence did you have?**

Mom and Dad were always there. They're the ones that got us involved in sports early on. By the time I was six years old, I was playing T-ball, and I was all into baseball up until I got into about high school. From that point on, I was into football, pretty much. Football, baseball, basketball. Dad worked at the Naval Air station. Mom was a stay at home mom.

- **Who was your favorite team and player growing up?**

When I was growing up, we always watched Miami. I watched the 17-0 season. I was partial to them. I watched Dallas a lot. The Landry years were great. I watched Madden when he was coaching with the Raiders for many years. I watched a lot of football, but I didn't have one particular favorite.

- **You mention the coaches, did you watch the coaches a lot?**

You think about those teams back then. It was more of a team sport. You had Bart Starr, Larry Czonka, Bob Griese, and everybody was always talking about the coaches. They were just as big a part of the game as the players were. To me, it's the media blowing the players out of proportion, but there are big-time coaches still coaching the NFL. You know Landry is always wearing his hat and tie and the whole way he dressed. You know Don Shula; you knew what he was going to be wearing on the sidelines. You watch these guys. You knew if somebody watched the play and, all of a sudden, they click over to the coach and you say, "Oh, man, he's mad now. I wouldn't want to be that player coming off the field."

- **Who was your college coach in Florida?**

Charlie Pell. He passed away about seven, eight years ago.

- **Was Bobby Bowden in Florida State then?**

Yes, he was.

- **How hard was he to play against?**

Bobby tried to recruit me to go to Florida State when he knew I was planning on going to Florida. They were trying to keep me from going to Florida, but Bobby was an icon down there at Florida State. He's been there for thirty-some-odd years, I guess. But, between Florida State and Miami and the University of Florida, you have three perennial powerhouses in one state. At the University of Florida, we had a tough schedule being in the S.E.C. Georgia, Kentucky, Vanderbilt, LSU, Mississippi, Old Miss, Alabama, Auburn, Tennessee. We didn't have easy games down there.

- **It's been said that the Ohio State/Michigan and Cleveland/Pittsburgh were the two best rivalries in sports today. What are your thoughts?**

I'd say Florida/Florida State, Florida/Georgia, Florida/Alabama, Florida/Auburn, Florida/Tennessee, and Florida/Miami.

- **Do they play the same kind of schedule they played back then?**

The divisions have changed a bit. Florida State used to be an independent. Now they've gone to the ACC. Teams do this for a lot of reasons. Mainly money. The way I look at it, it's always each conference plays a little different style of football compared to the next. The SEC, when I was growing up, was always run first and throw last. Now the SEC is throwing and running is secondary. They do both very well. Football is probably the most changed in the Pros. In the Pros, to some aspect, heck, the high school, they were still running the wishbone. We played Bear Bryant my freshman year in college. They were still running the wishbone. You know, things change, times change, depending on the player, and what sells tickets, for the most part.

- **What is the difference between the right and left guards and tackles?**

Mainly, it was in the stance, the numbers, and which side the ball was running. But, back when I was in Cleveland, I could play four positions, actually five, if I needed to. I could play every position on offensive line. There were a couple of games where they put me at tight end to run out the clock. I was a blocking tight end. To me, physically, I had skills because I worked at it. Mentally, the game was preparation, concentration, execution. I prepared very well, concentrated very well, and executed very well. It was very rare I got physically beat on a play and I didn't get beat mentally very rarely. It didn't happen. I mean, in my last three years, even when I was playing with Mike Babb as center and Cody Risien next to me, I could pick the scheme up and was calling the blocking scheme as well as Mike Babb. He knew when he'd call the blocking scheme I was going to say 'yes' or 'no' and correct him if it was wrong. Then when Mike left and I was still a right guard, I was calling the blocking scheme and then Bellichick came in. They moved me out to right tackle. I was the right tackle and I was calling the blocking scheme for the entire line. I was mentally into the game and it didn't affect my playing though. I could look at the field, look at the defense, and I could make a blocking scheme call and be done with it. I anticipated what was going to happen. I could see what the quarterback was looking for and expect the audible.

- **You're a very quiet individual, but are classified as one of the best linemen the Browns ever had. What made you so special?**

I grew up no nonsense, work hard, get your job done, and finish what you start. In college, when I was in the Pros, it was the same way. Know what you're doing, go out and perform, execute and make something happen. Plus, I hated to lose. I couldn't stand losing. I just can't stand losing. That's why my wife and I don't even play card games or board games together anymore. If I lose, I get mad. On our honeymoon, we played cards. I got mad because she beat me and that's me. So, we don't play cards together anymore.

- **Where were you born?**

Mobile, Alabama.

- **How long have you been married?**

Twenty years.

- **What was it like to play for Marty Schottenheimer?**

The Shotzy Nautzy. Marty was an X's and O's, cover all your bases, work hard, play hard, fundamentally sound, tough, team, mentality, played a lot on emotion, that was Marty.

- **Some players have said that guys actually quit the team because his practices and spring training or workouts were too tough for them.**

Well, they didn't go to Pine Forest High school where I went and go through some of those practices. They didn't go through Charlie Pell practices in college. When I got to Pros, going to training camp to me was sort of like being on vacation for five weeks. I got fed three square meals a day plus snacks, got to take a nap during the middle of the day, got to go out and work on my job. Marty had long days, he had hard practices but you know what? It was nothing different then what I had been exposed to my whole playing career. There were marathon three-and-a-half hour practices down in Florida on Astroturf. You talk about hot! You know, it would be ninety to a hundred degree days and that Astroturf would be a hundred twenty degrees for three hours. Well, I'll tell you what. Good thing I had tough coaches in high school. They were just as nuts and crazy as you can imagine. You run out there and you get it done.

- **Is that why Florida, Ohio, and Pennsylvania schools have some of the best Pro athletes?**

Well, it's the way they were raised and what's expected of them when they were growing up and playing.

- **What was it like to play for Bud Carson?**

Bud was more of a defensive coach. When he became a head coach, he didn't keep quite the organization he had with Marty. Bud was more of a fly-by-your-seat kind of guy. He didn't have the discipline that Marty had. Marty was very disciplined, on everybody and everything. Bud was more lax. It showed, his second season. The first, we still had the carryover from Marty. The training regime, the principles, the ethic to work hard, toughness. The second year was when it really hit. That and not having quality guys behind you. The draft didn't help. You started having attrition, players retiring or getting hurt. You didn't have quality players stepping in. That's what hurt Bud. He's still a great coach. He just didn't have what he was lacking, that one thing in personnel and in work ethic that was applied a little bit.

- **Back to Marty for a little bit. Why was he really fired?**

You know what, I don't really know. I heard rumors it was mainly geared around his brother Kurt. I think Modell wanted Marty to fire Kurt and Marty wasn't going to fire his brother. That was a rumor.

- **Well, the whole thing, in the public eye, was that Marty wanted to call the offensive plays and Modell wanted an offensive coordinator.**

Well, remember when Lindy Infante was here. I mean, that was like my second year in Cleveland. Well, you can't get a better offensive coordinator. Look at what we did that year!

- **He's proven that several times.**

Yeah. We had to cut the same scheme. I think Marty and the team kept Lindy Infanty's scheme, the rest of my time in Cleveland.

- **Was Bernie Kosar a really good smart quarterback?**

Absolutely.

- **Would it have been better if he'd had a little better skills?**

When Bernie would take the line of scrimmage, I knew what he was thinking. Bernie was mentally on top of the game. Physically, he could throw the ball well. Only thing I didn't worry about Bernie doing was running anywhere. When you have a quarterback where you don't worry about him running anywhere, you will know where the pass is supposed to be coming from. All we had to do was keep #19's jersey clean—if you keep #19's jersey clean, depending on play scheme, passing route, link of drop, on the pass that Bernie's three- to seven-foot drop, he'd get the ball off, and it'll move down the field.

- **He held the lack of interception record for how many years?**

That's what I'm saying. Bernie was excellent. We knew where Bernie was, knew what we could do. All we had to do was keep the defenders away.

- **Most of the players I've talked to who had Belichick as a coach felt that he progressed tremendously to the point where he is at right now.**

Absolutely.

- **He had a learning process, like a new player does. Tell us about that.**

Well, I had the misfortune—and fortune—of being seated next to Belichick in the offensive meeting. He ran controls for the film room breakdown and made corrections this way. They didn't have to ask me if this was what I thought about something, and at other times I thought, Bill was trying to outthink the other coach or the situation. There was a game plan that we had one time, when we went to play Thanksgiving Day with Detroit. The whole week we worked on giving wide splits. "We're going to run the football because we knew that they were weakest at the top of the run." The first three plays he calls are pass plays. Some we hadn't run in three weeks. That was one of the times where he over-thought the situation. What we'd planned on and what we worked on, he'd overthought it. You know, that's my opinion. Who knows if I'm right or wrong, but that's the way we'd worked at it. I could always see the wheels turning in his head. Early on, he wasn't real pleasant to be around. Sometimes he was. But other times, he wasn't. He wasn't like Marty, like a motivator. Yet, he was going to get the best you had.

- **Do you think he has matured now that he has these Super Bowl rings?**

That was a maturity process in New England, developing his own personality and his own way of doing things and schemes and he's very successful at it. He's developed that. He was starting to develop that in Cleveland before the team moved. It was getting there, but it wasn't quite right yet. It took him going away and then coming back again and being in New England to figure out that the situation just didn't work for him. He had the players that worked for him.

- **Does it take a while to get the right players into the scheme of things?**

Oh, absolutely. Every coach has a little bit different philosophy on how they want things done. Back when I was still in Cleveland, when Bill was here, he even changed his way of doing things. You know, you can always change your philosophy or change your scheme to match the players that you have in order to win but if you have a certain plan, you have your own scheme that you want, it's like running into a brick wall. You know, if I'm going to run into a brick wall, you know, I'm going to hurt my head. I'm going to hurt something and the brick wall is going to win. Well, in my opinion, he ran into a brick wall too many times and you know he's not going to break through it. If you have a jackhammer or sledgehammer or something like that, if you don't have a tool to run through the wall, go round it. You find a side door, you find another wall, and you go around it. In my mind, if our team had played what our team was capable of at that time, we'd have probably been more successful.

- **Then you went to Pittsburgh.**

Well, I got traded from Cleveland to Green Bay in training camp. I wasn't cut. Bill traded me so there wouldn't be an uproar. Went to Green Bay for a couple, three or four weeks, was released and then signed with Pittsburgh.

- **Who was the coach in Green Bay at that time?**

Well, he just lost the Super Bowl—Mike Holmgren. He was on top of it. He was a good guy. I liked him. I liked the way he worked and the way he thought and what he did to try and win.

- **Why didn't you make it there?**

It was a numbers game. They had two tackles holding out and they thought about bringing me in. By bringing me in, they put more pressure on them to sign.

- **And pretty much, that was their scheme of things.**

Yeah, that was the way I thought.

- **How'd you get to Pittsburgh, then?**

Went back home for about a couple weeks.

- **You say home. Florida, or…?**

Cleveland. Still lived in Cleveland. I had my agent trying to get me some shots. I went down to see Sam Wyche, coach at Tampa, to see if they needed a player and it was about three, four, five weeks in the season, and I said, "Well, I'm going to call Bill Cowher." I knew Bill for a few years. I called Bill and talked to him and told him I was available. Well, he didn't realize I was so he said, "Let me call you back in a day or two." So, he called back in a day or two and said, "Can you come down to Pittsburgh for a physical?" I said, "Sure." Came down, had the physical, and next week I signed on with Pittsburgh. I was in Pittsburgh a month and a half, two months.

- **The reporters have you down for three games. 1993. Pittsburgh.**

I was there for, about, six weeks, seven weeks, so I may have been active for three games with Pittsburgh, yeah.

- **And Cowhers was coach?**

Yes. He had a player out with a League drug suspension.

- **Who was that?**

Carlton Hassling. He was the Olympic wrestler. After that, I retired.

- **Because of your knees? Or was that just part of it?**

Not much interest. People interested in me, no more. And when you get out and see the defeat of the teams, they think you're just washed up, so I retired and got out and started a business and I've been going ever since.

- **But, you had eight good years.**

Eight and a half.

- **Who are the players that you enjoyed playing with?**

All of them. For the most part, everybody. When I was playing, how we played, it was more like family. When you first got on the team, you were part of the family. The '85 squad all the way up to the high 90's squad in Cleveland, you were part of the family. Things have changed in the last couple of years, you know, but the closer-knit groups were the '85, '86, '87, '88, and '89 squads. Those were the closest knit. Everybody knew everybody's wives, kids, hung out together, grew up together, worked together.

- **Your '89 squad was one of your best, right?**

It was pretty good, yes.

- **Well, in your best year, how did you guys compare to the '64 squad?**

Well, the '64 squad won.

- **Which year do you think was your best as a team?**

I think the drive year was probably better. Denver was coming to Cleveland, we're playing. We have home field advantage. We got confident. We just scored and there was two minutes left on the clock, or a little less. They had the ball on what, the ten-yard line? Me and Cody Rison were just hanging and banging over there, disappointed. We just kept our heads down the whole time. We were like, "Come on, defense." You hear the crowd yell and scream, then you look up and try and catch what's going on. That was a heartbreaker. I mean, I take my hat off to John Elway. He was the clutch player. We had actually given them too much time to work with. It's sort of like the way we got in the playoffs. We beat the Jets with a double-overtime game. They scored too fast on that last drive and gave us too much time on the clock to go back down and score. So, the "Drive" was a heartbreaker. "The Fumble" was probably even worse because I was so close to recovering that ball. Jeremiah Castille was out covering left to Webster Slaughter, out on the left, and I hadn't watched the game yet. Jeremiah Castille was covering Webster Slaughter. Webster was supposed to run an out pattern, like the one with corner, but I don't think he did. I don't know. I didn't watch the game. I haven't even watched the film. I've never watched it. This is what I've been told. Webster didn't do what he did, catch Bill, sniff the run. He came in, and, well, he didn't make the hit on Earnest Byner. Ernest caught the fumble and then still was able to recover the ball about a foot from him. I mean, it's almost like ten inches away from getting the ball in the end zone. It was letting the air out of the balloon. I was just deflated. Just like that.

- **Are the Browns fans the greatest in the NFL? Why are they good fans?**

Yes, they are. Win, lose, or draw, they're right there. Yes, that's the game. They come prepared every week. I have four season tickets. I go to every home game. Win, lose, or draw.

- **You can say that because you've been a couple places.**

Oh, yeah.

- **You're a fan as well as a player, too.**

Oh, yeah. Well, my son never watched his dad play, but my daughter did. She'd take her friends to the game. He's ten, now. I took him to the game so he could sort of see what I used to do.

- **What were your feelings when the Browns left Cleveland?**

Well, at that time, I was in the middle of my business, getting it off the ground in my business, couple years I was working like a fiend, so when they left, I knew it ripped the heart out of everybody. So, I don't have time to worry about it, because I was getting my business started. As soon as they came back, we made sure we had tickets to go to the games. It's family.

- **So, do you still feel like you're part of the organization?**

Yes and no. Yes, because I have so many memories, and yes because people still remember me. And yes, because I still see all my old buddies and old playing partners. So, yeah.

- **You said, "Yes and no." Why did you say, "No?"**

Well, I'm not a player anymore and that means you're not a part of the intimate, inner core. You're out of the loop. You're a fan looking in with experience and knowledge of how the game is played and supposed to be played, but you're not in that loop anymore.

- **Should you be?**

Well, you know what, there are so many guys from past teams that have so much knowledge. If you take that knowledge and put an electrode on my head and put it on another lineman's head and transfer all that knowledge I had back when I played to the current group coming up.

- **Did Jim Brown and other players have an influence on the players?**

Somewhat, because I knew of them because they were former Browns players. We never really talked to them about...well, sometimes we'd be out at functions, like charity functions or golf outings and stuff, and if you're riding around with Dante Lavelli, or if you're riding around with Bob Gain, or Dick Schafrath, or you stand up for those other guys that are always around, and hey, "What'd you guys used to do for that or for this? What was your training regimen like or certain running plays, what'd you all try to do?" It's that knowledge factor. If you can apply it to what you're doing, currently, and you have different eras. Football doesn't change, but it does change. Like Lombardi said, you know when he had that big speech, that "It's all about running, throwing, catching, blocking, and tackling." It's the game. So, you break it down and then there's different ways of doing it. Different schemes, speed levels, size-wise people change. They get bigger. They get faster. Each scheme's a little different.

- **Who gave you the most trouble? Who was your nemesis?**

All I can say is, every day, in practice, Carl Hairston lined up across from me. Here was an old Pro who knew all the tricks. He'd teach me something new. I'd see something new from him, or Clay Matthews, or those guys. Next thing you know, your shown blocks and they'd pull something different on you. You know, I learned more plotting against my own guys in training camp my first couple years than I had to worry about being in games.

- **Would the Browns ever have come back to Cleveland if it hadn't been for the fans?**

It would have been one of those situations like John Elway. If there hadn't been such a push by the fans to get the team back, it would have been a long time before the team ever developed.

- **Where's the hardest place to play due to the fans?**

There's always the Domes, no matter which dome it was. New Orleans wasn't too bad, because their fans weren't really that loud all the time because their quota wasn't that good. But, these other teams, they had some wild fans. When they started rocking that dome, I mean, the noise level could come from anywhere.

- **What's the funniest story of your NFL experience?**

[Laughing.] Probably my funniest one is with Mike Baab. I had a lot of good times, we were sitting there, and—I can't remember what game it was. It may have been the Jets game. We're sitting there and there was a television camera and I'm sitting there and I had my hand on my knee, taking a blow, and Mike was always a nervous person. He'd be sitting down and his legs would always be bouncing around. He was my roommate, we'd all be sitting on a plane, the whole thing. Best man at my wedding, the whole thing, you know. Mike was always a nervous person. I'm sitting there, trying to get a blow, and I look down at Mike's feet. His feet are sort of bouncing around. I sort of look at him and I got my hands on my knees. Bent over and got my hands on my knees and I sort of look at him. And his mind's coming up and I look up, and I look at his face, and he's sitting there shaking. You know, he's like all fired up. He's just sitting there shaking. You know, he's about to hyperventilate, I think. I stand up and look at him, and I look him in his face. He sees me looking at him, and I kept looking at him and he goes, "What, What. What? What's wrong?" I said, "Man, you got the biggest booger I've ever seen in your right nostril." He reached over to his left nostril and blows his nose to clear his nose out, and I started laughing and all of a sudden he calms down and he goes, "Thanks. Thanks, thanks for showing me that. Thanks." It's one of those times. It's one of those crazy things that happen. It's something I'll never forget. It settled Mike down. Biggest booger I've ever seen.... I don't know if you'll be able to print that or not.

- **What was the saddest thing that ever happened to you on the field? The saddest thing you saw on the field?**

We had a wide receiver here, I can't remember his name, and I think we were playing down in Houston. There was a kid, only been on the league for a few years. He came across on a slant trying to cross the middle, and he threw the ball up, and he broke his neck. Seeing that guy lying out on the field—I can't, for the life of me, remember his name. I can picture his face right now, but I can't remember his name. No. It was in the late 80's. Anyway, he got his neck broken right on the field, right there. They carted him off. That's one of those experiences, that's sort of like, "That can happen to me." Other scariest, most life-threatening thing that happened to me was, that was right after the fumble year. After we lost to Denver on the Fumble. We get on the bus, everybody got on the plane. Everybody's cool, pretty much in the dumper and the crapper, because you know we couldn't, there's no celebration. So, we get on the plane, and we start taxiing down the runway, and the pilot's thrusting the throttles forward and we're flying down the runway and the next thing you know he slams on the brakes about two feet from the end of the runway. We all look around at each other and the pilot comes on, and the pilot comes on, he's Continental. He comes on, "We at Continental take your safety seriously, and I noticed we have a high throttle leak and I shut it down." We all looked around at each other and we're like, "Oh, shit. We almost died." He takes the plane back to the terminal and we get off the plane and they shut the bar down and Don Bertum, the team physician, walks into the bar and makes them open it and puts his credit card down and says, "Give them whatever they want." That really brought us back to what was important. We lost the game, but we almost died. A lot of people don't know about that. Some of the guys forgot about it and they go, "Oh, yeah. That did happen." It's one of those things that wasn't a bad moment in our careers, but it was a truth where God's knocking on the door, going, "Hey, it's not all bad, guys."

- **What do you think when people say, "It's just a game."**

A game. It's a way of life, though. I mean, I've spent almost, let me think here, looking at four years of high school, four years of college, USFL, eight years in the NFL, I put eighteen years of my life in playing the game. It wasn't a game. It was a way of life.

- **Do you miss it?**

Oh, yeah, absolutely. I dream about it sometimes. Flashbacks. I think about that every so often. I'll be doing something or driving somewhere and something will pop into my head about a game or practice or lifting or somebody said something back in the day, you know, just certain stuff. For eighteen years of my life, that was it. In one of those years, I played in 1985, I played USFL, had one training camp, played four pre-season games, sixteen other-season games, and three playoff games, had two weeks off, went to another training camp and another four pre-season games, another sixteen games, and another playoff game. I spent a whole year of my life playing football.

- **Gotta love it, don't ya?**

Yeah, forty-three games played in one year.

- **Forty-three games?!**

Main year in '85, in USFL, both the running backs we had down in Tampa rushed for a thousand yards. I came to Cleveland in '85. Both the running backs ran for a thousand. Then Tampa, in the USFL, was Greg Boone and Gary Anderson. Then in Cleveland, it was Kevin Mack and Earnest Byner.

- **Tell us about the Pittsburgh/Cleveland rivalry because you got to live both sides of the fence.**

Didn't know anything about it when I got up here. I had no clue until the first game. After that, I knew all about it. Knew everything about it.

- **You said the first game. The first game between each team?**

Yep. Love to hate 'em.

- **Love to hate 'em. So, what was it like on the opposite side of the field?**

Well, with Pittsburgh, when you go out to practice, it's black and cold. Here I am facing guys in practice that I've played games with. In first practice, I'm getting all fired up. I'm hitting people like its game time. They're like, "Hey, Dan. Chill out. You're on the same team." It just took a little bit for me to get used to being on that squad and wearing those colors. Then when we came back to Cleveland to play, it was really strange to be on the other sideline and have the fans who cheered for me all those years booing me, calling me traitor, throwing phones at me, you know, all that stuff.

- **Do the fans actually show respect for you because of your skills?**

What, in cussing me out? Uh, no, I just think that was too much beer.

- **I understand, about how the fans should just let the guy play.**

Yes, if the player comes to the stands, then he's asking for it.

- **Are guys like that really professionals, though? Professional means, there's a degree of professionalism in the game. Is that being lost?**

No, it's still there. I just think there's a lot of players out there who are in it for themselves. There's no I in team. They have the "I" on their jersey, but they don't have "TEAM" on their jersey.

- **Does that come clear down to the college level?**

College and high school. There are more high school games that way. Hey, lots of college coaches have to coach college players differently now than when I was playing because they've all got that attitude. They're watching the guys in the Pros do it and they figure they can do it.

- **Are players worth their salary? Should they be more fan-conscious?**

They should definitely be more fan-conscious. Whether or not they're worth their salary, they're getting what the market pays. They're getting ten times more than I got my last year, if not more. Sometimes twenty times more, sometimes thirty times more.

- **Value is whatever it is. It's just whatever you want to be able to be paid. But, do you think it's starting to get out of hand?**

Well, I've never agreed with the first guy on draft choice getting paid millions and millions of dollars right out of college and having never stepped on the NFL field before. There's a salary cap that should have been first timers get this much, second timers get this much, third timers get this much, right on down the line, and then, after the year's gone, then put a lot of incentives on there so that they can make the money that they're close to making what the guys who've been playing are making.

- **As a rookie, did you have to chase down the frozen turkey?**

I did that in Cleveland, and I wasn't even a rookie.

- **How far did you have to go in Cleveland?**

Down on Broad and 83, somewhere down there. In Wooster, I believe it was. Somewhere down in Wooster. I couldn't find a certain place and I called the equipment man with the truck, and I said, "Hey, where's this place at?" He said, "Oh, you got to go this way." After I got off the payphone, I go five more rounds, and you know what? I did find the turkey.

- **Who was the one who got on the phone and told you it was a joke?**

Nobody did.

- **Were there any other type of rookie "hazing" you went through?**

No. Because I'd been with the USFL for a couple years.

- **You pretty much knew what it was.**

When I was in New York with the Jets, we just had to get up and sing during dinner and stuff like that. But not in Cleveland. I didn't have to worry about it. Did have to do a little rookie things, I had to go through the whole experience, but, you know, it was no big deal. I didn't care.

- **It's part of the team, isn't it? It makes you part of the team?**

You know, just got to do rookie things, you know, like the last week of training camp where you sing, something like that.

- **Do you have a most memorable game in your career?**

They all flashback in my head over the years.

- **The different situations?**

Sometimes I'll think about, "There's one you played San Diego and got killed." Pittsburgh at home. I think it was the first game of the season. We beat them like 51-3 or 51-7 or something like that. It was Bud Carson's first year. There are games like that that pop out. Not any particular game, though. I played just about every stadium in the country, but not any particular game stands out any more than any others.

- **Was the Astrodome field as bad as everybody said it was?**

I hated it. But I say what field was worse than the Astrodome or New Orleans, it was Philadelphia. They just have a turf field and they play baseball in the same field. Whenever you have a team on a football field that also has baseball in the off-season, there were gaps where the infield stuff was at. There was about a half-inch wide gap in there and it was like, two or three inches deep. You could catch your foot on that and there was a lot of stuff you could do to get hurt on it.

- **Was it hard to play Municipal Stadium for the same reason? None of the guys have ever complained about Municipal Stadium.**

No, nobody ever complained about playing in Cleveland, other than in the winter time when the field was—there was many years that by the time the end of the season rolled around, you had no grass left in the middle of the field and they'd try to put new sod down and that didn't work. They painted the grass green, or they painted the dirt green. But, I liked playing in that condition because by the end of the year the field got so, well, the elements were like the way football was supposed to be played. There were times we'd play the field would be foggy, it would be mud pit, the next time we played it'd be frozen over. There were many games I used to wear Astroturf shoes. We'd be out there with no thermal underwear on and Astroturf shoes.

- **Do you work now?**

I still work hard but I have more employees now.

- **What are your hobbies today?**

Not too many, other than we do travel a lot. Business runs in cycles, so there are three or four months out of the year where we slow down to the point where we can take off, and I love to play golf.

- **Tell us a little bit about your job.**

It's called *Let's Entertain Party Rental*, it's the name of the company. It's a full-service party business. Tables, chairs, dishes, glasses, flatware, linens, moonwalks, dunk tanks, chocolate fountains, margarita machines, everything. Right now I have a 40,000 square foot building, five acres of property, eight trucks, about twenty employees. I'll have about thirty by June 2007.

- **Do you go on a lot of the trips yourself?**

I'm in the truck all the time. I'm in the truck every day. I drive twenty-four-foot trucks. We have about 6000 chairs and 600 tables. Huge inventory! I enjoy doing it.

- **How is your health now?**

Two artificial hips, need to have my right knee replaced (*which he did in 2007*); other than that, everything else is good.

- **What did you get out of your NFL experience?**

A lot of joy and a lot of pain.

- **Was it worth it? Would you do it again?**

Absolutely. Do it again, yep; but about ten years later, to make about twice as much money.

Barry Taylor & Dan Fike

Dan Fike				
Guard/Tackle 1985-1993				
Florida				
Season	Team	Games	Other Stats	Total Points
1985	CLE	13		0
1986	CLE	16	Fum Rec: 1	0
1987	CLE	12		0
1988	CLE	16		0
1989	CLE	13		0
1990	CLE	10		0
1991	CLE	16		0
1992	CLE	16		0
1993	PIT	3		0
Career		115		0

Dan Fike at a Cleveland Browns practice

24

John Buddenberg

Do everything you do in life to the best of your ability. Learn the techniques. Have determination. Have faith in yourself and you can be successful in any endeavor. John Buddenberg realized, with all the wide-bodies on the offensive and defensive lines, his small chassis would put him at a disadvantage in the NFL. But John had quickness, was a great technician, and was determined he could play the game. The mismatch in size put a limit on his ability to earn a starting spot in the NFL. John never made it onto the field during the regular season as a Cleveland Brown rookie, but he has earned a respect from the players as though he had battled in all the games. And it shows as he sits in the new Cleveland Browns Stadium, surrounded by other alumni such as the likes of Al "Bubba" Baker, Cleo Miller, Don Cockroft, Greg Pruitt, Dan Fike, and others. John enjoys talking with the other alumni about the games and stories from their Cleveland playing days. John's favorite childhood team was the Pittsburgh Steelers, so he was okay with getting an opportunity to go play across the river in Pennsylvania for his second year as a Pro. Being taught by Chuck Noll, after his move to the dreaded Steelers, was an honorable learning experience. Chuck Noll was a disciple of Paul Brown and still taught some of Paul's attitudes and "old school" values at Pittsburgh. After that year, moving to Atlanta in his third season, he spent a year protecting QB Brett Favre. Brett's rookie card with the Falcons shows John blocking to keep his quarterback shielded from defenders. In Atlanta, John found himself behind a starting lineup of All Pro linemen. After three years on and off with the Falcons, and their decision of two first round offensive tackle draft picks (Bob Whitfield & Lincoln Kennedy), John decided to move on to the Canadian Football League in '94. There he was able to play as a starter again for a couple years and had a lot of fun. But after two seasons with the Sacramento Goldminers and San Antonio Texans, having a family, and now almost thirty, he decided to take off his jersey for the last time. He moved onto the next chapter of life, took his hardworking ethics to the business world, and kept the same determination to do his best in his new career with Philips Semiconductors.

- **What it was like to walk on the field the first time as a Browns player?**

Coming from a small college like Akron, I was honored to have the opportunity to try out for an NFL team, but being drafted by the Browns was beyond any of my expectations. I felt privileged to be able to go out on the field with the players I've always looked up to as heroes. And, for that team to be local in the state I grew up in, I was excited that my family and friends could come see me play. It was the greatest feeling you could ever imagine.

- **When did you decide you wanted to be a professional football player?**

I was always an undersized, overachieving type of player. When I wanted to go to college, out of Bellaire High School, I wasn't quite big enough to be a lineman, so I walked-on with the Zips as an outside linebacker. Coach Jim Dennison soon moved me to offensive tackle and I earned a starting position and scholarship. It was probably my junior year at Akron when I realized I may have the talent to play after college. Coming out of Akron as a senior in 1989, I was a small, 255-pound left tackle—again undersized for my position. There were big linemen like Tony Mandarich in the same graduating class, and I didn't know if I was really big enough to be an NFL player. I always worked hard to do my best and had goals set to get as far as my opportunity would allow. I didn't know if I would get a chance to show what I could do in the NFL until I got drafted. The scouts and the coaches who had seen my abilities must have felt I had enough talent to be in the league.

- **And then you were drafted by Cleveland?**

Yes, in 1989. It was the same year as Eric Metcalf.

- **What did you do after that?**

I went to the Steelers in '90, thinking I would have a better chance to earn a position. I didn't make the team and ended up getting cut. I signed with the Atlanta Falcons in '91. They sent me under contract to play spring football in the World League for the Sacramento Surge('91/'92). At Atlanta, I was one of the guys the Falcons kept around, on and sometimes off the roster for three seasons ('91 -'93). At one point in '92, I was released for a week to make room for Deon Sanders as he was coming back from playing Major League baseball. *(Sanders went on to be elected to the Pro Football Hall of Fame.)*

- **So you were in professional football for five years?**

Five years around the NFL then in 1994 I had gone back out to California to play in the Canadian Football League for the same owner and coach as the World League. It was fun to be a starter again. I played in Sacramento (Goldminers) in '94 and San Antonio (Texans) in '95. The team had transferred to San Antonio before the '95 season.

- **Was there any one person that inspired you to play football?**

My uncle played for a college in West Virginia, but no one in my family played at a major college or professionally. My dad didn't play football, but as for my inspiration, he was always my biggest fan. I remember once back at Bellaire when we were playing vs. Martins Ferry.... I was an OLB (outside linebacker) and chasing the QB down from the backside. My dad—you could see him in the game film—was jumping up and down on the sideline for me to get the sack. I remember the Bellaire coaches rewinding that play multiple times on the film and we all had a good laugh. My dad liked to take pictures and thru college I had always got him a sideline pass so he could be down there with us. He was my biggest fan.

- **You said that your uncle played at a small college in West Virginia.**

My uncle (my mom's brother, Ed Roth, from Wheeling) played on the line at West Virginia Tech in '68-'72.

- **Tell us about your parental influence.**

I grew up in Bellaire, Ohio, we had a close family. All of my relatives lived in Bellaire or across the river in Wheeling, W.Va. My dad was an electrician and my mom was a nurse at Bellaire Hospital. We grew up in a good, moral family. My father was strict, but he just wanted us to do the right things. Unfortunately, he passed away suddenly in '95 and I lost my biggest fan. We still have a close family today. My mother (Carol), sister (Sheri), brother (Tulsa), and their families all live within a mile from me in Massillon. I feel my drive to be successful started early when I was young, but I always strived to stay a small town guy.

- **Did they attend a lot of games?**

Yes. My sister also went to the University of Akron and I first met my wife, Donna, at Akron. With my parents and grandparents, they attended all the Akron home games at the Rubber Bowl. They also went to as many of the away games that they could drive to, but it was tough for them to travel to the far locations from Bellaire. It was great for my professional career to start out locally in Cleveland. They came to all of the Browns and Steelers games while I was on the teams. Then, thru my last three playing years, my wife and I had started our family. We had two boys (John in '93 and Michael in '94). I was proud to know that they were there watching me from the stands as I was on the field playing.

- **Bellaire; they pull a lot of nice, professional athletes out of that area.**

Yes, we have had a great football tradition in Bellaire. The Ohio Valley is a strong football area that produces a lot of athletes. Other professionals from Bellaire are:
    - Nate Davis - Current Ball State Quarterback (going to NFL)
    - Jose Davis - Indiana Firebirds (AFL), Colorado Crush (NIFL)
    - Andy Doris - Houston Oilers
    - Mike Basrak - Pittsburgh Steelers
    - Ed Burgy - New York Mets

- Mac Cara - Pittsburgh Steelers
- Todd Goodwin - New York Giants
- Joey Galloway - Seahawks, Cowboys, Buccaneers
- Ron Lee - Baltimore Colts
- Clyde Thomas - British Columbia (CFL)
- Nick Skorich - Pittsburgh Steelers, Cleveland Browns (Coach)
- Lance Mehl - New York Jets
- Ben Taylor - Cleveland Browns, Green Bay Packers

• Who was your favorite player growing up?

I grew up through the 70's and graduated at Bellaire High school in '84. Being that Bellaire is only forty-five minutes from Pittsburgh and the Steelers were winning Super Bowls...for this, I grew up a Steelers fan. Jack Lambert was my favorite player at that time and, ironically, he was also undersized compared to the other players for his position. He played much bigger on the field than he weighed. Then coming from Akron, when I was drafted by Cleveland, I quickly got to learn and see first-hand the quality of the Cleveland Browns organization. As soon as I went to the Browns, I realized that this is a first-class organization and they care about their players. I truly converted to become a Browns fan.

• Why is that?

The Browns are just a good organization with the best fans. Cleveland takes care of their people. The Browns carry the motto: "Once a Brown, always a Brown." When you have played with other teams, you do not see the passion throughout the whole organization that the Browns have. No team in the league continues the relationships with their alumni and are as close to the ex-players as the Browns are. The Browns players have always been blue collar, hardworking and respected. The Alumni directors involve the local players to participate in activities as Browns alumni representatives. Even like myself, only being here as a rookie on the practice squad, they asked me to be involved as an alumni. The Browns welcome all players back, even if we spent a lot of our career with other teams. They had given me a call to ask if I wanted to participate in local alumni activities. It is nice to live close and to be able to give back and support the communities.

• Do you still feel like you are part of the organization?

Yes, definitely. The Alumni department involves all local ex-Browns players equally and they work around our busy personal schedules. No other NFL team organizes and involves their alumni like the Browns. If it were not for this, a lot of players would be forgotten after their playing days.

• And that is because of?

It's because the guys in the alumni relations dept are the best. With Dino Lucarelli, Anthony Dick, and Bob Markowitz keeping in touch and scheduling alumni players to be involved in activities throughout the year. We do what we can to help promote the image of the Browns and it also helps us as alumni to stay involved. Since my playing days, I've moved on and have a job/career and a family that keeps me busy, but I still enjoy doing all I can do to help in the community as an ex-Brown's representative.

- **Alumni personnel say you're very active with the Browns Backers Clubs, going to the games, doing signing sessions and other functions.**

Yes, from my standpoint, it's great to live close enough to Cleveland and an honor to participate in the alumni, community, and game functions. The Browns alumni relations department lets us know about the Browns Backer events that we can support. There are always many guys donating their time. It's great for us to see the other guys, tell stories from our playing days, and feel the camaraderie. At one time, I'd been asked to speak to the Atlanta chapter Browns Backers while still playing as a Falcon. The Browns Fans just wanted me to tell some stories from my days in Berea.

- **Who was your high school coach? What kind of influence did he have?**

My high school head coach was Mike Sherwood. John Magistro and Bruce Stoltz were my position coaches. Coach Sherwood had played QB at WVU so he brought a lot of knowledge and experience to our program at Bellaire High. He only coached a few years before he became Athletic Director, and John Magistro took over and led Bellaire for twenty years. We had a good strength and lifting program at Bellaire and were taught to be tough. We were hardnosed, had a good work ethic...we never quit. I graduated from Bellaire in 1984.

- **Sherwood took over the Ohio Valley Greyhounds in Wheeling, WV?**

Yes, I know Coach Sherwood, Coach Magistro, and Lance Mehl all were coaching the Greyhounds for a while. I had gone to a few of the games, and it was fun to watch the excitement generated in the indoor football league. The wall makes a difference on the smaller indoor field and I do not want to know how it feels to run into it at full speed.

- **Who was your college coach and what influence did he have on you?**

My first college coach ('84 & '85) was Jim Dennison. Coach D. was a great coach and had been with Akron for many years. He is, and was, always very well respected. The type of blue collar coach that I was used to. He taught us the power of having inner strength…"PMA" (Positive Mental Attitude). You have to believe in your ability, your preparation, and know your game plan assignments to be successful. He taught me how to focus and channel my abilities to be the best. Just like the story of the little engine who thinks he can: I think I can, I think I can…. The ability to believe was especially influential to me since I was only 220 lbs when I first started as Akron's left tackle. I needed to be a skilled technician and find a way to win versus my bigger—sometimes 285 lb—opponents. In 1986, the University of Akron brought in Coach Jerry Faust from Notre Dame. Coach Faust helped Akron move the program to Division 1 in 1987 where we played football at a higher level. Coach Faust had assembled a great coaching staff that taught us more technique and strategy. Many of the coaches we had came with major college experience and are still today seen on television, coaching with Division 1 programs across the country. We did not win a lot of games moving up to Division 1, but I strived to play to my best in every game. My senior year, we played Auburn, who was ranked in the Top 10 at the time. It was a great experience to be at a school the size of Akron and able to line up and play against such big-time programs. Walking out on the field at Auburn, the grass was as nice as a golf green compared to the old indoor/outdoor carpeting we had at the Rubber Bowl. I had to line up against a group of All-American defensive linemen. I played especially well in this game, and the experience helped me prove to the NFL scouts that I could play on their level. We sent the Auburn game film to all of the NFL teams and scouts that were interested.

- **How were you acquired by the Browns?**

I was drafted in the tenth round.

- **How does turf make a difference from artificial turf to real grass?**

I imagine for spectators artificial turf is probably the preferred surface since there is no mud and it is a cleaner and faster game. But for a player, playing on the older turf we had, the game was quite different from playing on a natural grass surface. The older turf we played on in the 80's and early 90's was pretty much just indoor/outdoor carpet with a thin cushion between it and the hard concrete. It was a hard surface and was very sticky for shoe/foot traction. This had a good and bad impact on the game. The game was faster, being that the sticky surface allowed players to accelerate and move laterally without slipping. Even for linemen, the game was noticeably quicker. When you plant your foot, it sticks like glue and you can change direction. But, being able to change direction so quickly put a lot of strain on the hips, knees, and ankles of the players. This caused more injuries from the wear and tear on these joints. Also, there were the "turf burns." Falling down on the older turf peeled off the skin on your arms and knees. In the shower, it would burn then it would scab over in a couple days. Playing on grass was a lot different. Although the game was slower, it was easier on our joints, and it didn't hurt as much when you fell on the ground. As a lineman in the trenches, I enjoyed playing on both surfaces. Getting muddy and sliding around on rainy days was fun at times, and the defensive end coming off the corner wouldn't be as fast. But, since I was a smaller lineman, I liked being able to utilize my quickness advantage when playing on turf. The new turf on the fields today looks and feels very much like natural grass. It allows some give when you plant to change direction, and it is much softer than the old turf. It feels very much like natural grass and is the best of both worlds as a playing surface for today's athletes.

- **Tell us what it was like to play for Bud Carson.**

Marty Schottenheimer had just left Cleveland to go to Kansas City and Bud Carson was in his first year as the Browns coach in 1989. He appeared to be under pressure to win his first year here. Art Modell was a vital part of the everyday life of the Browns; we saw him at practice all the time, talking to Coach Carson. Being a rookie, I didn't get to know Coach Carson well, but I respected him and what he has done. I know that he had developed the "Steel Curtain" back in the 70's and, obviously, he knew defense. Initially, I was in awe of just being part of the team and professional atmosphere in Cleveland. I had built a good relationship with the offensive line coach (Hal Hunter), and the players were all friendly.

- **It sounds like you stepped up in quality coaches every year.**

Yes, I would agree that they all were quality coaches. Bud Carson was a respected coach and had a great defensive mind. He was the brains behind the dreaded Pittsburgh defense in the 70's. Then 1990 was one of the last couple years at Pittsburgh for Chuck Noll. It was honorable to spend the short time that I did with him and the team. During that year, Todd Blackledge's father, Ron Blackledge, was the offensive line coach. In the off-season, he had back surgery, and he was out during training camp. Generally, the head coach oversees the whole team, but Chuck Noll stepped in personally to coach the offensive linemen. He was the positional coach for us, and it was great to be in the OL meeting room with Chuck Noll critiquing each of us on technique and our footwork every day. Then, in Atlanta, Jerry Glanville was at the helm. It was a great experience, but it was a bit of a circus atmosphere. He was leaving tickets for Elvis and racing his car around the parking lot. There were also all kinds of celebrities hanging out with the team. MC Hammer, Hank Jr., James Brown, and Evander Holyfield would visit us in the locker room on a regular basis. The stereo was cranked up before the games in the locker room as we were dressing, and we had the run-and-shoot offense. We were a good team, and made it into the playoffs each year. My roommate and friend those years was Bill Goldberg (YES...the Wrestler). Brett Favre was also on the team in '91. We had a lot of fun those years.

- **Looks like you had a tough way to go to earn a position.**

I know, I found myself in that position with every team I was on. They were all very good linemen, and most were All-Pros. My forte was being quick and a good technician. Since I was only 230-255lbs in college, and got up to 260-275 lbs as a Pro, I was always light. I found myself able to dominate a lot of the lineman in college, but it was a different story in the NFL. Everyone was so much bigger and faster. When I was in Cleveland, I saw that they had bigger tackles—Cody Risen and Tony Jones—and both were very good. In searching to find a team where I could better fit in with my abilities, I decided to sign with the Steelers where they had John Jackson, Tunch Ilkin, Terry Long, and new draft pick Justin Strzelczyk. They weren't as big as the Browns linemen, but were more mobile type of guys. Pittsburgh's offense liked to trap block, run sweeps outside, and run screen plays. I saw that I could learn from the great Pro Bowl technician Tunch Ilkin who was a lighter lineman like myself. Unfortunately, I didn't make the team that year. The following year ('91) I ended up going to Atlanta, and I was able to stick with the Falcons for a few years. The linemen there were very talented as well. They had three all Pro first round drafts: Mike Kinn, Chris Hinton, and Bill Fralic. I found myself behind these All Star's, and still struggling to find where I could fit into a position. I was always in the shadow. Then in '92 they drafted Bob Whitfield and in '93 Lincoln Kennedy...both first round draft Offensive Tackle's .Atlanta really invested in the OL and backbone of their offense. We had five first round offensive linemen on the squad. I sometimes compare that talent to any OL of today. They were a very talented group.

- **What players did you enjoy playing with?**

Bernie Kosar was one of the first class guys I met while with the Browns. He was close to all of the offensive linemen and kind to us rookies coming into the league. Eddy "The Assassin" Johnson was also a veteran who helped us adjust to our new life as professional athletes. He was the nicest guy you could meet. Eddie led by example and showed us that we needed to be involved in the local community. Clay Mathews was hardnosed on the field, but personable and another nice guy. In Cleveland, I was good friends with safety Kyle Kramer (from Bowling Green) and free-agent Bobby Lyons from St. Clairsville. My closet friends while with the Atlanta Falcons were Bill Goldberg, Louis Riddick, and Bill Fralic.

- **Tell us a little bit about Eddy Johnson.**

Even though it was later in his career ('89), he was the first to corral all of us rookies together to help us to understand the transformation of becoming a professional. He talked to us about getting involved in the community and being role models to the young fans that looked up to us. He showed us how to keep a good image outside of football by signing autographs for fans, visiting blood drives, children in the hospitals, fundraisers, golf outings, and even fishing trips—not unlike some of the same things we still do today through the Alumni Dept. Eddie was a guy you could respect on and off the field. He was a nice person and a good player. A year before he passed away from cancer, he had come to Jackson Township to sign autographs for the youth football program where I was coaching and my son's team. My son still has Eddie's picture up in his bedroom.

- **Tell us about Bernie.**

Bernie was a good guy. He was one of the big stars on the team in '89. I was a rookie and obviously looked up to him. In pre-season, when we were to play the Steelers, Cody Risen had an injury and could not play left tackle so I got the opportunity to start as left tackle to protect Bernie's blind side. In the locker room, I was a bit nervous, but was ready to step up to the challenge. Bernie came over before the game and said, "John, don't worry if you get ten holding penalties, I won't let the coaches get mad at you…. Just don't let your guy hit me from the blind side." Being a rookie, I wanted to capitalize on the opportunity and kept my opponent from getting to Bernie. My guy didn't get to our QB, nor did I get a holding penalty. Bernie thanked me after the game for doing a good job. (*Note: Usually in the pre-season, younger players or rookies only played the second half, not when the starting QB was in the game.*)

- **Is there anybody else you enjoyed playing with?**

I always tell stories that my claim to fame was being with my roommates. While I was in Pittsburgh, I was Neil O'Donnell's roommate, and for the years in Atlanta, I was Bill Goldberg's roommate. Bill went on to become a Pro wrestler and movie star. I also had made many other friends in Atlanta: Bill Fralic, Louis Riddick, Tracey Eaton, Tim Green, and others.

- **Do you ever talk to Bill Goldberg?**

I haven't for a number of years but, coincidently, a few weeks ago his publicist requested my contact information for Bill. I left a message and expect we will talk and catch up soon. Bill and I first met and became friends when we played in the World League with the Sacramento Surge together in the spring of '92. We were the league Champs that year. We both finished Sacramento's season and came to the Atlanta Falcons training camp with only a six-week summer break. It was tough competing to make the team that year with such a short break between seasons. After football, we went in different directions. I see him hosting television shows and occasionally in movies, but haven't talked with him for a few years.

- **What kind of leadership role did you take on the field?**

In college, I strived to be a "lead by example" guy. I wasn't usually very vocal, but I tried my hardest to be the hardworking technique player that the other players look up to. In the NFL with the Browns, the Steelers, and the Falcons, I tried to learn as much as I could from the All Pro linemen I was behind. I found myself always in the shadows of very talented linemen, and I tried to pick up new skills from each of them to better myself. When I went to the Canadian League in '94 and '95, I strived again to lead by example in the trenches as a skilled technique player.

- **Who was your nemesis? Who did you have the most trouble with?**

In college, I found that most opponents were one dimensional—either strong & powerful or quick and fast. I could work different skills to handle either type of player. In the NFL, the guys were much bigger, stronger, and faster. The type of player that gave me more trouble was the players that could run around you and run over you. The best guys that I had faced were: Michael Dean Perry, Chris Doleman, Keith Millard, Clay Mathews, Greg Lloyd, Reggie White, and Charles Mann. They all were good defensive linemen with the combination of speed and strength.

- **Did Jim Brown and the players before you have any influence on you?**

Yes, how could a football player not look up to Jim Brown's accomplishments on the field? I have only met him a few times. Obviously, Eddie Johnson was a good influence on every young player. Other influential players to me that I looked up to and tried to learn from were guys like Cody Risen, Tony Jones, John Jackson, Tunch Ilkin, Mike Kinn, Bill Fralic, and Chris Hinton. I learned a lot from each of them through the years that made me a better player. They were all respected guys, and I looked up to them.

- **Tell us about Brett Favre.**

Even though Brett Favre was just a rookie in Atlanta, we quickly noticed he had the personality to be a team leader. He was a personal guy and team player who worked hard. He had such a strong arm that he broke a few of the receiver's fingers with his passes. Everyone got along with Brett. Obviously, it's the biggest trade that Atlanta wished they never made to Green Bay. Green Bay really made out on the deal. He was just a rookie and Atlanta had many other veteran quarterbacks at that time that had a lot of experience. Brett Favre came in under them and never had a chance to show much of his abilities in Atlanta during that year. I don't know how happy he was about the move initially, but going to Green Bay and focusing on football is what Brett did—the rest is history. Atlanta lost the future Hall of Fame player.

- **Tell us about your feelings when the Browns left Cleveland.**

That was the darkest day in Ohio sports history. We were watching the news about Art Modell's unhappiness in Cleveland, but I couldn't believe it actually happened. I know that there were a lot of issues and reasons… they were fighting for a new stadium that Cleveland couldn't commit to at the time. I could not believe we lost the team to Baltimore. I didn't watch much football that year and quickly became a "Raven hater." It is great that Cleveland fought to keep rights to the name, records, and the team colors. It is good to have a new team. We made history with the first time the NFL resurrected a team. It would never have been the same if the new team had a different name and colors. It's behind us, but I still do not like the Ravens.

- **Cleveland/Pittsburgh has been said to be the best rivalry in Pro sports. Tell us about your experiences and your comments on that.**

My experiences started very early in my life. Growing up directly between the two great cities (Bellaire), it was always my favorite game of the year, no matter how good or bad either team was. I grew up a Steelers fan, mainly because they won the Super Bowls when I was young and they were always on our local networks. Then getting drafted by the Browns, I did not hesitate to convert and become a Brown. I felt honored to be in the NFL and happy the Browns wanted me. My first professional start was a pre-season game against the Steelers. It was great to play. All of my family and friends were either at the game or watching on television. I couldn't believe the hype and the feeling of everyone's excitement for the game. Then the next year, I ended up going to the Steelers for minimum pay, and now found myself on the other side of the fence. Even though the Steelers are a good organization, too, I had already begun to bleed Brown. Now, knowing the history behind the organization, the fan base, and the Browns Backers all over…. There's no team in the league loved as much as the Browns. I do know one thing about the Browns Backers: They are the best fans and they are everywhere. As I said before, I was in Atlanta playing for the Falcons and the Browns Backers from Atlanta called me and asked, if I could come speak to their group. I said, "Are you sure? I'm the enemy." They said what all the Browns fans say, "Once you're a Brown, you're always a Brown. We'd like you to talk to us about your experiences when you were with the Browns. We don't need to talk about the upcoming game." That was very respectable to be honored as a player and not as this week's enemy. They were a great group, and I really enjoyed spending time with them. It was very nice evening.

- **Browns fans have been labeled with the distinction of several negative plays. Is it because of the history of the Browns?**

It may be because they're so passionate about the team, and want them to win. We've never had our dynasty years on top as so many other teams have had. Pittsburgh had their years, San Francisco had theirs, Dallas had theirs, the Patriots, and the Colts had their years on top. So, many teams have had their two, three winning years on top of the league, and we haven't made it yet. Even though we've had good teams and we've been close, we've never been in the Big Game. Someday our Browns will get their Super Bowl ring, and we all will be very happy.

- **Before the Super Bowls started, no one that could touch our records.**

Yes, we dominated back before the NFL started the Super Bowls. I do not think we are jinxed to win a Super Bowl, but one year we need to get the recipe right. Then we'll have our well-deserved days on top. Browns fans are so passionate about our team that they want each year to be "the year." It gets frustrating for all of our great fans and their continued anticipation of a Cleveland Browns championship.

- **Do you still feel like you're part of the Browns organization?**

Definitely. When we got the Browns back, I was asked to get involved as a local alumni player. I was a bit hesitant to get involved because I only played here as a rookie and had played with other teams for most of my Pro career. But the Alumni department welcomed me as they do with every alumni so I do feel a part of it and would do anything to help them out.

- **Are Cleveland Browns fans the best in the NFL?**

By far. They are passionate and you feel it when you go to the games. The stadium roars with cheers, and the dawg pound is always rumbling.

Also, as I said about the Browns Backers groups, you see there are chapters everywhere. No other team has such a following. When I was in Sacramento during my Canadian League playing years ('94-'95), I talked with the Browns Backers chapter out there. I went with them at times to see the game at their sports bar. It was just like being in Cleveland. Everybody had their Browns jerseys on, and cheering every time we had a good play. You don't see that kind of following for other teams all over the country like the Browns have.

- **What's the funniest story in your NFL experience?**

I wouldn't say it's funny, but one neat story from my rookie year is: I was out to dinner at a Cleveland restaurant with a couple college friends. They were asking me questions like, "What's it like to be a part of the Browns? We know you as our friend—an Akron guy—but do the Browns players know you? Do you sit in the same room with the guys we see on TV? Do they know your name? Do you talk with them?" I'd said: "Of course, the guys are friendly and even though they're big stars, they're still normal people. We all talk and hang out together. Yes they know who I am. There are not that many new guys to the team and we all know each other." They then ask, "Now, about Bernie...does he say 'hi' to you and would he know your name?" I replied, "Of course, yes, he knows me." Ironically, about five minutes later Bernie walks into the same restaurant. He looked over from across the room and waved to us before he went and sat down at his table. My friends said, "Oh, my goodness. It's Bernie Kosar and he waved at you. He does know you...." Then shortly after that, Bernie came over to our table and sat down with us. I introduced my friends to him. He had talked with us for a few minutes, bought us a drink, and then returned back to his family's table. Needless to say, they were speechless the rest of the evening. Bernie and most all of the Browns players in 1989 were good people. When you transition from a small college to the NFL, it is a big step. I never knew anyone who played Pro football before. Players from big colleges like Ohio State, Michigan, have three to four of their teammates and friends each year going to the NFL. They see Pro's all the time, but coming from Akron I had never met guys like Eddy Johnson, Bernie, Slaughter, Langhorn, Minnifield, or Dixon until I was on the team with them. Actually, the first Pro game I had ever been to was the first Browns preseason game of '89, and I got to play in it.

- **Tell us about your turkey hunt.**

The veterans didn't make us do too much, they weren't too hard on us. They made the rookies stand up individually on a table in the dining room at training camp and sing a song to everyone as they finished dinner. It was embarrassing for most of us (me included). Many of us didn't know the words to any Top 40 songs.

- **Did that make you feel more a part of the team?**

Obviously, it was humbling and embarrassing. You had to stand on the table and get everyone's attention before beginning your song. Then when the team and coaches are looking and listening, we had to sing something. After the first few guys did it and everybody laughs, the nervousness wears off a little. We did have a few guys who thought they were above doing it, and didn't feel they were going to get up there and sing. But, after a little "veteran influence," they completed their songs, too. It is part of being with the team, and you sure are relieved when it is over. You do feel closer to the group afterwards.

- **What's the saddest thing that happened while you were in the NFL?**

While in the Canadian League, we had a free weekend during our by week. One of our defensive backs, Junior Robinson from East Carolina, had gone home to see his family for the weekend. While home, he was in a car accident and died. Junior Robinson was a great teammate and a very nice person. He had a young family. This was a terrible event and we all miss him. During my career, I hated to see a player get hurt. You'd hear the sound of a knee ligament snap during a play. It makes a distinctive sound, and you know someone just got hurt. Also, it was scary knowing that that it could have been me at any time. During a game in the '89 season, I had seen Clay Mathews rip open his forearm on a goal line play when he caught it on a helmet snap. It tore the skin on his arm like you catch your jeans on a sharp corner. It was big enough that the trainers were lifting the flap of skin up and squirting antibiotic fluid underneath it. He came off the field, they cleaned and wrapped it up. He then went in for the rest of the game. After the game, he got stitches (a lot of stitches). Through the years, you see a lot of your friends get injured. Football is the greatest game in the world, but is also the most brutal on your body.

- **Should he be in the Hall of Fame?**

I would think so. Clay Mathews was in the Pro bowl and played consistent good football for many years. He had a good career, and he was a guy who was respected and well liked amongst the team. As we know, he ended up in Atlanta, too. I now enjoy seeing his son, Clay Mathews III, play for USC as his father once did...although USC is an enemy to our beloved Buckeyes. He has the same spirit and "never quit attitude" that Clay had here with the Browns. *(Clay III has since started in the NFL as an All Pro defensive end for the Green Bay Packers and his other son is a linebacker for the Philidelphia Eagles.)*

- **Are players worth their salaries? Should they be more fan conscious?**

Minimum salary in 1989 seemed like a lot of money to us players just out of college, but there were none of us set for life and retiring after a couple years in the league. The veteran players then felt that the team's ownership was not paying enough, and the financial balance should be better between the owners and players. Now today, players are making a whole lot more. To make minimum salary today for a few years in the NFL, a player that is conservative could be pretty well off after a football career. But, sadly, there now is Personal Seat Licenses fees, high ticket prices, and television contracts pushing toward Pay-per-view games. It is hard to expect the fans to continue to keep paying more to see and cheer for their team. Today, it is difficult for anyone to take their family to see a game. We need to keep our fans, who are following the team every week, and cheering for the big plays and TD's.... The type of fans that are making all the noise from the dawg pound when the opponent is backed up against the end zone in the fourth quarter.

- **Should players be more fan conscious?**

As a player, I strived to never forget where I came from and that the fans are most important. Players should put their fans first and always make time for them. Pro athletes are role models to young people. By the nature of being on television, kids and fans look up to the athletes. They should always be conscious of their actions while in public. That's one thing that Eddie Johnson showed us when we came to the Browns. He was the veteran that showed us rookies the right way of being a part of the community. He'd say things like, "Come on over here with me, let's sign a few autographs after practice," and "It's for the kids." Otherwise, as rookies, we may not have realized the need for when to make time to see the fans. Even though we may have been tired after practice, Eddy was a leader by his actions, and, obviously, he was well liked in the community. He helped us understand our role as professionals, too. I recently went to the Cleveland Sports Banquet, and Bill Walton was the host. He had told all kinds of stories through the evening, but in closing, at the end of the banquet, he said: "Of all of this I've said tonight, it's nothing without the fans. If I didn't have fans, and the teams I was on didn't have fans, we wouldn't have gotten to where we were."

- **What hobbies do you have today?**

I have always been a diverse person and enjoy many hobbies. I like to do woodworking and have made cabinets, beds, various pieces of custom furniture, and remodeled a few houses. Every year I'm working on a new project. I also like to fish and go boating with the family. We have a boat and we take it out every chance we get. I enjoy golfing occasionally. I also like to make homemade sausage, and use my mother-in-law's recipes to make Italian dried meats like suprasatta and capacola. I can't forget that I also enjoy coaching football to the kids. I've coached my two sons and in the local youth football program for eight-plus years.

- **Explain your job today.**

From Akron University, I received a Bachelor's degree in Electronic Engineering. I got my first job in 1997 with Philips Semiconductors, and have been a sales engineer for them through today. I support customers in the Ohio and Western Pennsylvania territory who are doing electronic circuit designs or building electronic products with circuit boards inside.

- **Did you get your degree before you graduated?**

No. I had attended Akron University from '84 until the spring of '89, when I was drafted by the Browns. At that point, I was six classes short of my degree. Then after the 1995 season and my football career was over, I returned to Akron in '96 to complete the classes to graduate. I was then hired as a sales engineer with Philips in the spring of '97. Working at Phillips Semiconductors, we are one of the top ten ranking electronic chipmakers in the world.

- **So, you spend a lot of time on the road then?**

Yes, somewhat; I travel to support the customers in Ohio and through Western PA. So, I spend a lot of time on the road driving up to three hours away, but I'm usually home in the evening to see my family. I've been doing it for quite a while, and the travel is not too bad.

- **What did you get out of your NFL experience?**

I would say I am honored to have had the opportunity and abilities to get to the NFL. I was always an undersized player. Even my college line coach told me when I was a senior, "You're probably not big enough for the NFL so you might want to look at the Arena Football League." I used this as a motivator and strived to find a way to make it. I had ambitions and goals to try the NFL if I had the chance and I got the opportunity from the Browns. Obviously, there is a lot of fame on and off the field when you are in the NFL. Looking back at the years I played, I have many memories, experiences and made many good friends that I will never forget. With my career, I was happy to play as hard as I could and get as far as I did, but I never took steroids, injections, or took anything that would harm my body. Now almost fifteen years after I hung up my cleats, I am glad that I am still healthy. Playing professional football was a great chapter in my life, but I never forgot who I was or where I came from…. Just a small town guy from Bellaire. I've now moved on to the next chapter with a career in the business world and have a great wife and family.

John Buddenberg with his two sons in Atlanta

GO BROWNS!!

About the Authors

Barry Taylor

Barry Taylor has been a Cleveland Browns fan since he attended Marietta Senior High in Marietta, Ohio. As a high school athlete, his dream of playing professional baseball was denied by extensive knee surgery. At Fairmont State College, in Fairmont, West Virginia, he was a springboard diver in his freshman year until he broke his eardrum on a rip entry during practice. Barry then turned his sports-minded focus to slow-pitch softball where he soon became the District 12 Umpire and Chief in Ohio, then the ASA Commissioner of the same district. Twenty-five years later, he retired from the Softball and Plumbers and Pipefitters Local 168 due to a knee replacement and other injuries. However, bored with his retirement, Barry wanted more in his life. A good friend had told him that, with his sports knowledge, he should write a book. He'd already read one of Rich Wolfe's books, *For Browns Fans Only*, and had put on three golf tournaments where he'd met several professional football players so he knew the stories they told were priceless. He knew how the everyday fan would never be able to hear these kinds of stories and how much they would enjoy doing just that, so with that in mind, he started interviewing players to create this book to share with Cleveland Browns Fans around the world. Web: www.ilovemybrowns.com.

Shannon Duffy

Author Shannon Duffy was born and raised in Southeastern Ohio. She currently lives in Southern California with her two sons, cat, a pack of coyotes, a family of raccoons and one lone skunk. When not role playing as Mother Nature, she enjoys being in the great outdoors and spending time with her family. Aside from *If You Wore the Uniform...You're a Brown*, her published book credits include the best-selling Young Adult novel *Stormy Knight: Prom Queen of the Undead* and *The Couples Guide to Pregnancy & Beyond*. She has been quoted by CNN numerous times, as well as iVillage and *Parenting Magazine*. Visit her online at www.shannonmarieduffy.com

Coming Soon!!

If You Wore the Uniform
You're a Brown

Volume 2

More great pictures!
More great stories!

Go Browns!!

by Barry Taylor
& Shannon Duffy

www.ILoveMyBrowns.com

Made in the USA
Monee, IL
24 May 2021